EDUCATING EXCEPTIONAL CHILDREN

Third Edition

Annual Editions

A Library of Information from the Public Press

Cover illustration by Mike Eagle

The Dushkin Publishing Group, Inc.
Sluice Dock, Guilford, Connecticut 06437

The Annual Editions Series

Annual Editions is a series of over thirty-five volumes designed to provide the reader with convenient, low-cost access to a wide range of current, carefully selected articles from some of the most important magazines, newspapers, and journals published today. Annual Editions are updated on a regular basis through a continuous monitoring of over 200 periodical sources. All Annual Editions have a number of features designed to make them particularly useful, including topic guides, annotated tables of contents, unit overviews, and indexes. For the teacher using Annual Editions in the classroom, an Instructor's Resource Guide with test questions is available for each volume.

PUBLISHED

Africa
Aging
American Government
American History, Pre-Civil War
American History, Post-Civil War
Anthropology
Biology
Business
China
Comparative Politics
Computers in Education
Criminal Justice
Early Childhood Education
Economics
Educating Exceptional Children
Education
Educational Psychology
Environment
Global Issues

Health
Human Development
Human Sexuality
Latin America
Macroeconomics
Marketing
Marriage and Family
Personal Growth and Behavior
Psychology
Social Problems
Social Psychology
Sociology
State and Local Government
Urban Society
Western Civilization, Pre-Reformation
Western Civilization, Post-Reformation
World Politics

FUTURE VOLUMES

Abnormal Psychology
Death and Dying
Drugs, Society and Behavior
Computers in Business
Computers in Society
Congress
Energy
Ethnic Studies
Foreign Policy
Geography
Judiciary
Middle East and the Islamic World
Nutrition

Parenting
Philosophy
Political Science
Presidency
Religion
South Asia
Soviet Union and Eastern Europe
Twentieth Century American History
Western Europe
Women's Studies
World History

Library of Congress Cataloging in Publication Data
Main entry under title: Annual editions: Educating exceptional children.
    1.   Handicapped children—Education—Addresses, essays, lectures.   2. Gifted children—Education—Addresses, essays, lectures.   Title: Educating exceptional children.
ISBN 0-87967-593-4   371.9   79-644171

Manufactured by The Banta Company, Menasha, Wisconsin 54952

1985

Editors/ Advisory Board

To The Reader

In publishing ANNUAL EDITIONS we recognize the enormous role played by the magazines, newspapers, and journals of the *public press* in providing current, first-rate educational information in a broad spectrum of interest areas. Within the articles, the best scientists, practitioners, researchers, and commentators draw issues into new perspective as accepted theories and viewpoints are called into account by new events, recent discoveries change old facts, and fresh debate breaks out over important controversies.

Many of the articles resulting from this enormous editorial effort are appropriate for students, researchers, and professionals seeking accurate, current material to help bridge the gap between principles and theories and the real world. These articles, however, become more useful for study when those of lasting value are carefully *collected, organized, indexed,* and *reproduced* in a *low-cost format,* which provides easy and permanent access when the material is needed. That is the role played by *Annual Editions.* Under the direction of each volume's *Editor,* who is an expert in the subject area, and with the guidance of an *Advisory Board,* we seek each year to provide in each *ANNUAL EDITION* a current, well-balanced, carefully selected collection of the best of the public press for your study and enjoyment. We think you'll find this volume useful, and we hope you'll take a moment to let us know what you think.

During the last decade, tremendous progress was made in guarantying equal educational opportunities for handicapped children through the passage of individual state laws in the early 1970s and finally in the passage of the federal law P.L. 94-142, The Education for All Handicapped Children Act of 1975. Those supporting passage of this law envisioned equal treatment of handicapped and nonhandicapped children in the schools, nondiscriminatory testing and placement practices, more representative decision-making practices (including parents), and greater acceptance of handicapped individuals in our society-at-large with lifestreaming of handicapped individuals into our communities being the ultimate goal.

In some ways, our progress has far surpassed the intent of P.L. 94-142. In other areas, we have only begun to grapple with the many complexities in educating handicapped children within the context of the public schools. The issues are not simple, nor are many of the solutions. Special educators, regular classroom teachers, and supportive personnel are in key roles for creating and carrying out these solutions.

In the 1980s, much remains to be done. Teachers, whether they be special or regular educators, need to learn more about handicaps—what they are (and are not), and what effects handicaps have on a child's learning and development. Each section of this book contains information about the various handicapping conditions, so that teachers can have up-to-date, accurate information to help combat the myths and fears many children and their parents have about handicaps.

Several of the articles address the difficult attitudinal and social issues of bringing handicapped and nonhandicapped children together in the schools. Too many children are coming to school without positive, realistic expectations for their handicapped peers.

The remaining articles present ideas and methods for teaching handicapped children. There are many simple adaptations that can be made in materials or methodologies which allow the handicapped child to participate in the same classroom activities as nonhandicapped children. Many of the methodologies will not only help handicapped children, but will also help nonhandicapped children learn more efficiently.

It is hoped that this book will be informative, interesting to read, and helpful in your teaching. It is also hoped that the ideas presented in this book will help prepare you for the many challenges in teaching children, whether they be handicapped or not.

Let us know your opinion of this anthology by filling out the article rating form on the last page of this book.

Ian A. Nielsen

Ian A. Nielsen
Program Manager

Contents

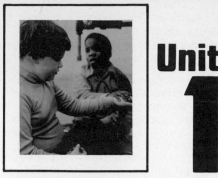

Unit 1

Mainstreaming: Basic Concepts and Issues of Implementation

Four articles examine the status of special education programs and services for the nation's exceptional children.

Unit 2

Attitude Change Strategies: Helping Nonhandicapped Children Understand Their Handicapped Peers

Eight selections discuss the need for developing strategies for interaction between handicapped and nonhandicapped persons, methods for making the interaction successful, and include an annotated bibliography.

The concepts in italics are developed in the article. For further expansion please refer to the Topic Guide and the Index.

Unit 3

Teaching the Visually Impaired Child

Five articles discuss mainstreaming and the special needs of visually impaired children.

Unit 4

Teaching the Hearing Impaired Child

Four selections detail the hearing mechanism, special needs of the hearing impaired, and teacher strategies.

The concepts in italics are developed in the article. For further expansion please refer to the Topic Guide and the Index.

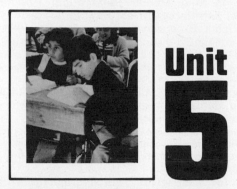

Unit 5

Teaching the Physically Impaired Child

Five selections examine the educational implications of physical impairment, the effect of medication on learning, the use of microcomputers, and the value of programs to teach the nonhandicapped about the needs of handicapped classmates.

Unit 6

Teaching the Mentally Retarded Child

Six articles discuss the identification, incidence and prevalence of mental retardation, children with Down's syndrome, special learning programs, and include a bibliography of writings by mentally retarded individuals.

The concepts in italics are developed in the article. For further expansion please refer to the Topic Guide and the Index.

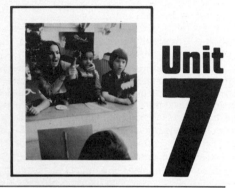

Unit 7

Teaching the Learning Disabled Child

Four selections present strategies for addressing the special needs of the learning disabled.

Unit 8

Teaching the Emotionally Disturbed and Behaviorally Disordered Child

Five articles discuss mainstreaming and strategies for teaching children with emotional and behavioral problems.

The concepts in italics are developed in the article. For further expansion please refer to the Topic Guide and the Index.

Unit 9

Teaching the Gifted and Talented Child

Five selections analyze the current status of gifted education programs.

Topic Guide

This topic guide suggests how the selections in this book relate to topics of traditional concern to students and professionals involved with educating exceptional children. It is very useful in locating articles which relate to each other for reading and research. The guide is arranged alphabetically according to topic. Articles may, of course, treat topics that do not appear in the topic guide. In turn, entries in the topic guide do not necessarily constitute a comprehensive listing of all the contents of each selection.

TOPIC AREA	KNOWLEDGE (These articles provide information about a handicap or about a special education concept.)	ATTITUDES (These articles contain personal experiences of exceptional persons or discussions about changing children's attitudes toward handicaps.)	TEACHING (These articles contain practical suggestions about how to apply special educational principles to the teaching of exceptional children.)
Classification/ Labeling	1. Executive Summary 2. The 1984 Annual Report to Congress 13. Mainstreaming Children with Visual Impairments 27. What Is Mental Retardation? 37. The Psychology of Mainstreaming Socio-emotionally Disturbed Children	6. Changing Attitudes 8. Toward More Success in Mainstreaming	9. Integrating Disabled Children
Continuum of Educational Settings	13. Mainstreaming Children with Visual Impairments 29. Learning Through Outdoor Adventure Education	31. An Analysis of EMR Children's Worries About Mainstreaming	9. Integrating Disabled Children 10. The Parent Connection 29. Learning Through Outdoor Adventure Education
Due Process (PL 94-142)	1. Executive Summary 2. The 1984 Annual Report to Congress	8. Toward More Success in Mainstreaming	
Educable Mental Retardation (EMR)	30. Changes in Mild Mental Retardation	31. An Analysis of EMR Children's Worries About Mainstreaming 32. Speaking for Themselves	
Effect of the Handicap on Learning and Development	13. Mainstreaming Children with Visual Impairments 26. Is There a Child with Epilepsy in the Classroom? 28. The Child with Down's Syndrome 37. The Psychology of Mainstreaming Socio-emotionally Disturbed Children	8. Toward More Success in Mainstreaming	7. Providing Opportunities for Interaction 9. Integrating Disabled Children 11. Involving Students in the Planning Process
Emotional and Behavioral Problems	37. The Psychology of Main-streaming Socio-emotionally Disturbed Children 39. Educator Perceptions of Behavior Problems of Mainstreamed Students 41. Child Abuse and Neglect	39. Educator Perceptions of Behavior Problems of Mainstreamed Students	38. Skill-Streaming 39. Educator Perceptions of Behavior Problems of Mainstreamed Students 40. Reducing Stress of Students in Conflict
Gifted and Talented	42. Our Most Neglected Natural Resource 44. Special Children 46. Will the Gifted Child Movement Be Alive and Well in 1990?	43. The Teacher as Counselor for the Gifted	45. A "Social" Social Studies Model for Gifted Students
Hearing Impairments	19. The Hearing Mechanism	21. There's a Deaf Child in My Class	18. Poor Learning Ability . . . or Poor Hearing? 20. Notetaking 21. There's a Deaf Child in My Class
Identification of Handicaps	9. Integrating Disabled Children 12. Books About Children with Special Needs 15. Teaching Partially Sighted Children 19. The Hearing Mechanism 27. What Is Mental Retardation?	41. Child Abuse and Neglect	8. Toward More Success in Mainstreaming 18. Poor Learning Ability . . . or Poor Hearing?

TOPIC AREA	KNOWLEDGE (These articles provide information about a handicap or about a special education concept.)	ATTITUDES (These articles contain personal experiences of exceptional persons or discussions about changing children's attitudes toward handicaps.)	TEACHING (These articles contain practical suggestions about how to apply special educational principles to the teaching of exceptional children.)
Individualized Education Programs (IEPs)	11. Involving Students in the Planning Process		9. Integrating Disabled Children 11. Involving Students in the Planning Process
Interaction Between Handicapped and Nonhandicapped	6. Changing Attitudes 25. Learning About Disabilities	5. Don't Stare—I'll Tell You Later 6. Changing Attitudes 7. Providing Opportunities for Interaction 9. Integrating Disabled Children 25. Learning About Disabilities	7. Providing Opportunities for Interaction
Learning Disabilities	33. Recognizing Special Talents in Learning Disabled Students 34. Teaching Learning Disabled Children to Help Themselves	34. Teaching Learning Disabled Children to Help Themselves 35. How Do We Help the Learning Disabled?	34. Teaching Learning Disabled Children to Help Themselves 35. How Do We Help the Learning Disabled? 36. Mainstreaming
Least Restrictive Environment	3. Where Is Special Education for Students with High Prevalence Handicaps Going? 30. Changes in Mild Mental Retardation	5. Don't Stare—I'll Tell You Later 6. Changing Attitudes 9. Integrating Disabled Children	8. Toward More Success in Mainstreaming
Mainstreaming	13. Mainstreaming Children with Visual Impairments 22. Integrating the Physically Handicapped Child 36. Mainstreaming 37. The Psychology of Mainstreaming Socio-emotionally Disturbed Children	6. Changing Attitudes 8. Toward More Success in Mainstreaming 31. An Analysis of EMR Children's Worries About Mainstreaming	4. Staff Development 9. Integrating Disabled Children 39. Educator Perceptions of Behavior Problems of Mainstreamed Students
Mental Retardation	27. What Is Mental Retardation? 28. The Child with Down's Syndrome	29. Learning Through Outdoor Adventure Education 31. An Analysis of EMR Children's Worries About Mainstreaming 32. Speaking for Themselves	29. Learning Through Outdoor Adventure Education 31. An Analysis of EMR Children's Worries About Mainstreaming
Physical and Health Impairments	22. Integrating the Physically Handicapped Child 25. Learning About Disabilities	25. Learning About Disabilities	23. Children on Medication 24. Comprehensive Microcomputer Applications for Severely Physically Handicapped Children 26. Is There a Child with Epilepsy in the Classroom?
Special Education Programs/Services	1. Executive Summary 2. The 1984 Annual Report to Congress 3. Where Is Special Education for Students with High Prevalence Handicaps Going?		4. Staff Development 10. The Parent Connection
Technology and the Exceptional Child			16. Technology and the Handicapped 24. Comprehensive Microcomputer Applications for Severely Physically Handicapped Children
Visual Impairments	13. Mainstreaming Children with Visual Impairments 17. The Visually Handicapped Child	14. Some Thoughts on the Education of Blind Children	15. Teaching Partially Sighted Children 16. Technology and the Handicapped

Mainstreaming: Basic Concepts and Issues of Implementation

Public Law 94-142, The Education for All Handicapped Children Act, has been a reality since 1975. Schools have had a chance to put into practice the legal mandates guarantying handicapped children a free public education. The law intends that handicapped children be educated alongside their nonhandicapped peers in the least restrictive environment. The battle to assure individualized educational plans, due process procedures, and nondiscriminatory testing was hard-fought. While ensuring the right to an education is a dramatic advance, serious questions are being raised about the best way to educate these children. Although some of these questions remain unanswered, we have learned much during these initial years.

The articles in this section examine the present state of P.L. 94-142, and also discuss related issues, such as the importance of staff development. Implementing an effective mainstreaming program revolves around seven basic concepts: right to a free public education; appropriate education; least restrictive environment; continuum of service; individualized educational programs (IEPs); supportive services; and due process procedures.

For the federal government to mandate a program that is designed to involve all students in our educational process was a monumental step. To bring this program to effective reality, however, involves many areas of difficulty, including incorrect classification, inappropriate educational programming, the deleterious effects of labeling, and inadequate staff development programs. These essential problems are addressed in this section.

The lead article, "Executive Summary—Sixth Annual Report to Congress on the Implementation of Public Law 94-142," assesses the status of special education programs and related services for the nation's handicapped children. The following article analyzes the Executive Summary. The author maintains that while there has been progress in improving services to handicapped children, stabilizing local, state, and federal funding of special education programs and services remains to be accomplished. "Where Is Special Education for Students with High Prevalence Handicaps Going?" examines the different types of handicapped students served, and notes that over four million students have been involved in special education services in recent years. "Staff Development: A Key Ingredient of Effective Mainstreaming" stresses that teachers must be trained to overcome the many problems encountered when handicapped students are integrated into regular classrooms.

Looking Ahead: Challenge Questions

How has the mainstreaming program, instituted by P.L. 94-142, impacted on the exceptional child? What are the continual problems encountered by this program?

What kind of students are categorized as exceptional? How have they fared in the past years?

What is needed for developing an effective staff to handle exceptional students? How have these needs been addressed?

Executive Summary

Sixth Annual Report to Congress on the Implementation of Public Law 94-142: The Education for All Handicapped Children Act

U.S. DEPARTMENT OF EDUCATION, 1984

■ This is the sixth *Annual Report to Congress* on the status of education and related services for the Nation's handicapped children and youth in fulfillment of the provisions of Part B of the Education of the Handicapped Act (EHA-B) (20 U.S.C. §§1401, 1411, *et seq.*), as amended by P.L. 94-142. In Section 601(c), Congress stated the purposes of the Act, which are: (1) to assure that all handicapped children have available to them a free appropriate public education, (2) to assure that the rights of handicapped children and their parents are protected, (3) to assist States and localities to provide for the education of all handicapped children, and (4) to assess and assure the effectiveness of efforts to educate handicapped children.

The report is submitted by the Secretary of Education in accordance with the provisions of Section 618, which requires that the impact of the program authorized by the Act be evaluated and that updated information, including information regarding the number of children requiring and receiving a free appropriate public education, be provided annually. The Education of the Handicapped Act Amendments of 1983, P.L. 98-199, have modified the reporting requirements in a number of respects. This report, however, was prepared to cover a period of time during which the previous version of Section 618 was controlling. The report provides, as have previous reports, current information which describes the progress that has been made in meeting the purposes outlined in Section 601(c) of the Act.

Number of Students Served

● The number of handicapped children who are receiving special education and related services continues to rise as it has each year since the initial child count in 1976–77. The 1982–83 total of 4,298,327 served by the States under the provisions of EHA-B and P.L. 89-313 is an increase of 65,045 (or 1.5 percent) over the previous school year, and 16 percent since 1976–77. The number of handicapped children served in proportion to the number of children enrolled in preschool through twelfth grade rose from 10.47 percent in 1981–82 to 10.76 percent in 1982–83. This overall increase becomes more significant when compared with the Nation's total school-age population, which has been steadily decreasing in the past decade.

● Variations continue in the number of children served within the different handicapping conditions. Large increases in the number of learning disabled children served overshadow the decreases in number of children served in most other categories. Since 1976–77, the learning disabled population has grown by 119 percent. This rate of growth appears to be slowing, in part due to increased efforts by States to assure that children are not erroneously classified. The category of emotionally disturbed has also increased, possibly as a result of the increased capacity of State educational agencies (SEAs) and local educational agencies (LEAs) to provide services, especially at the local level.

● The total number of multihandicapped and other health impaired children served has declined, although this is not uniformly true within the States. Some of this decline can be attributed to definitional and procedural changes in reporting, especially in a few populous States. During the past year and since 1976–77, the number of children served in every other category except visually handicapped has decreased. Trend data from National totals is often at odds with the data from individual States. Therefore, many factors, such as population shifts and procedural or definitional changes, must be exam-

From *Exceptional Children*, November 1984, pp. 199-202.

ined in order to account for changes in the number of handicapped children served.

Services for Children from Birth through Age Five

- The implementation of the Education of the Handicapped Act, as amended by P.L. 94-142, has brought concomitant increases in the nature and extent of programs to provide education and related services to the population of young handicapped children. Early intervention with handicapped children results in a significant decrease in services required later; in some cases it eliminates or reduces the services which would otherwise need to be provided when the child enters school, thereby resulting in notable cost savings.

- States continue to report increases in the number of preschool-age handicapped children served, especially those aged three through five. This age group represents nearly a quarter of the total increase in the number of children ages three through 21 who received special education services last year. Since 1976–77, there has been an increase of more than 23% in the number of preschool children served.

- Thirty-eight States now mandate services to at least some portion of the preschool handicapped population from birth through age five. The specific ages and areas of handicap for which services are provided vary among States; however, a larger percentage of the three- through five-year-old population is reported to be served in those States which mandate services than in those that do not.

- Four Federal initiatives—EHA-B, the Preschool Incentive Grant Program (20 U.S.C. §1419), the State Implementation Grant Program, and the Handicapped Children's Early Education Program—have played a critical role in encouraging preschool programs. The number of States choosing to participate in these preschool programs has more than doubled since fiscal year (FY) 1978. A recent National analysis of the impact of demonstration and outreach programs found the accomplishments of the HCEEP projects to be "greater and more varied than those of any other documented education program identified."

Services to Secondary- and Postsecondary-Age Students

- A noticeable expansion of services to secondary- and postsecondary-age handicapped students has occurred, in part due to (1) increased recognition of the importance of a successful transition from school to work and community life; and (2) the need to preserve educational gains from earlier education. Information from selected States indicates a more rapid growth in services at the secondary level than for younger school-aged children. The 1982–83 child count data indicates an increase of 9% from the previous year for postsecondary-age students aged 18 through 21, and an increase of 70% over the number served in 1978–79. Although all States have mandates to provide services to handicapped students through age 17, 24 States have mandates to serve handicapped youths through the age of 21 if they have not graduated from high school. In addition, many States permit local schools to provide services at least through age 21 even when a mandate does not exist.

- There is a growing trend toward expansion of vocational services and use of community resources to provide vocational skills to secondary- and postsecondary-age handicapped youth. Through such programs, there is also greater opportunity to receive education with and interact with nonhandicapped students.

- Through combining resources from other public and non-profit service agencies and prospective employers, financing of programs for older handicapped youth is being shared among other human service agencies and the private sector.

- The Education Department will assist the expansion and improvement of transitional services for handicapped children and youth through development of curriculum materials, research on the accessibility of employment training, follow-up studies of secondary-age students, demonstration and dissemination of successful practices, communication between the education community and the business community, and development of workable interagency agreements.

Services to Institutionalized and Previously Institutionalized Students

- Over the past decade, judicial and professional decisions have led to dramatic reductions in the enrollment of handicapped children in State institutions. Many States have now adopted policies to keep or return students to their home communities whenever possible, thereby avoiding institutional placement. Local educational agencies are increasing their resources to assist with previously institutionalized students.

1. MAINSTREAMING

- Changes in SEA, other State department, and LEA policies and practices for provision of educational services to students who remain in institutions suggest improved capability to meet the needs of these handicapped students.
- The primary source of Federal support to children in State-operated or State-supported schools is P.L. 89-313. These funds can also "follow" children who leave the State programs to enter local programs. The number of children supported in LEAs has increased by 700% since 1975 to a total of 49,601 in 1983.

Personnel

- Overall, there was a slight increase between 1980–81 and 1981–82 (the two most recent years for which data are available) in the total number of special education and related services personnel.

Least Restrictive Environment

- Fewer than 7% of all handicapped children are educated in either separate schools or separate environments. Of the more than 93% who are educated in regular schools, about two-thirds receive their education in the regular classroom with nonhandicapped peers.
- The overall proportion of handicapped students served in various settings has remained relatively stable over the years. However, through the development of a continuum of placement options within LEAs, there have been changes within specific handicapping categories to serve children in less restrictive settings. This is particularly notable for the visually handicapped, emotionally disturbed, orthopedically impaired, and hard of hearing and deaf. Placement and review procedures designed to improve the quality of the placement decision-making process is an important factor in assuring education in the least restrictive environment.

Procedural Safeguards

- The use of mediation as a process to bring about a reconciliation between schools and parents before going to a due process hearing is evident in a large percentage of States. However, the extent to which mediation serves to deter the need to go on to the hearing stage is unclear.

Protection in Evaluation

- Concern over the continually rising number of students counted as learning disabled has stimulated concerted State efforts to assure the consistent application of eligibility criteria and to strengthen the capacity of the regular education program to address learning problems.

Funds for Serving all Handicapped Children

- States use a mixture of resources—Federal, State, and local—to finance services for handicapped children and youth. EHA-B funds are important in both the support of administrative activities in SEAs, including support of personnel, and in the funding of direct and indirect services at the local educational agency level, including exemplary demonstrations, and resource and information systems.
- Numerous studies of the structure of education finance have demonstrated the complexities of attempting to determine the cost of providing education and related services to handicapped children and youth in the States. Case studies were conducted by SEP in 1983 to examine the available expenditure data from four selected States. Development and use of more sophisticated accounting systems is contributing to the increased availability of detailed cost information in some States.
- Through various discretionary programs and through the monitoring of State plans and administration of EHA-B funds, Special Education Programs continues to provide technical assistance to the States as required by Section 617(a)(1)(A) of EHA-B.

Impact and Effectiveness of EHA-B

- Special Education Programs continues to conduct special studies, as required by Section 618 of EHA-B, to determine the extent to which the purposes of the Act are being met. A longitudinal study of selected local educational agencies recently concluded that the impact of EHA-B has been primarily positive and that the law has been a major factor in effecting change in special education, specifically through increasing the scope and comprehensiveness of special education programs and related services at the local level.
- State and local educational agencies are also recognizing the need to have good evaluation information with which to make decisions affecting special education within the States. They are supporting numerous studies relating to policies, procedures, and cost and effectiveness of the provision of special education and related services.

6

The 1984 Annual Report to Congress: Are We Better Off?

Abstract: The U.S. Department of Education 1984 Annual Report to Congress on progress in achieving the intent of P.L. 94-142 gives cause for thought and questions in the minds of local special education practitioners. Questions concern the extent to which there has been locally perceived progress in improving services to handicapped children, meaningfully characterizing that progress for critical audiences, and major initiatives yet to be addressed. In the opinion of the author, there have been both substantive and substantial improvements in local special education programs and services, in part attributable to the provisions in P.L. 94-142. Stability in local, state, and federal funding for programs and services remains a major area demanding attention.

DAVID E. GREENBURG

DAVID E. GREENBURG is Executive Director, Council of Administrators of Special Education, Inc., Indianapolis, Indiana.

The past six years have seen a shift from the initial procedural activities to implement this legislation affecting all handicapped children (PL 94-142) to a strengthened concern for the quality and comprehensiveness of special education programs.

■ With those words, Madeleine Will, Assistant Secretary for Special Education and Rehabilitative Services, U.S. Department of Education, introduced the 1984 Annual Report to Congress (U.S. Department of Education, 1984) concerning progress in the states and localities toward achieving the intent of EHA (the Education for All Handicapped Children Act, P.L. 94-142). With some areas of exception (referenced in the following paragraphs), those words accurately characterize progress made in the education of handicapped children over time—if shifts of emphases and concerns are acceptable as demonstrations of progress.

Each successive annual report to Congress on the implementation of P.L. 94-142 gives increased cause, particularly to local special education administrators, to consider current program efforts and accomplishments as well as those attended primarily before the enactment of that legislation. Surely few would contend there has been no substantive change in their professional lives or in the educational lives of those students identified previously and/or currently as handicapped by definition of the law. Change is not necessarily progress however. The questions before the field include: Has some measure of progress toward the stated purposes of P.L. 94-142 been achieved? How might that measure best be demonstrated? What major initiatives still need to be addressed?

STUDENTS SERVED

The U.S. Department of Education has consistently referred to increases in the number of handicapped children receiving special education and related services as evidence of progress toward the stated full services goal. The 1984 report addresses that issue first and sometimes defends special education enrollment increases given the generally decreasing

1. MAINSTREAMING

total school population and variations in growth among exceptionalities and among states and localities. Evidence in the report does point to overall increases in 35 states and territories and overall decreases in only 19, but in 21 of the 52 states and territories for which data are given, changes were less than 2%. If the 65,045 overall increase in numbers of students served (1982–83 over 1981–82) were distributed among the 15,912 school districts in the U.S. (Grant & Snyder, 1983), it would reflect a net increase of some four students per district, less than one per school (.76) if distributed among the 85,431 public elementary and secondary schools.

Following prior encouragement to conduct extensive childfind efforts and increase the number of handicapped children served, it is unlikely a local special education administrator would find such increases excessive. Further, those data might be considered from the view of one who hears firsthand the continued requests from general educators for some form of special assistance in educating "this other child." Granted, there is no evidence to indicate anyone is willing to accept "runaway" increases in special education enrollments. The reported change in the learning disabilities definition in New York (resulting in some 40% of the current year national increase in learning disabled population) is further documentation that states are still grappling with handicapping condition eligibility criteria. The 1984 report does describe the overall childcount as "relatively stable" while addressing variances among areas.

Of note in the report are increases in the numbers of preschool-age and of secondary- and postsecondary-age handicapped persons served. In the preschool area, the report states that there were few education programs for the handicapped "before passage of EHA-B," that there are now more such programs through multiple-agency cooperation, and that programs for handicapped and high risk infants are "in a stage of intense development." Given the expansion of state education agency (SEA) and local education agency (LEA) roles with the enactment of P.L. 94-142, and the subsequent overlap with and redefinition of some agency roles in identifying, evaluating, and serving preschool handicapped children, such would seem natural developments during a period of increased resources. The strength of local commitments and efforts in this area may be tested, however, as demands for staff and space to serve traditional school-age populations become greater in the future.

PERSONNEL

The report refers to a National Association of State Directors of Special Education (NASDSE) survey indicating respondent states need more qualified personnel in the preschool area, but it does not link that need with priorities that may be demanded in the future when greater shortages in personnel to serve all handicapped children are anticipated. The report also cites a 1982 study which indicated the activities of the Handicapped Children's Early Education Program (HCEEP) have had positive outcomes and impacts. Again, from a local administrator perspective, such might be expected in that the HCEEP is designed to support experimental and demonstration projects. Local personnel input to both the Council of Administrators of Special Education (CASE) (Training and Model Exchange Project) and to NASDSE (FORUM Project) has indicated that model program descriptions and demonstrations are the most helpful forms of program development assistance.

The concerns expressed above regarding future continued local commitment to preschool programs for handicapped children do not extend to anticipated maintenance of effort in services to secondary- and postsecondary-aged handicapped persons. While there has been growth in this area over 6 years, that growth has been at a decreasing rate in each of the most recent 4 years. Local administrators consistently have listed this area as a top program development concern in surveys of the past 5 years for the CASE Research Committee and the CASE Training and Model Exchange Project. Further, the trend noted in the 1984 Report to Congress of using staff and other resources from the community to provide vocational training opportunities is well proven in vocational education and could relieve some of the future staffing pressures likely to exist in preschool programs. In spite of expressed local needs regarding secondary/vocational program development and renewal, there may be concern about the report statement that "The Department plans to give highest priority to the improvement of programs and services that will help handicapped individuals make a successful transition from school to community." Clearly an Office of Special Education (OSEP) initiative is in order and seems well under way, but there is, at the same time, a caution that the initiative be placed in the proper perspective among various needs in the field.

LEAST RESTRICTIVE ENVIRONMENT

To this reader, the 1984 Report to Congress section on least restrictive environment can best be described as inadequate and not truely reflective of local effort. It is likely the data are no easier to report or collect than the concept has been to implement, but it seems unreasonable to give evidence of progress with phrases such as "large numbers of handicapped students continued to be served in less restrictive settings" (than what?) and "the overall proportion of students served in various settings has remained relatively stable over the years" (with specific exceptions). It is doubtful the examples of placement options listed (regular classes, separate classes, separate schools, and other) would be considered an appropriate full continuum by any monitoring agency. Further, while the report cites certain state and local policies and practices that have apparently contributed to improved least restrictive environment (LRE) decision making, they include no reference to the considerable personnel development efforts in many localities which have also contributed to improved LRE decision making. For future reports, OSEP may wish to consider case study data (as used in other sections) to demonstrate continuum development and design as well as impact of local comprehensive systems of personnel development on LRE decisions and on the evolution of general education service options.

PROCEDURAL SAFEGUARDS

In a somewhat different way, the report discussion of progress in achieving procedural safeguard provisions of EHA-B is also disquieting. That section is based largely on a 1983 NASDSE study of mediation in 38 states in which the analysis of responses was inconclusive concerning the impact of mediation on the number of hearings eventually held. Such data may only demonstrate the need for further study of situations in which mediation is used to identify factors common to successful and to unsuccessful mediation. If available, it may also be instructive to review year-by-year summary data that include the party initiating the hearing (parent or school), the nature of the hearing issue, and the frequency of finding appeal.

EVALUATION

The report section on protection in evaluation focuses on eligibility criteria and standards for placement decisions. That focus may be interpreted to reflect a deemphasis of concerns regarding nondiscriminatory and/or multi-disciplinary evaluation accompanied by a re-emphasis of concerns regarding inappropriate over-identification of children as learning disabled. While such is probably not necessarily true, there is some relief in noting the suggested OSEP initiative deals with providing

"relevant technical assistance" toward LEA and SEA development of standards for placement decision making. From the perspective of a local special education administrator, the prospect of developing and implementing placement standards is infinitely more positive than a "cap" on the percent or number of children of a given handicapping condition for which the planning unit can anticipate financial support.

ASSISTANCE

There is considerable discussion in the 1984 Report to Congress concerning fiscal and technical assistance to states and localities. The portion on finance reiterates the federal allocations and serves well to demonstrate variances in special education funding procedures among cited states. While they may read that portion with interest, most local administrators' funding formula concerns are primarily state-specific. A statement of reaction may be appropriate relative to report comments on OSEP technical assistance to states. Clearly, the Division of Assistance to States (DAS) has SEA's as a primary constituency and cannot be expected to provide ongoing technical assistance directly to localities. At the same time, there is variance across the SEA's in the consistency or effectiveness with which OSEP-generated technical assistance reaches all localities, just as there is variance among the localities in making effective, productive, or appropriate use of information received. There is certainly nothing newsworthy in this matter. It may be sufficient (and not necessarily related to the 1984 Report to Congress) to state a reminder that effective communication linkages are critical if handicapped students are to benefit from current developments in the field. Further, one cannot strongly enough endorse the report's expression of need for further federally sponsored research, development, and demonstration efforts.

PROCEDURAL CHANGES

Summarily, the 1984 Report to Congress cites specific impacts of EHA-B over the 6-year period, including changes in LEA procedures (child identification, parent notice and consent, multi-disciplinary evaluation, IEP's, and due process), increases in the scope and comprehensiveness of programs, and increases in the range of handicapped conditions of children identified and served. Most local special education administrators would agree program expansion indicates progress to the extent that provisions have been made for handicapped children previously unserved in the public education community. Further, in spite of the concomitant complexities, most would agree there was a need in some areas for procedural changes.

The concluding section of the 1984 Report to Congress concerns procedures used by state and local education agencies in local special education program evaluation. Several examples of program evaluation are cited and include (a) SEA development and implementation, (b) SEA development and LEA implementation, and (c) SEA technical assistance with LEA development and implementation. It might be pointed out there are also models of LEA development and implementation with or without other external technical assistance. The report notes several advantages to evaluations performed by LEA personnel such as cost efficiency, validation and improvement of programs, incorporation of locally specific items, and prior familiarity with programs. Other advantages of locally designed program evaluation processes might include insight about local readiness for accepting and acting upon program evaluation findings, master contract provisions that may govern data collection strategies, and community resources that may be implicated. In the 1983 CASE Planning Study, program evaluation was noted as one of the major concerns of local special education administrators.

CONCLUSION

To return to the questions noted at the outset, it is this individual's perception that not only has there been progress toward achievement of the stated purposes of P.L. 94-142, but more importantly, there has been progress toward improving the futures of handicapped children and youth. Despite the sometimes difficult group and individual confrontations and negotiations, mere public attention has raised the general level of awareness concerning the uniqueness and potential of some previously disenfranchised members of society. Much progress made in special education is difficult to document in the short term and cannot remain dependent on descriptions of procedural changes or on data concerning numbers of children served or personnel trained. While such may contribute to the necessary data base for proving effort, attention must focused on longitudinal studies involving those persons purportedly served. There are several areas to which attention must be directed, but one overshadows all others. In a 1971 study of local special education directors, Kohl and Marro noted a primary concern was "continued federal aid to special education." In the 1983 CASE Planning Study, the primary respondent concern was "reductions in fiscal support from federal, state/province, and local sources." At a 1982 international meeting of special educators, one participant from the United Kingdom observed funding seemed an overriding factor in the initiation and continuation of services to the handicapped in the United States. Clearly some stability in funding of local programs must be achieved if attention is to be directed toward long-term program outcomes.

Finally, when considering the changes that have occurred in recent years in the administration of local special education programs (primarily through the provisions of P.L. 94-142) this former local director recalls the time slightly more than a dozen years ago when a child was identified as handicapped and assigned to a special education class on a principal's telephone call reporting a single test score. The child may have been referred for evaluation a year or more previously. There was no confirmation the child's parents were fully informed. Often there was not yet a written evaluation report. There certainly was no individual plan for the child's education. Are we better off than we were before? In my view, the answer can only be "yes."

REFERENCES

Grant, W. V., & Snyder, T. D. (1983). *Digest of education statistics 1983–84.* Washington DC: U.S. Government Printing Office.

Kohl, J. W., & Marro, T. D. (1971, March). *The special education administrator: A normative study of the administrative position in special education.* U.S. Department of Health, Education and Welfare (Report). Washington DC: Bureau of Education for the Handicapped.

U.S. Department of Education. (1984), *Sixth annual report to Congress on the implementation of Public Law 94-142: The Education for All Handicapped Children Act.* Washington DC: U.S. Department of Education.

Where Is Special Education for Students with High Prevalence Handicaps Going?

Abstract: In recent years, more than 4 million handicapped students received special education services supported in part by federal monies supplied for compliance with provisions specified in Public Law 94-142. The numbers of different types of handicapped students served was the focus of this research. Data from 50 states indicating the proportion of students classified in 10 categories of exceptionality were compiled and analyzed. Analysis of average percentages of students served in each handicapping condition for the 1978–1982 time period indicated consistent increases in numbers of learning disabled students, consistent decreases in numbers of speech impaired and mentally retarded students and relatively constant numbers of emotionally disturbed students and students with physical handicaps. Similar trends were evident when data were analyzed across geographical regions of the country; however, considerable variability in numbers of students classified was evident when data from individual states were analyzed. The significance of the findings was discussed with regard to alternative answers that arise when considering what the data mean and what professionals can and should do about them.

BOB ALGOZZINE
LORI KORINEK

BOB ALGOZZINE *is Professor of Special Education and* LORI KORINEK *is a doctoral candidate, University of Florida*

■ On November 29, 1975, it became a handicapped student's right to be provided a free, appropriate education. At that time, then President Gerald R. Ford signed the Education for All Handicapped Children Act (Public Law 94-142) which mandated that each state develop a plan describing in detail the policies and procedures that would be used to ensure that handicapped students between the ages of 3 and 18 be served by September of 1982. The purposes of the Act are described in Section 601(c); they are (a) to assure that all handicapped children have available to them a free, appropriate public education, (b) to assure that the rights of handicapped children and their parents or guardians are protected, (c) to assist states and localities to provide for the education of all handicapped children, and (d) to assess and assure the effectiveness of efforts to educate handicapped children (USDE, 1984, p. v).

United States Department of Education figures indicate that, during the 1982–83 school year, approximately 4.3 million students received special education services paid for in part by federal monies provided as a result of compliance with the provisions of P.L. 94-142 (USDE, 1984); the number served has increased each year since states began reporting the data (i.e., since October, 1976). The federal government recognizes 10 categories of handicapping conditions (Ysseldyke & Algozzine, 1984). Students classified as Speech Impaired, Learning Disabled, Mentally Retarded, Emotionally Disturbed, Other Health Impaired, Orthopedically Impaired, Deaf and Hard of Hearing, Visually Handicapped, Multihandicapped, or Deaf-Blind are eligible for

1. MAINSTREAMING

special education services provided by P.L. 94-142 (USDE, 1980; 1984). Professionals have developed definitions to guide identification practices for each group of students. Approximately 11% of the school-aged population is classified into one of these special education categories and is provided special education as a result of the classification practices (USDE, 1984).

The number of handicapped students counted at any given time is referred to as a prevalence estimate. It is an estimate because students enter and leave programs every day and there is no way of knowing exactly how many are being served at any one time. The best estimates come from data supplied to the federal government under the provisions of P.L. 94-142; specifically, states must supply "child count" data which are compiled and reported in government documents. Of interest in this research were the numbers of students with various handicapping conditions being served. It was reasoned that an analysis of these data would provide useful information for policy makers and other professionals relative to the nature of the various conditions. For example, knowing that a category size is growing or shrinking has implications for personnel in teacher preparation programs and state departments of education as well as for local school district administrators.

METHOD

Available Data

Data on the numbers of students served for each handicapped condition were available in the mandated annual reports to Congress on the implementation of P.L. 94-142 compiled by the U.S. Department of Education, Office of Special Education for school years 1977–78 through 1981–82. Each report listed by state and by handicapping condition the numbers of children aged 3–21 years served under P.L. 94-142 and P.L. 89-313 (Title I) for the respective school year. For recording and reporting purposes, the year the school year ended was used to designate the different sets of data (e.g., 1977–1978 school year = 1978 data).

Data Analysis

Numbers of students served in each state for the 1978–1982 school years were tallied for data analysis; numbers served in each handicapping condition as well as the total number for each state were compiled. The percentages of students served were then calculated by dividing the number in a category by the total number served. These data were summarized using descriptive statistics to analyze trends.

Specifically, the average percentages of students served in each category were compared for the 5-year time period and the relationships between the numbers of students served across the time period were evaluated. A distinction was made between low and high prevalence handicaps for purposes of subsequent discussion. Those categories in which definitions are based on physical (as opposed to psychometric) differences among children contained relatively small numbers of students; *low prevalence* categories included children classified as Other Health Impaired (OHI), Orthopedically Impaired (OI), Deaf and Hard of Hearing (DHH), Visually Handicapped (VH), Multihandicapped (MH) and Deaf and Blind (DB). Definitions and eligibility criteria based primarily on psychometric results (e.g., IQ scores, achievement test scores, behavior ratings, and so on) are used in classifying students as Speech Impaired (SI), Learning Disabled (LD), Mentally Retarded (MR) and Emotionally Disturbed (ED): These categories were referred to as *high prevalence* handicaps.

RESULTS

The average percentages of students served in each handicapping condition for the 1978–1982 time period are presented in Table 1; the corresponding graphic representation of these data is presented in Figure 1. Low prevalence handicaps account for less than 10% of the students served; the percent served in any one of these categories during different years varied very little. More than 90% of the students were classified in four high prevalence handicapping conditions (i.e., SI, LD, MR, ED); definite trends were evident in the percentages of students classified in specific categories in different years. The number of ED students (as reflected in the percentage of all handicapped students) remained relatively constant (6–7%); however, the LD population increased approximately 12% while the combined SI and MR populations decreased by a similar amount over the time period studied.

The relationships between the percentages of students served in each category and the passage of time were evaluated. Specifically, the percentages of students served in each category for each state were plotted over the 5-year time period and the slope coefficients obtained for these data were compared. The slope coefficients reflect the rate of change in the percentages of students served in any category for the corresponding passage of time (i.e., 1 year).

The observed increases in the average percentages of students served in LD programs and the decreases in those served in SI and MR

FIGURE 1
Services to Handicapped Students, Ages 3–21

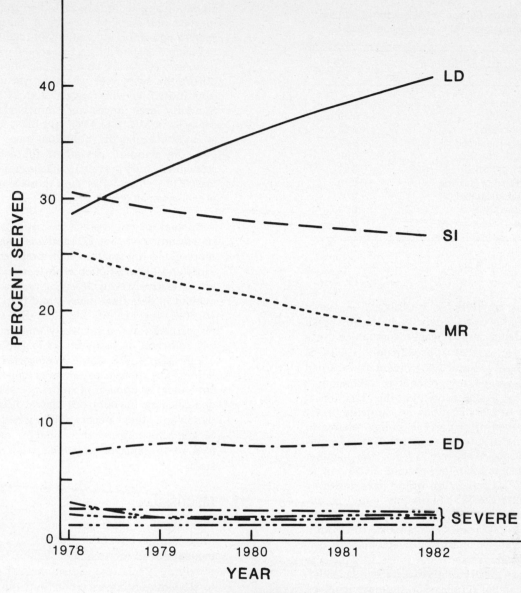

TABLE 1
Average Percentage of Students Served During 5-Year Time Period

	School Year				
Category	*1978*	*1979*	*1980*	*1981*	*1982*
Speech Impaired	30.54	29.10	28.03	27.12	26.40
Learning Disabled	28.77	32.49	35.60	38.16	40.40
Mentally Retarded	25.93	23.34	21.57	19.73	18.47
Emotionally Disturbed	6.85	7.55	7.38	7.63	7.68
Other Health Impaired	2.95	1.75	1.67	1.51	1.34
Orthopedically Impaired	1.88	1.45	1.40	1.34	1.35
Deaf and Hard of Hearing	2.27	2.18	2.03	1.99	1.89
Visually Handicapped	0.96	0.82	0.78	0.75	0.72
Multihandicapped	—*	1.47	1.71	1.82	1.88
Deaf-Blind	—*	0.07	0.08	0.09	0.10

*Data were not reported during 1978 school year.

TABLE 2
Rate of Yearly Change Predicted Based on Data
Compiled for 1978–1982 School Years

Category	Slope Coefficient
Speech Impaired	−1.03
Learning Disabled	2.89
Mentally Retarded	−1.85
Emotionally Disturbed	0.17
Other Health Impaired	−0.33
Orthopedically Impaired	−0.11
Deaf and Hard of Hearing	−0.10
Visually Handicapped	−0.05
Multihandicapped	0.39
Deaf-Blind	0.02

programs are reflected in Table 2. A yearly increase of approximately 3% in the number of LD students served was accompanied by a yearly decrease of approximately 1% in SI students served and 2% in mentally retarded students served. It is, of course, impossible to know the extent to which the data reflect changes in classifications for students previously served or changes in policy relative to new students entering programs. The ED population increased at a rate 17 times less than that for the LD population. Put another way, in 10 years the LD population would have grown by 30% while the ED population would be approximately 2% greater and the MR population would be *decreased* by almost 20%. And, while changes in some low prevalence categories were greater than those in ED, these effects are greatly diminished when considering the actual numbers of students involved (e.g., 3 times as many are served in ED programs as in *any* low prevalence category).

Similar patterns of classification and service delivery were evident across geographical regions. The trends present when the data from all states were summarized were also shown when data were grouped using states within the four Bureau of Census regions (i.e., Northeast, North Central, South, and West). Large, consistent increases in the numbers of students classified as LD were indicated in data from each geographical region. Similarly, corresponding decreases in numbers of students classified as MR and SI were evident, as were relatively even patterns of classification for ED and students with low prevalence handicaps.

When numbers of students in high prevalence categories in individual states were com-

pared, large variability in percentage served among states was indicated. For example, speech impaired students constituted 26% of all handicapped students classified and served in 1982 and from 14 to 46% of the nation's special education students were identified as SI in any one state during that school year. The national average for students classified as LD during the same year was 40%, yet the data from individual states ranged from 25 to 62%. Similarly large ranges were indicated in percentages of MR (7 to 45%) and ED (1 to 27%) students classified by individual states; in general, the standard deviations for data from students in high prevalence categories were at least 2 to 3 times larger than those in any low prevalence category.

An analysis of classification patterns among states indicated that ED students most often represented the smallest high prevalence category and LD most often represented the largest. A relatively even classification system was evident in data from many states (e.g., 28, 16, 16, 19% for LD, SI, MR, and ED students respectively) and a relatively uneven system was indicated in many others (e.g., 56, 27, 7, 3% for LD, SI, MR, and ED categories respectively). The uneven pattern was usually present when the number of students classified in one category (usually LD) was at least twice that in any other category and/or when the LD, SI, and MR categories accounted for more than 85% of the special education students in a state.

DISCUSSION

What do these data mean and why are they important? It could be argued that they provide evidence of an increasingly effective system of providing specialized educational experiences to students failing to profit from the experiences provided in regular education. Those supporting this argument would believe that there are more handicapped students "out there" than are currently identified; and that until *all* handicapped children are served, the system is believed ineffective. They might point to increases in the number of learning disabled students as evidence of improved diagnostic strategies and decreases in the number of mentally retarded students as proof that medicine, early intervention, parent programs, and technology are paying dividends in the education arena.

It could also be argued that the data are reflective of an increasingly ineffective system, one in which most decisions are made based on anything but the characteristics and needs of the students. Those supporting this argument would point to the growth in LD and corresponding shrinkage in MR as evidence that social, political, legal, and economic factors greatly impact the practice of special education. They might argue that there really aren't more learning disabled students and fewer retarded students but that it has become more profitable and socially desirable to find more or less of each.

There is support for both arguments. As indicated in the 1984 USDE Report to Congress,

> Reasons for this rapid growth in the number of children served as learning disabled ... include improved assessment procedures, liberal eligibility criteria, social acceptability for the learning disabled classification, and a lack of general education alternatives for children who experience problems in regular classes. (p. 5)

Special education prevalence figures are influenced by a complex set of interacting factors evident in the professional literature (Ysseldyke & Algozzine, 1982). There is ample evidence to suggest that learning disabilities are easier to find today than several years ago and that this is largely due to changes in underlying concepts, definitions, and diagnostic strategies (Lerner, 1981; Mann, Davis, Boyer, Metz, & Wolford, 1983; Mercer, 1979; Sabatino, 1983; Tucker, Stevens, & Ysseldyke, 1983). At the same time, changes in the MR definition reduced the number of students eligible for services and pushed many into classes providing LD services after some reclassification (Mascari & Forgnone, 1982; Polloway & Smith, 1983).

Data are also readily available indicating that medical advances have reduced the likelihood of individuals being born retarded, that diagnostic decision making in the area of learning disabilities is capricious, that few differences exist between low achievers and LD students, that the LD label is more preferable to the MR diagnosis and that diagnostic "bounty hunting" favors finding students in some categories more than in others (Algozzine & Ysseldyke, 1983; Epps, Ysseldyke, & Algozzine, 1983; Neisworth & Smith, 1978; Robinson & Robinson, 1976; Ysseldyke & Algozzine, 1983; Ysseldyke, Algozzine, Shinn, & McGue, 1982). Data, then, support two apparently divergent conclusions, both of which are reflected in the results presented here. While we believe there are occasions when two competing, seemingly contradictory arguments can be correct, we also believe this is not one of them.

If the numbers we have analyzed reflect actual growth, then questions such as the following must be addressed: Who profits from the growth? How much growth will be tolerated? How will personnel preparation programs keep pace with these changes and what impact do they have on the future of special education? The learning disability category is growing at a rate of approximately 3% of the special education population a year. At that rate of progress, all currently classified students in high prevalence categories would be classified LD by around the year 2001. Of course, that will not happen, because somebody will see what is going on and take steps to change it. For example, federal, state, or local officials will place a "cap" on the number of LD students who can be served, or eligibility criteria will be rewritten with the expressed purpose of limiting the numbers of students served. This type of action, of course, will provoke considerable discussion and one can expect to see "task forces" convene in attempts to standardize practice. Once again, the best minds in special education will come together to reaffirm problems and issues and recommend appropriate courses of action for deciding who shall be entitled to special educational services—all such action, of course, predicated on the assumption that special education is better than regular education for all these students.

If data indicate ineffective decision making, educational practice characterized by whim and chance, then the question of who receives and who profits takes on special significance. For example, what are the characteristics of students currently in special education programs? Are students being served different from those not being served? Are students with real handicaps being deprived of services because upper limits are such that simple redistribution within the system benefits "highly profitable" categories more than others? If students in need of services are not being identified or are being reclassified based on anticipated benefits to the system rather than the students, then the injustices at the heart of the social and political efforts that resulted in passage of P.L. 94-142 still exist. And what if the services are not effective? As Gerber (1984) indicated,

> Over 1.6 million American school children are being treated as learning disabled, and their school experiences are often drastically changed without unequivocal demonstration that such changes benefit them over the course of their public school education or produce desirable, long-term life outcomes. (p. 222)

In the educational world of such unknowns, why isn't more done in "regular" classes and does not being in a "special" class really add to a hidden handicap?

The extent to which there are unserved students in America's public school system is not evident in the data we analyzed. That important differences exist in numbers of students served is obvious. The question of who shall be included in special education programs must be addressed. We are reminded of an argument made earlier by E. P. Cubberly:

> We know now that the number of children of superior ability is approximately as large as the number of the feeble in mind, and also that the future of democratic governments hinges largely upon the proper education and utilization of these superior children. One child of superior intellectual capacity, educated so as to utilize his talents, *may confer* greater benefits upon mankind, and be *educationally far more important*, than a thousand of the feebleminded children upon whom we have recently come to put so much educational effort and expense. (1922, p. 451, emphasis added)

Clearly, there is no simple answer to the question of whether so much special education (i.e., for so many students) is justified. So what does all of this mean? We think it means that it is time to quit viewing eligibility decision making as a technical problem. It means putting an end to efforts to try to find better ways of defining concepts and conditions that cannot be defined and may not exist (e.g., "hidden handicaps"). It means recognizing that social, political and economic factors create the problems. It means that fundamental examination of the concepts and assumptions that drive assessment and decision making in special education is needed. It means it is time for a careful examination of public policy on the education of handicapped students. The Mother Liberty mentality that established America's first special class homes for the down-trodden and disabled may now be an outdated perspective that has made today's special classes overpopulated havens for the hard-to-teach.

REFERENCES

Algozzine, B., & Ysseldyke, J. E. (1983). Learning disabilities as a subset of school failure: The oversophistication of a concept. *Exceptional Children, 50*, 242–246.

Cubberly, E. P. (1922). *A brief history of education.* Boston: Houghton Mifflin.

Epps, S., Ysseldyke, J. E., & Algozzine, B. (1983). Impact of different definitions of learning disabilities on the number of students identified. *Journal of Psychoeducational Assessment, 1*, 341–352.

Gerber, M. M. (1984). The department of education's sixth annual report to Congress on P.L. 94-142: Is Congress really getting the full story? *Exceptional Children, 51*, 209–224.

Lerner, J. (1981). *Learning disabilities.* Boston: Houghton-Mifflin Company.

Mann, L., Davis, C. H., Boyer, C. W., Metz, C. M., & Wolford, B. (1983). LD or not LD, that was the question: A retrospective analysis of child service demonstration centers' compliance with the federal definition of learning disabilities. *Journal of Learning Disabilities, 16*, 14–17.

Mascari, B. G., & Forgnone, C. (1982). A follow-up study of EMR students four years after dismissal from the program. *Education and Training of the Mentally Retarded, 17*, 288–292.

Mercer, C. D. (1979). *Children and adolescents with learning disabilities.* Columbus, OH: Charles E. Merrill.

Neisworth, J. T., & Smith, R. M. (1978). *Retardation.* New York: McGraw-Hill.

Polloway, E. A., & Smith, J. D. (1983). Changes in mild mental retardation: Population, programs and perspectives. *Exceptional Children, 50*, 149–159.

Robinson, N. M., & Robinson, H. B. (1976). *The mentally retarded child* (2nd ed.). New York: McGraw Hill.

Sabatino, D. A. (1983). The house that Jack built. *Journal of Learning Disabilities, 16*, 26–27.

Tucker, J., Stevens, L. J., & Ysseldyke, J. E. (1983). Learning disabilities: The experts speak out. *Journal of Learning Disabilities, 16*, 6–14.

United States Department of Education. (1980). *To assure the free appropriate public education of all handicapped children: Second annual report to Congress on the implementation of Public Law 94-142: The Education for All Handicapped Children Act.* Washington, DC: Department of Education.

United States Department of Education. (1984). *To assure the free appropriate public education of all handicapped children: Sixth annual report to Congress on the implementation of Public Law 94-142: The Education for All Handicapped Children Act.* Washington, DC: Department of Education.

Ysseldyke, J. E., & Algozzine, B. (1982). *Critical issues in special and remedial education.* Boston: Houghton-Mifflin.

Ysseldyke, J. E., & Algozzine, B. (1983). LD or not LD: That's not the question. *Journal of Learning Disabilities, 16*, 29–31.

Ysseldyke, J. E., & Algozzine, B. (1984). *Introduction to special education.* Boston: Houghton-Mifflin.

Ysseldyke, J. E., Algozzine, B., Shinn, M. R., & McGue, M. (1982). Similarities and differences between low achievers and students classified learning disabled. *The Journal of Special Education, 16*, 73–85.

Staff Development: A Key Ingredient of Effective Mainstreaming

Margaret C. Wang
Eva D. Vaughan
Joan A. Dytman

Margaret C. Wang *is Professor of Educational Psychology and Senior Scientist and Director of the Adaptive Learning Environments Unit at the Learning Research and Development Center (LRDC) at the University of Pittsburgh.*
Eva D. Vaughan *is a Center Associate at LRDC.* **Joan A. Dytman** *is Adjunct Assistant Professor of Educational Psychology at the University of Pittsburgh and a post-doctoral Fellow at LRDC.*

■ Enactment of the "least restrictive environment" mandate of Public Law 94-142 in 1975 established a nationwide standard for the integration of exceptional students in regular classroom settings. Great strides in this direction have been made over the past decade. Nevertheless, the restructuring of regular classroom environments to accommodate the diverse needs of individual students has been a major obstacle (Reynolds & Wang, 1981). The need for restructuring is underscored by the past failure of conventional general education programs to provide appropriate instructional accommodations for special needs students. If

Effective mainstreaming requires an environment in regular classes where special needs students are integrated socially and academically with their general education peers.

headway is to be made, however, in educational restructuring that is aimed at the effective instructional and social integration of special needs students, the roles and functions of specialized school personnel and regular classroom teachers must be redefined. Systematic provision of staff development is a key ingredient of successful change along this line (Wang, 1982).

Research and experience have consistently suggested that staff development programs which provide ongoing training support for helping school staff to develop required implementation expertise tend to be associated with effective school improvement in general and effective mainstreaming in particular (Wang & Gennari, 1983). Certain features have been identified as characteristic of effective staff development efforts. First, they are adaptive to the training needs and interests of individual staff (Melle & Pratt, 1981); Merten & Yarger, 1981; Miller & Wolf, 1979). They also adopt a programmatic approach to addressing day-to-day implementation problems, rather than being in the genre of "one-shot" inservice programs that occur in contexts different from the staff's daily work (Emrick & Peterson, 1977; Huberman, 1981; Melle & Pratt, 1981). Other identified features of effective staff development include strong support from central and building administrators; active participation by school staff in decisions regarding staff development goals and procedures; and systematic involvement of all personnel whose work is either directly or indirectly affected (Charters & Pellegrin, 1973; McLaughlin & Marsh, 1979; Merten & Yarger, 1981; Weatherley, 1979).

In a review of over 100 studies of staff development, Lawrence (1974) concluded that teachers prefer (a) individual staff development over large-group sessions, (b) active staff involvement over passive-receptive involvement, (c) demonstration of skills with supervisor feedback over provisional skills for future use, and (d) an integrated program of staff development activities over isolated training sessions. The consensus of research in this area is that teachers need frequent contact and continuous support in their efforts to solve both short-term and long-range problems (e.g., Cruickshank, Lorish, & Thompson, 1979; McLaughlin & Marsh, 1979; McNergney, 1980; Miller & Wolf, 1979; Perry, 1980; Zigarmi, Amory, & Zigarmi, 1979).

One of the primary goals of the work discussed in this article was to develop and test a systematic staff development approach that incorporates the features described above and is also designed to support the

programming and role changes required for greater accommodation of special needs students, as well as their general education peers, in regular classes. In the following sections, this staff development approach is described in the context of a mainstreaming program that was implemented in a large urban school system. First, the mainstreaming program is discussed to provide information on its goals and the nature of the educational environment in which teachers and students were expected to operate. Next the program's built-in, staff development support system is described and evidence regarding its effectiveness in helping to achieve desired implementation and student outcomes is summarized. Finally, some of the implications for educational practice and research are outlined.

Staff development efforts that address day-to-day implementation problems facilitate the restructuring of regular classrooms to accommodate special needs students.

THE ALEM AS A MAINSTREAMING PROGRAM

The Adaptive Learning Environments Model (ALEM) was the educational program implemented in the mainstreaming classrooms that provided the setting for the study described in this article. Implementation of the ALEM as a full-time mainstreaming program is based on several principles and assumptions regarding effective instruction and learning. These are summarized briefly as follows:

- A basic condition for effective mainstreaming is the establishment of environments in regular classes where special needs students are integrated socially and academically with their general education peers, and where special and general education students alike are provided with equal access to available instructional resources and equal opportunities to succeed socially and academically.

- As individuals, general education students as well as special education students learn in different ways and require varying amounts of instruction and time to learn. Thus, educational programs that recognize the "special" needs of each student in the regular classroom, and make instructional provisions to accommodate those needs, are a direct application of the principle of "appropriate" educational services in the "least restrictive environment." When instructional provisions are made available by regular and specialized professional staff to meet the "special" learning needs of each individual student, in the same setting, and on a regular basis, general and mainstreamed special education students alike are more likely to experience learning success. Moreover, in such environments the focus is on educational intervention rather than placement, and individual differences tend to be viewed as the norm rather than the exception.

- Provision of adaptive instruction requires use of a variety of instructional methods and learning experiences. Essentially all learning involves both external and internal adaptation. External adaptation occurs in the ideas and tasks that are to be learned and in the modes and forms in which new task content is presented to the learner. Internal adaptation takes place in the mind of the learner as new tasks are assimilated and internal mental structures are modified to accommodate the tasks. Thus, the twofold goal of adaptive instruction is to make instructional provisions that are adaptive to individual differences in students and to foster students' ability to effectively assume self-responsibility for making necessary adaptations in their learning environments, in their learning process, and in management of their own learning and classroom behaviors.

- Effective mainstreaming requires the establishment of functional linkages and integrated services among

Staff programs motivate teachers to view individual differences as the norm rather than the exception and to gear their instruction accordingly.

classroom instructional staff and specialized professionals who currently work, for the most part, in separate special education and compensatory education entitlement programs. The roles of both general and special education staff must be renegotiated, with the focus on those specific functions involved in effectively adapting school learning environments to the needs of individual students. The role of special education teachers, for example, would include consultation with general education teachers, as well as the provision of direct instructional services for special education students in regular classes. General education teachers, on the other hand, would be the primary instructors for both general education students and mainstreamed special education students in regular classrooms.

Implementation of the ALEM as a mainstreaming program incorporates these principles and is aimed at the effective provision of learning experiences that are adaptive to student differences in regular classroom settings (Wang, 1980a). Toward accomplishing this objective, the ALEM's design systematically integrates aspects of individualized prescriptive instruction that facilitate basic skills mastery (Bloom, 1976; Glaser, 1977; Rosenshine, 1979) with aspects of informal education that foster self-responsibility (Johnson, Maruyama, Johnson, Nelson, & Skon, 1981; Marshall, 1981; Peterson, 1979). Specifically, the ALEM includes twelve critical program dimensions. Nine of the dimensions are related to the process of providing adaptive instruction. They are Creating and Maintaining Instructional Materials, Developing Student Self-Responsibility, Diagnostic Testing, Instructing, Interactive Teaching, Monitoring and Diagnosing, Motivating, Prescribing, and Record Keeping. Three of the dimensions—Arranging Space and Facilities, Establishing and Communicating Rules and Procedures, and Managing Aides—are related to supporting implementation of adaptive instruction in the classroom. In addition to the twelve critical dimensions, implementation of the ALEM is supported by a school- and district-level delivery system that consists of four major components: an ongoing, data-based staff development approach; instructional teaming; multi-age grouping; and a parent involvement program.

Each school day, general education students and mainstreamed special needs students in ALEM classes receive instruction from general education teachers in all subjects on a full-time basis. The services of special education personnel are integrated with implementation of the ALEM in regular classrooms, and they range from the provision of consultation for general education teachers to direct instruction on an individual basis for students with special needs. As with many conventional special education programs, the focus is on upgrading achievement in mathematics and in reading and other language arts. Equally important, the ALEM fosters the development of greater self-management skills for all students.

Students in ALEM classrooms work in small groups, in large groups, and by themselves. They move from one learning task to another at individually varying paces. The progress of each student is monitored by the teacher, and only upon satisfactorily completing a task is a student able to move ahead to another task that is different and/or more difficult. Teachers work individually and in teams, as needed. Students often collaborate in teaching and testing each other, but all activity is observed closely by teachers and each student has access to teacher help when it is required. More detailed descriptions of the ALEM can be found in several other publications (e.g., Wang, 1980a; Wang & Birch, 1984; Wang, Gennari, & Waxman, in press).

THE ALEM'S STAFF DEVELOPMENT COMPONENT

The establishment and maintenance of an innovative school program like the ALEM require not only detailed specification and understanding of the program's design and operating features, but also staff development that supports day-to-day operation of the program in the classroom. The Data-Based Staff Development Program provides a systematic mechanism for identifying and accommodating the training needs associated with the programmatic and personnel role changes required for effective implementation of the ALEM. It is designed to help school personnel to become increasingly self-sufficient in monitoring and diagnosing their implementation needs as well as more proficient in establishing and maintaining a high degree of implementation of the ALEM.

The Data-Based Staff Development Program consists of three components: a training sequence of three levels; a set of measures for assessing the degree of program implementation; and a delivery system that enables school staff to provide ongoing inservice support to meet the needs of individual staff. The three training levels are shown in Figure 1. Level I provides basic working knowledge of the curricular content and procedures incorporated in the ALEM. In Level II, more intensive training is provided in specific staff functions. Level III is a clinical training component tailored to the needs of individual staff. Training at Levels I and II generally is completed in a total of five, half-day sessions prior to classroom implementation. Training at Level III is ongoing in-service training designed to help school staff to continually improve and upgrade their classroom implementation. It is primarily at the third level that the interactive process of assessment, feedback, planning, and training occurs. (For more detailed discussions of the Data-Based Staff Development Program, see Wang, 1981 and Wang and Gennari, 1983.)

IMPLEMENTATION OF THE ALEM IN AN URBAN SETTING

In 1982–83, the ALEM was implemented in five schools of a large urban school system as a full-time mainstreaming program for mildly handicapped students who previously had been served in a "pull-out," self-contained, special education program. The implementation and outcomes of the ALEM are discussed here, especially insofar as they reflect the operation and effectiveness of the Data-Based Staff Development Program.

The Setting

The five schools that participated in the study are located in three community school districts of the New York City Public Schools. Although they vary in ethnic composition, all three districts contain a significant number of low-income students; the proportions of Title I–identified students in the districts in 1982–83 were 12%, 19%, and 70%, respectively.

The ALEM was implemented in 26 first- through fourth-grade classrooms across the five schools. The instructional staff consisted of 26 classroom teachers (general education); one half-time paraprofessional for each classroom; and four education specialists (one of whom was shared by two of the schools). The classroom teachers ranged in teaching experience from 2 to

FIGURE 1
The Data-Based Staff Development Program

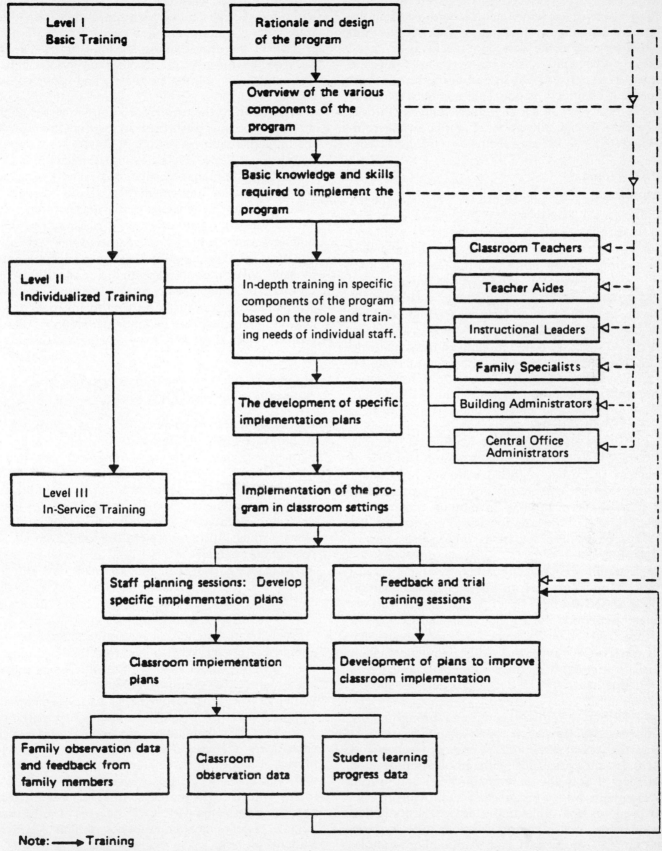

Note: ──► Training
      ---► Re-training

1. MAINSTREAMING

32 years, with an average of 17 years. The education specialists (two certified in general education and two in special education) were assigned from among teachers in the participating schools; they were trained to monitor program implementation, coordinate staff development planning and activities, and provide consultative services to the classroom teachers.

The 26 participating classes ranged in size from 21 to 31 students. Approximately five students in each classroom were identified as educable mentally retarded, learning disabled, or socially-emotionally disturbed. All of the special education students were mainstreamed in the ALEM classrooms on a full-time basis.

Staff Development

In late August, 1982, just before the beginning of the school year, the staff of all five schools—general and special education teachers, administrators, and paraprofessionals—attended three days of pre-implementation training (Levels I and II of the Data-Based Staff Development Program). First, an overview of the ALEM's goals and major components was provided (Level I). The next level of training focused on those skills required to implement the ALEM in the classroom (Level II). Specifically, training addressed how to use individualized learning materials for adapting instruction to individual students, how to share responsibility with students for managing the instructional-learning process, and how to develop activities for exploratory learning. Hands-on training also was provided whereby teachers actually rearranged furniture and storage space in their own classrooms for ease of movement and access, labeled materials for student use, and set up exploratory learning centers. The overall emphasis of pre-implementation training was on the practical know-how needed to get through the first days and weeks of school—in other words, how to get the program started.

Preparation for Level III training (ongoing, inservice training support) began during pre-implementation training. Based on their observations of the teachers during this period, the education specialists worked with the instructional leaders from their respective assigned schools, and with ALEM implementation specialists, in identifying the additional training needs of individual teachers and developing teacher-specific implementation plans.

Inservice training support continued throughout the school year. The education specialists made frequent visits to the ALEM classrooms to observe teachers and students; to help teachers with problems related to instruction of both the general education and special needs students; and, when needed, to provide instructional services for individual students. Information from informal classroom observations was used to plan group and individual staff training. For example, if many or most teachers in a particular school experienced difficulty with a certain aspect of implementation, the education specialist might schedule that topic for discussion at the next staff meeting. If an individual teacher showed weakness in a particular area, the education specialist might plan appropriate individualized training. Figure 2 shows a page from an education specialist's monthly training log for Teacher XX. The log provides information on observed teacher behaviors, suggested training strategies, and expected outcomes.

In addition to their frequent informal observations, the education specialists used an instrument known as the Implementation Assessment Battery for Adaptive Instruction (Wang, 1980b; Wang, Catalano, & Gromoll, 1983) to obtain objective, quantitative measures of the degree of implementation of the ALEM's 12 critical program dimensions in the 26 classrooms. The Battery was administered in each classroom at three different points in the school year—October, February, and May. The resulting information was incorporated in staff development planning for individuals and groups. The objective was to provide teachers with a self-monitoring tool for improving their capabilities to achieve higher degrees of implementation of dimensions in which they were experiencing difficulty.

MAJOR FINDINGS ON THE ALEM'S IMPLEMENTATION AND EFFECTS

Findings on the implementation and effects of the ALEM as a full-time mainstreaming program in the participating classrooms are summarized here to illustrate the effectiveness (albeit indirectly derived) of the Data-Based Staff Development Program as an integral support component. Data in three categories—program implementation, classroom processes, and student learning outcomes—were collected from all five participating schools to assess the effectiveness of the mainstreaming program and its staff development component. (A more detailed description of the design and findings of this study can be found in Wang, Peverly, and Randolph, in press.)

Program implementation was found to improve consistently across all five schools from the beginning to the end of the school year, with most teachers achieving a high degree of implementation of the ALEM by winter or spring. Improvements in implementation were accompanied by positive changes in classroom processes and interactions for general and special education students. For example, greater frequencies of teacher-student interactions for instructional, rather than management, purposes were observed in classrooms with a high degree of implementation (compared to classrooms with lower degrees of implementation), as were greater amounts of time spent by students on-task.

The ALEM also was found to have a positive impact

FIGURE 2
Sample Monthly Training Log

LOG

School: J.J.

Teacher: X X

District: A

Date: November 6, 1982

Grade: 2

Time: 9:50 – 10:30

Observed Behavior	Strategy Suggested	Expected Outcome
Math skills introduced without use of concrete aids.	Use concrete aids to introduce new skills.	Concepts are introduced with manipulatives. Less time is spent teaching a skill.
Students marked self-scheduling folder on their own.	Only aide or teacher marks self-scheduling sheet.	Students ask teacher (aide) to check their self-scheduling sheet/order work has been completed.
Paper/pencil tasks used in math explorations.	Include math activities — math bingo.	More hands-on tasks are included.

Follow Up: An observation of XX's class has been scheduled for November 13.

1. MAINSTREAMING

on the learning outcomes—academic and attitudinal—of both the general education and the special education students. Scores on standardized achievement tests were used to measure achievement gains in mathematics and reading. Although they lagged somewhat behind the general education students, the special needs students averaged grade-equivalent gains of 1.04 in reading and 1.08 in mathematics. These are about equal to the expected gains based on national norms for general education students, and approximately twice the expected gains for comparable groups of handicapped students. In addition, results from measures of student attitudes showed few differences in affective outcomes for both groups of students in the ALEM classrooms. Both groups indicated a willingness to accept responsibility for their classroom performance, as well as positive attitudes toward their classes.

The problems that many of the general education teachers had expected in dealing with special needs students rarely were noted in the ALEM classrooms. The adaptive curricula and the program's instructional-learning management system, combined with the staff development support, were identified by the participating teachers as important factors. The extent to which the special needs students were successfully integrated into classroom life, instructionally and socially, was evidenced not only by improved classroom processes and interactions but also by the fact that, at the end of the school year, approximately 30% of the mainstreamed students were recommended by their teachers for decertification. The average decertification rate across the districts for students with similar special education classifications in self-contained special education classes was 2.8%.

Teacher perceptions of the ALEM's effects on students and teachers were viewed as another indicator of the success of the program's staff development approach. In their general assessment, 85% of the teachers in the ALEM classrooms felt that implementation of the program had been a professionally rewarding, challenging, and stimulating experience for them. A large majority also felt that the ALEM enabled them to get to know their students better. Although the teachers expressed some reservations about the program's record-keeping demands, a majority (67%) disagreed that the individualized approach to instruction placed too heavy a demand on their time and effort. In terms of the program's effects on students, 85% of the teachers who responded to a survey of teacher attitudes indicated that students in their classrooms seemed to feel better about themselves as a result of their experiences under the ALEM. A majority of the teachers also felt that the provision of learning options and individualized instruction resulted in lessons matched appropriately to each student's academic level and in improved academic performance.

IMPLICATIONS

The work described here, as well as the other studies cited earlier, suggests that effectively designed and implemented staff development programs lead to the increased ability of general and special educators to work together in mainstreaming settings to improve educational services for general and special education students alike. With ongoing, inservice training support, school staff can successfully adapt curricula to individual student needs, while also promoting students' self-management skills. The outcomes of these efforts include positive classroom processes, achievement gains, and increased self-esteem in students, as well as positive attitudes and increased efficacy in program implementation for teachers.

Despite the admitted constraints against making generalizations based on findings from a single program, the positive results of the study seem to suggest that innovative educational practices can be successfully implemented with ongoing staff development support. In fact, a large majority of teachers in the study were found to be able to develop areas of expertise that traditionally have been attributed to a rare breed of "master" teachers. Thus, there is evidence to support the opinion that it is time to shift attention from demonstrating the need for, and positive outcomes of, effective staff development programs to the study of how to implement such programs as support systems for innovative improvement efforts in a variety of school settings.

REFERENCES

Bloom, B. S. (1976). *Human characteristics and school learning*. New York: McGraw-Hill.

Charters, W., & Pellegrin, R. (1973). Barriers to the innovation process: Four case studies of differential staffing. *Educational Administration Quarterly, 9*(1), 3–14.

Cruickshank, D. R., Lorish, C., & Thompson, L. (1979). What we think we know about inservice education. *Journal of Teacher Education, 30*(1), 27–31.

Emrick, J., & Peterson, S. (1977). *Evaluation of the National Diffusion Network*. Menlo Park, CA: Stanford Research Institute.

Glaser, R. (1977). *Adaptive education: Individual diversity and learning*. New York: Holt, Rinehart, & Winston.

Huberman, M. (1981). *Exemplary Center for Reading Instruction (ECRI), Masepa, North Plains: A case study*. Andover, MA: The Network.

Johnson, D. W., Maruyama, G., Johnson, R., Nelson, D., & Skon, L. (1981). Effects of cooperative, competitive, and individualistic goal structures on achievement: A meta-analysis. *Psychological Bulletin, 89*, 47–62.

Lawrence, G. (1974). *Patterns of effective in-service education*. Tallahassee: Florida Department of Education.

Marshall, H. H. (1981). Open classrooms: Has the term outlived its usefulness? *Review of Educational Research, 51,* 181–192.

McLaughlin, M. W., & Marsh, D. D. (1979). Staff development and school change. In A. Lieberman & L. Miller (Eds.), *Staff development: New demands, new realities, new perspectives.* New York: Teachers College Press.

McNergney, R. F. (1980). Responding to teachers as individuals. *Theory Into Practice, 19,* 234–239.

Melle, M., & Pratt, H. (1981, April). *Documenting program adaption in a district-wide implementation effort: The three year evolution from evaluation to an instructional improvement plan.* Paper presented at the annual meeting of the American Educational Research Association, Los Angeles.

Merten, S., & Yarger, S. (1981, April). *A comprehensive study of program estimates, staff services, resources, and policy board operations in 37 federally funded teacher centers.* Paper presented at the annual meeting of the American Educational Research Association, Los Angeles.

Miller, L., & Wolf, T. E. (1979). Staff development for school change: Theory and practice. In A. Lieberman & L. Miller (Eds.), *Staff development: New demands, new realities, new perspectives.* New York: Teachers College Press.

Perry, R. H. (1980). The organizational/environmental variables in staff development. *Theory Into Practice, 19*(4), 256–261.

Peterson, P. L. (1979). Direct instruction reconsidered. In P. L. Peterson & H. J. Walberg (Eds.), *Research on teaching: Concepts, findings, and implications.* Berkeley, CA: McCutchan.

Reynolds, M. C., & Wang, M. C. (1981). *Restructuring "special" school programs: A position paper (LRDC Publications Series 1981/24).* Pittsburgh, PA: University of Pittsburgh, Learning Research and Development Center.

Rosenshine, B. V. (1979). Content, time, and direct instruction. In P. L. Peterson & H. J. Walberg (Eds.), *Research on teaching: Concepts, findings, and implications.* Berkeley, CA: McCutchan.

Wang, M. C. (1980a). Adaptive instruction: Building on diversity. *Theory Into Practice, 19*(2), 122–127.

Wang, M. C. (1980b). *The degree of implementation measures for the Adaptive Learning Environments Model.* Pittsburgh, PA: University of Pittsburgh, Learning Research and Development Center.

Wang, M. C. (1981). *The use of the Data-Based Staff Development Program to improve program implementation.* Pittsburgh, PA: University of Pittsburgh, Learning Research and Development Center.

Wang, M. C. (1982, November). *Continuing professional development: An adaptive approach.* Keynote address delivered at the annual national conference of the Teacher Education Division of The Council for Exceptional Children, Nashville.

Wang, M. C., & Birch, J. W. (1984). Effective special education in regular classes. *Exceptional Children, 50*(5), 391–399.

Wang, M. C., Catalano, R., & Gromoll, E. (1983). *Training manual for the Implementation Assessment Battery for Adaptive Instruction.* Pittsburgh, PA: University of Pittsburgh, Learning Research and Development Center.

Wang, M. C., & Gennari, P. (1983). Analysis of the design, implementation, and effects of a data-based staff development program. *Teacher Education and Special Education, 6*(4), 211–224.

Wang, M. C., Gennari, P., & Waxman, H. C. (in press). The Adaptive Learning Environments Model: Design, implementation, and effects. In M. C. Wang & H. J. Walberg (Eds.), *Adapting instruction to student differences.* Chicago: National Society for the Study of Education.

Wang, M. C., Peverly, S., & Randolph, R. (in press). An investigation of the implementation and effects of a full-time mainstreaming program. *Journal of Remedial and Special Education.*

Weatherley, R. (1979). *Reforming special education: Policy implementation from state level to street level.* Cambridge, MA: MIT Press.

Zigarmi, P., Amory, J., & Zigarmi, D. A. (1979). A model for an individualized staff development program. In A. Lieberman & L. Miller (Eds.), *Staff development: New demands, new realities, new perspectives.* New York: Teachers College Press.

The research reported herein was supported by the Learning Research and Development Center, which is supported in part by funds from the National Institute of Education, and by the New York City Board of Education. The opinions expressed herein do not necessarily reflect the positions or policies of these agencies, and no official endorsement should be inferred.

Attitude Change Strategies: Helping Nonhandicapped Children Understand Their Handicapped Peers

Probably the single, most important factor influencing the success or failure of mainstreaming, and later of lifestreaming, is the attitudes of nonhandicapped persons toward those who are handicapped. Our attitudes affect the way we view handicapped persons, which in turn affects the way handicapped persons view themselves. Our expectations of what handicapped persons can do may be too limited, thereby causing us to limit opportunities and life experiences needed for them to participate fully and function independently in society.

Children need to learn that handicapped children are more like than different from themselves; that handicapped children are people first, who happen to have a disability. Children need to gain factual information to replace false myths, and to have first-hand experiences to gain an understanding of what the disability is really like instead of repeating harmful stereotypes based on the biases and misconceptions of other uninformed persons in their lives.

The first article, "Don't Stare—I'll Tell You Later!" shows how some adult reactions can jeopardize healthy, honest, and open responses of children to the whole issue of disabilities.

The articles in this section show how educators can use attitude change strategies in classroom settings. Activities should be planned in advance to ensure opportunities for interaction between handicapped and nonhandicapped children. "Changing Attitudes" discusses some of the methods used for integrating handicapped children into the classroom more effectively. Cooperative work projects, joint play activities, and human differences training are suggested by the Stainbacks and Jaben in the third article. "Toward More Success in Mainstreaming" maintains that when peers are trained to assist handicapped children, they not only provide role models for them, but also develop in themselves sensitivity, appropriate expectations, and natural interactions. The benefits of mainstreaming on children who are not disabled is explored in "Integrating Disabled Children." The article explains that the nonhandicapped children may learn to become more sensitive to and accepting of individual differences. It also stresses the importance of teachers' attitudes on this process.

The necessity of a total educational and living experience for exceptional children is important if their assimilation into society is to be successful. "The Parent Connection: Enhancing the Affective Component of Parent Conferences" examines a model for developing a positive and whole-living experience for handicapped students.

Several good materials are available now to help children deal with handicaps. "Books About Children with Special Needs: An Annotated Bibliography" addresses selection criteria and use of children's books for sensitizing and educating children about handicaps.

Looking Ahead: Challenge Questions

How do children learn stereotypes and develop misconceptions about handicaps?

In what ways do these stereotypes and misconceptions affect children's behavior with handicapped persons?

What attitude change strategies can educators employ in reversing negative attitudes?

How do cooperative, competitive, and individualistic climates affect children? Which climate would you establish and why?

What is handicapism? Where does it come from? What can be done about it?

DON'T STARE—
I'll Tell You Later!

Hoyt Anderson

Hoyt Anderson, born with cerebral palsey, is a 31-year-old free lance writer who lives in California. Despite his mobility and speech impediments, he has volunteered since his early teens to help other physically disabled young people, in both educational and recreational programs. Mr. Anderson is the author of *The Disabled Homemaker*, a book on daily living skills for the physically impaired person, published by Charles C. Thomas Publishers in Springfield, Illinois.

Mary Jo, a teenage polio victim, hopped down the aisle of a supermarket on crutches. Five-year-old Jimmy stared at her, watching every step. Finally he asked, "What's wrong with you?"

His mother stopped, grabbed him, reprimanding him sharply, "Shh . . . Don't stare—I'll tell you later!" She dragged him away without ever explaining Mary Jo's handicap.

This is a common occurrence. Many parents don't know how to explain a person's disability to a child and invariably avoid doing so. Dr. William Rader, a psychiatrist, points out: "People are under the misconception that it would be embarrassing or hurtful if a person's disability were discussed in his presence. Even though nothing is said, there is actually communication. Because of this silence, the parent is saying to the child, 'You should feel sorry for that person; there is something bizarre about him! Don't hurt his feelings! Don't discuss his disability! Pretend it doesn't exist!'"

Some adults react negatively to the disabled. When Mrs. Boyer took her son Willie shopping (fifteen-year-old Willie had an abnormally large head and was confined to a wheelchair), an elderly, white-haired woman approached and asked her, "What's wrong with your boy? Does he have water on the head?"

Willie, not hard of hearing, quickly responded, "Lady, lady—I have muscular dystrophy. My head is not completely filled with water because I have an IQ of 120!"

Other adults are more understanding, but don't really know how to explain a person's disability to their children. They feel inept at handling the situation and therefore ignore it. However, the child's curiosity about the handicapped is often satisfied in other ways.

Mrs. Jones and Johnny walked into the library. While they were looking for books, Johnny spotted eight-year-old Brian, wearing thick glasses and a protective helmet and walking with three-pronged crutches.

"What's wrong with him?" Johnny asked.

Mrs. Jones, ill at ease and not wanting to make a scene, ignored Johnny's questions and continued browsing through the books. She looked up in a few minutes and saw Johnny talking to the boy. They were laughing and playing together. Apparently, Johnny realized Brian could be his friend and that his differences didn't matter.

Thinking it over on the way home, Mrs. Jones realized she had done the wrong thing. After all, Brian was no different from any other child, except for his physical handicaps. Basically, all children are innocent, warm and loving.

Children's Attitudes

As Dr. Rader points out: "A child is very accepting usually—much more so than an adult, because a child is much less biased. In reality, the parent could learn a great deal from the child by observing his behavior with the handicapped person in a situation where there has been no negative input in the initial phases and the disabled person feels comfortable about himself. Then you will find that the handicapped person and the child will feel comfortable with each other."

Sometimes the situation isn't as easy as in Johnny's case. Often children react negatively towards handicapped people. Two German psychologists, Gerd Jansen and Otto Esser, made a three-year-study of 1,000 school children and observed that younger children had a greater aversion to the handicapped than older children. Esser explained this by saying that older youngsters learn to pity the handicapped.

These psychologists also interviewed 1,060 adults and found that 90% didn't know how to approach a handicapped person. Obviously, this same group would not know how to explain a disability to a child. With this in mind, let's look at how people with handicaps themselves handle children's questions.

Jack, a veteran paralyzed from the waist down, sat in a wheelchair on his front lawn. Mike and David, playing hide-and-seek across the street, suddenly saw Jack. They came over to where he sat.

"Why do you sit in that funny chair?" asked Mike.

"I noticed you wheeling yourself around," added David. "Can't you walk?"

"I was shot in the spine when I went to war," Jack explained. "The doctors removed the bullet, but now I must use a wheelchair to get around."

Satisfied, Mike and David asked no more questions and went back to their game.

Another handicapped person handled a situation like this: On the beach, Bob and Peter were building sand castles. A man wearing a hearing aid strolled by.

"What's that tiny wire and that box in your shirt?" asked Mike.

"I can't hear too well," the man replied. "This helps me to hear. I call it my radar equipment.

This man's good humor helped explain his disability. Many times these situations seem awkward, but a joke is always a good response. Without being serious, this man got his message across.

Often children will hesitate to ask questions in the presence of their parents. One evening Mrs. Combs asked Doris, an amputee, to babysit with her daughter, Susie, but didn't tell Susie Doris had only one leg. After Mrs. Combs left, Doris and Susie were playing on the floor when the phone rang. Since Doris' crutches lay across the room, she hopped over to the phone and answered it. Susie followed her, also hopping. Susie asked "Why do you have only one leg?"

"When I was a little girl I was very sick. My leg became infected with germs. The doctor had to take it off."

"Why?"

"To save my life."

"Oh. Okay, let's play a game."

This explanation satisfied Susie and no more was said.

A one-armed man explained his disability like this:

Michael and his father walked into a supermarket. Michael pulled back. He saw a man with a hook for his hand.

"Why does that man have a hook?" asked Michael. While his father hesitated, the amputee walked over and spoke.

"When I was younger I caught my hand in a machine at the factory where I worked. The nerves and muscles were damaged and the doctor removed my arm, replacing it with an artificial one. It's attached with a strap around my shoulder behind my back. I can pick up money and even light a match."

He showed Michael how his hand worked. Michael then seemed less afraid, since he could now understand the disability.

Later at home, Michael told his mother, "You know, there are many different people in the world, but lots of them are nice."

Blind people answer these same questions. Five-year-old Joey and his mother went to the zoo, where he saw Lisa, a blind college student.

"Mommy look. That lady's using a cane. Why, mommy, why?"

"Never mind. Be quiet!"

"But mommy, that lady is using a cane and bumping into things!"

"It's not nice to stare at people. Come on, let's go look at toys."

Joey hung back as his mother started walking away. Lisa, hearing Joey's questions, walked over to him and said: "Hey Joey, want to know why I use a cane?"

Shy but curious, Joey answered, "Yeah. Why do you?"

"When I was born I couldn't see. I don't know exactly why. But I can do almost anything you can. I use this cane to know if there's anything in front of me."

"Will you ever see?"

"I don't know. Maybe someday."

Dr. Rader believes handicapped people should answer children's questions. "I feel it is very important to have a handicapped person involved in the situation," he says. "It makes it much more real and much more meaningful. If this is done, it would be almost impossible for the handicapped person to be rejected or bring on a greater problem."

Some Suggestions

If a child asks his parent about the handicapped person, it will be up to the parent to explain. Here are some suggestions to help:

1. *Respond to your child's questions promptly.*

As Dr. Rader points out: "The matter should be handled at the moment, so there isn't any suspicion of anxiety or any big deal made out of it. If you

2. ATTITUDE CHANGE STRATEGIES

wait until later, then you are saying in a nonverbal way there is some kind of a problem that couldn't be dealt with at the time."

For example, when Johnny asks his mother, "Why does that man have a stiff leg?" she might reply, "I don't know. Maybe he was hurt in some way."

Answering the child's questions immediately, while the situation is fresh in his mind, is the best time for learning to take place. This response eliminates any negative feelings the child may have toward the disabled person, and it prevents him from shunning handicapped people in the future.

2. *Develop empathy for the disabled.*

Five-year-old Doris Wilson asked her mother, "Why does Kenny sit in that chair with wheels?"

Mrs. Wilson tried to create an understanding of Kenny's disability. "Doris, Kenny can't walk."

"It must be awful not to walk. He seems so lonely."

"Yes. Some people don't play with him because he can't walk."

"Why? That's silly. He's a nice boy."

"I know. Try to think what it would be like if you couldn't walk. Then treat Kenny as you would like to be treated."

Children are sensitive to what's going on around them. If parents make an effort to build understanding of people's problems, this can be a way to explain handicaps.

3. *Tell your child a disability doesn't make a person less of a person.*

Jane, six, saw a man with a scarred face. "Mommy, mommy, is that man's face scarred because he did something bad?"

"No, Jane. Something happened to him. His injury doesn't make him a bad person. Just because he has a deformed face doesn't mean he's evil."

Often children are afraid of handicapped people. Explaining that their disability makes no difference in their personality can alleviate this fear.

4. *Explain they will meet many different kinds of people.*

"Why does he limp and lean over to one side when he walks?" asked Kathleen when she saw a boy with cerebral palsy.

"There are many different kinds of people in the world. Some have black skin, others have brown," explained her mother. "Remember Tommy's accident? He walked on crutches a few weeks. This made him different. Many people have accidents or injuries they never overcome, but all people have feelings—just like you!"

5. *Use language that a child can understand.*

Bobby, four, stopped his mother in the middle of the street and asked why a man used a cane to walk.

"Oh, he's probably been sick or hurt."

Bobby could understand this explanation and asked no more questions.

For older children, use the terms "handicapped" or "disabled." You might tell a story like: "Remember when John broke his arm and wore a cast? For a time he couldn't write. He was *handicapped*. That man we saw yesterday who couldn't walk also was *handicapped*, or *disabled*. He was trying to live the best way he can."

These two words should become a part of a child's vocabulary, because they are used often.

6. *Explain in simple words the medical aspects of a disability.*

Six-year-old Danny asked, "Why does Shelly have to sit in a wheelchair? Why can't she walk?"

"Because when she was born, her spine, the big bone in her back, was not formed properly. It's called 'spina bifida.'"

7. *Show a child what a disability is like by helping him experience it.*

"Gee, I wonder what it's like to be blind like Suzy," John Williams said to his mother. Mrs. Williams wrapped a towel around John's eyes. "This is how the world looks to blind people all the time," she said.

John aimlessly stumbled around the house for two hours. Finally he began to feel things and sense where he was going.

"Being blind must really be tough," he said. "It must take real guts for Suzy to do what she does."

8. *Expose children to the handicapped.*

Fifteen-year-old Sharon and her mother were making plans for a Christmas party.

"We'll invite Sue, David, Linda, Bobby . . ." said Sharon's mother.

"Whoops! Did you say Linda? Do we *have* to invite her? All she does is sit in that wheelchair. She can't dance. She's just a drag."

"Now look, Sharon, if I'm going to help you with this party, we're going to invite Linda. It's not fair to invite the others and not her."

"Yes, but, but . . ."

"No but's. We're inviting her—or no party!"

On the night of the event everyone came. Linda wheeled her chair into the house and sat in a corner. Soon Sharon noticed three of her friends talking with Linda; so she walked over and joined them. Before long, Sharon and Linda were laughing and enjoying themselves.

"You know," said Sharon as she and her mother were cleaning up after the party, "I'm sure glad we invited Linda. She really knows a lot about sewing. She can't walk, but she doesn't let that stop her from leading a useful, happy life."

9. *Tell your child not to hurt handicapped people's feelings.*

Mrs. Morgan looked out and saw her son, four-year-old Jimmy, walking pigeon-toed behind a man who limped.

"Come here Jimmy! Come here!" she shouted.

Jimmy stopped and came up to her.

"What were you doing?" she asked.

"Just having fun. That man looks so funny!"

"That's not nice. That man can't help the way he walks. He has feelings just like you and I. Maybe he feels bad about the way he walks."

Often young children are unaware of what they are doing. Sometimes if you point it out to them, they will understand.

10. *Ask your child to befriend at least one disabled person.*

At noon every day Danny sat talking to Joey, who stuttered. Danny, a fifth grader, came home from school and asked his mother, "Why don't the kids in my class like Joey? Why don't they ever play with him? He learns slowly, but he's sure a nice boy."

"Many of your classmates probably think Danny is so different they don't want to be around him. They can't understand he's still a person who needs friends. You understand his needs and so continue to treat him as your friend."

11. *Finally, keep composed when explaining a person's disability to a child.*

Children are often sensitive to the reactions of their parents; adults should always remain calm in this situation. Remember, a child's questions show he is curious and aware of the world about him. Answer questions straightforwardly. The more confident you are, the more likely he is to accept your answers.

I know. I have cerebral palsy.

Changing Attitudes

Joan Kilburn

Joan Kilburn, *the developer and director of the Better Understanding of Handicapped Children program, has a master's degree in special education and has taught mentally retarded and learning disabled students. She is active in community programs for exceptional children and adults who are developmentally disabled.*

■ Attitudes of the nonhandicapped population toward persons with disabilities play a deciding role in the ultimate success or failure of endeavors to integrate handicapped persons more fully into society. Better Understanding of Handicapped Children, a community education program sponsored by the Easter Seal Society of Marin in San Rafael, California, was developed in 1980 to deal with attitudes that present barriers to the full participation of an individual with a disability.

The project helps school children and adults become more aware of the needs and capabilities of persons who are handicapped. It is designed to encourage people to look at their own responsibility in integrating the disabled into the mainstream. The project's goal is to promote awareness and change attitudes so that mainstreaming will have a positive base from which to build.

CHANGE CAN HAPPEN

Two components stand out as essential in changing negative attitudes and increasing awareness. The first element is having people who are disabled act as their own advocates. The second is to provide structured opportunities for nonhandicapped and handicapped people to interact. If both elements are present, attitudes are more likely to change in positive directions. These methods are more effective than using simulations only or showing pictures of disabled persons to stimulate discussion. Asking a nonhandicapped person to talk about the handicapped is, at best, a weak approach. When a disabled person interacts with the nondisabled in a structured situation, positive attitudinal change can and does result.

WHAT WE DO

In the Better Understanding program, students interact with the disabled instructor in a variety of experiential activities. The children become active learners. The atmosphere fosters insight and provides a basis for discussion in which information, personal experience, and feelings are shared and clarified.

In the Elementary Classroom

Regular classroom programs for kindergarten through eighth grade consist of two meetings, one week apart, taught by a team of two instructors, one of whom is disabled. The curriculum features four major components.

Personal experience. Instructors share their own experiences about being handicapped, candidly and sensitively. Questions are answered and myths disspelled during these interchanges.

Simulation stations. Hands-on activities help students comprehend what it is like to be disabled and how the environment or an activity can be adapted to minimize the difficulty caused by a handicap. At the hearing station, students learn about sign language and finger spelling, as well as how to talk to someone with a hearing loss.

At the vision station, students learn about Braille, try writing with a slate writer and a Braille writer, wear special glasses to "see" what it is like to have low vision, and try to play games adapted for blind persons. At the movement station, students go through an obstacle course using wheelchairs, crutches, walkers, or canes; they also learn how to help someone using a wheelchair.

At the learning station, students try to read stories in which letters have been reversed or words misspelled.

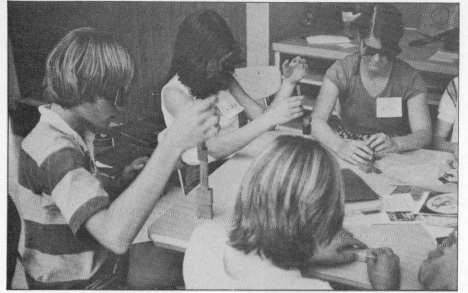

Vision simulations promote better understanding of disabled persons.

Kevin, a Better Understanding instructor, talks about what it is like to have cerebral palsy.

They gain an appreciation of what it is like not to fully understand discussions or explanations. Activities are designed to be beyond the comprehension of the children, which can create frustration, boredom, daydreaming, or restlessness. The next step is exploring with the students how to change the activities to help a retarded person learn.

Adventure game. This is the climax of the course. The game poses the problem of how to get a group of people, half of whom are "disabled" (blindfolded, in wheelchairs, or on crutches) across an imaginary chasm. It is set up so that students have to work cooperatively. There is movement and excitement—as well as frustration, until the group discovers how to work as a unit.

Wrap-up. The final session consists of sharing more information and discussing what the students have learned. By this time, confidence and friendliness have been established between the instructors and the students. The children now feel comfortable asking questions that are important to them, but were embarrassing to ask at the beginning.

At the High School Level

At the first of two meetings, students participate in a "What If . . ." exercise. Each student draws a card which describes some type of disability. The class then discusses what it might be like to have that handicap. This is followed by a personal account of a disability

2. ATTITUDE CHANGE STRATEGIES

and its effects, related by an instructor from the Better Understanding program. The meeting ends with simulation activities illustrating the instructor's disability. The second meeting features more simulations about other disabilities and ends with a discussion period.

Adult Workshops

A disabled person serves as a speaker and resource person at workshops for teachers and other educators. Simulation exercises are presented, as well as exercises designed to prompt people to look at their own attitudes in a nonthreatening setting. At longer workshops (3 hours or more), methods to adapt classroom activities or games are demonstrated and practiced. The emphasis is to develop a process to be used in the classroom to change activities so that all students can participate fully, regardless of differences.

CONTINUING TO GROW

During the first year of operation, we learned that additional follow-up visits were helpful. Even though each teacher is given a handbook of related activities that can be easily incorporated into the ongoing curriculum, a stronger follow-up program was necessary to assure further study.

Now, about a month after the original course is presented, a follow-up session is scheduled, led by a Better Understanding instructor. A variety of activities are available. The classroom teacher and the Better Understanding instructor select enrichment activities that enhance the interests and concerns of the class.

Enrichment Activities

Values clarification and the role-playing exercises about disabilities are popular, and create lively discussion among class members. A Better Understanding instructor guides the activity and clarifies when appropriate. Many thoughts and ideas are scrutinized, such as:

How would a disability affect me?

How would I cope with it?

How would others react?

What would I be doing?

How would my parents feel?

As part of the follow-up repertoire, cooperative games demonstrate how to adapt a game to include a child with a disability. The students look at what everyone in the group can do and then at how a particular disability will make participation difficult. The challenge is to figure out how to change the rules or the process so that everyone will be able to play.

Michael shows fifth-grade students how he reads using Braille.

Someone is chosen to play the role of a handicapped person if no one in the class is disabled. In deciding as a group how best to change the game, members work together and check out suggested changes with the handicapped person, who is encouraged to enter the discussion. We have found that, often, upon assuming a handicap role, the person stops participating. We discourage this stereotypic response. Cooperating and practicing a skill is stressed, rather than being competitive or "the best."

Mini-workshops feature simulation activities about a specific disability. Students select one workshop to attend rather than rotating, as they did in the original course. The children like this format, as they are able to use the materials for a longer period of time.

Other classroom enrichment activities include field trips to facilities serving people with disabilities, writing or research projects, and community surveys about accessibility.

Aware-News

In order to maintain contact, a newsletter is published monthly and sent to classrooms which have participated in the Better Understanding program. *Aware-News* contains regular features which teachers can use as a basis for classroom projects. One feature, "What Would You Do? . . .", poses situations about a particular disability. For example:

Imagine that you are paralyzed and use a wheelchair . . . you need to go shopping and you have to use the bus. Could you do it? Could you get on the bus? How could you find out? What would you do?

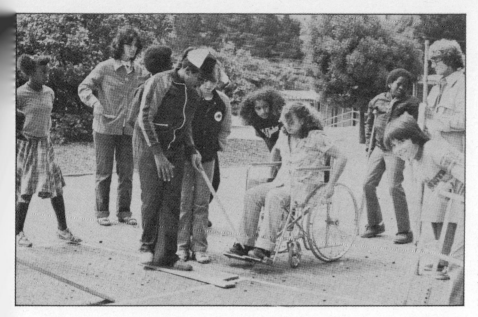

Students from Martin Luther King School, Marin County, participate in an adventure game. Feet, wheels, and crutch tips all must touch the boards to avoid falling into the imaginary chasm of hot, sticky tar!

Imagine that you are retarded. A group of kids your age is playing ball. The kids never pay any attention to you, but you would like to play. What would you do? Suppose you ask to play and one of the kids says, "Go away, 'retard,' leave us alone!" What would you do?

A true-and-false section of the newspaper is used as a vehicle to provide information about disabilities, and a section on sign language also appears each month. In addition, each issue contains an interview with a disabled student to illustrate that he or she has similar interests and problems as everyone else; the interview also exposes problems created by insensitive people. Students are encouraged to contribute articles about disabilities, as well. Each issue presents a balanced treatment of a variety of specific disabilities—physical, hearing, visual, retardation, and learning.

WHERE WE'VE BEEN

During the past three years, the Better Understanding program has been presented in approximately 225 classrooms in Marin County and the San Francisco Bay area. Children completed pre- and post-session written evaluations, when appropriate for the grade level. In kindergarten and some primary grades, teachers conduct an oral survey of the children's reactions and perceptions.

Student responses indicate that the program has significant impact upon their attitudes toward disabilities. Typical comments are:

"I used to be kind of afraid, but now I learned not to be." "I thought handicapped people were dumb until these classes." "Now, I won't make fun of them and laugh at them." "I really learned a lot about 'normal' people teasing each other, saying, 'You retard.' And that it makes a real retarded person feel bad." "You opened my eyes—instead of feeling sorry for a disabled person, I will try to make him feel good."

OBSERVATIONS

Being comfortable and open about a disability is the first step toward change. The next step is using processes to help a group change. The ultimate goal is to adapt the environment so that each student or adult, whether disabled or not, can participate actively, and with satisfaction.

The most dynamic aspect of the Better Understanding program is the key role played by disabled persons, who act as leaders and role models not only for nonhandicapped persons but also for those who are disabled. This is often the first time students with special needs have ever seen another disabled person in a leadership role. Our observation is that the student usually finds it easier to talk with classmates about disabilities after the awareness program. Communication is opened up for all students, and interaction in a more confident and relaxed manner is the ultimate reward.

Providing Opportunities for Interaction Between Severely Handicapped and Nonhandicapped Students

WILLIAM STAINBACK
SUSAN STAINBACK
TWILA JABEN

■ The trend to provide programing for severely handicapped students in regular public schools rather than segregating them in special schools and institutions is gaining widespread support. One of the benefits of integrating handicapped and nonhandicapped students is the possibility for increased interaction between the two groups. This interaction benefits both the handicapped and nonhandicapped students (Bricker, 1978; Brown, Branston, Hamre-Nietupski, Johnson, Wilcox, &Gruenewald, 1979; Haring, 1978; Sailor & Haring, 1977; Stainback & Stainback, 1980).

Severely handicapped students are given opportunities for more expanded and normalized learning experiences. Nonhandicapped students are provided unique opportunities to learn first hand about human differences and similarities and how to approach and interact with handicapped members of society. Such interactions can also reduce nonhandicapped students' fear of the handicapped and promote understanding and acceptance.

Thus, it is important for teachers to arrange the environment so that opportunities are actually available for interaction between severely handicapped and nonhandicapped students. In this article, the authors discuss several ways opportunities for interaction can be provided. The purpose in discussing them is to point out several critical factors that should be considered when providing opportunities for interaction.

PROVIDING OPPORTUNITIES FOR INTERACTION

There are numerous ways to provide opportunities for interaction. Described here are three ways that are practical and easy to implement. These are: (a) cooperative work projects, (b) prearranged play sessions, and (c) human differences training. All three methods require planning and cooperation between special and regular class teachers.

Cooperative Work Projects

There are projects that need to be accomplished in any school that both severely handicapped and nonhandicapped students can work together to complete. The projects should be set up so that all students involved can contribute to their successful completion. Examples of some possible projects include decorating a school wall or bulletin board, planting flowers or shrubs on the school grounds, rearranging the cafeteria for an assembly, or making props for a school play.

An example of how a cooperative work project could be implemented follows. A special and regular classroom teacher might coordinate times at which their students could work together on designated projects. Following this the handicapped and nonhandicapped students would be jointly responsible for actually planning and carrying out the project(s) under the guidance of their teachers. One project might involve the planting and maintenance of a flower garden on school grounds. Discussions involving the students and teachers would have to take place to determine where the garden should be planted, what flowers should be included, and how to arrange the students' time schedules to give them opportunities to work on the project. After the planning stage, the garden project could get under way. From one such project other joint projects and activities could be planned.

It should be noted that the severely handicapped and nonhandicapped students should be approximately the same chronological age and should work on age appropriate activities. While many professionals in the past have felt that it was not possible, due to mental age functioning, for severely handicapped students to work on age appropriate activities, this belief is changing (Brown, Branston, Hamre-Nietupski, Pumpian, Certo, & Gruenewald, 1979). There are numerous age appropriate projects or activities to which severely handicapped students can make a meaningful contribution. A few examples were cited above. Also, the projects selected should be real and functional. It would be a mistake to have the students work on a "made up" project, one that has no real meaning or purpose. We have found that most students' enthusiasm wanes quickly when they are faced with nonfunctional, meaningless tasks. In short, any project selected should be age appropriate, worthwhile, and challenging to both the nonhandicapped and severely handicapped students.

Prearranged Joint Play

Joint play sessions can also be used to enhance positive interaction behaviors between the severely handicapped and nonhandicapped students. This method involves an organized play situation in which the regular and special teachers cooperatively plan group games and activities that both of their classes can jointly participate in during at least some of their recess periods. The games selected should be positive, high probability activities that are age appropriate for the students. The games selected should also be arranged so that successful participation can be expected from both the handicapped and nonhandicapped.

Games that are not complicated yet unique and enjoyable are particularly useful. The games chosen, although not unnecessarily complicated, should present a challenge to both the severely handicapped and nonhandicapped. Often those involving the influences of the physical environment are fun, challenging, and a good learning experience. One set of games that meet these criteria for most children are parachute activities. One way to play a parachute game is to place a ball in the center and have the children grasp the edge of the parachute. The object of the game is for the children to knock the ball off by lifting their arms and hands and getting air under the parachute. While this game can be played without an excess of rules and complicated movements, it is an enjoyable novel experience for most children and presents a challenge to them. It should be noted that for children who have poor grasp or arm movement in either of the classes, this particular activity may not be applicable or may require modification. The physical as well as other abilities of the children involved should influence game selection.

A word of optimism about what severely handicapped students can do should be inserted here. Unfortunately, we sometimes determine that a game (activity or project) is too complex for some students, especially severely handicapped students, when it is *not* too complex or difficult. The real problem is our own inability to adapt the activity and/or physical/social environment so the student(s) can participate (at least partially) and/or to provide the students with the kind of assistance necessary for them to participate. Brown, Bramston-McClean, Baumgart, Vincent, Falvey, and Schroeder (1979) have pointed out that severely handicapped students have been excluded or excused from numerous activities because they could not perform "adequately". They also outlined ways in which severely handicapped students can participate or partially participate in activities we may consider too complex or difficult for them. The reader is referred to Brown and associates (1979) for additional information.

Finally, to carry out joint play successfully, training some severely handicapped students in appropriate play behavior may be necessary. This training may also be needed for some members of the nonhandicapped class. Both decreasing inappropriate play behavior—such as refusal to play, lack of sustained play, and/or throwing toys or objects—as well as the building of appropriate behaviors such as learning to play cooperatively and sharing, may need to be included in play training sequences. Fortunately, there has been a great deal of recent research and ideas published about how to decrease inappropriate and teach appropriate play skills (e.g., Wehman, 1977; 1979; Wehman & Marchant, 1978). Such training sequences may considerably influence the potential success of the prearranged joint play approach to interactions.

Human Differences Training

Both regular and special education teachers should provide their students with information regarding human differences as well as similarities. Special education teachers who have been trained to deal with human differences should make an effort to assist regular teachers in integrating such training into their classrooms, in addition to incorporating such training into their special education classes. Although some of the human differences training described might be carried out while the severely handicapped and nonhandicapped are in their separate classrooms, the training is designed to promote understanding and increased interactions among severely handicapped and nonhandicapped students. Also, if possible,

based on variables such as schedules, classroom location, and activities selected, several of the organized activities may be done together, so the teachers can share the duties involved while providing additional opportunities to their students for shared experiences.

Teachers can assist their students in learning about human differences in many ways. These can include such activities as role playing and having handicapped guest speakers, films, and discussions. For example, students can role play a difference they have noticed in some children and/or experience a handicapping condition for a day. A child may be blindfolded to simulate blindness. Another child may *not* be allowed to talk and be required to figure out how to communicate without his voice or hands. Still another child may be confined to a wheelchair for a day. Along with informative films, film with no sound or garbled sound can be used and the children can be required to explain and/or answer questions about the film's content. Discussions in groups where individual students explain their own differences and describe how others react to them and how they deal with these reactions is a good activity. Objectivity and positiveness about human differences must be stressed throughout the learning sequences since pity and/or negative attitudes can interfere with positive interactions.

Human differences training can be included in both regular and special classrooms as an integral part of various subject areas rather than as an isolated component. Supplemental reading assignments for reading practice can be selected regarding some aspect of human differences, language arts can include a project to learn and practice sign language, and social studies can evaluate jobs in the community that can be done by individuals with various handicaps. The inclusion of these activities and projects into various curricular areas should begin early for all students before barriers to human differences due to lack of understanding develop.

CONCLUSION

Opportunities for interactions between severely handicapped and nonhandicapped students can be provided at all levels of schooling. For example, at the high school level, severely handicapped and nonhandicaped students might interact during lunch, in some vocational training related activities, and in certain science projects such as collecting various types of leaves from trees to be analyzed.

Also, it should be emphasized that the methods outlined in this article are only meant to serve as examples of how interaction can occur between severely handicapped and nonhandicapped students. There are numerous other ways interactions can occur. Opportunities for interactions should be available in the hallways, restrooms, when riding the bus, and in many classroom activities such as certain academic tasks, art, music, and physical education activities. Other ways include having birthday parties, show and tell times, and rest times together. The number of possible ways is almost endless. The specific methods used will depend on factors such as the age of the children, the cooperative spirit of the special and regular teachers, and the organizational structure of the school. Fortunately, there are many creative and talented teachers who are continually coming up with excellent ideas about how severely handicapped students can become integrated members of the general public school population.

2. ATTITUDE CHANGE STRATEGIES

Finally, it should be noted that providing opportunities for interaction—as important as it is—may be in some cases only the first step. Some severely handicapped and nonhandicapped students may fail to interact when given the opportunity (Guralnick, 1980). Teachers may need to encourage and reinforce interactions. Also, selected nonhandicapped students acting as change agents can model, prompt, and/or reinforce, when necessary, the socialization skills of severely handicapped students. In addition, some nonhandicapped students may need to be instructed in how to best initiate interactions with the severely handicapped students, as well as how to respond to the interaction attempts of the severely handicapped students. The reader is referred to Fredericks, Baldwin, Grove, Moore, Riggs, and Lyons (1978) and Strain and Kerr (in press) for more detailed information about methods of promoting interactions among handicapped and nonhandicapped students.

REFERENCES

Bricker, D.D. A rationale for the integration of handicapped and nonhandicapped preschool children. In M.J. Guralnick (Ed.), *Early intervention and the integration of handicapped and nonhandicapped children.* Baltimore: University Park Press, 1978.

Brown, L., Branston, M., Baumgart, D., Vincent, L., Falvey, M., & Schroeder, J. Utilizing the characteristics of a verity of current and subsequent least restrictive environments as factors in the development of curricular content for severely handicapped students. *AAESPH Review*, 1979, *4*, 407-424.

Brown, L., Branston, M., Hamre-Nietupski, S., Johnson, F. and Wilcox, B., & Gruenewald, L. A rationale for comprehensive longitudinal interactions between severely handicapped students and nonhandicapped students and other citizens. *AAESPH Review*, 1979, *4*, 3-14.

Brown, L., Branston, M., Hamre-Nietupski, S., Pumpian, I., Certo, N., & Gruenewald, L. A strategy for developing chronological age appropriate and functional curricular content for severely handicapped adolescents and young adults. *Journal of Special Education*, 1979, *13*, 81-90.

Fredericks, B., Baldwin, V., Grove, D., Moore, W., Riggs, C., & Lyons, B. Integrating the moderately and severely handicapped preschool child into a normal day care setting. In M.S. Guralnick (Ed.), *Early intervention and the integration of handicapped and nonhandicapped children.* Baltimore: University Park Press, 1978.

Guralnick, M. Social interactions among preschool children. *Exceptional Children*, 1980, *46*, 248-253.

Haring, N.G. Progress and perspectives. In N.G. Haring and D.D. Bricker (Eds.), *Teaching the severely handicapped.* Seattle WA: American Association for the Education of the Severely/Profoundly Handicapped, 1978.

Sailor, W., & Haring, N.G. Some current directions in education of the severely/multiply/handicapped. *AAESPH Review*, 1977, *2*, 68-87.

Stainback, S.B., & Stainback, W.C. *Educating children with severe maladaptive behaviors.* New York: Grune & Stratton, 1980.

Strain, P., & Kerr, M. Modifying children's social withdrawal: Issues in assessment and clinical intervention. In M. Hersen, R. Eisler, & P. Miller (Eds.), *Progress in behavior modification* (Vol. 10). New York: Academic Press, in press.

Wehman, P. *Helping the mentally retarded acquire play skills: A behavioral approach.* Springfield IL: Charles C Thomas, 1977.

Wehman, P. Instructional strategies for improving toy play skills of severely handicapped children. *AAESPH Review*, 1979, *4*, 125-135.

Wehman, P., & Marchant, J. Improving free play skills of severely retarded children. *American Journal of Occupational Therapy*, 1978, *32*, 100-104.

Toward More Success in Mainstreaming: A Peer Teacher Approach to Physical Education

M. RHONDA FOLIO
ANNE NORMAN

A frequent concern of physical educators is the lack of time they are able to devote to the handicapped child mainstreamed in a regular class group of 30 or more children. A variety of techniques have been used to increase the amount of individual attention these children receive. The peer teacher, or peer tutoring, concept has been one approach which made mainstreaming a huge success in our model physical education project—Project PERMIT (Physical Education Resources for Mainstreaming and Inservice Training).

Project PERMIT is funded by BEH as part of the Special Education's program assistant grant at Tennessee Technological University. The project is housed at Sycamore Elementary School in Cookeville, Tennessee. The major purpose of the project is to provide inservice training assistance and demonstration in mainstreaming in physical education. Inservice is offered via 1 day or 1 week workshops through the exemplary program at Sycamore Elementary School. This is the third year of a 3 year funding cycle. Participants in workshops over the last 2 years have been principals, regular and special education teachers and physical education teachers. The project also serves as a practicum placement for special and physical education majors at Tennessee Technological University. The project will be presented at the national meeting of the American Alliance for Health, Physical Education and Recreation in Boston, Spring 1981. It is hoped that, if funding is continued, ongoing inservice will be provided to a select group of teachers so that the exemplary program can be implemented.

IDENTIFYING AND TRAINING PEER TEACHERS

Upper elementary grade children are selected and trained to become peer teachers. Their primary role is to assist the physical education instructor with mainstreamed exceptional children, as well as with any other children in the class who may be having difficulty. Peer teachers may be used in a variety of ways, including skill demonstrations, assisting with equipment, record keeping, and working individually with ex-

ceptional children while instruction continues. Several procedures and guidelines were followed in implementing the peer teacher program.

1. Student selection is based on the following personal qualities:
   a. Leadership capabilities
   b. Student's acceptance of others
   c. Maturity
   d. Motor skill (student need not be gifted in this area)
   e. Ability to follow instructions
2. Miniworkshops are conducted with selected peer teachers. The workshop content includes:
   a. Orientation on skills to be taught
   b. Observation of the teaching process in classes with which the peer teachers will be working
   c. Instruction in simple techniques of rewarding student performance
   d. Peer teacher workshops are held for peer teachers. Each teacher is required to attend four ½ hour workshops. Instructions are given about handicapped students; i.e., "Mentally retarded children are just like any other children, they require longer to learn and in more steps." General statements such as these are usually required to orient peer teachers.
   e. Instruction includes having peer teachers do most of the basic skills the handicapped students will do. These include basic motor skills of locomotion, balance, object manipulation including throwing, catching, striking and kicking. Additionally, basic and simple problem solving activities are used such as, "How many ways can you balance on three body parts." Another important component taught is perceptual motor development. Students are taught basically to receive stimuli, process the information and make appropriate motor responses.
   f. Games are used to teach cooperation among students. New games are used which eliminate the competitive aspect and emphasize sharing and cooperation.

BENEFITS OF PEER TEACHING

The peer teachers, usually fifth and sixth grade boys and girls, seem to have an inborn ability to relate to other children,

2. ATTITUDE CHANGE STRATEGIES

especially those who are younger than themselves. They seem to sense when to give assistance and just what amount of help is needed and appropriate. Peer teachers also serve as excellent models for both handicapped and regular students. Their assistance allows the physical education teacher to keep contact with the entire class. Many disruptive behaviors are eliminated, since those having difficulty are receiving help and tend to maintain on-task behavior.

The effects of the peer teacher role on the mainstreamed child are many. The handicapped child benefits from an atmosphere of positive regard. A positive attitude on the part of other class members is fostered as they see the peer teacher actively relating to the handicapped child. A cooperative effort develops among students in assisting the handicapped child, as well as a sensitivity toward appropriate degrees of assistance. A direct line of communication is forged between the regular student and the handicapped student. The most obvious change is the increase of peer expectations, as regular students broaden their perceptions of the abilities of handicapped students.

COMPLEMENTARY PROGRAM FEATURES

The following concepts and techniques employed in Project PERMIT also contribute to the success of the mainstreaming program:

Personal Space Concept

Each student has a personal space on the gym floor, within which he or she can move to the full extent of individual abilities. No one is allowed to move in another person's space. This approach avoids the use of highly structured formations and allows more individual movement to occur.

Movement Exploration

Some example activities include having students move from one point to another in as many different ways as they can. The same principle can be applied when working with balance. The teacher might ask students to balance with a partner as many different ways as they can using only two body parts or one body part. If working with objects, the teacher might ask students to bounce a ball using only one body part or two body parts.

Personal Equipment

Personal equipment involves distributing equipment to match the child's motor ability or motor maturity. For example, when developing the skills of ball handling and control a child will be given a ball which matches his or her abilities. A nerf ball, which is soft and has little bounce, would be given to a child with slow reactions, uncoordinated movements, or visual impairments. On the other hand, a child with less refined movements, uncoordinated movements and immature motor patterns would use a beach ball rather than a typical rubber playground ball.

Station Training

Stations are developed for particular skills, such as balance or agility, again allowing students to progress at individual rates. Stations are sequentially arranged from least difficult skill to most difficult skill, with each child completing the circuit during a class period. Objectives are developed for each station.

Stations may be used to develop any sequence of skills such as a throwing sequence or catching sequence. Stations were usually developed for physical fitness. When they are applied to specific or groups of motor skills they allow an individual to progress at his or her own rate. Generally about six stations are used at one time. This is usually the number that can be managed in an average class where students are mainstreamed. Figure 1 illustrates how stations can be used to develop a sequence of balance skills. Stations can be thought of as "mini" learning centers. The diagram contains six stations for balance. Station one requires the student to complete a 4, 3, 2 point balance stance with or without assistance. Station two requires students to complete a balance stance on a balance board for at least 5 seconds. Station three requires students to balance on the board while tossing a bean bag to a partner. Station four requires students to walk in a variety of directions between taped lines on the floor. Each taped line makes a shape. Station five allows students to walk on 6 inch wide boards on the floor alone, then with an object in each hand. Station six actually permits students to walk on a raised balance beam in a variety of directions. If students are less skilled these stations can be made even more simplified. Figure 2 includes a sample activity card. Activity cards may be distributed to peer teachers monitoring each station. Generally four to six children can be assigned to each station. On a given signal, students can rotate to the next station.

Children may record their individual accomplishments on charts, score cards, and record sheets. Peer teachers assist students at each station and may help maintain student records.

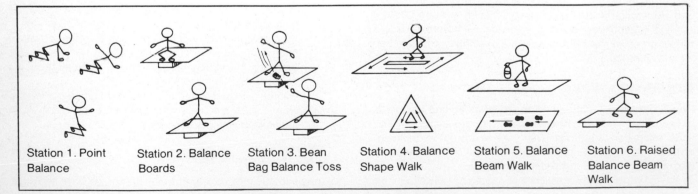

Station 1. Point Balance Station 2. Balance Boards Station 3. Bean Bag Balance Toss Station 4. Balance Shape Walk Station 5. Balance Beam Walk Station 6. Raised Balance Beam Walk

FIGURE 1. Stations Training for Balance.

Station 3—Bean Bag Balance Toss
Objective: Toss and catch a bean bag at least three times without losing balance
Materials: Two bean bags
Two balance boards
Activities: One student stands on each balance board. Students may also sit if standing balance is poor. Toss the bean bags back and forth until each student has at least three successful trials or catches. Students waiting their turn can practice tossing and catching while standing on one foot or both feet.
Variations
Toss the bean bag high or loss it low. Increase the distance between balance boards. Toss a different item, such as a beach ball or balloon.

FIGURE 2. Sample Station Activity Card.

Positive Interaction

Implementing a positive approach in the learning environment creates a nonthreatening and affirmative classroom atmosphere. The approach used in our project was based on the RAID model (Bailey & Morton, 1970), a classroom management model constructed according to the following principles:

- **R= Rules.** Rules in the physical education classroom are established with help from students, thus allowing children to know and to help formulate clear statements of expected behavior. Rules are stated in positive terms (e.g., "Put equipment away" instead of "Don't leave equipment out").

- **A= Approval.** Approve or reward those students who follow the rules. Approval may be signaled by nonverbal gestures, verbal praise, or special treats such as free time or individual choice of activities. Peer teachers seem to demonstrate a natural ability for rewarding desirable behavior (Folio, 1980).
- **I= Ignore.** Children who do not follow the rules are ignored. This technique, in order to be most successful, must be paired with the preceding principle of rewarding those who do follow the rules.
- **D= Disapprove.** Disapproval is shown when student behavior threatens to injure self or others, or when behavior disrupts the learning process for the group. Disapproval is shown by removing rewards or by temporarily removing the child from the activity.

Project PERMIT found these techniques, coupled with the peer teacher program, to be particularly successful for use in elementary physical education classes with mainstreamed children having mild to moderate handicapping conditions. Careful planning and organization on the part of the teacher helps make mainstreaming a positive and relatively nonthreatening experience for the handicapped child.

Everyone benefits from the peer teacher model. Exceptional students receive the individual attention they need. The classroom teacher is free to reach more students. Last, but not least, peer teachers themselves gain in leadership abilities, peer interaction skills, and the knowledge that they are making a valued contribution to the educational process.

REFERENCES

Bailey, R. E., & Morton, J. H. *RAID: A formula for positive classroom management.* Clearwater FL: Pinellas County School Board, 1970.

Folio, R. *Mini workshops in peer teacher instruction.* Cookeville TN: Project PERMIT, Tennessee Technological University, 1980.

Integrating Disabled Children

Mary Frances Hanline

Mary Frances Hanline, M.A., is a lecturer in Special Education at San Francisco State University, and a doctoral candidate at both the University of California, Berkeley, and San Francisco State University, in California.

Disabled and regular needs children are enrolled in many early childhood programs. This integration is supported by legal-legislative, psychological-educational, and social-ethical arguments (Bricker 1978). All disabled children have the right to a free public education in the least restrictive environment. Parents must be involved in educational decisions about their child. The potential benefits for disabled children who observe and interact with their nondisabled peers form the foundation for psychological-educational arguments. Social-ethical arguments supporting integration are based on humane treatment of disabled people, the detrimental effects of segregation, and the potential for creating more positive attitudes toward people with disabilities.

Normally developing children may benefit from integated settings by learning to be more accepting of individual differences through repeated contact with disabled children, as peer interaction has the potential to influence children's attitudes and behavior (Apolloni and Cooke 1975). Some adults have been concerned, however, that

---

Integration seems to have no detrimental effects on the social or cognitive play behavior of young normally developing children.

---

nondisabled children might imitate socially inappropriate behaviors exhibited by disabled children or might not develop at the expected rate. Although research on the outcomes of integration focuses predominately on the effects of integration on disabled children, there is a limited amount of research regarding nondisabled children. What are

the effects of integration on normally developing young children? How does this research affect programs for young children?

Imitative behavior

The fear that integration will lead normally developing children to imitate socially unacceptable or developmentally immature behaviors which disabled children may exhibit has often been expressed. Such behavior, however, does not seem to occur spontaneously in either free-play or structured teaching situations (Peck et al. 1978; Peterson, Peterson, and Scriven 1977). Regular needs children are more likely to imitate another nondisabled child than a developmentally delayed playmate. If, however, a nondisabled child does imitate a disabled peer, it is appropriate, not inappropriate, behavior which is imitated. Such reciprocal imitation may facilitate social integration, thereby increasing the chances that disabled children will become more accepted by their peers.

Developmental progress

Another concern about integration at a preschool level is that nondisabled children may not make adequate developmental progress. Research, however, indicates that normally developing young children attending integrated educational programs make expected progress in the areas of language, cognitive, motor, perceptual, and social development (Bricker and Bricker 1977; Bricker, Bruder, and Bailey 1982).

The teacher-student ratio in classrooms serving developmentally delayed children is usually low. Teachers can individualize curriculum to a greater degree than may be possible in regular classes. All children, therefore, receive more individual attention, which may help to develop a positive attitude toward school and learning. Students also have more occasions to be praised, which can help develop pride in accomplishments and motivation for further learning.

Social and play behavior

Most research studying the outcomes of preschool integration has focused on the amount and type of social interactions that occur between special and regular needs children. These studies indicate that nondisabled children prefer to play with other nondisabled children rather than with their developmentally delayed playmates (Guralnick 1980; Peterson 1982). Although overt rejection of disabled children by their normally developing peers is rare, nondisabled children more frequently initiate eye gaze toward, smile at, touch, vocalize to, sit next to, and choose as playmates other nondisabled children than disabled classmates.

Michael D. Sullivan

Disabled children can be perceived by nondisabled children as being competent.

Successful integration depends heavily on the attitude of teachers.

In addition, when developmentally delayed children are the only available playmates for nondisabled children, isolate play (such as talking to self and playing with toys alone) occurs more often than socially interactive play. The presence of a disabled child does not alter the play of two nondisabled children (Peterson and Haralick 1977).

Integration over the course of a school year seems to have no detrimental effects on the social or cognitive play behavior of young normally developing children (Guralnick 1981).

However, simply placing disabled and nondisabled children in the same classroom does not insure that these children will play together and learn from one another.

A basic level of social interaction is necessary for all children to benefit from the processes of attitudinal change, friendship formation, and observational learning. Structured educational programming is needed to insure that social interactions do indeed occur. Teachers can prompt and reinforce desired social behaviors such as sharing, helping, and cooperating (Fredericks et al. 1978; Allen 1980; Cooper

and Holt 1981). Nondisabled children can learn to initiate social interactions with and reinforce appropriate behaviors of their disabled playmates (Strain 1977). Both of these strategies produce an increase in cooperative and socially interactive play with no detrimental effects on the nondisabled child.

Although preferring to play with other normally developing children, nondisabled children do, however, behave in ways which indicate they are sensitive to the needs of their disabled classmates. They will adapt their verbal interactions in a way that insures that their delayed peers will understand messages (Guralnick and Paul-Brown 1980). The children are also gentle with their disabled classmates, often attempting to help, teach, encourage, and give affection to these children (Ipsa and Matz 1978). When nondisabled children are educated side-by-side with their disabled peers, they have the opportunity to nurture others by teaching the developmentally delayed children skills such as dressing themselves or putting their materials away when they are finished.

Implications for practice

The most important practical finding from research assessing the effects of early childhood integration is that social interactions between nondisabled and disabled children do not occur spontaneously. In order for such interactions to occur, they must be encouraged by the teacher. Whenever a teacher observes a disabled and normally developing child playing together, this behavior can be praised with statements such as, "You two are playing together so cooperatively!" Other behaviors which promote friendships should also be praised. For example, "Tom and Aisha are sharing their crayons. They are good friends to each other." Walking together, hand-holding, and sitting together are other behaviors which should be encouraged in a similar manner. Nondisabled children usually respond to such praise by repeating the appropriate behaviors at other times.

In addition to encouraging social interactions with praise, interactions can also be encouraged through organization of the physical environment. Dolls and doll houses, blocks, balls, dishes, and sectional trains encourage socially interactive play because they can be used by more than one child at a time. Arranging play sessions so that only two or three children play together in one area of the classroom can also encourage cooperative play. The children in these small groups should be socially compatible and similar in developmental functioning. Seating nondisabled and disabled children next to each other during snack, music, art, and other larger group activities can also encourage social interactions.

Imitation can be encouraged by the teacher. Providing duplicate toys during play sessions allows an opportunity for children to imitate each other and for this imitation to be praised by the

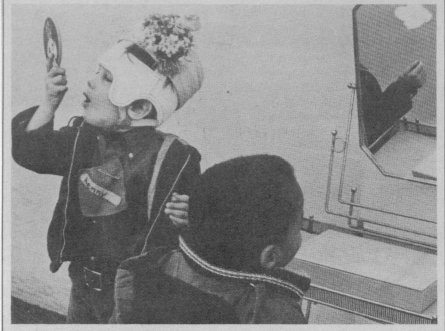

Teachers must encourage social interactions between disabled and nondisabled children.

Rose G. Engel

teacher. "Derek and Julian both are making interesting patterns with their colored blocks." Games such as "Monkey See, Monkey Do" and "Simon Says" also promote imitation. Verbal imitations, as well as imitation of motor responses, should also be encouraged. For example, "Jessica, can you say 'milk, please' like Amy?" or "Let's sing every word of the song like Brian does." It is important to encourage imitation of *appropriate* behaviors. Reciprocal imitation can also increase positive social relationships.

In order to encourage both friendship formation and imitation behavior, it is important that disabled children be perceived by nondisabled children as being competent. If a disabled child can carry a ball to the playground or pass out snacks, allow the disabled child to lead these activities at times and call it to the attention of other children. ("David is doing a splendid job passing out cookies to all of us, isn't he?") Some developmentally delayed children may need individual guidance in appropriate toy use or verbal greetings. Nondisabled children could be involved by modeling a skill for the developmentally delayed child. Such an approach would increase the skills of the delayed child while allowing the nondisabled child the opportunity to see how well the delayed child can learn.

Successful integration depends

heavily on the positive attitude of teachers. Teachers must communicate honestly and openly about disabilities. It is important that negative attitudes about disabling conditions are not conveyed by words, expressions, voice tone, or other behaviors. Teachers should try to stress similarities, not negative differences, among the children. Explain that Sarah cannot hear well (a difference), but she is able to play and learn with other children (a similarity) because a hearing aid helps her to hear (a positive approach to a difference). Or explain that Brad has cerebral palsy and needs leg braces to help him walk. Teachers must be careful not to overprotect disabled children or expect nondisabled children to assume too much of a teaching and helping role. Teachers should display the attitude that each child is equally appreciated if integration is to be successful. Souweine, Crimmins, and Mazel (1981) offer many practical ideas for incorporating these strategies.

Conclusion

The major potential impact of integration on nondisabled children is that they may learn to be more sensitive to and accepting of individual differences. Research on social interaction indicates that acceptance does occur if it is encouraged and reinforced. Nondisabled children will develop friendships with many children and see themselves as part of a group in which responsibilities are shared. Fears that normally developing children will imitate inappropriate behavior of developmentally delayed children or not make progress developmentally are not supported by research. Developmental gains for nondisabled children in integrated settings occur at the expected rate, and these children do not seem to imitate inappropriate behaviors of their disabled peers.

Although these findings are reassuring, more extensive and longitudinal research is needed. The majority of the literature on early childhood integration presents an optimistic outlook. However, integration of disabled and nondisabled children will most likely not be beneficial to any individuals if teachers, parents, and children are not prepared and supported throughout the year. The decision to educate disabled and nondisabled children together must be made in the best interests of the individual needs of each child and family.

Bibliography

Apolloni, T. and Cooke, T. P. "Peer Behavior Conceptualized as a Variable Influencing Infant and Toddler Development." *American Journal of Orthopsychiatry* 45, no. 1 (1975): 4–17.

Allen, K. E. *Mainstreaming in Early Childhood Education.* Albany, N.Y.: Delmar, 1980.

Bricker, D. D. "A Rationale for the Integration of Handicapped and Nonhandicapped Preschool Children." In *Early Intervention and the Integration of Handicapped and Nonhandicapped Children,* ed. M. J. Guralnick. Baltimore: University Park Press, 1978.

Bricker, D. D. and Bricker, W. A. "A Developmentally Integrated Approach to Early Intervention." *Education and Training of the Mentally Retarded* 12, no. 2 (1977): 100–108.

Bricker, D. D.; Bruder, M. B.; and Bailey, E. "Developmental Integration of Preschool Children." *Analysis and Intervention in Developmental Disabilities* 2 (1982): 207–222.

Cooper, A. Y. and Holt, W. J. "Development of Social Skills and the Management of Common Problems." In *Early Childhood Education: Special Problems, Special Solutions,* ed. K. E. Allen and E. Goetz. Rockville, Md.: Aspen Systems Corporation, 1982.

Fredericks, H. D.; Baldwin, V.; Grove, D.; Moore, W.; Riggs, C.; and Lyons, B. "Integrating Moderately and Severely Handicapped Preschool Children into a Normal Day Care Center." In *Early Intervention and the Integration of Handicapped and Nonhandicapped Children,* ed. M. J. Guralnick. Baltimore: University Park Press, 1978.

Guralnick, M. J. "Social Interactions Among Preschool Children." *Exceptional Children* 46, no. 4 (1980): 248–253.

Guralnick, M. J. "The Social Behavior of Preschool Children at Different Developmental Levels: Effects of Group Composition." *Journal of Experimental Child Psychology* 31, no. 1 (1981): 115–130.

Guralnick, M. J. and Paul-Brown, D. "Functional and Discourse Analysis of Nonhandicapped Preschool Children's Speech to Handicapped Children." *American Journal of Mental Deficiency* 84, no. 5 (1980): 444–454.

Ipsa, J. and Matz, R. D. "Integrating Handicapped Preschool Children with a Cognitively Oriented Program." In *Early Intervention and the Integration of Handicapped and Nonhandicapped Children,* ed. M. J. Guralnick. Baltimore: University Park Press, 1978.

Peck, C.; Apolloni, T.; Cooke, T.; and Raver, S. "Teaching Retarded Preschoolers to Imitate the Free Play Behavior of Nonretarded Classmates: Trained and Generalized Effects." *Journal of Special Education* 12, no. 2 (1978): 195–207.

Peterson, N. L. "Social Integration of Handicapped and Nonhandicapped Preschoolers: A Study of Playmate Preferences." *Topics in Early Childhood Special Education* 2, no. 2 (1982): 56–69.

Peterson, N. L. and Haralick, J. G. "Integration of Handicapped and Nonhandicapped Preschoolers: An Analysis of Play Behavior and Social Interaction." *Education and Training of the Mentally Retarded* 12, no. 3 (1977): 235–245.

Peterson, C.; Peterson, J.; and Scriven, G. "Peer Imitation by Nonhandicapped and Handicapped Preschoolers." *Exceptional Children* 43, no. 4 (1977): 223–224.

Souweine, J.; Crimmins, S.; and Mazel, C. *Mainstreaming: Ideas for Teaching Young Children.* Washington, D.C.: National Association for the Education of Young Children, 1981.

Strain, P. S. "An Experimental Analysis of Peer Social Initiations on the Behavior of Withdrawn Preschool Children: Some Training and Generalization Effects." *Journal of Abnormal Child Psychology* 5, no. 4 (1977): 445–455.

The Parent Connection:
Enhancing the Affective Component of Parent Conferences

Sharon Roberds-Baxter

Sharon Roberds-Baxter *is the home-school interventionist for low-incidence programs in Wood County, Ohio. She is a counselor to students with severe behavioral handicaps, a consultant in affective areas to teachers in low-incidence classes, and a liaison and counselor to parents.*

■ We have all received instructions, read guidelines, and attended workshops on the legal mandates of IEP meetings. We know the procedures and the content. But seldom are we told how to get parents willingly and actively involved, how to relieve teacher fatigue and stress, or how to cope with the strong emotions present at the session.

The focus of the Parent Connection model is on the *process* of a parent conference. The goal is to create a bond between teacher and parents which invites an open and positive exchange of information and encourages an alliance of home and school. Thus, the model is based on techniques that (a) enable teachers to feel confident and at ease while leading the meeting, and (b) encourage parents to feel wanted and necessary to the procedure.

THE MODEL

Educators invite a parent connection by engaging in behaviors which cluster into three categories: structure, teacher well-being, and parent comfort (see Figure 1). The behaviors listed in the first category (*structure*) help alleviate stress. A structured framework frees teachers from concern about content detail and allows them to concentrate on the interpersonal dynamics of the situation. In the second category, behaviors are described which enhance *teacher well-being*, and enable teachers to enter a parent meeting feeling calm, confident, and attentive. The third category (*parent comfort*) lists strategies that encourage psychological comfort in the parents. Parents who feel respected, understood, and important to the conference procedure will participate eagerly and intelligently in the process.

Designing the Structure

A first step toward planning a structure is to gather information about each family. As teachers, we are familiar with individualizing instruction for students; we can also use our creativity to individualize a parent conference as we decide on locations, time constraints, get-acquainted topics, and subjects to be included on the agenda.

Some questions to be considered are: Is there a topic which may need extended time? Are there many topics to cover? Which subjects must be discussed and which can wait, if necessary? Should I schedule a particular family for early in the morning while I am fresh? Will the parents be more comfortable in the informal environment of the teachers' lounge; will they want to meet in the classroom where their child spends six hours a day; or will they respond best in an atmosphere of power and authority represented by the principal's office?

Design a structure that works for you. Choose a location for each conference which will further your goal. Create a flexible agenda which assures participants that essential tasks will be accomplished, important topics will be raised, and time will be available for new directions to develop. Keep within your time constraints; you deserve to have time for yourself between sessions. About seven minutes before the meeting is over, let all participants know how much time is left, briefly review the remaining items, and decide together if another session is necessary.

After each conference, take time to jot down notes on ideas that will make next year's annual review easier or more productive. Did you learn new information about the child or family? What were your impres-

FIGURE 1
The Parent Connection:
A Flow Chart of Activities

	Structure	Teacher Well-Being	Parent Comfort
Before the conference		Practice relaxation and visualization.	
			Make positive contact.
	Gather family information.		
	Decide time constraints.		
	Decide location.		
			Send personal messages home.
		Review delicate issues.	
		Set personal goals.	
			Check presentation for jargon and technical terms.
	Prepare objectives. Prepare agenda. Prepare environment.		
		Center	
During the conference	Present agenda and objectives.	Be straight with your feelings and thoughts.	Provide get-acquainted time.
	Keep to time constraints.		Listen actively. Use facilitating questions.
	Mention 7 minutes to end of meeting.		Remember the grief issue.
After the conference	Record notes.		
		Reward yourself.	
			Continue positive contact.

sions of the parents? What elements of your personal style, or someone else's, facilitated or hindered progress? What questions do you want to ask of someone else? Use your intuition, creativity, and intelligence to choose items which are important to record before the next conference blurs the image.

Teacher Well-Being

Personal growth activities such as relaxation and visualization, setting personal goals, and rewarding oneself result in teacher confidence and the ability to focus on the present. The resource section at the end of this article provides references which describe the following activities more fully.

Relaxation. Relaxation is a strategy which teachers will find helpful in many areas of their lives. Physical tension and psychological stress are inseparably entwined. Reducing physical tension eases emotional strain and results in greater personal effectiveness and self-assurance. Relaxation techniques help people pin-point the situations in which their tension develops; what the onset of tension feels like; and where tension is most likely to be experienced in their body.

Visualization. Visualization exercises are useful for changing behavior. Relaxing your body and then picturing yourself doing well in a difficult situation is a beneficial rehearsal for real events. During visualization, imagine yourself moving, talking, and acting only in productive ways. Whenever self-defeating thoughts or behaviors enter the picture, change them; in your imagination you practice by doing things perfectly. You may choose to picture yourself responding nondefensively, speaking less often, showing concern, or being assertive.

Focus on Delicate Issues. Coping with delicate issues that you want to raise in a parent meeting offers another opportunity for self-understanding and personal development. If there is an issue to be discussed that may cause embarrassment, anger, or defensive-

2. ATTITUDE CHANGE STRATEGIES

ness, spend time thinking through how you will communicate it to the parents.

One suggestion is to approach the topic without apology and without euphemistic jargon. Be direct, specific, caring, and realistic about the seriousness of the problem. Try your ideas on other people to get their reaction. Get feedback on the words and your manner of speaking. Go over your presentation until it comes smoothly and naturally.

Goal Setting. Set individual goals for honing your interpersonal skills. Do you want to hear accurately what parents say and feel, be certain parents are involved in setting classroom objectives, or become aware of nonverbal signals? Choosing one goal for a whole day of conferences, or a separate objective for each conference, should help polish your interpersonal skills. Make this goal a part of a visualization activity or centering exercise; jot it down at the top of your copy of the agenda, or share it with another participant and ask for feedback at the end of the meeting. Setting specific goals and working toward accomplishing them are effective methods for programming personal growth and enhancing your physical and emotional well-being.

Centering. Centering is a technique that enhances psychological integration; to be centered is to have intellect and intuition working in harmony. Centering can take from two minutes to an hour, and can be used prior to parent conferences for relieving tension, renewing energy, building intuition, sharpening senses, enhancing self-image, or strengthening attentiveness.

As you integrate mind and body, you will feel balanced, more responsive to the environment, and emotionally strong. Allow yourself a few minutes for centering before every conference. You will develop an inner stillness that facilitates clear thinking and productive behavior.

Rewards. Finally, for your well-being, reward yourself. Send a message of appreciation to yourself after every conference. Identify the things you did well and spend a few minutes feeling good about them. Recognize that you don't have to be perfect, and appreciate yourself for learning from strategies that didn't work. Set a tangible reward for your work and caring.

Parent Psychological Comfort

You can engage in behaviors that invite parents to feel relaxed, important, and accepted. For instance, you can begin to build rapport with parents soon after school starts by sending them messages which stress the positive traits of their child. You may write a few sentences at the top of a paper the child is taking home, make a brief telephone call, or write a separate note. Make the message positive and honest; there will be opportunity later to discuss behavioral problems or academic difficulties. Make contact with every family at least three times a year. When it is time for a conference, parents are likely to attend more willingly if positive communication has been part of the school-home interaction throughout the year.

Verbal Interactions. When parents arrive for a meeting, allow time for getting acquainted. Schedule time for sharing coffee and talking informally. Draw on information you have gathered to identify conversational topics such as a hobby, a new baby, a place of business, or a change of careers. Choose topics that establish parents as unique individuals and reflect your interest in them as persons.

To be fully involved partners, parents must view themselves as having equal status with educators. Specialized language creates barriers. During the meeting, invite positive feelings in parents by carefully choosing the language you use. Using technical terms or jargon may confuse and irritate parents. One suggestion is to record what you are going to say. Let someone who is not an educator check it for acronyms and jargon. Go over the presentation often enough that you can be crisp and precise.

Facilitating questions may be used to encourage participation from reluctant parents. Questions may take the form of: How do you feel about that? Does that fit with what you see at home? What would you suggest about this? Are there any other topics you would like to discuss this afternoon?

The parent sees the child in roles different from those we see in the classroom. To understand our students, we need to know how they behave outside the school. Facilitating questions can elicit pertinent information as well as encourage parents to take an active part in our educational efforts.

Active listening. Parents with special children often experience strong emotions that may spill over at a school meeting. How educators cope with their own feelings can determine whether or not a parent connection will be formed. Active listening is an interpersonal skill which communicates to parents that we are interested in what they have to say, will work to understand what they mean, and are comfortable with the feelings underlying their message.

Active listening clarifies word meaning, conveys attentiveness, elicits information, and facilitates sharing of feelings. It is the process of feeding back to the parent our interpretation of what was said, including the emotion behind it. The parent, then, can confirm or correct our understanding.

Parent Message: "I just can't understand why Janet is the way she is!"

Active Listening: "You sound very sad about Janet's disability."

Parent Response #1: "No, I can handle her slowness. It's the distance she puts between us that hurts me."

OR

Parent Response #2: "Yeah, I really am down. I'm so tired of coping."

Active listening is appropriate whenever emotion is evident in the parent. If you anticipate a strong response to a topic you are going to raise, allow time in the agenda for parents to react and for active listening to their response. Trying to solve problems through a layer of heavy feelings is like swimming against a current. Thus, you may need to set another date to discuss a solution to the problem.

Active listening is effective when you are confronted with the recurring grief of parents with special children. The parents of a handicapped child have suffered a loss. They have lost the dreams, fantasies, and hopes which they cherished for their child, and they must move through the same stages of grieving which people experience after a death. Grief can be a positive process which allows growth, but it is, nevertheless, very painful. It is especially difficult for parents of handicapped children as they experience loss anew at various stages in their child's development. When other children of their child's age start to school, begin dating, graduate, or marry, parents of special children are reminded of their loss and their grief is rekindled.

A parent's reaction to teachers at a school conference may be influenced by the grieving process. You can help by recognizing that it is normal for parents to experience denial, guilt, and depression. Accept all their feelings as a normal expression of their need to understand why their child is handicapped.

THE PARENT CONNECTION

Regular contact, get-acquainted time, facilitating questions, active listening, and acceptance of grief are all methods for inviting parents to feel respected, wanted, and necessary to the conference procedure. Rapport formed in an atmosphere of respect for each other's uniqueness as well as our collective similarities can bind parents and educators into a strong alliance. The Parent Connection Model identifies areas in which teachers can use their natural creativity to enhance their own well-being and invite a positive response from parents so that school and home can work together as a powerful force for the benefit of handicapped children.

RESOURCES

For relaxation:

Benson, H., & Klipper, M. Z. *The relaxation response.* New York: Morrow, 1976.

Corbin, F., & Corbin, E. *How to relax in a busy world.* Englewood Cliffs NJ: Prentice-Hall, 1962.

Watson, D. L., & Tharp, R. G. *Self-directed behavior: Self-modification for personal adjustment.* Monterey CA: Brooks/Cole, 1977.

For visualization and centering:

Hendricks, G., & Wills, R. *The centering book.* Englewood Cliffs NJ: Prentice-Hall, 1975.

Hendricks, G., & Roberts, T. B. *The second centering book.* Englewood Cliffs NJ: Prentice-Hall, 1977.

Stevens, J. O. *Awareness: Exploring, experimenting, experiencing.* Moab UT: Real People Press, 1971.

For active listening:

Egan, G. *You and me.* Monterey CA: Brooks/Cole, 1977.

Gordon, T. *T.E.T. Teacher effectiveness training.* New York: Peter H. Wyden, 1974.

It's My IEP: Involving Students in the Planning Process

Ellen B. Gillespie
Ann P. Turnbull

Ellen B. Gillespie *is a Regional Administrator for the Office of Mental Retardation in Louisiana. Dr. Gillespie has taught mentally retarded adolescents, worked as a public school mental health consultant, served as program development specialist for a residential center, and worked as an evaluation specialist for the Louisiana Department of Education.*

Ann P. Turnbull *is Acting Associate Director of the Bureau of Child Research and Associate Professor in the Department of Special Education at the University of Kansas. Her areas of special interest include working with families of handicapped children, developing and implementing IEP's, and mainstreaming.*

He knows how to tell what he likes and doesn't like and what he wants to do. It does no good to decide something for someone else. If he decided, maybe he would be more eager to do it.

> —Mother of a 12-year-old
> physically handicapped student

If she were told it was to help her, it would give her a sense of importance in planning her own life. She is maturing and she needs to feel some responsibility for her education and her life.

> —Guardian of a 17-year-old
> emotionally handicapped student

W. could get ready to explain his past history and his feelings about how he has not been able to learn and has tried to keep up. It would help him know how far he has come.

> —Mother of a 17-year-old
> learning disabled student

LOOKING AT THE LAW

Public Law 94-142 provides for the participation of the student, "whenever appropriate," in meetings to develop the individualized education program (IEP). Although a great deal of progress has been made by education agencies in implementing parent participation in educational planning, very little has been done to include students with special needs in planning their own programs. The potential of this involvement for furthering students' growth, maturity, and the exercise of appropriate power over their own lives is tremendous.

P.L. 94-142 regulations specify those persons who should be involved in the IEP meeting. They include a representative of the school other than the child's teacher who is responsible for providing or supervising special education, the teacher, the parents, and the child, "whenever appropriate." While most persons are aware that school officials and parents are involved in IEP planning, many are not aware that the student may be included in helping to develop the IEP.

CRITERIA FOR STUDENT PARTICIPATION

The words "whenever appropriate" have seldom been defined by policymakers. Only a few articles have suggested criteria for deciding when it is appropriate to include students. The student's age, severity of handicap, and ability to handle the situation have been suggested as possible considerations (Winslow, 1977).

More recently, student interest in participating has been recommended as an important criterion. In a study designed to elicit ideas from those who are most affected by the IEP, 47 special education students (12 years of age and older) and their parents were asked to cite considerations in deciding when to include a student (Gillespie, 1981). Respondents were classified by their schools as learning disabled, educable mentally handicapped, seriously emotionally handicapped, or physically handicapped.

More than 75% of the students and 90% of the parents said that they were unaware of the possibility of involving students in IEP meetings. When asked about their attitude toward student participation, both parents and students expressed positive feelings. Over 90% of the parents and over 75% of the students reported that they either completely agreed or mostly agreed with the idea of student involvement.

Student Opinions

Very often, individuals who agree with a general concept fail to find that it applies to them personally. In this case, however, over 70% of the students said that they believed it was a good idea for them to attend their own IEP meeting. Almost 90% of parents indicated that involvement of their child would be appropriate.

Student responses to questions concerning why they should attend their own IEP meeting were varied.

> I would like to go, but the first time would be hard. It would be good so that if you have some feelings you could ask them if they could change it a little bit, and you could ask for help.
> —17-year-old physically handicapped student

> The teachers and parents get everything out and students have feelings and want to get them out, too.
> —13-year-old emotionally handicapped student

> I could learn more about why I'm in a special class.
> —14-year-old EMR student

DECIDING WHEN TO INVOLVE A STUDENT

Each year, parents of students with special needs receive notification from the school that an IEP meeting will be held to discuss goals, objectives, and services for the student. Most local education agencies conduct these meetings in the spring or early fall. P.L. 94-142 requires that the first IEP meeting be held within 30 days of the time a student is determined to be in need of special education services (*Federal Register*, 1977).

Once parents have been notified, it is advisable that some preparation take place. Parents can make significant contributions to the development of the IEP by giving information about the student's interests, abilities, and behavior at home. They may also serve an important advocacy function for the inclusion of specific goals, objectives, or related services. As part of the preparation for the IEP meeting, it is important to consider whether the student himself should be involved.

The decision to involve the student should be based on individual characteristics, rather than on labels or classifications. The following considerations can assist parents and teachers in deciding whether a student could benefit from IEP involvement:

- *Communication.* Does the student understand conversation conducted in simple language? Can the student communicate preferences and interests either verbally or nonverbally?

- *Comfort.* If the meeting is conducted in a nonthreatening way, will the student feel reasonably comfortable? If disagreements occur, how will he or she react? Some uncertainty is always present in new situations, but a few students may feel completely uneasy in a formal setting with school officials and parents.

- *Interest.* Does the student understand what the meeting is about? When the meeting is explained, does the student want to attend? As parents and teachers, do you feel that the student's involvement could be beneficial, either to you and other IEP committee members, or to him or her?

If parents and students decide that it is appropriate for the student to attend, the teacher can work with them in a coordinated fashion to help them prepare the student for the conference.

PRACTICAL SUGGESTIONS

The accommodations necessary to involve a student effectively in the IEP meeting should serve to make the meeting more comfortable and to encourage active participation by parents. As a result, the IEP which is developed will usually be a more personalized document, reflecting the individuality of the person whom it concerns.

Suggestions for Parents

- Ask your child if he or she would like to attend the meeting. Explain why the meeting is being held and who will be there.
- Inform your child at least one week in advance that he will be able to attend the meeting.
- Show your child last year's IEP (if available) and review what was included.
- Request copies of the evaluation report and a draft copy of the teacher's recommendations for the IEP in advance of the meeting. Make notes of questions, comments, or concerns. Review this information with your child, and tell him generally what you plan to say at the conference.
- Discuss with your child issues to be covered at the

2. ATTITUDE CHANGE STRATEGIES

IEP meeting such as goals, objectives, placement, and related services. If you and your child differ in what you consider to be appropriate, pinpoint these differences as much as possible before the meeting. Share your viewpoints with each other and work hard to develop compromises acceptable to both of you. Remember that it can create discomfort for both of you to strongly disagree with each other in the IEP meeting.

- Stress that everyone's ideas are welcome in the meeting.
- Caution your child that all of his suggestions may not be followed, but that his thoughts are valuable.
- Gather as much information as possible from your child about his present educational program. It may be helpful to make a list of specific questions and to discuss each question with him.
- Help your child make a list of three things he likes about school, three things he would like to change, and three things he wants to learn to do in the future.
- Discuss the meeting at home among family members (perhaps using role-playing).
- On the day of the meeting, review the purpose, the persons who will be there, and the list of ideas about school you developed together.
- Make sure your child takes his list of ideas to the meeting.
- Help your child feel comfortable in the meeting by talking with him and encouraging him to talk. It may be necessary to ask him questions about items on his list.
- After the IEP meeting has been concluded, tell your child that you are proud of him for helping to make some very important educational decisions.

Suggestions for School Personnel

- Schedule the meeting at a time convenient for all parties, including the student.
- Allow enough time for the meeting so that all participants can share their views.
- Realize that, in order for the IEP to reflect the views of the group, more than one meeting may be needed.
- Inform all IEP committee members that the student will be present.
- Work with the parent to help the student prepare for the meeting in advance by making a list of information to share.
- Consider having students who have previously participated in their own IEP conferences with success share suggestions with students preparing to participate for the first time.
- If a draft IEP has been developed, review it with the student in advance of the meeting.
- Begin the meeting by introducing each person and

asking the person to explain his role. Whenever possible, ask the student to share some information about himself—his age, class, etc.
- Conduct the meeting in an organized but informal manner.
- Resist the temptation to use jargon which parents and students may not understand.
- Phrase suggestions positively and emphasize the strengths of the student.
- Address both the child and the parent in the meeting, not just one or the other.
- When the student or parent makes a contribution to the meeting, actively reinforce their participation by telling them that their contribution was helpful.

- Carefully explain the goals, objectives, and services to be provided.
- Ask questions of the student and parents about each aspect of the program.
- Structure questions in an open-ended manner and avoid leading questions.
- Ask the student and parents to share their list of the student's ideas about school.
- Discuss these ideas and include them whenever feasible.
- Make sure that all persons present understand and agree with the information contained in the final IEP document.
- Have the student sign the IEP, as well as the parent.
- Provide a copy of the IEP and minutes of the meeting to the parents (and to the student, if appropriate).
- After the meeting is concluded, tell the student that his participation was valuable.
- As lessons and assignments are later given to the student, relate them back to the IEP. Assist the student in seeing the connection between IEP meeting decisions and the instructional program.

REFERENCES

Federal Register, August 23, 1977, 42475-42518. Education of handicapped children: Implementation of Part B of the Education of the Handicapped Act. Washington DC: Office of Education, Department of Health, Education and Welfare.

Gillespie, E. B. *Student participation in the development of individualized education programs: Perspectives of parents and students.* Unpublished doctoral dissertation, University of North Carolina at Chapel Hill, 1981.

Winslow, L. Parent participation. In S. Torres (Ed.), *A primer on individualized education programs for handicapped children.* Reston VA: Foundation for Exceptional Children, 1977.

Books About Children with Special Needs: An Annotated Bibliography

What to look for when selecting children's books about handicapped persons.

Bonnie Lass
Marcia Bromfield

Integration of children with special needs into regular classrooms must be done thoughtfully and with preparation. Both teachers and children should become attuned to special needs students in as many ways as possible.

One of the most logical ways to broaden awareness is to stock the classroom library with books dealing with handicapped people. However, not all such books are helpful. Some of them perpetuate false stereotypes.

Because of the stereotypes that unfamiliarity fosters, attitudes toward handicapped people are often negative. Wolfensberger (1972) discussed a number of stereotyped roles into which handicapped persons have historically been cast. They have been seen as perpetual children, menaces to society, subhuman or superhuman, and objects of pity, charity, or ridicule.

Many of these stereotypes are found in children's books as well as in the mass media and in adult literature. Since literature is one important vehicle that can affect and change attitudes, appropriate, accurate portrayals of children with special needs are essential.

This article suggests children's books that give handicapped persons a "fair shake," and presents criteria for discriminating between books that foster positive attitudes and those that are negative portraits.

The criteria used for book selection follow. Examples of literature we cannot recommend accompany the standards as illustrations. These criteria will enable teachers to select books about special needs children even if they are not cited in the bibliography.

Criteria for book selection

Books were chosen because, both in text and illustration, they:

1. Promote empathy rather than pity. *The Blue Rose* by Gerda Klein was omitted from the list because of its "tear-jerker" qualities. The little girl, retarded and afflicted with cerebral palsy, is described as "like a bird with shorter wings [who] has to be protected."

2. Portray the handicapped person as human rather than romanticized. *At the Mouth of the Luckiest River* by Arnold Griese was not included because its clubfooted hero needed to be superhumanly resourceful, making peace between Alaskan Indians when adults could not.

3. Describe admiration and acceptance rather than ridicule. *He's My Brother* by Joe Lasker, a popular book of this genre, depicts Jaime, a learning disabled child, who is ridiculed by peers, accepted only by younger children and family. This is a poor model for the treatment of learning-different children within the classroom.

4. Present an accurate portrayal of the behaviors associated with a specific handicap. *Lisa and Her Soundless World* by Edna Levine describes deafness as "T.V. with the sound turned off." Often, however, deafness is quite different. For instance, deaf people sometimes hear at certain frequencies but not at others.

5. Were judged interesting for a designated age group in plot, characterization, and language. Some books on the handicapped are "preachy"—educative but nonmotivating, better for a report on the handicapped than as recreational reading. Using *Lisa and Her Soundless World* as an example again, we find no action or plot but instead a clinical description of hearing loss.

6. Present the handicapped child in a realistic setting when possible. *Howie Helps Himself* by Joan Fassler depicts physically disabled children in a special school. The current practice is to place such children in regular schools, so we have excluded this book from our list.

7. Emphasize similarities rather than differences between handicapped and nonhandicapped children. *The Blue Rose*, mentioned previously, not only promoted sympathy but also an image of the handicapped child as qualitatively different. Analogies between the child and a "kitten without a tail," and fish who have a language and music of their own were made. She was even compared to a being from another planet!

From *The Reading Teacher*, February 1981. Reprinted with permission of Dr. Marcia Bromfield and the International Reading Association.

2. ATTITUDE CHANGE STRATEGIES

These are unfortunate metaphors that cannot promote acceptance of handicapped children as peers.

The above criteria are important in selecting books about handicapped people. When used, they help to insure that a positive, unstereotyped view will be promoted. Unfortunately too few books met these standards. The bibliography that follows should be longer, and the hope is that more sensitive, well written, and realistic books will soon be available.

At Boston College, Chestnut Hill, Massachusetts, Lass teaches courses in developmental and remedial reading and is particularly interested in methods and materials for learning-different students. Also at Boston College, Bromfield teaches special education courses to undergraduates and coordinates the Special Education/Alternative Environments Program.

References

Fassler, Joan. *Howie Helps Himself*. Chicago, Ill.: Albert Whitman, 1975.

Fry, Edward. "Fry's Readability Graph: Clarifications, Validity, and Extension to Level 17." *Journal of Reading*, vol. 21 (December 1977), pp. 242-52.

Griese, Arnold. *At the Mouth of the Luckiest River*. New York, N.Y.: Thomas Y. Crowell, 1973.

Klein, Gerda. *The Blue Rose*. New York, N.Y.: Lawrence Hill and Co., 1974.

Lasker, Joe. *He's My Brother*. Chicago, Ill.: Albert Whitman, 1974.

Levine, Edna. *Lisa and Her Soundless World*. New York, N.Y.: Human Sciences Press, 1974.

Wolfensberger, Wolf. *The Principle of Normalization in Human Services*. Toronto, Ont.: National Institute on Mental Retardation, 1972.

Acceptable books about children with special needs

Book	Readability level*	Handicap	Synopsis
Joan Fassler. *One Little Girl.* Human Sciences Press, 1969.	4th grade	Mild mental retardation	Laurie can do many things but is considered a slow child in school. After a psychologist says that she is slow at some things, fast at others, but quite happy with herself, everyone begins emphasizing her strengths rather than worrying about her weaknesses.
Phyllis Gold. *Please Don't Say Hello.* Human Sciences Press, 1975.	5th grade	Autism	Eddie is autistic, and new in the neighborhood. With the love and support of his parents and an older brother and his friends, Eddie begins to emerge from his shell. Particularly noteworthy is the appreciation shown for his special talents, such as jigsaw puzzling.
Frank Jupo. *Atu, the Silent One.* Holiday Press, 1967.	5th grade	Muteness	Atu, an African boy of the Bushman tribe, communicates through sign language and pictures drawn on rock or in the sand. He is valued for his unique contribution to the tribe instead of ridiculed for his lack of speech.
Ada Litchfield. *A Button in Her Ear.* Albert Whitman and Co., 1976.	3rd grade	Hearing impairment	This book humorously portrays the misunderstandings that occur because of Angela's unidentified hearing loss. After a visit to a doctor, she is fitted with a hearing aid. When she comes to school wearing it, her teacher enthusiastically has her demonstrate it for the class. Positive attitudes toward hearing loss as well as Angela's spunkiness make this a highly recommended book.
Jeanne Peterson. *I Have a Sister—My Sister Is Deaf.* Harper and Row, 1977.	4th grade	Deafness	A deaf child is shown doing the things typical children do: going to school, watching television, climbing trees, and playing on a jungle gym.
Harriet Sobol. *My Brother Steven Is Retarded.* Macmillan, 1977.	4th grade	Mental retardation	Beth has conflicting feelings about her retarded older brother; she loves him and takes pride in his accomplishments but is embarrassed by his looks and behavior. A realistic, complex, and unromantic view of mental retardation, illustrated with striking photographs.

(continued on following page)

(continued from preceding page)

Sara Bonnett Stein. *About Handicaps: An Open Family Book for Parents and Children Together.* Walker and Co., 1974.	2nd grade	Cerebral palsy	This excellent book examines the fears Matthew, a nonhandicapped child, has about his friend Joe's cerebral palsy. The format is unusual; one part of the book is for children and a corresponding part is for adults to help stimulate discussion. Both photographs and words sensitively portray a friendship between a handicapped and non-handicapped child.
Glendon Swarthout and Kathryn Swarthout. *Whales to See The.* Doubleday, 1975.	6th grade	Learning disabilities	A group of 6th graders from a special class have a rare adventure: a day on the ocean viewing gray whales' migration shared with another class of "normal" children. Both groups learn about whales, seafaring, and each other.
Bernard Wolf. *Anna's Silent World.* Lippincott, 1977.	6th grade	Hearing impairment	Through photographs and text, the reader learns about Anna, a deaf girl very much in the mainstream of life. She goes to school with hearing children, takes dancing lessons, and has friends. In addition to showing the life of deaf children, this book provides much information about deafness.
Bernard Wolf. *Connie's New Eyes.* Lippincott, 1976.	5th grade	Blindness	This nonfiction book begins with the story of a young girl raising a seeing eye dog and then introduces us to Connie, a 22-year-old blind woman who gets the dog. Connie is capable and independent. Her social activities are typical for a woman her age. Also, she is a competent teacher of handicapped preschoolers. Both text and photographs make this a highly recommended book.
Bernard Wolf. *Don't Feel Sorry for Paul.* Lippincott, 1974.	4th grade	Physical handicap	Paul was born with stumps for hands and one foot. This piece of nonfiction, illustrated with superb photographs, shows how he manages an ordinary boy's life of horseback riding, school, and a birthday party. The book dispels some of the myths and fears nonhandicapped persons have about prosthetic devices.
Frances Wosmek. *A Bowl of Sun.* Childrens Press, 1976.	3rd grade	Blindness	Megan, who is blind, has a close relationship with her father, a leather-crafter in a small seashore town. In order to send Megan to school, her father moves with her to Boston where they live in a communal house. The adjustment, both to the city and to increased social contacts, is difficult for Megan. Learning to become a potter, however, helps her smooth the transition.

*An estimate, using the Fry readability formula (Fry, 1977)

Teaching the Visually Impaired Child

Approximately sixty percent of all visually impaired school-aged children are being educated in regular classrooms (Report to Congress, U.S. Dept. of HEW, 1979). Mainstreaming is not a new phenomenon for this population of children, since visually impaired children have been routinely mainstreamed in large numbers since the 1900s. "Mainstreaming Children with Visual Impairments" examines the benefits of mainstreaming, describes the educational needs of visually impaired children, and discusses the practices and placement options being used today.

Because there are so few visually impaired children (prevalence estimates range from as few as one to as many as 17.5 per thousand), teachers don't often have contact with visually impaired children in their classrooms. This lack of experience and personal contact with visually impaired persons increases teachers' concerns about whether they can provide for the specialized needs of these children. In fact, as Rottman points out in "Some Thoughts on the Education of Blind Children," the greatest obstacle in educating these children is attitudinal, because our society evidences a lack of acceptance of blindness and shows limited expectations for what blind people can do.

Once these attitudinal obstacles are overcome, there are still issues of whether regular classrooms can adapt enough for these children and whether visually impaired children can receive the needed specialized work, such as braille reading, mobility and orientation training, and residual vision training. (Most blind children are not completely without sight; they have some residual vision that can be utilized for maximal visual efficiency.) Teachers are not expected to carry out this training because there are specialists who can meet these needs. However, in keeping with the least restrictive concept, visually impaired children do not need specialized training during the entire school day. Most of these children need exposure to the regular school curriculum, and need to be included with the same peer group they would have encountered had they not been visually impaired. A mixture of specialized work outside the classroom and regular work in the classroom is currently the preferred way of educating these children. "Teaching Partially Sighted Children" examines how reading and testing materials can be adapted for those who have partial vision.

The biggest problem in adapting the ongoing school program for visually impaired children is the need to get information through means other than visual. Visually impaired children also need help in learning words and concepts for visual phenomena for which they have had no experience. In this instance modern technology can be effectively employed. "Technology and the Handicapped" discusses how a successful program can be developed by using microprocessors for the visually impaired student.

Looking Ahead: Challenge Questions

To what extent should visually impaired children be mainstreamed?

What factors should be considered when mainstreaming these children?

How can materials be adapted for partially sighted and for blind children?

In what areas would they need specialized help?

What other adaptations are necessary?

Unit 3

Mainstreaming Children With Visual Impairments

S.C. Ashcroft

and A.M. Zambone-Ashley

Peabody College of Vanderbilt University

Mainstreaming is the most talked about trend in special education today. Children who are blind have been mainstreamed in educational programs since the early 1900s. Mainstreaming should be defined as educating children with handicaps in regular education programs with supporting help from specially prepared personnel. Before it was called mainstreaming, such programs were functioning effectively for children who are blind with the assistance of resource teachers and itinerant teachers. Today most children who are blind are being educated in local day schools with their normally sighted peers.

The merits of education in local day schools (mainstreaming) versus education in residential schools have been debated continuously since the 1830s. In 1866, Dr. Samuel Gridley Howe (cited in Irwin, 1955), founding director of Perkins Institutions said:

> all great establishments in the nature of boarding schools, where the sexes must be separated; where there must be boarding in common, and sleeping in congregate dormitories; where there must be routine, and formality, and restraint, and repression of individuality; where the charms and refining influences of the true family relation cannot be had—all such institutions are unnatural, undesirable, and very liable to abuse. We should have as few of them as is possible, and those few should be kept as small as possible.

Howe also said:

> with a view to lessening all differences between blind and seeing children, I would have the blind attend the common schools in all cases where it is feasible (depend upon it, one of the future reforms in the education of the blind will be to send blind children to the common schools, to be taught with common children in all those branches not absolutely requiring visible illustrations, as spelling, pronunciation, grammar, arithmetic, vocal music and the like.) We shall avail ourselves of the special institutions less and the common schools more.

Thus, the area of service to persons with visual impairments has been a pioneer in mainstreaming for many years. However, many educators of the visually impaired continue to believe that education in residential schools is superior to local day school education for large numbers of children with visual impairments whether multiply handicapped or not.

Who Should be Mainstreamed?

Today, mainstreaming is widely recommended for children with mild handicaps. Therefore, most discussions of mainstreaming deal with the education of children who are educable mentally retarded, children with learning disabilities, children with behavior disorders, and children with handicaps in speech. Frequently, children with more severe handicaps are excluded from discussions of mainstreaming: children who are blind, deaf, moderately or severely retarded, emotionally disturbed or multiply handicapped. However, there are those who believe that public schools should practice a "zero reject" philosophy and exclude no one from the mainstream. These professionals (not always "practitioners") believe that a child's failure to learn should not be blamed on the child or the disability, but on the school program which has failed to create conditions productive for successful learning achievement.

Children who are blind and have no other serious impairments, disabilities or handicaps, are among the most "integrable" or mainstreamable children with handicaps. Children who are blind with multiple disabilities are only somewhat less so. However, it must be remembered that mainstreaming does not mean enrolling children with handicaps in regular education pro-

Reprinted from *Journal of Research & Development Education*, Vol. 13, No. 4, pgs. 22-36, with permission.

grams without the needed understanding, acceptance, assistance, support, materials, equipment, and teacher education. Fully integrated education of children with handicaps will likely cost less both in the immediate and the long range future. Not all children, however, should necessarily be mainstreamed. The questions should really be which child can be successful in what type of program under what circumstances? Thus, no categorical answer regarding mainstreaming should be applied to all children, but each child should be considered in terms of his or her own unique circumstances and the environmental circumstances in which the child lives.

The position taken by the National Education Association in 1975 (Hyer, 1979) advocates mainstreaming under certain conditions. NEA's position was reflected in the 1975 resolution by the Representative Assembly:

The NEA will support mainstreaming handicapped students only when—

● It provides a favorable learning experience for both handicapped and regular students.
● Regular and special teachers are prepared for these roles.
● Appropriate instructional materials, supportive services, and pupil personnel services are provided for the teacher and the handicapped student.
● Modifications are made in class size, scheduling, and curriculum design to accommodate the shifting demands that mainstreaming creates.
● There is a systematic evaluation and reporting of program developments.
● Adequate additional funding and resources are provided for mainstreaming and are used exclusively for that purpose.

The Child With Visual Impairment

The term "visually impaired" implies a variety of conditions related to the state of the individual's visual system. The child with a visual impairment is usually labeled under one of two general categories: blind or partially sighted, for the purpose of delivery of special education services. In the United States, the accepted definition of blindness is "corrected visual acuity of 20/200 or less in the better eye, or a visual field of no more than 20 degrees in the better eye" (Vaughn & Asbury, 1977, p. 359). A child who is labeled "partially sighted" has a "corrected visual acuity of 20/70 or less in the better eye" (Vaughn & Asbury, 1977, p. 361) or the "visual field subtends an angle no greater than 140 degrees" (VonHippel, 1977, p. 15).

Another means of categorizing individuals with visual impairments for education is to refer to the child who is blind as a "braille reader," while the child who is partially sighted is called a "print reader"—either large or regular print, possibly under special conditions (Harley, 1963). While this mode of classification may be somewhat useful for educational purposes, the mode of

reading is usually selected based on: personal preference; motivation; teacher skill and preference; availability of low vision aids; and prognosis of the visual condition (Reynolds & Birch, 1977).

The state of the visual system can vary, with significant implications for the individual, in a variety of ways including: reduced visual acuity; limited visual field; defective color vision; and "extrinsic or external muscle imbalance" (Lowenfeld, 1973, p. 29). Two key factors related to the onset of a visual impairment have major implications for the abilities and needs of the child: age of onset; and manner of occurrence. It is generally agreed that age of onset has major impact on development, functioning, and learning. Children with severe loss of vision prior to the ages of five and seven are usually unable to draw on visual imagery, and rarely possess color concepts (Schlaegel, 1953; Blank, 1958). The manner and rapidity of the loss of vision has implications for psychological adjustment (Cutsforth, 1951; Lowenfeld, 1973), and adaptability. Consequently, knowledge of the visual acuity or field of vision does not necessarily communicate the child's optical abilities or impairments and certainly does not indicate his scholastic aptitude.

There are a variety of visual conditions, as well as wide variation in the way children utilize residual vision. Visual loss can occur peripherially or centrally. Many children have disrupted visual fields—that is, they may see as through a tunnel, see spots, or have blurred vision. Visual acuity may vary at different times and under different circumstances depending on such factors as fatigue, illness, or stress (VonHippel, 1977). The majority of children with visual impairments do have some residual vision and should be encouraged to utilize it. Residual vision is seldom harmed by use, but may deteriorate through lack of use.

A 1970 study by the Rand Corporation determined that twenty-one million children up to twenty-one years old required eye care. A child was considered visually impaired if he was unable to see well enough to read newsprint, or was in need of services specifically related to the visual disability. One hundred eighty thousand were identified as having sight loss, including 32,000 who were "legally," but not totally, blind. Thirteen thousand children were totally blind, or possessed light perception only (Kakalik, Brewer, Dougharty, Fleischauer, and Genensky, 1973). These data, though they represent an estimate, suggest the general magnitude of that portion of the population with visual impairments.

One must remember, in considering the needs of the child, that the "physical ability of youth, 0-21, to see. . . (as well as the functional ability to utilize the visual system) varies on a continuum" (Kakalik, Brewer, Dougharty, Fleischauer, Genensky, and Wallen, 1974, p. 5). Consequently, a child may see clearly enough at close range to read print, but be hampered in mobility and orientation (getting about in the environment). Kakalik, et al. (1974, p. 6) make the vital point that, while acuity ratings and other medically based definitions may give "some indication of who needs service, (they are) not refined enough to indicate the type of service required and (do) not include everyone who needs special services. . . a set of definitions is needed for each type of handicap, not a single definition." Thus, functional capability, need and capacity to benefit from service should form the basis for defining the child with a visual impairment (Kakalik, et al., 1974).

Visual impairment, then, can be regarded as any condition of the optical system which interferes with, or alters the pattern of development. The primary goal of education is the fostering of human development. Therefore, the child with visual impairments is particularly in need of an educational program which will meet the developmental needs of the total child, including those needs resulting from the visual condition. In addressing the developmental needs of the child with visual impairments, two key points must be remembered: approximately 80% of all blind and partially sighted children do have some remaining vision; and the visual impairment is but one of a multitude of characteristics of each child—such children are more alike than different from their more normally seeing peers. The similarities and differences of each child and his or her peers go far beyond just the visual impairment. Furthermore, each visual impairment is different in its characteristics, consequences and implications, depending upon the child.

Labels are to be avoided (Harley, 1963; Hobbs, 1975) because of their lack of utility in facilitating clear communication of a child's characteristics. Using visual acuity for the purpose of classification is possibly more applicable to the legal, medical, or rehabilitation professions, than for educators (American Foundation for the Blind, 1954).

In a book, *The Futures of Children,* Ashcroft (1975) stated:

> There is a growing recognition that the diagnosis and classification of blindness for educational purposes should be limited to children who have no measurable vision or such limited vision that it is nonfunctional as a major channel for learning. . . The label "partially seeing" has more and more been used to designate children whose serious visual disability impairs their learning efficiency but who, nonetheless, rely on vision and visual aids and utilize print as a primary medium or reading. (Ashcroft, 1975, p. 65)

Ashcroft also pointed out the growth of a trend away from reliance on "arbitrary, acuity-related definitions and classification systems" toward "educationally relevant criteria for defining and classifying children with visual impairments" (p. 66).

Several factors influencing this trend have major implications for the child with visual impairments: (Ashcroft, 1975)

a) While traditionally the labels of blind and partially sighted have only been applied to those children who had no other disabling condition, the increase in the number of multiply impaired children demands an assessment of, and attention to visual functions and educational prognosis;

b) Clinically based information including: age of onset, etiology, visual acuity, field of vision, and medical prognosis have been helpful, but limited in utility for educational programming. For example, educational setting can play a more significant role than acuity rating in determining the development of either print or braille reading skills;

c) The belief that encouraging the development and use of remaining vision is beneficial both to the visual system itself, and the child and his or her development and integration, has become an accepted fact.

Nature of the Problem

"When thinking of the causes of blindness, one must think anatomically and remember that visual loss can occur from obstruction to the light source anywhere from the outermost parts of the eye to the very depth of the brain" (Harley & Lawrence, 1977, p.5). When thinking of educational service for a child who is blind, one must think of the total child and the "ecological system" (Hobbs, 1975) in which the child participates. "For the most part, children with vision impairments who are enrolled in regular school programs (and academic tracks in residential schools for the blind) present a pattern of normal variations on traits other than vision" (Reynolds & Birch, 1977, p. 607). There is, as well, a variation in the visual trait. Yet, *cautiously* one can look at needs of the group of children with visual impairments which result from, but are not solely affected by, the visual condition.

Vision is considered the unifying sense. It is frequently claimed that as much as 90% of learning, by sighted persons, takes place through vision. The child who cannot see well is limited in learning through conventional modes of environmental and visual experience, and must be given opportunities to develop mobility, spatial orientation, appropriate concept development, social development, and acquisition of behavior through imitation (Cutsforth, 1951; Cratty & Sons, 1968; Cratty, 1971; Lowenfeld, 1973; Reynolds & Birch, 1977). The child with visual impairment will demonstrate few serious deficits, functioning effectively even in complex seeing environments.

For a variety of reasons, the majority of research on developmental and functional differences between persons who are blind or have sight has been carried out with individuals with congenital and near total blindness. The primary areas of differences demonstrated in the research on early development include: delays in conferring objectivity on persons and things, reaching and grasping, mobility, concept development, constitution of an "I" and "you," and the representation of self as "I" in play. Overall, however, educationally advantaged children who are blind are primarily aligned in developmental areas with children who have sight and usually function at a normal level by, or shortly after, school age (Fraiberg, 1977).

While serious visual impairments do not decrease the ability to process information, the quantity and quality of information is affected, thereby influencing development and functioning. Restrictions of visual input, and attenuating restrictions such as the range of experience, vary from child to child and account for unique needs and abilities of each child with a visual impairment. The degree and type of visual impairment and opportunities for learning determine the extent to which the child must rely on the other senses to obtain information about the environment. This reliance on alternate senses is further affected by the quality and amount of visual stimulation early in life.

Delay in cognitive and motor development can occur if sensory information is further restricted through limited opportunities, the reduction of motivation to explore, or additional impairments. Information available through other senses is limited in a variety of ways. Often items are inaccessible, too large, fragile, moving too fast, or too difficult to touch (Harley, 1963; Lowenfeld,1973). Misconception and lack of conceptualization can result from the inability to establish contact with objects to the necessary extent, particularly in the realm of incidental learning.

Other areas of ability which may differ from the sighted child include: verbal learning without conceptual basis through concrete experience (Cutsforth, 1932; Nolan, 1960; Harley, 1963); space perception and spatial relations (Worchel, 1951; McReynolds and Worchel, 1954; Senden, 1960; Fraiberg, Siegel, & Gibson, 1966; Juurmaa, 1967; and Hartlage, 1968); and abstract thinking (Tillman, 1967; Zweibelson & Barg, 1967; and Miller, 1969). Another area which may be problematic due to loss of vision is social skills (Cutsforth, 1951). The results of research on learning and development of children with visual impairments indicate that this segment of the population differs primarily in these areas due to "disadvantage in observing objects as a whole and in relating these objects to other parts of (the) environment" (Harley, 1963). Harley (1963), Lowenfeld (1973) and others call for an educational program which will provide concrete, practical experience, and ordered stimulation.

Educational Services

The education of children with visual impairments has had an interesting history in the United States. As early as 1828 (Frampton & Kerney, 1953), plans were made for education in residential schools, and shortly thereafter (1830) school founders recommended limitations of such residential schools in the hope that local programs, now called mainstreaming, could meet the needs of the children with visual impairments. Local day school programs for the blind, which had origins as early as 1834 in Scotland (Farrell, 1956), began in 1900 in this country. In 1908 the first program specifically for children who were partially seeing was established in London (Hathaway, 1959). By 1913, the first class for such children had been opened in Boston. In the same year, the cooperative system, combining special classes an integrative placement, already functioning for children who were blind, was extended to Cleveland for children who were partially seeing.

Local day school classes for children with visual impairments grew in number at a faster rate than residential schools beginning in 1949, and, since 1973, 60% or more of all children with visual impairments attended local day school programs in their home communities (Lowenfeld, 1973). Thus, the concept of "mainstreaming" the child with visual impairments has historically been a component of educational services.

With the inception of Public Law 94-142, the schools are mandated to provide an appropriate education for all children in the least restrictive, that is, the "most integrative," environment (Wolfensberger, 1972). The most appropriately integrative environment will vary for each child, his or her family, and community. In the school system, the ultimate integration for the child with visual impairment is in the "regular" classroom, in the "regular" community school system; the least integrative is in the residential institution, specifically organized for children with visual impairment, and providing an on-site, comprehensive need-meeting service delivery system. Within, and between each educational setting, is a wide gamut of environments, offering varying degrees of integration with a heterogeneous population.

Mainstreaming the Child with Visual Impairments

"The most conspicuous trend in the field of special education, and perhaps in all of education, is mainstreaming" (Reynolds, 1975, p. 39). Mainstreaming can be regarded as "the enlargement of the stream of regular education . . . to accommodate children who present special education needs" (Reynolds, 1975, p. 1); that is to make available to a child the most integrative educational setting appropriate to the needs, so as to foster "the positive interactions between handicapped and nonhandicapped learners" (Martin, 1975, pp. 3-4). Current legislative and social policy mandate that there be a wide array of educational settings available and that these settings be utilized. Indeed, Reynolds has stated "that the whole history of special education, the systematic attempt to educate exceptional children can be viewed in terms of one steady trend described by the term 'progressive inclusion' " (1975, pp. 43-44). One of the first groups of children offered special education through the public schools were children with visual impairments. "The efficacy of special classes for partially seeing or educationally blind has really never been tested. It seems that visually impaired children with normal or above intelligence, and no additional impairments, should be able to function adequately in regular classes, without need of special rooms" (Harley, 1963, p. 434). A large percentage of educators can anticipate a child with visual impairment in their classroom at some point during their careers (Scholl, 1978). Those educators who have past or current experience with children who have visual impairment "report benefit from mainstreaming" for the child (Scholl, 1978, p. 79).

In 1954, the American Foundation for the Blind (AFB) officially recognized three types of educational settings for school-age children with visual impairments: the public or private residential school; the regular school with a full resource or special class teacher available for the total school day; and the regular school with itinerary services available at regular intervals. AFB endorsed all three types of settings, with the understanding that the existence of one type not cancel out the existence of the others.

Current Practices

Reynolds and Birch (1977) listed prevailing practices in the education of children with visual impairments, with particular attention to those they felt could be changed or added to in the near future:

1. Children with visual handicaps are mainstreamed for academic instruction, but social mainstreaming is often lacking; calling for social integration as well as physical integration;
2. Children with visual impairments are taught mainly by cooperation with one or more regular teachers; calling for participation of all significant others in the planning of the educational program;
3. Special education teachers encourage regular classroom teachers to send handicapped children to resource room for much of their instructional needs; calling for a change toward a consultative role for the special education teacher;
4. The program for students with visual impairments is mainly academic; calling for integration of social opportunities, and support for participation in all school functions;
5. Residential schools for the blind operate often as comprehensive alternative programs; calling for a change in the role of the residential school to that of support in training the child and the teacher. (pp. 635-636)

"Current trends in 'mainstreaming' through services based on the cascade model (Deno, 1970) indicate that itinerant and resource room approaches will be more likely 'treatments of choice' for the future" (Wilson, McVugh, McMahon, Bauer, and Richardson, 1976, p. 83). Many educators strongly feel that "the regular classroom offers children with special limitations a more normal, natural learning and social environment" (p. 23) and that, in having the child who is visually limited in the regular environment, he or she may begin to learn the adjustment necessary for adult life at an earlier age. Mainstreaming is also necessary to enhance the acceptance of the child with visual impairments by children with sight (Alson, 1977).

Regular Classes or the Residential School?

A controversy has occurred in the past over the benefits of a residential school versus the public school, which can only be resolved on the basis of the needs of each individual child with visual impairments, and that child's family (Frampton & Kerney, 1953; Lowenfeld, 1973; Rottman, 1978). No one educational setting is best for all children, or even for a particular child throughout the educational career. Since the early 1960's there has been a trend toward the development of a continuum of educational programs for children with visual impairments (AFB, 1954) rather than dichotomous services among local day versus residential school programs. Every state (Jones, 1961) has some type of legislative provision enabling the development of residential or local educational programs, or both, for children who are visually limited. The present authors endorse a continuum of services, perhaps best exemplified early in the so-called "Oregon Plan" (Lowenfeld, 1959), and the New Jersey Plan (Taylor, 1959). In both these plans, day and residential school provisions are available in terms of the needs of the *individual child* rather than in terms of administrative expediency. Essential to the effectiveness of such plans is the flexibility of individual placements, and opportunity to modify the plans for an individual child when the situation calls for such modification. Placement in one type of program or the other should not imply total or permanent commitment to that placement.

Children with visual limitations, like all school aged children, are first and foremost the responsibility of general education. Only when it is clear that the regular educational provisions provided for all children are inadequate to meet the needs of children who are blind or partially seeing, should special programming be sought. Following a brief review of some essential and unique features of various administrative plans as they relate to educational provisions for the child with visual limitations, some guidelines for the regular classroom teacher are presented for additional understanding or educational planning of children with visual impairments.

Bledsoe (1971) outlined three types of residential

school programs for children who are visually limited: the classic type, providing a comprehensive educational program from kindergarten through the last year in high school; the center type, serving as an active resource for the community-integrated education of children with visual impairments; and the hospital type, providing educational services to children with multiple impairments including visual limitation.

Presently, self-contained special classes in the public school systems exist mostly at the primary level for children with visual impairments. Thus, children participating in these settings interact exclusively with others who have visual limitations. A variation of this setting occurs in programs where children predominantly are involved in the special class, but do experience some activities and settings with those who are sighted. For some children with visual impairments, the self-contained classroom may provide a means for intensive intervention at an early age, and gradual, coordinated mainstreaming in later school years.

Another type of educational setting available to children with visual impairments is resource room with regular classroom participation for most of the school day. With this type of educational programming the child predominantly participates in the integrated classroom, yet receives intensive instruction with other children with visual limitations in special skills areas. This program plan may be particularly useful to the child who needs to develop mobility and orientation, and/or braille reading skills.

A fourth educational setting for children with visual impairments is consultation and itinerant instruction within the integrated classroom. In this setting, the regular classroom teacher assumes responsibility for the child's educational development, and receives guidance and support, as well as supplementary child-direct instruction from specialists in visual impairment. This service design is effective in areas where there are few children who have visual limitations; children who are severely but not totally visually impaired; or children who are totally blind and are having few problems developing skills in mobility and orientation, braille reading, or the use of special equipment.

Educational services for children with visual impairments apparently vary by degrees, rather than categories, in the amount of integration occurring with children who have sight. Vision consultants are often available to the regular classroom teacher for guidance, support, and direction. Not so apparent is the fact that there is also a multitude of children with visual limitations participating in integrated classrooms, without the need of specialized assistance.

Educational Placement for the Child with Visual Impairment

Lowenfeld (1959) presented four categories of issues important in considering the selection of an educational placement for a child with visual impairments: the availability of other types of educational services in the child's home community; the family's ability to maintain the child in the home; the child's overall strengths and needs, and their integration with the resources of the local educational system; and the parent's, and child's preferred educational setting.

Within these four categories, there are many considerations for placement decisions. In relation to geographic availability, Jones and Collins (1966) found that approximately 75% of the students with visual limitations residing in the North Atlantic Region had local services available; 50% of the students had access to local services in the West and Southwest Regions; 35% in the Great Lakes and Plains Regions had local services available; while only 25% of the children in the Southeastern Region had services in their local communities. Children in integrated programs with itinerant and resource assistance exhibit similar or stronger academic achievement in many areas when compared with children in residential schools (Lowenfeld, et al., 1969: Stephens & Birch, 1969). Howell (1970) examined the extent of acceptance of children with visual impairments and found that generally these children were less accepted than children without visual limitations. He also discovered that: children who were blind were more readily accepted than children who were partially sighted; social status was generally lower during junior high school; and children who performed at an average academic level were less socially integrated.

"Nearly one-third of the visually handicapped graduates of residential and day high schools throughout the United States attend some college or university" (Dauwalder, 1964, p. 19). Lowenfeld (1973) suggested local high school placement may better facilitate college placement because small enrollments in residential high school programs often limit opportunities. He offers some specific considerations for the placement decisions which are equally pertinent in deciding placement at the elementary and junior high school level:

1. A home free of such serious problems that he will not be able to progress satisfactorily in his academic and personal growth;
2. Basic textbooks for each subject available to him in a reading medium he can handle efficiently at the time that he needs them;
3. All equipment and special materials that he needs for the study of his various subjects at home, with duplicates of heavy or bulky articles to keep at school;
4. Adequate reader service (preferably paid readers, so that he will not need to feel in debt for the privilege of having at his command the same information others are able to obtain);

5. A teacher-consultant who will arrange for the three preceding requirements, and who will be able to advise the student, his parents, and school personnel, as well as to arrange for additional services such as tutoring, mobility instruction or vocational counseling, at the time the need occurs.

6. Opportunity for and encouragement to participate in the extra-curricular activities that may enhance his social, emotional, and physical development. (p. 177)

The Role of Resources

A multitude of resources are available to teachers who have students with visual handicaps. Often, however, these resources may be difficult to locate. Frequently, a formal referral and information service exists to conduct the search for assistance. If no such service is available, the special education coordinator for the school system can assist in procuring materials and support. The department of vocational rehabilitation in many states can also supply information and direction, as can local teacher education programs. A social services staff is also an excellent source of information. The nearest state school for the blind is another source of direction and support. Some of the specific resources available to the teachers are:

1. *The special teacher.* This person is available for consultation, special instruction, support, and guidance in procuring aid and additional resources. One can generally identify the person in this role through the state and local boards of education.

2. *The special interest foundations* can provide a large quantity of information, suggestions, and materials. A partial list of these appear at the end of this chapter.

3. *Related professionals* such as ophthalmologists, optometrists, social workers, and special educators are often willing to provide information and consultation. Frequently, these persons are willing to interpret evaluation material; explain the nature of the child's visual impairments; describe and explain the operations and functions of visual aids; and speak to classes or parent groups on topics related to visual impairments.

4. *Volunteers and volunteer groups* are invaluable to any teacher. For the teacher who has a student with special needs resulting from visual limitations, the volunteer can: record materials; help to purchase materials; and fill in gaps the teacher may view as existent in her classroom program due to lack of time or resources. The "braillest" may be a volunteer or a paid person trained in the proper transcription of print materials to braille. This can be invaluable when materials of local interest and content are needed.

5. *Community settings* such as the public library, the chamber of commerce, the public transportation program, and churches are excellent sources of materials and activities.

6. *The state residential school* for the blind are not only good sources of information on other resources, but can provide suggestions for materials and activities.

7. *The family* is truly a useful resource, often overlooked during the rush of the school day. The family knows their child better than anyone and wants the maximum in quality services available for that child. They can provide pertinent information about the child, are often willing to provide an extra pair of hands, and are essential to continuity of programming and skill development across settings.

The classroom teacher cannot, and should not, attempt to meet all of a child's needs. A brief search will reveal many sources available to the teacher, child, and family in assuring effective and efficient integration into the "regular" classroom.

What To Do?

When a child with visual impairments is mainstreamed into the regular classroom, there are efforts which must be made to enhance the child's integration. These efforts are basically the same as those required for every new child in the class:

1. Introduction to the setting. The child should be familiarized with the design of the classroom and the school. This includes ample guided and unguided opportunities to explore. The child should learn the location of materials, desks, activity areas, the teacher's work station, and exits within the classroom. This learning or orientation can occur much more rapidly for the child with a very severe visual limitation if these places are presented sequentially, and from a focal point such as the child's desk. Often, through the use of a buddy system with peers, these activities can also serve as get-acquainted sessions for all the students, and satisfy the curiosity of children with sight. The special teacher, or a mobility and orientation specialist, can provide additional guidance in structuring this experience. When the classroom in familiar to the child, the school building and surrounding areas can be introduced. A good recreational activity can be structured around finding the gym, restrooms, and the playground and its equipment. Be sure to make the child aware of objects and obstacles such as water fountains and hall displays.

For the child with partial vision, placement within the classroom can be the key to his or her success. When viewing distance is determined, placement of the child's work area in relation to the chalkboard and demonstration areas should match this distance. The same is true for the degree of illumination. Some children need quite a bit; others cannot see in bright light and may need to work in dimmer areas of the classroom. For all children, minimum glare and maximum contrast in materials are vital.

2. Materials and equipment. Some children with visual limitations may need special materials and

equipment. These are available from a variety of sources. The special teacher or special education co-ordinator can assist the teacher in determining what the child needs and procuring those items. Through the use of braille and large print materials, braillewriters of one form or another, tape recorders, typewriters, magnification aids, the abacus, as well as more sophisticated electronic equipment such as the Optacon and Talking Calculator, the child with visual limitation can participate in lessons and classroom activities. Within the classroom, many steps can be taken to make the standard materials useful. A volunteer or student with sight can trace the handouts in dark ink, particularly if they are duplicated materials, so they are clear. These materials can also be transcribed into a large size. The teacher can verbalize what is being written on the chalkboard and demonstrated at the front of the room, and provide the opportunity for close examination before, during, or after the demonstrations. In selecting materials, remember: "If a child cannot see materials well enough to learn the intended concepts or skills, provide suitable tactile or auditory materials to teach these things." (VonHipple, 1977, p. 61). Some materials may be unpleasant to touch or smell for the child who cannot perceive the "eye-appeal." Careful, systematic introduction of materials can alleviate some problems that arise from initial distaste.

3. Physical recreation, recess, and special activities. Children with visual impairments are particularly in need of a large variety of physical activity. Not only does this facilitate good health and motor development, but it is necessary for concept and sensory development. Frequently, children who are visually limited have little opportunity or motivation to run, bend, stretch, and engage in expressive large movements. Tumbling, dancing, skipping, rolling, and reaching need to be taught to a child who cannot model these movements through observation. Running down a clear corridor where the child can maintain contact with a guide such as a wall or another child, helps to build confidence in both personal abilities and the environment. It is important to provide the child with ample opportunity to explore the chosen path first. The use of mats, balls, gym and playground equipment builds muscles and develops body concepts; develops tactile, kinesthetic and auditory sense awareness; and, develops use of residual vision. With physical demonstration, verbal cues, and some additional planning, the child who is visually limited can participate in all recreational activities. This child, too, needs the social, physical, and leisure skills learned through physical education programs.

4. Social Integration. The teacher has major impact on the acceptance of a visually impaired child by sighted children and true integration of the child into the regular classroom. It is an error to assume that "mainstreaming" occurs when the child with visual limitations is placed in the "regular" classroom. All of the children should be encouraged to be open and honest about their questions and feelings. Explaining the nature of the child's visual impairment and sharing special equipment that may be used with the children who are sighted, can reduce anxiety and curiosity. Each child, including the child with visual impairment can take an active role in helping to form the collection of children into a class. The teacher further facilitates "mainstreaming" by assuring that the child with a visual impairment has an equal opportunity to participate in classroom duties, privileges, and activities. Standards of behavior must not be different for the child with a visual limitation. Independence, self-sufficiency, and competence is the goal for the child who has a visual impairment, as well as for children with visual impairments. The means for meeting this goal is through development of the child's abilities in typical societal settings, through typical activities commensurate with his or her developmental level.

5. Curriculum. The overall curriculum and standards should not be different for the child with visual impairments. Some special substitutes for visual materials may be necessary, and the medium for reading may be different. The special teacher and other resources can assist with procurement of materials and the development of plans for their use. Fellow students are often very creative in producing substitutes for visual cues and materials. Involve all the students, including the students with visual impairments, in awareness of the need for some substitutions and the responsibility for supplying them.

6. Extra curricular activities. Mainstreaming does not occur until the child who is visually limited has an equal opportunity to participate in the extracurricular activities of the school community. Again, some planning, encouragement, and shared responsibility may be necessary to assure participation takes place. Helping the child to be aware of what is available, and assisting other school personnel in being aware of the child, as well as his or her visual limitations, is the first, and maybe the only necessary step.

7. The teacher's strengths and skills. Children with visual impairments also possess a multitude of other characteristics. The teacher's skills, experience, and common sense are as valuable in teaching this child as all other children. The teacher who is unfamiliar with visual impairments should recognize his or her feelings of anxiety and curiosity and take the necessary steps to abate or satisfy them. Seek assistance. Get to know the child well. Be honest with yourself and others. The teacher is also a part of a system made up of children, school, family, and community people. Draw on these system members for ideas, support, information, and assistance. The responsibility can be shared with all of them.

Mainstreaming is more than placement in a "regular" classroom. It is active involvement in the most integrative environment appropriate to a child's needs. A child with visual limitations is more than the visual impairments. A teacher knows what teaching a child is about, and that knowledge is applicable to all children.

8. The Individual Educational Plan (IEP). The Right to Education for All Handicapped Children Act, P.L. 94-142, requires that an educational plan be prepared for each child with an impairment after placement is decided by a multidisciplinary team. For the teacher, this is an invaluable guide for structuring his or her interactions with the child during the school year. Although some initial confusion may result concerning the development of such a plan, it must be remembered that the IEP is simply a recognition of the child's strengths and needs, how those needs are to be met, who is responsible for meeting each need, and what sort of timetable is to be attempted. The IEP is not inflexible; it can be changed if it appears inaccurate. Observe the child. Gather information about him or her. Identify the resources available in and outside of the classroom. Make a list of the child's needs and prioritize them. Based on those needs, select some goals—a realistic and conservative number—and operationalize them. List some appropriate activities which can facilitate meeting the goals. Identify the persons responsible for carrying out the activities, when to start on them, and how long it will take. Discuss it with the child, family, and other teachers. Be sure to review the plan frequently. Goals and activities are useful for assessment as well. While additional information and a certain form may be required in various educational systems, the essence of the IEP is similar to the lesson plan, only covering a broader span of time, goals, and activities. It is an excellent mechanism for assuring that what the teachers, child and family are doing is meaningful for the child and his or her development.

Common sense and basic skills coupled with some additional planning can make mainstreaming truly operational for the child, the teacher, the class, the school, and the family. Mainstreaming is specific to an individual child and his or her family's and community's needs and resources. It is recommended that resources include the full range of educational settings. Planning and implementation of a child's educational plan should involve all members of the child's ecological system, and include ongoing planning and evaluation.

Conclusion

Mainstreaming, the most talked about trend in special education today, has been practiced with children with visual impairments for almost 80 years. Its merits are still being debated, but most children who are blind continue to be educated in local day schools while about 40% continue in state and private residential schools. Decisions about the education of children with visual impairments must be made in terms of a wide array of information about the child, his or her environment, the schools, their capabilities, and other factors. A continuum of services should be available to every family. Ultimately, the question must be, "which type of program for which child under which circumstances." Thus, mainstreaming will continue to be available and will make its best contribution to the children who can benefit from it, as one of the more desirable, economic, and popular special education administrative arrangements.

References

Alson, M.L. Into the mainstream. *Instructor,* 1977, *87,* 222-224.

American Foundation for the Blind. *The Pinebrook report.* New York: 1954.

Ashcroft, S.C. In N. Hobbs (ed.), *The futures of children.* San Francisco: Josey Bass, 1975.

Blank, H.R. Dreams of the blind. *The Psychoanalytic Quarterly,* 1958, *27* 158-174.

Bledsoe, C.W. The family of residential schools. *Blindness,* 1971, 19-73.

Cratty, B.J. *Movement and spatial awareness in blind children and youth.* Springfield, Ill.: Charles C. Thomas, 1971.

Cratty, B.J. and Sams, T.A. *The body-image of blind children.* New York: American Foundation for the Blind, 1968.

Cutsforth, T.D. *The unreality of words to the blind. The Teacher's Forum,* 1932, *4,* 86-89.

Cutsforth, T.D., *The blind in school and society, a psychological study.* New York: American Foundation for the Blind, 1951.

Dauwalder, D.D. *Education, training and employment of the blind.* Pittsburgh: Western Pennsylvania School for Blind Children, 1964.

Deno, E. Special education as developmental capital. *Exceptional Children,* 1970, 37, 229-237.

Fraiberg, S. *Insights from the blind: Comparative studies of blind and sighted infants.* New York: Basic Books, Inc., 1977.

Fraiberg S., Siegel, B.J., and Gibson, R. The role of sound in the search behavior of a blind infant. In R.S. Eissler, et al. (eds.), *The psychoanalytic study of the child.* New York: International Universities Press, 1966.

Frampton, M.E. and Kerney, E. *The residential school: Its history, contributions, and future.* New York: Edwin Gould Printery, 1953.

Farrell, G. *The story of blindness.* Cambridge, Mass.: Harvard University Press, 1956.

Harley, R.K. In L. Dunn (ed.), *Exceptional children in the schools: Special education in transition.* New York: Holt, Rinehart and Winston, Inc., 1963.

Harley, R. and Lawrence, G. *Visual impairment in the schools.* Springfield, Ill.: Charles C. Thomas, 1977.

Hartlage, T.C. *The role of vision in the development of spatial ability.* (Doctoral Dissertation, Ann Arbor, Mich.: University Microfilms, No. 69-443, 1968.)

Hathaway, W. *Education and health of the partially seeing child* (4th ed.) New York: Columbia University Press, 1959.

Howell, S.J. *The sociometric status of visually handicapped students in public school classes.* Research Bulletin No. 20. New York: American Foundation for the Blind, 1970.

Hobbs, N. *The futures of children.* San Francisco: Josey Bass, 1975

Hyer, A. The view of P.L. 94-142 from the classroom. In Hunich, R. (ed.), *Educating all handicapped children.* Englewood Cliffs: Educational Technology Publications, 1979.

Irwin, R.B. *As I saw it.* New York: American Foundation for the Blind, 1955, 128.

Jones, J.W. The blind child in school. *School Life,* 1961, *43,* 7-10.

Jones, J. and Collins, A. *Educational programs for visually handicapped children.* Washington, D.C.: U.S. Government Printing Office, 1966.

Juurmaa, J. *Ability structure and loss of vision.* New York: American Federation for the Blind Research Series, No. 18, 1967.

Kakalik, J., Brewer, G., Dougharty, L., Fleischauer, P. and Genensky, S. *Services for handicapped youth: A program overview.* Santa Monica, Cal.: Rand Corporation, P.L. 1220-HEW, 1973.

Kakalik, J., Brewer, G., Dougharty, L., Fleischauer, P., Genensky, S., and Wallen, L. *Improving services to handicapped children.* Santa Monica, Cal.: Rand Corporation, R-1420-HEW, 1974.

Lowenfeld, B. The role of the residential school in the education of blind children. In G.A. Ahl (ed.), *Concerning the education of blind children.* New York: American Foundation for the Blind, 1959.

Lowenfeld, B., et al. *Blind children learn to read.* Springfield, Ill.: Charles C. Thomas, 1969.

Lowenfeld, B. (ed.), *The visually handicapped child in the school.* New York: John Day Co., 1973.

McReynolds, J. and Worchel, P. Geographic orientation in the blind. *Journal of General Psychology,* 1954, *51,* 221-236.

Martin, E. Integration of the handicapped child into regular schools. M. Reynolds (ed.), *Mainstreaming: origins and implications.* Reston, Va.: Council for Exceptional Children, 1975.

Miller, C.K., Conservation in blind children. *Education of the Visually Handicapped,* 1969, *1,* 101-105.

Nolan, C.Y. On the unreality of words to the blind. *Outlook for the Blind,* 1960, *54,* 100-102.

Reynolds, M. (ed.), *Mainstreaming: Origins and implications.* Reston, Va.: Council for Exceptional Children, 1975.

Reynolds, M. and Birch, J. *Teaching exceptional children in all America's schools: A first course for teachers and principals.* Reston, Va.: Council for Exceptional Children, 1977.

Rottman, R. Some thoughts on the education of blind children. In *Readings in special education.* Guilford, Conn.: Special Learning Corporation, 1978.

Schlaegel, T.J., Jr. The dominant method of imagery in blind as compared to sighted adolescents. *Journal of Genetic Psychology,* 1953, *83,* 265-277.

Senden, M. von, *Space and sight: The perception of space and shape in the congenitally blind before and after operation.* (P. Heath, trans.) Glencoe, Ill.: Free Press, 1960.

Scholl, G. Visually handicapped children in the regular classroom. *Teacher,* 1978, *95,* 79-80.

Stephens, T.M. and Buck, J.W. Merits of special class, resource, and itinerant plans for teaching partially seeing children. *Exceptional Children,* 1969, *35,* 481-484.

Taylor, J.L. *The itinerant teaching program for blind children.* New York: American Foundation for the Blind, Education Series No. 12, 1959.

Tillman, M.H., The performance of blind and sighted children on the Weschler Intelligence Scale for children. *International Journal for the Education of the Blind,* 1967, *16,* 65-74, 106-112.

Vaughn, D. and Asbury, T. *General opthalmology,* Los Altos, Cal: Lange Medical Publications, 1977.

Von Hippel, C. *Mainstreaming preschoolers: Children with visual handicaps.* Belmont, Mass.: Contract Research Corporation, 1977.

Wilson, J.D., McVugh, V.M., McMahon, J.F., Bauer, A.M. and Richardson, P.C. Early intervention: the right to sight. *Education of the Visually Handicapped,* 1976, *83,* 83-90.

Wolfensberger, W. *The principle of normalization in human services.* Toronto: Leonard Cramford, 1972.

Worchel, P. Space Perception and orientation in the blind. *Psychological Monographs,* 1951, *65.*

Zweibelson, I. and Barg, C.J. Concept development of blind children. *New Outlook for the Blind,* 1967, *61,* 218-222.

APPENDIX I
Sources of Materials and Information

American Foundation for the Blind
15 West 16th Street
New York, NY 10011

American Printing House for the Blind
1839 Frankfort Avenue
Louisville, KY 40206

American Thermoform Corporation
8640 East Stauson Avenue
Pico Rivers, CA 90660

Braille Book Bank
National Braille Association
85 Godwin Avenue
Midland Park, NJ 07432

Braille Circulating Library
2823 W. Grace Street
Richmond, VA 23221

International Business Machines (IBM)
Office Products Division
Parsons Pond Drive
Franklin Lake, NJ 07417

Reference and Information Section
Division for the Blind and
   Physically Handicapped
Volunteer Services Section
Library of Congress
Washington, D.C. 20542

Telesensory Systems, Inc.
2626 Hanover Street
Palo Alto, CA 94304
National Association for
   Visually Handicapped
305 East 24th Street
New York, NY 10010

Stanwix House
3020 Chartiers Avenue
Pittsburgh, PA 15204

National Aid to Visually
   Handicapped, Inc.
3201 Balboa Street
San Francisco, CA 94121

National Society for the
   Prevention of Blindness
79 Madison Avenue
New York, NY 10016

Recordings for the Blind
215 East 58th Street
New York, New York 10022

National Braille Press, Inc.
8820 Steven Street
Boston, MA 02115

Some Thoughts on the Education of Blind Children

Robert Rottman

Educators today will scarcely question the proposition that modern education is dedicated to the academic and social development of every student to the fullest extent permitted by his individual capacities; that its goal is the graduation of informed, responsible, self-confident, and self-reliant adult citizens who will participate in and contribute to their society. Educational programs for blind children, which serve a particular segment of that total group comprised by "every student," must, of necessity, be imbued with the same philosophy and committed to the same goals.

Blindness is a physical nuisance and a social handicap. Both of these currently inevitable characteristics begin to affect the life of a blind person from the moment his blindness becomes apparent to himself or to others, even if that moment occurs on the day of his birth. These characteristics of blindness together with their cumulative effect on the developing blind child, are of primary concern to the educator of blind children, for they must constitute the nucleus around which his understanding of the special problems of blind children and his provision for their solution will be formed. Given this understanding and these solutions to supplement a normal school curriculum, a blind child can be expected to achieve, upon graduation, those goals of knowledge, confidence, self-sufficiency, and responsible participation in the work and play of society for which public education today is striving.

The physical nuisance of blindness derives from the fact that most people can see and have organized the physical environment on the basis of the possession and use of vision. Sight is not essential to the performance of the tasks of daily living, but in a world geared to seeing the blind minority must employ "abnormal"—that is, not ordinary—ways of doing many things. Thus a blind infant identifies his mother by footstep, voice, scent, and feel, and his bottle by size, shape, temperature, weight, time of appearance, and—of course—contents. A blind toddler can distinguish the bathroom from the kitchen by size, location, smell, temperature, sound, and—again—contents. A blind child can read and write, in braille, by touch; or with recordings, by hearing.

A blind teen-ager can do geometry, apply make-up, choose clothes, and go out on dates through a variety of non-visual adaptations. A blind housewife can cook, sew, clean house and change diapers; and a blind man can run a lathe, wire a house, manage a business, conduct an experiment, teach a class, or argue and win a legal case.

All of these things can be accomplished without sight; all can be done as well without sight as with it. Sometimes the non-visual methods require equal or even less effort; often they demand extra time, extra concentration, extra exertion, or extra tension. But the important facts are that the methods exist and that they work, that they make of blindness at worst a physical nuisance, but not a physical deterrent.

The implication of these facts for educational programs for blind children is obvious. Such programs, however organized and wherever located, must teach blind children, in addition to the content of the normal school curriculum, the tools and skills which will enable them to fulfill independently, with competence and confidence, the physical demands, not only of school activities, but of normal daily living and competitive employment. This is both necessary and feasible. It is necessary for the simple reason that without such tools and skills, blind students will be extremely limited, if not totally lacking, in the ability to put their education to independent and constructive use. It is feasible because proven tools and skills do exist, and, when competently taught, fit easily and appropriately into the purposeful learning environment of the school; indeed are indispensable—even in school—if this environment includes the expectation of independence, responsibility, and self-direction on the part of students.

The basic physical tools and skills which can make a blind student independent and self-sufficient are not hard to conceive nor difficult to teach. They include such things as the mastery of a system for independent reading, writing, counting, and measuring, which for blind students means braille; the ability to travel independently under all circumstances, which for blind students means the skillful use of a cane plus the employment of other senses and common sense; and the general ability to do things for themselves, which for blind students means primarily the long-established habit of planning and organizing. Whether these tools and skills are learned, and, if learned, whether they are used will depend a great deal on the effect of the second significant characteristic of blindness.

Blindness is not only a physical nuisance, which can be readily overcome, but a social handicap which, in our present society, is not so readily removed. The blind as a group are handicapped socially, not because they are essentially inferior, maladjusted, or anti-social, but because people with sight, who constitute a vast majority, grossly over-estimate the physical and mental limitations imposed on the blind by their blindness, and regard the blind as necessarily helpless and dependent, kept alive by the charity of their more fortunate sighted brothers, unable to contribute their share of society's work, and, consequently unentitled to full participation in society's benefits. This feeling is rarely articulated in words, but it speaks for itself in the general actions and attitudes of the sighted toward the blind. The stereotyped concepts of helplessness, loneliness, and utter wretchedness which have been formed about the blind; the pity, wonder, or disgust with which they are regarded; the protective concern which their presence arouses; and the sheltered and limited activities which are organized to occupy their time all bespeak relegation to an inferior status in the eyes of society at large.

The influence of society's attitudes on blind children and blinded adults is strong and pervasive. It extends from infancy to advanced age, and, unless counteracted with a powerful and positive program of education and training, its effect is generally the discouragement of independence and initiative, the limitation of adaptive skills, the development of feelings of inferiority, and, too often, the ultimate acceptance and personification—and thus the perpetuation—of the very stereotype of which the blind are the victims. The over-protection of parents, the pity of friends and relatives, the pessimism of teachers and counselors, and the refusal of employers—all these are at the same time the result and the direct implementation of society's misconceptions about the limitations of blindness; all must be negated, and the strength and desire to resist and surmount them must be instilled in blind students if they are ever to fulfill their potential as self-supporting, fully participating citizens enjoying the same rights and assuming the same responsibilities as their sighted peers.

Tools and skills—while essential—are not enough in themselves to achieve this end, and no educational program for blind children can be considered adequate which confines itself solely to the physical adaptations made necessary by blindness. The major effort of a complete and effective program must rather be directed toward the development in the child—and in the homes, school, and community environment around him—of a full acceptance of blindness without shame and without loss of incentive or aspiration; a firm conviction of the right of the blind to equal status with their sighted peers; an unshakable belief in the ability of the blind to fulfill completely the physical, mental, and social requirements of equal status; a thorough understanding of existing concepts and attitudes about the blind and the barriers to equal status which they present; an unwavering confidence that these barriers to equality can be levelled; and

a positive, aggressive determination that these students are going to do the levelling. It cannot be emphasized too strongly that blind students must be equipped with the *confidence* as well as the *competence* to achieve independence and self-sufficiency in a sighted world as yet only too ready to support and "protect" them—at the cost of segregation, dependency, and social and economic inferiority.

All this, then, is to say that the major problems of blindness, at any age, stem from the mistaken attitudes held by the sighted toward that blindness, and from the economic and social impact of those attitudes on the blind. A sound program of education for blind children must first of all free itself from attitudes which limit and discourage; second, help blind students to develop the knowledge, the skills, and the inner strength to meet and overcome these attitudes when they encounter them—as inevitably they must—outside of school; and third, vigorously support and actively assist independent blind persons everywhere, and those who know their true abilities, in a great campaign to educate—and even, where necessary, to legislate—degrading and restrictive public attitudes out of existence.

What does this ringing statement imply for you as an educator of blind children in terms of the program you have organized or are now organizing? What must you do, in addition to meeting the blind child's curricular needs with appropriate special teaching tools and techniques, to instill the confidence and develop the competence so necessary to the survival of his social and economic equality and integrity in an unbelieving sighted world?

The answer lies primarily in the realm of attitudes, specifically in the formulation of a thoughtful, consistent, and vigorous campaign of education designed to accomplish three main objectives: (1) to enable the student to accept his blindness and himself as a blind person; (2) to establish firmly in his mind the conviction that he not only *can* but *should* lead a normal, happy, productive life in full and equal competition with his sighted peers; and (3) to help him to accept and master the tools, skills, and aids that will contribute to his ultimate equality, independence, and self-sufficiency.

With a few possible exceptions, no blind student likes or wants to be blind. Many resist the idea with great determination. Even those who freely call themselves blind may be fighting an inner battle against blindness, a battle that can take the form of hope for a miraculous operation; rejection of anything associated with the special needs of the blind; resentment against parents, school, or the entire sighted population; or the refusal to do anything for oneself. It goes without saying that preparation for life as a successful blind adult cannot begin until the student has come to accept himself as a blind person without loss of self-esteem, and to adopt, confidently and unashamed, the special modes of operating that blindness makes necessary. If the parents have handled their child's blindness well, the chances are that the school will need only to reinforce an accepting attitude already established. Unfortunately such instances will be rare, and on the school—as the second great influence in the life of the child—must devolve in most cases the imperative obligation of counteracting—and sometimes flatly contradicting—the home and other influences which have occasioned resistance to blindness in one or more of its forms.

Acceptance of blindness is not brought about in the school environment by repeated lectures on the acceptance of blindness. Instead, the nature of the school environment itself, and the child's relationship with his teachers, will serve as the primary media for an effective conversion. Resistance to blindness is subtly attacked from two closely related points of view, which might be expressed in simplified form as "blind people are normal" and "blindness is not a limitation." The first requires a sincere conviction on the part of the school as a whole, but of the child's teachers in particular, that blind people *are* normal. The very fact that special education programs are provided for blind children can indicate to a particular blind child that he is not unique, that society expects a certain percentage of its children to be blind and considers these children equally worth educating. If the word blind is used freely by the school staff, and the child's blindness treated with quite evident matter-of-factness, and with no lessening of requirements for him because of it; if his special tools and materials and the instruction in the special skills he needs to function adequately are provided as a matter of course; if his outside activities and interests are discussed without wonder, surprise, and undue admiration as they would be with sighted students; if even in the primary grades his future is spoken of with the expectation of a normal life made obvious in such phrases as "when you're in college . . .," "after you've been on the job awhile . . .," "your wife may have something to say about that . . .," "that will come in handy when you're doing your own cooking," or "wait until you're a parent yourself," then the student cannot help but consider himself a normal person. When it is apparent that the school staff, whose opinion in these matters he respects perhaps even more than that of his parents, is not particularly disturbed by his or anyone else's blindness nor holds toward him an attitude different from that bestowed upon his sighted age-mates, then one main objection to blindness is gone.

The second point of attack is closely allied to the first, and is even more important to the bringing about of a true acceptance of blindness. The unshakable conviction that blindness need not limit anyone from anything which makes life worthwhile is the key that unlocks the door of achievement for blind children and for blind adults. It is the foundation upon which every program for the blind which truly meets the needs of the blind has to be built. Blind students, from the very beginning, must be surrounded with this idea, with demonstrations of tools and methods used by blind persons in accomplishing seemingly difficult or impossible tasks; with accounts of the successes of blind persons in such occupations as those of electrician, chemist, physicist, classroom teacher, lawyer, businessman, salesman, farmer, machinist, and homemaker; with the simple, often-repeated statement itself: "Blindness need not bar anyone from anything important in life. Whatever has to be done, there's a way for a totally blind person to do it." (The idea of a totally blind person is important. The students who have the hardest time accepting blindness and the efficient methods of the blind are those with a slight degree of sight, insufficient for the visual performance of most tasks.)

The most effective avenue to the acceptance of blindness, however, is through actual contact with it. The school program should plan and provide numerous opportunities for blind students at every level to meet and talk with self-sufficient, self-confident blind adults from many occupational areas. In no other way can the absence of permanent barriers to normal life be brought home so effectively; in no more convincing manner can blind students learn the value of the skills they are acquiring in a school; from no more competent authority can they get answers to questions about blindness lying long unspoken in their minds;—and from no better source can they learn of the obstacles to integration imposed by society's misconceptions about blindness and the blind.

For these obstacles, too, are involved in the acceptance of blindness. The world of today, a little more sophisticated than it was twenty-five or a hundred and twenty-five years ago, would still rather build a recreation center to fill idle hours than an orientation center to restore self-esteem, self-confidence, and self-sufficiency; would still rather send a newly-blinded wage-earner or professional to a sheltered shop or a vending stand than return him to his former occupation; would still rather drop a daily quarter in a street corner musician's tin cup than trust a competent blind worker with a machine or a decision. The world of tomorrow, barring a miracle or a miraculously effective campaign of public education, will not be drastically changed ten, twenty, even fifty hears hence, in spite of the considerable progress that has been made so far by the blind as individuals and as a group. It is important that blind students, as they acquire a firm belief in their own capability, be also arming themselves for the fight to maintain this conviction and to convince the world around them in the face of disbelief, disappointments, and the constant temptation to surrender their dignity and independence in exchange for the meager security of permanent state aid or the limited offerings of a sheltered shop. Made aware from the first of the difficulties imposed by public attitudes, and thoroughly convinced of the injustice thereby done, blind graduates can be helped to develop, not bitterness or resentment, but a realistic evaluation of the hurdles ahead, a compelling sense of the need to surmount them and an aggressive determination not to fall victim to them.

One further consideration for educators in guiding blind

students toward their attainment of self-sufficiency remains to be discussed. This is the responsibility of providing for a thorough acquaintance with every available means to the desired end. The importance of a mastery of the physical skills of competence is self-evident. It is taken for granted that no self-respecting educational program would allow a normal blind student to leave without a high degree of proficiency in the reading and writing of standard English braille, considerable skill in the use of a standard typewriter, practice in the use of sighted readers and various types of recorded materials, and, above all, the ability to organize, keep track of, and otherwise assume responsibility for his own material possessions.

Likewise it is assumed that every program will provide for its students training in the skills of independent travel. Sometimes ignored, but of vital necessity in this regard, is the skillful employment of the long white cane, which gives protection and confidence in moving outside the familiar environment of home and school. Independent travel should be associated with the use of a cane in the minds of blind youngsters long before they begin actual instruction in cane travel techniques in the intermediate grades. Here again discussions with a competent blind adult, who carries his cane with pride and employs it with confident skill, can be of invaluable assistance to both student and teacher in gaining acceptance and appreciation of this indispensable tool of independence.

But the physical skills are not the only aids available to blind students in their efforts to achieve personal independence, competitive employment, normal family life, and the satisfying and constructive use of leisure hours. Society, while failing to recognize its own culpability, has long recognized the state of social and economic inequality in which the blind have traditionally lived. Many programs have been instituted by the states and the federal government, and by private organizations, to ameliorate this unequal condition in one way or another. These programs run the gamut from recreation centers to rehabilitation services, from monetary assistance to missionary efforts; from home teaching to sheltered "homes." Educational programs in which blind students are enrolled must assume the responsibility not only of informing them about every service, every aid to which they are legally entitled, but of helping them to develop, as a part of their overall philosophy of self-sufficiency, that fine discrimination which distinguishes between those offerings based on mistaken charity and the desire to relieve lonely, useless hours with time-filling palliatives, and those services which operate to equalize the opportunities for blind persons to take their places as self-reliant, self-respecting, contributing members of society.

Teaching Partially Sighted Children

Patricia Anne Davis

Patricia Anne Davis has been an itinerant teacher of blind and partially sighted children in Baltimore County, Maryland, for seven years.

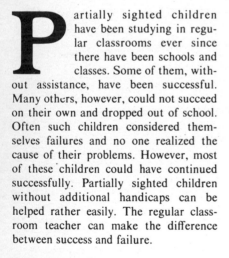

Partially sighted children have been studying in regular classrooms ever since there have been schools and classes. Some of them, without assistance, have been successful. Many others, however, could not succeed on their own and dropped out of school. Often such children considered themselves failures and no one realized the cause of their problems. However, most of these children could have continued successfully. Partially sighted children without additional handicaps can be helped rather easily. The regular classroom teacher can make the difference between success and failure.

Who Is Partially Sighted?

For educational purposes, the partially sighted child is described as one who is visually impaired but can read print, either regular or enlarged. Those children who use Braille are considered to be educationally blind. (The legal meanings of "partially sighted" and "legally blind" concern the school only for registering children for federal quota funds. Otherwise, all visually impaired print readers may be considered partially sighted.)

Most visually impaired children are identified in infancy or early childhood. Others are found through vision screening programs in the early school years. However, screening does not pinpoint all these children, and others do not become visually impaired until after they have begun school. Thus it is important for the teacher to be aware of the following characteristics that these children display and refer for vision screening any child who persistently shows them.

• Red, sore or watery eyes and recurrent eye infections.
• Eyes that do not look straight.
• Covering one eye to see.
• Squinting or frowning when looking.
• Appearing to turn the head away when looking.
• Seeking more or less light.
• Holding reading matter too close or constantly moving it back and forth.
• Skipping words or losing place in a book.
• Copying incorrectly from the chalkboard or from papers.
• Making many errors in seatwork though concept was understood.
• Having difficulty recognizing colors, interpreting pictures, sequencing or observing details.
• Having difficulty catching or hitting a ball and avoiding ball games.
• Bumping into or tripping over things.
• Crying excessively or being generally irritable or often frustrated.
• Complaining of headaches, stiff neck, blurred vision or trouble seeing.
• Being constantly restless and moving about in the classroom, repeatedly coming up to the teacher's desk.
• Being excessively anxious in open or unfamiliar places.
• Having difficulty recognizing or remembering others and making friends.

Classroom Adaptations: Distance Work

Most partially sighted children have very poor distance vision. This problem makes it difficult for them to see the chalkboard or to gain much detailed information from filmstrips or overhead projector images. You can make board work easier for these children by writing in large, clear print with white chalk. Reading script is more difficult than reading print for many of them.

Seat partially sighted children as close to the board as practical and away from any window glare. Many visually impaired children have eyes that differ in visual acuity, and they really use only one eye. If this is the case, know which eye the child uses and base your seating arrangement on this knowledge.

Some visually impaired children can see the chalkboard only if they sit at desks that are touching the board. Some even need to stand with the person who is writing. You may be able to tolerate such an arrangement for young children in small groups, but it is never very practical because the child near the board blocks the view of classmates. As an alternative, the visually impaired child could copy from your desk copy, or you could have another child make two copies—perhaps using carbon paper. Also, if there is a child in the room who cannot see the board, be sure to read aloud everything written on it. It is extremely frustrating for such a child to hear the teacher say, "Now, what can you tell me about this word?" The student begins to daydream or become restless and disturb others.

Follow similar methods with the overhead projector and filmstrips. For the overhead have someone read aloud all the projected words. Some teachers have solved the problem for filmstrips by obtaining two copies—one for the partially sighted child to watch up close on a filmstrip viewer while the rest of the class watches the other one.

Some partially sighted children—especially those with focusing problems—have extreme difficulty in copying from the board or screen. For each shift of the eyes from the board or screen to the paper they have to refocus. Because of the time lapse they constantly lose their place on the board and have to reread the passage many times before getting it all copied. This procedure is arduous and frustrating, and it's not worth the effort. Therefore, it's important to devise an alternate way for the child to get the work.

Unless you are sure that distance reading is not a real problem, never require a visually impaired child to take a test from the board or the overhead. Instead, provide a typed or printed copy of the test.

Classroom Adaptations: Class Work

It sometimes disturbs teachers to see how close visually impaired children hold their books and papers. Some read with their noses or chins actually touching the page. Partially sighted children do not harm their vision by reading in this way and should be allowed to place reading material wherever they want it. However, if the children read for long periods in awkward positions, they may become tired or stiff or get headaches. Try to limit the amount of reading required of them. You might substitute listening to a tape for a reading assignment.

Many visually impaired children can read regular size print—especially at the first- and second-grade levels when the print is rather large anyway. Most children who can read regular print prefer to do so. Others want to have some large-type textbooks, at least at home. Large-type copies of many school textbooks are available from the American Printing House for the Blind (1839 Frankfort Ave., Box 6085, Louisville, KY 40206). Federal funding provides these books for children whose best corrected vision is 20/200 or lower. [For more information write Ralph E. McCracken at the American Printing House.] Sometimes a hand-held magnifier will help.

Reading materials that offer the greatest contrast between the print and the paper are easiest for partially sighted children to see. Black print on white paper with fairly large letters and good spacing is best. The purple ink used in commercial duplicating machines is generally difficult. You can make duplicated copies that are easier to read by using white paper and giving the visually impaired child the darkest, clearest ones. You can also improve the readability of these sheets by using black masters and primary or at least pica type with good spacing. Elite or fancy type, handwriting, crowded letters, colored paper and blurred or faint copies all add to the partially sighted child's difficulties.

Most children with impaired vision need more time to complete their work than do children who see normally. Because they often have difficulty focusing, they are unable to skim a reading passage. When a visually impaired child seems always to finish well behind the others, try reducing the quantity of work you require from him or her. However, don't lower your expectations about the quality.

Testing may pose some special problems. Clearly typed teacher-made tests should not cause any particular difficulty except for the time factor. So that the child can finish the test in a reasonable amount of time, you may prefer to orally test some partially sighted children.

Standardized tests that require separate answer sheets may be especially difficult for partially sighted children. The mechanical task of keeping their places on the answer sheet and in the test booklet is difficult and time-consuming for these children; the sustained reading is tiring. When they realize that they cannot finish the test in the time allowed, they often become anxious and begin marking answers at random. It's important to be aware that, generally, the mechanical problems involved in taking a standardized test will cause a child's scores to be lower than her or his ability and achievement would indicate.

Special Subjects

Most special subjects do not require extensive modification for partially sighted students. It is a surprise to many teachers to see how well some children with extremely low vision can draw, for example. Others, as with any group of children, do not draw well and dislike art or prefer other kinds of art projects.

Most visually impaired students can participate fully in industrial arts and home economics classes. Even totally blind students can learn to use most tools—including power tools—effectively. However, it is important for the teacher to take the time to instruct partially sighted children separately in the use of tools. In this way he or she will be sure that the child is able to use them correctly. One point to remember is that some visually impaired children are afraid of fire and of striking matches. This can be overcome, but teachers may prefer to exempt visually impaired children from the task if they seem very fearful.

Physical education may present a few special problems. The attitude of partially sighted children toward this subject differs widely. Some want to participate in every activity; others do not want to take part at all. Therefore, the teacher has to exercise careful judgment. Contact sports and rough games are not advisable for persons with certain types of visual impairments, and limitations should be noted on their medical records. In these cases teachers must be responsible for finding out what these restrictions are.

Even when there are no medical cautions, some activities are difficult for most visually impaired children. It is hard for such a child to track visually a fast moving ball or other small object required by some games. A child who never knows where the ball is becomes frustrated and fearful in ball games. You may want to give partially sighted children who have no medical restrictions a choice about playing ball. Some want to play and do so fairly well. Others prefer to watch or be scorekeeper.

Some visually impaired children do not want to take part in any physical activity, usually because they are excessively fearful. However, except for medical reasons, don't automatically exempt these children from physical education. It may help them to lead as integrated a life as possible if you encourage them to try activities in safe situations—running with a partner, for example—until they develop more confidence. Urge visually impaired children with no medical restrictions to take part in all playground activities—climbing, swinging, sliding and so on.

One additional problem contributes to the reluctance of some children to play outdoors. People whose visual impairment is caused by certain conditions—notably albinism and achromatopsia—are extremely sensitive to light. Children with these conditions may need to wear sunglasses inside and special protection outside. Don't press them to play in bright sunlight or in snow if they do not want to. In addition, children with albinism are very susceptible to sunburn and must be protected from overexposure.

Understanding a Partially Sighted Child

The emotional needs of partially sighted children are like those of all children. They need acceptance, praise when they are doing well and encouragement when they are having difficulty. They need to succeed and to be part of a group. In addition, all children with disabilities need to learn to accept their limitations realistically without losing their self-esteem. A sensitive teacher will have little difficulty working with a partially sighted child. Here are a few practical hints:

1. Have a private talk with the child. As soon as possible after you and the children have become acquainted with each other, have a private conversation with the partially sighted child. This will give the child a chance to express without embarrassment his or her preferences for seating, lighting, size of type and any other concerns. Specifically tell partially sighted children that they have permission to move without asking when they cannot see something. Once you establish this privilege, make it the child's responsibility to carry through with it.

If the child is receiving special education services, you may be required to meet with his or her parents early in the year to plan the Individual Education Program. Even if this is not the case, a parent conference can be very useful. You will gain valuable insights by learning how parents feel about their visually impaired child and what their expectations are. Also, parents are often willing to help by copying duplicated work sheets, reading to the child and so on.

2. Do not call attention to the child's disability. Most children, especially as they approach adolescence, resent anything that publically points out their differnce from others. It is generally wise to avoid saying things like, "Can you see that?" "Move up where you can see."

Try to determine, without asking, whether a partially sighted child is seeing printed or displayed material by observing the quality of his or her work. When a tenth-grade biology teacher asked a partially sighted boy in her class, "Can you see that?" each time she put a slide on the screen, the student answered positively. When it became apparent that he had not been seeing the slides, the teacher was puzzled about why he had not told the truth. In fact, the student thought he was telling the truth. He could see that there

was a slide on the screen. He simply did not know that the normally sighted person could see a great deal more.

Some teachers get overly concerned about glasses for children with poor vision. In the case of the partially sighted, glasses may or may not help, depending on the impairment. Usually, when they do help, children wear them willingly. If a child seems to have a physical problem with his or her glasses, and puts them on and takes them off all the time, you should probably suggest a vision check. If he or she seems to have a psychological problem with glasses, your private talk may reveal the cause. Otherwise, don't worry about keeping glasses on a child.

3. Call the child by name. Many visually impaired children cannot see facial expressions or gestures. Also remember that a smile or a frown from across the room will have no effect.

Occasionally, a teacher calls a child's name and then points or gestures rather than stating what is wanted. The partially sighted child wonders why the teacher called and then said nothing further. Sometimes these children hesitate to raise their hands with a question because they do not know whether the teacher's back is turned. On the other hand, because they do not know when the teacher's back is turned, they may complain that the teacher never pays attention to them. If you notice that the child's hand is raised, acknowledge the child by name right away, possibly adding, "I'll be with you in a minute."

4. Be aware of signs of the child's frustration. Most teaching is visual. Therefore, visually impaired children are at a great disadvantage, and much of their school experience is frustrating. Children show their inability to cope in different ways, so you have to be alert to the reactions of the individual child. One of the most common reactions of visually impaired children to work that is difficult to see is to refuse to do it. If a child frequently says, "I can't do this because I can't see it," investigate in a nonpunitive manner. The child may have another problem. He or she may not understand the work or may lack confidence.

Special Help

Once a partially sighted child has been identified, it is important that the school find out whether any appropriate special services are available. Outside services can be extremely helpful to you in giving the children the support they need. Generally, special education is

available only for those children whose best corrected vision is 20/70 or lower. For the partially sighted child in the regular classroom, the two most common types of help come from consultants and itinerant teachers. An educational consultant usually visits several times a year, provides materials and meets with the classroom teacher, the child and the parents. He or she is then available on call, does evaluations and supplies liaison service to other agencies.

The itinerant teacher does the same things but visits more frequently—daily in some cases. He or she may provide some of the following services:

1. Assesses visual functioning, not visual acuity. Determines where the child must sit to see the board, what kind of lighting is needed, what size type is best and to what extent the child sees color.

2. Supplies special materials and equipment, such as large-type books, magnifying devices, tape recorders and tapes and special desks. He or she may also recopy tests and other classroom materials if the material is supplied in time.

3. Reinforces or teaches special skills that are causing difficulty or that are especially necessary for the partially sighted child. For example, children who cannot see the board require excellent listening skills. Most visually impaired children need some assistance in learning to make the most efficient use of their residual vision. Some need special help with handwriting and, possibly, instruction in typing or effective study skills.

4. Counsels the child in matters relating to the handicap of visual impairment, as well as advising the parents, the teacher, the school staff and other personnel. The itinerant teacher also serves as a liaison to other special services, such as vocational evaluation or orientation and mobility, which are needed by some partially sighted children. In addition, he or she attends all staff meetings concerning the child and, quite often, serves as the child's advocate in educational matters.

In the final analysis, however, the most important person in the educational life of a partially sighted child is the classroom teacher. If you accept the child as a fully participating class member, the other children will take your cue. If you expect the child to learn and succeed—and set up conditions that contribute to this—the child will develop confidence and skills, and will not seem very different from the other children.

Technology and the Handicapped

Talking computers help blind students hear what they cannot see.

John M. Williams

Mr. Williams, a free lance writer, is President of Technical Communications, Sterling, Virginia.

Jeane Blazie and John Eulenberg are among many nationally known computer scientists developing talking microprocessors and terminals so that blind, visually impaired, speech impaired and other handicapped people can receive an education regardless of the severity of their disability. Their efforts are paying off, but there is still a long way to go.

"Many people believe that the synthetic speech used in talking terminals, typewriters, calculators, microprocessors and other talking products has been around for about a decade. Actually, synthetic speech was developed about fifty years ago. It has only been within the last ten to twelve years, particularly the last five years, that there has been a rising demand from teachers and teaching institutions who have seen for themselves the multiple benefits that synthetic speech offers to blind and visually impaired students. In future years, the demand for these products will rise more dramatically," says Blazie, president and co-founder of Maryland Computer Services, Inc., Forest Hill, Maryland.

Eulenberg, director of the Artificial Language Laboratory in the Computer Science Department at Michigan State University, adds, "Synthetic speech is producing a revolution throughout our entire educational system."

Teachers of handicapped children agree. "Synthetic speech has had tremendous impact in recent years in making it possible for our blind or visually impaired students to go through the same educational system that nondisabled students participate in," says Mrs. Phyllis Brunken, Communications Specialist, Nebraska School for the Visually Handicapped in Nebraska City.

The Nebraska School for the Visually Handicapped was founded in 1875 by Samuel Bacon, who stated, "Education for the blind should provide not just for a living but a life." The school continues to work toward that goal. It is a pioneer in the use of electronic equipment for visually handicapped persons. Through vocational grants, donations, trust funds, business grants and general funds, the school has developed a program to meet the following goals:

● Using the equipment tutorially to provide drill and practice in areas such as mathematics, spelling, social studies, science, and language arts;

● Using the equipment in the instruction of a computer literacy course;

● Teaching the skills for a career in computer technology;

● Career planning through the use of computer career searches; and

● Applications of technology, espe-

Reprinted from *American Education*, June 1984, U.S. Department of Education.

75

cially synthetic speech, to personal use to enhance the independence of the visually handicapped person.

To achieve these goals, the school purchased a talking terminal to interface with the computer. The talking terminal is also used as a talking typewriter to reinforce accuracy in typing. In one particular instance, a young man with motor disabilities would type "kkk" rather than a single "k." After 20 minutes of using the terminal, this problem was eliminated.

The school serves as a resource to blind and visually handicapped people in Nebraska and surrounding states. They come to test the types of equipment being developed for use by blind and visually handicapped students and adults to see if it will meet their needs or solve some of their vocational problems. Other schools interested in starting similar programs have often sent their representatives to observe the students and the school's program.

How speech is produced

Some talking terminals and computers are programmed to speak in much the same way a child is taught to read phonetically. Its speech is produced by a synthesizer board which is capable of producing 64 different phonemes (a sound that distinguishes one utterance from another, such as "th" and "sh", and long and short vowels). A microprocessor converts letters and groups of letters into digital codes corresponding to the phonemes. The result is synthetic speech.

Talking computers and terminals are meeting the demands of blind and visually impaired students in record numbers. As the need increases, they will become an even more effective way for handicapped people to have independent access to information.

"Our blind and visually impaired students have the same access to information as our nonhandicapped students at Catonsville Community College (CCC), and now have many more opportunities available to them in education and other careers because of the talking products we have at the college," says

Bill Hadlock, coordinator of Services for Blind and Visually Impaired Students at the college in Catonsville, Maryland.

The Baltimore County Board of Education established CCC in 1956. Its 26 blind and visually impaired students use a variety of speech products to help them with their class work. CCC's Board does what it can to encourage the use of such products and to purchase them.

"The synthetic speech used in our talking terminal enables me to hear what I cannot see," says a blind CCC student. "When I leave here to further my education, I am confident I will be competitive with the other teachers when we graduate, because synthetic speech—or rather talking computers—elimi-

---

Talking computers and terminals are meeting the demands of blind and visually impaired students in record numbers.

---

nates the traditional reasons employers have thrown at blind people for not hiring them. The most obvious one is, 'How can you work if you cannot see?'"

More than 2,300 miles away from CCC at Arizona State University (ASU), blind and visually handicapped students, as well as those with either learning disabilities or orthopedic impairments, are using talking products.

"Students, particularly disabled ones, have to learn to view technology as their equalizer or compensator. They have to embrace it and master it. Having done so, they are the equal of nondisabled people," says B. J. Maxson, counselor for Visually Impaired Students, Disabled Student Services, at ASU. "Our students are working very hard and very well with technology. Many of them have an easier time with it than nondisabled students. This is attributed to their in-

dividual drives and because they have more at stake than nondisabled people do."

Last summer, ASU purchased a talking computer which has become a marvelous, productive tool for the students who use it. "I have more versatility than I would have if I were using a non-talking computer. I can write, edit and proofread my own reports with it," says a blind student.

"There are a number of features that people should look at when they go out and purchase a talking computer," says Maxson. "Good speech quality, user definable speech, intelligent terminal capabilities, information retrieval capability, the number of languages that can be used with it, such as COBOL, BASIC, FORTRAN, Pascal and others, storage capability, and the flexible disk drives it can use. Also very important is whether it can produce braille."

Maxson believes that the technology must be made known and utilized in more schools. ASU, for example, has developed a statewide information program on the technology it has for disabled students, particuarly its talking computer, to attract more blind and visually impaired students.

Spreading the spoken word

As more talking computers are being used with favorable results, teachers and administrators are looking for support from teaching organizations to help them to persuade other teachers to investigate the use of talking computers and to incorporate them into their curriculum. One such organization that has taken a leadership role in this area is the Council for Exceptional Children (CEC).

The Council for Exceptional Children is a strong advocate for the use of synthetic speech in all educational grades to help handicapped or gifted children, or both. "Synthetic speech has a unique and expanding role in assisting blind, visually impaired, and especially those students with communication disorders," says John Grossi, project director.

CEC believes that it is everyone's

responsibility to meet the challenge that computer technology presents to special education. They stress that a cooperative effort must be initiated among administrators, teachers, school boards, and the community at large to see that computer technology is utilized in their schools to achieve the maximum benefit for disabled or gifted children.

"In no other field does the state-of-the-art promise so much or change so rapidly. Existing uses are almost limitless, and new ones are being created all the time," adds Mr. Grossi.

He is aware of workshops being held across the country on various uses of talking computers. Two that he would recommend are: "Making Microcomputers Talk for Blind and Speech Handicapped Students," by Peter B. Maggs, University of Illinois at Champaign; and "The Microcomputer as an Efficient Speech Output Communication Aid," by G. Evan Rushakoff, Department of Communication, New Mexico State University at Las Cruces.

"John Eulenberg is another person people should contact," adds Mr. Grossi. "His work in developing talking computers is phenomenal. The benefits to speech-impaired people are a major breakthrough. His artificial language laboratory is amazing."

The Artificial Language Laboratory, established in 1971, is a research laboratory within the Department of Computer Science at Michigan State. Its program of multidisciplinary studies is aimed at researching particular applications to address human communication needs. The lab has been involved with mass market applications of computer-based processing technology, such as two-way interactive cable television. The bulk of the lab's efforts are directed at meeting the needs of persons with severe communication handicaps. It is supported by local foundations, United Cerebral Palsy of Jackson County, and some of the school districts in the state.

More and more research is being done in colleges and universities on applying synthetic speech to assist handicapped people. Colleges and universities are also buying talking computers, terminals, typewriters, and calculators to help handicapped students get the most out of education. Those colleges and universities are:

> California State University at San Diego
> Valparaiso University, Valparaiso, Indiana
> St. Joseph's University, Philadelphia/Pennsylvania
> Arizona State University at Tempe
> California State University at Long Beach
> Cuyahoga Community College, Cleveland, Ohio
> Fairleigh Dickinson University, Teaneck, New Jersey
> Evergreen State College, Olympia, Washington
> Highline Community College, Midway, Washington
> Memphis State University, Memphis, Tennessee
> Catonsville Community College, Catonsville, Maryland
> North Carolina State University at Raleigh
> Stanford University, Palo Alto, California
> University of Wisconsin at Platteville
> University of Central Florida, Orlando
> University of South Florida, Tampa
> Taft College, Taft, California
> Vanderbilt University, Nashville, Tennessee
> University of Illinois at Champaign
> Valencia Community College, Orlando, Florida

Another leader in this area is the federal government, which has historically funded projects dealing with different applications of talking computers.

Federal involvement
Dr. Paul Andereck, Education Specialist, Special Education Programs with the U.S. Department of Education, describes the work the federal government has undertaken to promote and fund research programs in the area of synthetic speech to assist handicapped people. He cites the results of three cases:

The work of Dr. David Lunney of East Carolina University in North Carolina involved analog instruments in a chemistry laboratory. For example, ph meter readings were hooked to a microcomputer which changed the readings to a synthesized voice so that a blind student could hear the instrument readings. Similar kinds of changes from analog readings to auditory signals for blind persons can be generalized from Lunney's work.

Dr. Wesley Wilson of the University of Washington worked with non-vocal paralyzed people who learned the Morse Code and then could signal either a dot or a dash by any two body parts that could

---

Synthetic speech is producing a revolution throughout our entire educational system.

---

move. If necessary, this includes inhaling and exhaling through a straw. The Morse Code was converted by a microcomputer to printer language, or to synthetic voice, or to signals that turn a switch on or off on lights and radios. He programmed his computer to guess ahead, so that the subject seldom has to complete a word or a sentence.

Wilson's procedure has been tested on a variety of non-vocal children who used other ways of communication before this development. His method has proved clearly superior.

Dr. Peter Maggs of the University of Illinois uses a microcomputer to take digital data and drive a commercial voice synthesizer. His software permits such readily available equipment to be used as talking terminals for blind people in many computer terminal situations, whether for education, business, or social purposes. His work also involves translating to foreign languages. Such a talking terminal has wide usage in the lives of young blind adults.

Andereck sees the role of the federal government as continuing to lead in this area. He says, "The federal government will continue to explore new educational delivery systems from high technology tools available. To make them affordable and versatile is very important to handicapped persons."

Synthetic speech will play a major role in reshaping the lives of disabled people. Properly used, it will open up career opportunities for them in business, government, education, and in other professional and nonprofessional fields.

Of course business is the major leader in this field, working with disabled people, special education teachers, and researchers to produce the best synthetic products. Business is also working to bring down the cost of the products. Talking computers or terminals can run from $3,000 to $11,000 depending upon the brand name and the peripherals accompanying it—including software.

"Businesses have discovered there is a market out there, particularly in the education area. Education is the place to start to shape the lives of disabled people so they can become active citizens," says Blazie.

The Visually Handicapped Child

Infancy through Pre-school Age
The importance of vision stimulation

William V. Padula, O.D.

and

Susan J. Spungin, Ed. D.

The majority of children who are visually handicapped are not blind but have useable vision. Unfortunately, there are visually handicapped children treated as if they are blind and never given the opportunity to function as sighted individuals. Since vision is learned, all children must develop it through use. A child with a visual handicap may have difficulty developing it and have special needs that require types of aids and techniques to allow the child the opportunity to use his/her vision.

Why is vision so important?

Simply considering the physiology of the eyes, 70% of all the sensory nerves in the entire body come from the eyes. These nerves give information that not only enable us to see, but also reinforce our ability to coordinate movement, maintain balance, think, problem-solve and many other actions. For the child, vision is an extremely important process and greatly affects and influences the child's development.

When a child has an impairment to his or her sight, this means that the child's ability to function and perform in the environment has been affected because of either a reduction in acuity (reduced ability to see clearly) and/or a restriction in the child's field of vision (scope or peripheral extent of sight) and that is not correctable with ordinary eye glasses.

A child is considered **visually impaired** if he/she has 20/70 acuity or less in his/ her best corrected eye. The child is considered **legally blind** if he/she has 20/200 acuity or less in the best corrected eye or a 20° field of vision or less. Visual acuity is a measurement used to describe the smallest size detail that a person can see at a particular distance. For example, a child with 20/200 acuity would have to be within 20 feet of the same object that another child with so-called normal acuity (20/70) could see from 200 feet away.

A child who is visually handicapped may qualify for federal or state funding to provide a special education program designed to meet his/her visual needs. The definitions of visual impairment and legal blindness are not functional ones. These definitions only use acuity and/or field measurements as a means to determine eligibility for services. Both of these measurements (visual acuity and visual field) do not indicate how the child uses his or her vision to function in their environment. A child may have better than 20/70 acuity (ie. 20/40) but have a significant interference with processing and understanding what they are seeing. In turn, that child's performance and functional abilities are affected.

Although the standard criteria used for classification (ie. legal blindness, visual impairment, etc.) is based on acuity and field measurements, the child's ability to use his/her vision effectively depends on many other factors. These classifications are a means to identify groups of people, however, generalizations about whether a person can or cannot function must be avoided. For example, two children who are the same age, may function quite differently. This is because their ability to use their remaining vision may vary. Therefore, the impairment is not the diminished acuity level or the field restriction, it is rather the interference with how the child uses his/her remaining vision. The acuity and field measurements do not relate function and performance. Function and performance relate to a complex interaction between the senses, the motor system, and the child's ability to perceptually manipulate these processes to establish meaningful relationships.

When there is a visual handicap, the child's performance and learning abilities will often be affected. This is because the child's dominant means for learning has been interfered with. In turn, delays in the child's development may result because the learning process has been interfered with. This doesn't mean that the child can't utilize other senses to learn with. If the child can compensate for his/her visual loss through high intelligence and a suitable environment to learn of other means, then a developmental delay may not occur. However, for the majority of visually handicapped children, visual interferences can greatly interrupt and delay their development.

Even before the child is born, the visual system is matching information received through other senses regarding position and balance to establish basic experiences which the child, after birth, will utilize to develop new relationships. After birth, the visual process leads in establishing perceptual experiences and learning necessary for normal development. Through the visual process, the child actively probes the environment, matching information through motor and sensory functions. In early development, the infant monitors all sensory and motor information and attempts to relate all information to his/her visual

world. Once the information is matched visually, the infant develops a relationship and, in turn, a perceptual experience that is stored as a reference base to compare to new situations. In this way, development proceeds by the establishment of perceptual experiences and because of the general physiology and nature of the child, development progresses primarily as a function of vision with the strong support from the other senses.

This does not mean that the totally blind child, who has lost the ability to see will not develop. The totally blind child, depending on factors of other physical abilities, intelligence, and environmental surroundings will compensate for the loss of vision by utilizing other senses to match information to develop the relationship to establish perceptual experiences. However, delays in development will occur because the child must wait for other physiologic sensory-motor functions and perceptual processes to mature to a level that meaningful relationships can be established.

For the visually impaired child, delopment will progress depending on the amount of interference created by the impairment. It is important to note that the amount of visual impairment (ie., acuity and/or field loss) is not directly proportional to delay in development. This is because the child will attempt to maximize his or her residual vision and depending on factors of other physical abilities, intelligence, and environmental surroundings may not demonstrate consistent development delays. The acuity loss (lowered ability to see clearly) or the field loss (constriction to the scope of a vision) does not mean that the child has a lesser ability to function. Function and development will depend on the three factors previously mentioned and how the child can adapt and compensate for the impairment.

The Multi-handicapped child

Over 50% of visually impaired children have additional physicial handicaps. These may range from severe gross motor impairments to minor impairments of fine motor control. Just because a child is physically impaired, it must not be taken for granted that the child is retard-

ed or lacks the potentials for advanced learning. Again, the physical impairment (sensory and/or motor) is not directly related to an inability to develope the skills needed for learning. The latter depends upon the child's ability to adapt and compensate for the physical impairment by utilizing other motor and sensory processes to experience with. Therefore, delays in developement depend on whether the child can adequately manipulate his/her environment motor and sensory function to grasp meaningful relationships.

When a child has a visual handicap together with other physical impairments, delays in development become more predictable. The child will require comprehensive plans of care from a multi-disciplinary team of professionals to help the child adapt, compensate and overcome his/her physical restrictions. It is important that one member of this multi-disciplinary team be a vision specialist (optometrist and/or opthalmologist) who understands low vision and the developmental needs of the child. The vision specialist should also work with other members of the team (ie. educator, physical therapist, speech and hearing specialist, etc.) to design therapy programs and prescribe whatever may be needed to improve the child's visual abilities to improve visual functioning. In this way, the child will be maximizing use of his or her vision which can then be used for learning and supporting normal development.

What can be done? — Low Vision

By understanding the importance of vision for the development of the child, when a visual impairment is suspected, the child should be taken, without delay, for a complete visual examination to a qualified optometrist or ophthalmologist. It may be determined that the child only needs glasses to improve his/her vision. In this case, glasses will be extremely important to support the development and the factors mentioned previously. A visual examination can be performed at any age, including early infancy. If a visual impairment is diagnosed, plans should then be made for the child to have a low vision examination. This examination is different from a routine visual examination, for this form of examination determines what can be done for the child beyond conventional glasses such as prescribing special optical aids that will improve the child's ability to see.

Optical aids vary in type. They range from simple hand held magnifiers to special types of telescopes and microscopes small enough to be mounted on glasses or even a closed circuit TV. The purpose of these aids is to magnify what the child is looking at so that he/she may be able to utilize his/her residual vision effectively to read, watch TV, spot signs, and street lights at a distance, and otherwise function visually. The optical aids vary in type and power, and the doctor specializing in low vision will be able to evaluate the child's vision and determine which type and power optical aid will be most effective.

Low vision services do not end with the prescription of an optical aid but begin there. A low vision examination performed as early as possible allows a team of professionals from many fields (low-vision specialists, educators, therapists, orientation and mobility specialists, etc.) to plan ahead for what the child's needs will be. Special programs can be designed to enable the child to maximize use of his/her vision. As previously discussed, some visually handicapped children are unable to use their residual vision effectively and, in turn, the impairment actually interferes with their development. The reason for this is that the child has never learned how to use his or her vision and, in turn, has suppressed it. For this child, a program of vision stimulation designed specifically for the child's needs and abilities, could be developed. Vision stimulation can be developed for children of any age. Of course, the younger the child the earlier his/her vision can be habilitated, thereby causing less of an interference with development.

According to Faye, Hood and Sprague (1975), all children whose vision measures light perception or better are candidates for a low vision evaluation and for utilization of low vision instruction and should receive both as long as they have vision problems. However, since vision is learned, a child will sometimes appear totally blind but actually have useable vision because that child has never learned to use his/her vision. Therefore, every child, regardless of whether it is believed the child is blind or not, should be given the opportunity to receive a low vision examination. Low vision services offer a comprehensive, multi-disciplinary approach toward affecting and improving the child's vision. Prescribed low vision optical aids together with other specially designed programs can allow the child to function visually to his or her maximum potential.

The next article will examine specific needs of the visually impaired child. Also, we will discuss the roles of professionals serving these children and various other resources in the U.S. for materials.

Teaching the Hearing Impaired Child

The primary area of concern in educating deaf children is language. Hearing impaired children are like hearing children in all other areas, including physical development, learning and thinking, and intellectual abilities. Because these children tend to participate less in communication interchanges and have more difficulty with initial learning of verbal symbols due to the interference of the hearing impairment, language skills tend to be delayed. The problem is more severe with children who have a hearing loss prior to their language development than for those children experiencing a loss after language development has begun. In no way are these children less bright or capable. It is crucial, however, that the child's enviromental opportunities are as broad as possible to compensate for the child's lessened auditory learning opportunities or else the child will be academically delayed due to loss of life experiences. Some children's hearing losses are mild and can easily be confused with low motivation or lack of ability. It is important for teachers to notice the signs of undetected hearing losses, or else these children will slip further behind and not realize why they are not learning. "Poor Learning Ability . . . or Poor Hearing?" provides a checklist for teachers so that they will know what signs to look for and how to respond to children who have hearing impairments. "The Hearing Mechanism" diagrams the hearing apparatus, demonstrates how hearing loss occurs and how hearing is tested using an audiometer, and explains causes of common hearing impairments.

In teaching deaf (or partially deaf) children, communication between teacher and student, or between hearing and hearing impaired students can be difficult, especially during lectures, group discussions, or audio-visual presentations. Few teachers are proficient in using sign language, so interpreters and notetakers are often used in classrooms for hearing impaired students. "There's a Deaf Child in My Class" offers several good suggestions for preparing classroom teachers for mainstreaming a deaf child, while "Notetaking: A Necessary Support Service for Hearing-Impaired Students" discusses the importance of notetaking in the learning process.

There are a variety of communication systems available for deaf students. The oral method teaches deaf students to lip read, produce speech, and trains them to use any residual hearing for maximal interpretation of speech and production of language. The advantage of this system is that deaf students can learn to communicate with hearing individuals in a predominantly hearing world. Unfortunately, only one-third of a person's words can be correctly identified using lipreading (since so many sounds look alike when spoken), and learning to produce speech intelligible to a hearing person is a difficult and painstaking process.

Manual methods (involving fingerspelling and a sign language system) allow communication between deaf individuals, but is not useful with the majority of hearing persons who do not know a sign system.

The current preferred way of educating deaf students is to use total communication, which involves all the above methods of communication plus non-verbal communication methods to enhance understanding.

Looking Ahead: Challenge Questions

How can hearing impairments be distinguished from other learning problems?

How does hearing occur? How are hearing losses caused? What do audiograms show about a person's hearing?

What communication systems are used by the deaf and what types of support people are available to assist the deaf in communicating?

How can deaf students play musical instruments?

What adaptations would need to be made in a classroom where deaf students were mainstreamed?

Poor Learning Ability . . . or Poor Hearing?

Lawrence B. Mollick
and Kenneth S. Etra

Lawrence B. Mollick and Kenneth S. Etra are practicing ear, nose and throat specialists in Great Neck and Glen Cove, N.Y.

Jennifer, in many respects, is an ideal pupil. She sits quietly in class, paying close attention to what is being said. She almost never misbehaves. Her good conduct, however, does not result in good grades. Jennifer's test scores are surprisingly low.

Timmy is less of a mystery. He, too, is not doing well in school, but it's not hard to see why. He simply doesn't pay attention. Despite all efforts to draw him out, he ignores most of what is going on in class, preferring to daydream or to draw pictures (which he does extremely well) in his notebook.

Jennifer's and Timmy's problems appear to be altogether different. But, in fact, they stem from an identical source: both children are hard of hearing.

We often think of hearing loss as a problem of the elderly. But current statistics indicate that approximately *half a million* American children between the ages of six and 12 suffer from hearing loss to some degree (Office of Demographic Studies, Gallaudet College, Washington, D.C.). And in the past 10 years it has been shown again and again that poor hearing is the cause—often unsuspected—of a wide range of childhood problems, from bad grades to inadequate social adjustment. For example:

• In a 1969 test, American children with impaired hearing were found to be badly delayed in their language development ("Effect of Chronic Otitis Media on Language and Speech Development" by V.A. Holmes and L.H. Kunze, *Pediatrics,* Vol. 43, 1969, p. 833).

• In 1972, a study of 14,000 seven-year-olds in Great Britain showed that those with hearing loss were not only poorer in reading ability, but also "more clumsy" and "less stable" than other children ("School Attainment of Seven-Year-Old Children With Hearing Difficulties" by C.S. Peckham, M. Sheridan and N.R. Butler, *Developmental Medicine in Child Neurology*, Vol. 14, 1972, p. 592).

• In 1973, Eskimo boys and girls with impaired hearing scored "significantly lower" than others in tests of verbal skills ("Long-Term Effects of Otitis Media: A 10-Year Study of Alaskan Eskimo Children" by G.J. Kaplan, J.K. Fleshman and T.R. Bendman et al, *Pediatrics*, Vol. 52, 1973, p. 577).

During the elementary school years children pass through a crucial period of cognitive development. It is the concluding phase of what psychologist Jean Piaget termed the "concrete operations period." In this period the child masters the thought patterns that prepare him or her to move ahead into mature conceptual thinking. To be hard of hearing at such a time is a handicap that may result in life-long damage. Yet the condition frequently goes undiagnosed, largely perhaps because the signs of hearing loss are not always what you might suppose.

In Timmy's case, an alert teacher or parent might suspect that his inattentiveness was the result of poor hearing and ask that auditory testing be done. But how many would guess that a "model student" like Jennifer had the same problem . . . that her extreme attentiveness was due to the fact that she had to watch her teacher's lips in order to know what was being said?

Recognizing a Problem

You, the teacher—admittedly already overburdened with non-teaching tasks—will be in a good position to recognize this problem. And in many ways you are the person best able to do so. On school days, you actually spend more hours with children than their parents do. And even more important, you work with the children at a higher level of awareness. You often need to focus your attention directly on a particular youngster, as a parent may not do. Hence you are more likely to notice subtle differences in response. Here are some questions to ask yourself:

• Is the child abnormally attentive like Jennifer or abnormally inattentive like Timmy? Either extreme can be a sign of trouble.

• Is the child behind in speech development? Distorted or immature speech may be the result of distorted hearing. By the age of six a youngster should be able to pronounce clearly such blends as *th, tl, gr, br* and *pr*. More difficult sounds, such as *thr, sk, st, shr, z, sh, ch* and *j*, may not be mastered until age seven or eight.

• Does the child have frequent colds and ear infections? If the answer is yes, then you should watch this child closely for signs of impaired hearing. Approximately 80 percent of all hearing loss in children is *conductive*—that is, it comes from an impediment of some kind that interferes with the transmission of sound inside the ear. Infections often produce such impediments. Fluid in the middle ear is a common cause of problems.

• Is the child subject to allergies? They can produce swollen tissues in the nose and ear area, leading to faulty hearing. Signs of allergies, however, can vary widely. Among the more visible ones are dark circles under the eyes (possibly indicating presence of fluid in the tissue and middle ear), red eyes, a chronically runny nose or frequent sneezing. A teacher also should watch for what is known as the "allergic salute"—rubbing the palm of the hand upward over the mouth and nose. In children with allergies, this gesture sometimes become habitual.

• Has the child had measles, mumps or rubella, either recently or in the past? Despite the existence of preventive vaccines, these diseases are still around, and all three can lead to impaired hearing. It is not uncommon to discover a boy or girl who had one of these diseases as a small child, and whose hearing loss remained unsuspected until he or she started school.

• Does the child rely on gestures when speech would be more effective? Some hearing-impaired children develop gestures into a virtual sign language. One child we know became almost a mime—and the class clown—before it was finally realized that, far from being a natural show-off, he was a partially deaf child.

• Does the child come to school with bruises about the face? The battered child suffers many forms of damage, both physical and psychological. Not infrequently, there is a loss of hearing due to blows on the head which displace delicate bones inside the ear.

• Does the child often ask you to speak louder or give inappropriate answers to your questions? These, of course, are the most obvious of indications that he or she hasn't heard well.

The Need for Prompt Action

As these questions suggest, many cases of hearing loss come from conditions that produce pressure inside the ear—allergies, infections, even enlarged adenoids.

This means that many cases are frequently temporary in nature and often respond readily to treatment. (Even the stubbornest cases of fluid in the middle ear—the commonest cause of hearing loss in children under 10—can be relieved by a simple operation that creates a tiny hole in the eardrum. An inserted tube allows the fluid to drain.) This does *not* mean, however, that you can disregard danger signs, or that it is safe to "wait and see" before speaking to the school doctor or to the parents.

Some of the conditions, if left untreated, will worsen, so that what might have been a temporary loss of hearing becomes a permanent one.

An equally important reason for prompt action is the child's own urgent need not to be out of touch with the world, even for a short time. During the next 12 months, you, as an adult, will take in only a limited amount of new information compared to the child, with so much more to learn. He or she will be taking in new information at an incredibly rapid rate. Interfere with this learning for even a few months and you can create a serious handicap in terms of misunderstood lessons and social isolation.

In guarding against this danger you, the teacher, are the child's first line of defense.

If there's a child in your class who is hard of hearing . . .

Due to the growing implementation of mainstreaming, more and more classroom teachers have hearing-impaired children in their classrooms. For such youngsters, school can be a pleasant experience—and a far more productive one—if you observe the following rules:

1. Always turn and face the class when you have something to say. Don't "teach to the chalkboard." It may seem easy and natural while you're writing on it, but avoid it at all times.

2. Use preferential seating. Seat youngsters with hearing losses near the front of the classroom, close to your desk. A child with a bad left ear should be seated on your right as you face the class, a child with a bad right ear on your left.

3. Pay attention to your diction. Actors know that voices are projected not by speaking louder but by emphasizing the consonants. Sounds like "h" and "th" require special emphasis to be understood by a hearing-impaired person.

4. Be vigilant to make certain you're "getting through." A student's degree of participation in class is one index of good hearing. The child who appears disinterested simply may not be hearing everything that is said.

5. Stay in close touch with the parents. They can tell you whether medical treatment is improving the child's condition and what the long-term outlook is.

6. Help the child overcome any self-consciousness. If it is necessary to refer to the child's handicap, always do so in private, never in front of the class.

7. Allow the child to participate in appropriate activities. Being overprotective when there is no need stifles a child. There's no reason for a youngster who wears a hearing aid not to take part in active sports—keeping the aid on—if he or she wishes. Never compel a youngster who wants to join in a game to remain on the sidelines if there is no medical reason for it.

8. Schedule regular private conferences with the children. Some youngsters talk freely about their problems, others do not. Handicapped children, especially, should always have the opportunity to speak up. In listening, you may discover new ways to be helpful.—*L.B.M.* and *K.S.E.*

The Hearing Mechanism

James W. Sherbon

The author is assistant professor of graduate music education in the school of music at the University of North Carolina, Greensboro.

Auditory perception is a fundamental requisite for musical response (behavior). The paramount and undisputed fact about the manifestation of musical behavior caused by the traditional auditory stimulation route is that if there is no hearing there is no music. It is obvious that when permanent hearing loss is present, individuals are handicapped in their ability to receive musical stimuli.[1] The discouraging aspect of hearing loss, and particularly total deafness, is that little is being done to avoid this state by personal awareness of the function and care of the hearing mechanism.

For over a decade, musicians have voiced concern about the auditory dangers resulting from noise pollution. But we have done literally nothing about controlling these threats to our pleasures and livelihood, with the exception of such awareness tactics as promoting the sale of earplugs, attempting to persuade individuals to turn down the gain on their amplifiers, and publishing repeated warnings that the next generation of musicians may be deaf.

Americans are often difficult to understand. We are generally concerned with physical fitness, yet we neglect or purposely avoid routine examinations of our eyes, teeth, and hearing despite the fact that early diagnosis often results in cure and control. Do you know how well you hear? When did you last have your hearing tested—elementary school, military service, or can you even remember? Do you know where your areas (specific frequencies) of auditory sensitivity or lack of sensitivity (tonal lacunae) lie?

Common sense indicates that there is some degree of association between hearing efficiency and musical behavior. It has been demonstrated that a temporary threshold shift in hearing can occur as a result of prolonged exposure to the sound normally encountered in an orchestra rehearsal,[2] although there apparently is little association between hearing efficiency and performance on measures of musical behavior.[3] Adler implied that as a result of compensating for a hearing defect, an individual may become a better musician.[4] As yet, however, there is a lack of empirical evidence to support hypotheses directed toward musical achievement in relationship to hearing efficiency.

An examination of the hearing mechanism and some of the factors involved in hearing problems may offer encouragement for a regular schedule of hearing maintenance. It may also help us, as music educators, to become more aware and understanding of our own and of our students' hearing as it affects musical behavior. As musicians, we should be especially aware of pathological implications related to hearing. The reasons are obvious—the protection and conservation of hearing for both self and others. Music educators are in a unique situation in that we constantly employ the hearing mechanism in our daily work. (Some individuals suggest there is a dichotomy between hearing and listening. This point, which will not be discussed in this article, emphasizes the importance of hearing efficiency. We have to hear before we can listen.)

---

[1] Work is now being done with the totally deaf and vibratory stimuli. See Joan Dahms Fahey and Lois Birkenshaw, "Bypassing the Ear: The Perception of Music by Feeling and Touch," *Music Educators Journal*, Vol. 58, No. 8 (April 1972), pp. 44–49.

[2] R. O. Jones and R. Pracy, "An Investigation of Pitch Discrimination in the Normal and Abnormal Hearing Adult," *Journal of Laryngology and Otology*, Vol. 85 (August 1971), pp. 797–798.

[3] James W. Sherbon, "The Association of Hearing Acuity, Diplacusis, and Discrimination with Music Performance," *Journal of Research in Music Education*, Vol. 23, No. 4 (Winter 1975), pp. 249–257.

[4] Paul R. Farnsworth, "Further Data on the Adlerian Theory of Artistry," *Journal of General Psychology*, Vol. 24 (January 1941), p. 447.

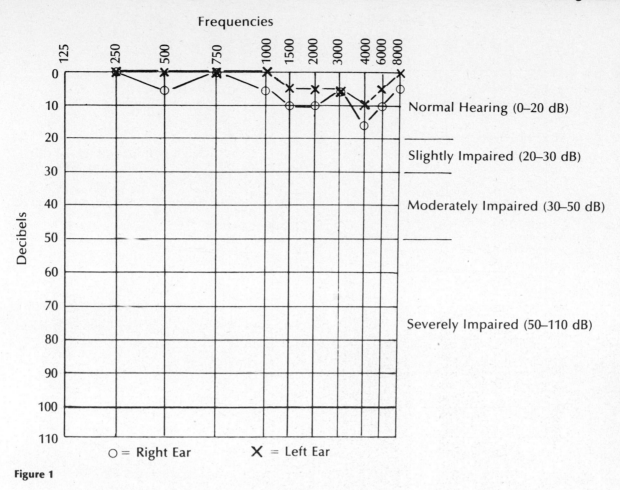

Figure 1

Hearing problems and music implications

The hearing mechanism (ear) is one of the most complex, intricate, fragile, and amazing parts of our body. Sound pressure waves cause the eardrum to sympathetically vibrate, which in turn mechanically sets three tiny bones (ossicles) in motion, thus transmitting the message of sound stimuli to an organ approximately the size of the tip of an index finger—the inner ear (cochlea). Through a series of complex actions (mechanical, hydraulic, and neuro-electric) the inner ear sends electrical firings to the brain, and we are able to simultaneously hear the many timbres, intensities, and frequencies of an entire symphony orchestra. It is easy to visualize that a mechanism as complicated and fragile as the ear can be subject to many external and internal sources of abuse and malfunction.

There are two general classifications of hearing malfunction. The first is *common hearing loss* and the second is *diplacusis*. These broad and sometimes ambiguous areas are not mutually exclusive and cover a wide range of pathological and environmental connotations.

Hearing loss is defined as the lack of auditory acuity as compared to established norms.

It is often difficult to determine an exact point whereby an individual may be classified as suffering from hearing loss because of differences in testing conditions and equipment, audiometric procedures, and testing standards. Specific cutoff points are often avoided by employing a continuum to describe the magnitude of loss. The independence of the two ears adds a further complication in hearing assessment. It is not uncommon to find individuals with one normal ear and one that shows hearing loss. Results of audiometric tests (audiogram) from an individual with normal hearing will show corresponding linear profiles for the two ears (Figure 1). If loss is present in one or both ears the audiogram may show unrelated profiles for the ears (Figure 2). This illustrates another problem in the assessment of hearing. Since humans tend to have a favorite ear, it becomes increasingly difficult to state any quantitative summary information regarding an individual's total hearing. For purposes of providing descriptive data, readings are often averaged for both ears or results of the better ear are used. It is interesting to observe musicians when tuning and their use of a favorite or better ear. The turning of the

4. TEACHING THE HEARING IMPAIRED CHILD

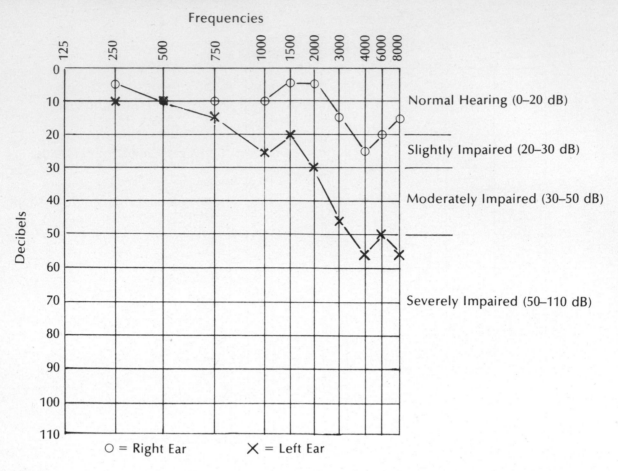

O = Right Ear   X = Left Ear

Figure 2

head so that the favorite or better ear is directed toward the sound is particularly noticeable with cello and double bass players.

Routine audiometric testing in the schools is often administered under adverse conditions. It is not uncommon for tests to be given in a less than ideal environment: a school cafeteria, gymnasium, classroom, or hallway. The procedure is often hurried and inefficient. An audiometric testing procedure most often used in the schools is the sweepcheck method. An audiometer is precalibrated to produce sinusoidal tones at intensity levels slightly above normal hearing levels for each frequency to be tested. A sweep is made across a frequency band, and subjects simply indicate if tones are heard at specific testing frequencies. This procedure only identifies individuals who cannot hear tonal stimuli at the frequencies tested and gives no indication of the true hearing sensitivity. The sweepcheck procedure is efficient and expedient in discovering individuals who may have a hearing loss in the speech hearing range but excludes many factors, such as extreme frequencies and absolute hearing thresholds, that may be of importance to the perception of musical stimuli.

A second testing procedure is termed the threshold method and produces a relatively accurate hearing profile. Similar equipment is used, but an attenuation process allows absolute hearing thresholds to be determined so that individuals with supersensitive hearing can be identified as well as those with a hearing loss. It may be important to a music teacher to know that, for example, a student has normal hearing except for a 4,000 Hz dip (lack of hearing acuity in the 4,000 Hz range). Of particular significance musically is the fact that audiometric testing seldom is administered above 8,000 Hz, thereby omitting at least an entire octave that is well within the hearing capabilities of most individuals. Similarly, standard testing usually does not include frequencies below 250 Hz (the lowest piano tone is approximately 27 Hz). In view of these audiometric limitations it might be musically significant to have data showing accurate and inclusive individual hearing profiles.

Diplacusis is a common hearing malfunction that may be unfamiliar to the general public. For purposes of definition it should be stated that there are essentially three classifications of diplacusis: (1) *Diplacusis binaur-*

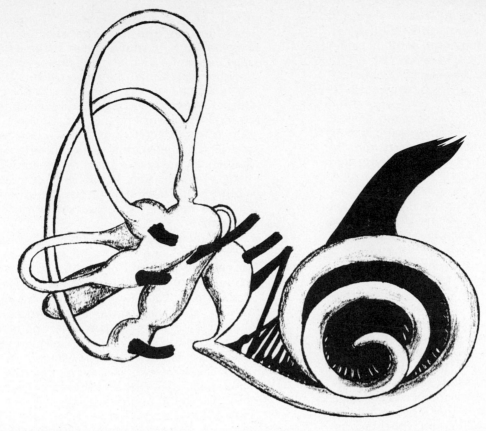

The highly complex nerve structure of the inner ear (in black) allows us to differentiate minute variations in timbres, intensities, and frequencies.

alis echotica, in which a sound is processed at different times by the two ears and thus perceived as an echo; (2) *diplacusis monauralis dysharmonica*, in which a single tone is perceived as two pitches by the same ear; and (3) *diplacusis binauralis dysharmonica* (binaural diplacusis—usually referred to as diplacusis), the perception of two different pitches between the ears from a single tone.[5] The first two classifications are not recognized as common hearing problems, although individuals often experience some of these described symptoms when suffering from any of a multitude of ordinary ear, nose, and throat disorders. The third classification (hereafter referred to as diplacusis) is quite common and present to some extent in most humans. This should not be surprising since each ear is essentially an independent hearing mechanism.

Diplacusis is similar to hearing loss in that numerical criteria have not been established specifying the presence or absence of this malfunction. (We are able to measure quite accurately the decibel deviation from the norm to determine hearing thresholds and, probably more accurately, the perceptual frequency dif-

ference between the ears when measuring diplacusis.) It would be relatively safe to generalize that all individuals have some pitch deviation between the two ears, but at what point this deviation would be defined as diplacusis is not clear.

Diplacusis, if it is congenital, apparently creates only minor problems for musicians even when the difference is as great as a major third or perfect fourth due to a natural compensation process. When diplacusis is provoked by ear problems such as infection or common colds, a pronounced distortion of sound is often experienced and difficulties with accurate tonal perception and intonation are commonly encountered. Music teachers should be aware of these possibilities and not be unknowingly critical of students' erratic performance (for example, placing the blame for sudden intonation problems on lack of attention) when in fact it may be impossible for a student to center a tone. Audiometric testing procedures seldom include tests for diplacusis.

As previously mentioned, humans tend to develop a favorite ear as they do a favorite eye, hand, or foot. This ability apparently compensates for deviations of pitch between the two ears—for critical and sensitive perception we listen primarily with one ear. That neural processing may aid in this compensation is

[5]George E. Shambaugh Jr., "Diplacusis: A Localizing Symptom of Disease of the Organ of Corti," *Archives of Otolaryngology*, Vol. 31, No. 1 (1940), p. 160.

shown by the tendency to isolate one pitch from two sources of slightly different frequencies or the establishment of a pitch center within a wide vibrato. Therefore, except for sudden malfunctions, the extent of a handicap to musicians resulting from diplacusis is thought to be minimal.

Instrumental teachers often spend considerable effort and time in prognostic testing and matching students with particular instruments. Factors such as lips, teeth, and hand size and shape usually receive the most attention in the area of physical concerns. Seldom does hearing efficiency receive attention. Should a student with severe diplacusis be counseled against playing stringed instruments? Should a student with a right ear hearing loss play the horn? We do not know the answers to these questions, but it is certain that we would not place a student who has a severe hearing loss in the back of a classroom. Therefore, simple logic would rule against placing students with hearing problems on such instruments as tuba or percussion because of the placement of these instruments in the typical band/orchestra seating arrangement. This greater physical distance further handicaps the student in that it becomes more difficult to hear the conductor's verbal instructions. This is a nonmusical consideration, but nevertheless a very important aspect that is often overlooked by the music teacher.

Causes of hearing malfunctions

We experience changes in hearing acuity from day to day and often more frequently. Usually a direct result of a present physical or environmental condition, these changes may be insignificant in routine daily life but become highly critical in situations that require sensitivity such as listening to or performing music. If the causes of the temporary fluctuations reach a magnitude (period of time or severity/intensity) beyond the physical limitations of the hearing mechanism, permanent damage will result. We have all experienced temporary threshold shift from sudden or prolonged exposure to sound. In some circumstances repeated or prolonged noise exposure may lead to permanent hearing loss. For example, paradoxically, while sound is the musician's business, sound may also be one of the worst enemies of efficient hearing. Thus the concern for noise pollution and the control of excessive sound in general. We cannot turn our ears off as we close our eyes; therefore the hearing mechanism is never at rest—awake or asleep. As with other parts of our body, fatigue becomes a limiting factor when the hearing mechanism is overworked. Thus the rock musician suffers a hearing loss (temporary or permanent) in the ear(s) exposed to amplification, and the band director who is bombarded with sound five or six hours a day may encounter similar problems.

Some factors that may also cause a temporary change in hearing acuity with possibilities of permanent damage are wax buildup against the eardrum, inflammation or infection, colds, eustachian tube congestion (which restricts compensation in the middle ear for ambient atmospheric pressure changes), and perhaps medication. It should be the responsibility of the musician/teacher to be informed of these dangers and take appropriate precautions.

Permanent hearing loss is often a result of pathological and exposure factors experienced over a period of time or in excessive amounts. Most individuals will or have experienced presbycusis, which is hearing loss resulting from the natural aging process. Although there may be experiential and medical (in addition to temporal) factors involved in the cause, apparently little can be done to avoid or treat this common affliction. We should be aware that as individuals grow older, it is common for hearing acuity to decrease, usually in a descending pattern starting with the higher frequencies. Because it is not unusual (a conservative estimate) for individuals over fifty-five to be insensitive to frequencies above 10–12,000 Hz (slightly over an octave above the high C on the piano), they may not hear many of our music sounds, especially the upper partials, that are of importance to the perception and recognition of specific tone qualities.

Since the introduction of antibiotics, many common causes of permanent hearing damage have been minimized—for example, middle ear infection. Modern medical techniques enable physicians to correct what would otherwise be permanent hearing loss. In recent years otologists have perfected procedures that can temporarily improve hearing as well as permanently repair damaged parts of the hearing mechanism. These procedures include such techniques as the replacement of tubes in eardrums to relieve middle ear pressure, eardrum repair, and replacement of ossicle parts. Little can be done beyond the use of medication to treat inner ear problems. This small, intricate, and complex organ is often the victim of numerous abuses and disorders that result in hearing loss beyond the help of the surgeon's scalpel. Diplacusis is often a result of sensory cell damage within the cochlea, therefore a permanent condition. Medical science may offer hope to those who suffer from any severe hearing loss or deafness (conductive or sensory) because we may soon commonly see successful electrode implants that carry sound stimuli directly to, or beyond, the auditory nerve.

Little known to the layman is the possibility of damage to the hearing mechanism from improper or unfortunate use of medication—particularly some classified as antibiotics. Severe and permanent (mainly cochlear) damage has resulted from these drugs, commonly known as ototoxic, which generally, although not exclusively, include the mycins. Research studies are available that deal with hearing and streptomycin,[6] neomycin,[7] tobramycin,[8] kanamycin,[9] and others. By no means should individuals avoid these drugs, but it is wise to be aware of dangerous side effects. Some variables involved in ototoxicity include factors such as body weight, dosage, kind of medication, interactions with the physical condition and other drugs, body/system status, and kidney function. Most physicians are extremely knowledgeable about the implications involved in prescribing any medication that may have ototoxic effects; however, it is a wise practice to inform physicians, who may be unfamiliar with an individual's medical history, of any hearing problems (past or present) when drugs such as the mycins are prescribed.

Hearing knowledge is important

Any descriptive attempt toward a topic as extensive and technical as musical implications in relationship to hearing efficiency may result in a superficial overview or a voluminous pathological-behavioral treatise. At the risk of jeopardizing the contextual value of the subject, an overview has been presented to provide brief but important information that will be of value to the music educator. As with many topics dealing with human characteristics, it should be understood that generalizations must be made with caution because of individual differences. There are many elderly individuals who do not suffer any noticeable hearing problems, and conversely, there are children with severe hearing handicaps. The most important message is do not take hearing for granted. Be aware of hearing conservation techniques as well as behaviors possibly resulting from hearing malfunction. We should take advantage of our work with the medium of sound and encourage this awareness as well as personal knowledge of hearing that can lead to possible solutions of often unidentified musical and disciplinary problems. Music educators, know your characteristics and the hearing abilities of your students. The difference in communication and musical results may be surprising.

[6]Roger E. Johnsonbaugh, Hazel G. Drexler, Irwin J. Light, and James M. Sutherland, "Familial Occurrence of Drug-Induced Hearing Loss," *American Journal of Diseases of Children*, Vol. 127 (February 1974), pp. 245–247.

[7]Louis D. Lowry, Mark May, and Peter Pastore, "Acute Histopathologic Inner Ear Changes in Deafness Due to Neomycin: A Case Report," *Annals of Otology, Rhinology, and Laryngology*, Vol. 82, No. 6 (November-December 1973), pp. 876–880.

[8]Thomas B. Logan, Jiri Prazma, William G. Thomas, and Newton D. Fischer, "Tobramycin Ototoxicity," *Archives of Otolaryngology*, Vol. 99, No. 3 (March 1974), pp. 190–193.

[9]Emilia Krochmalska, "Effect of Industrial Noise and Ototoxic Antibiotics on Cochlear Function," *Acta Otolaryngologica*, Vol. 77, Nos. 1–6 (January–June 1974), pp. 44–50.

Notetaking: A Necessary Support Service for Hearing-Impaired Students

Jimmie Joan Wilson

■ Notetaking, the "unseen support service" for hearing-impaired students, is becoming more accepted in mainstreamed public school programs on all levels. At the National Technical Institute for the Deaf (NTID), which has been on the campus of the Rochester Institute of Technology since 1967, notetaking has been formalized and validated as an important support service. Many students find it to be more useful than interpreting in the classroom. Particularly for oral students, or for any students in the public school, notetaking may be the *only* appropriate classroom support.

From the time students begin to learn to read, notetaking can meet several needs:

1. Clarification of classroom procedures and materials.
2. Reinforcement of reading and study skills.
3. Information for tutoring.
4. Information of daily classroom proceedings for the classroom or substitute teacher.
5. Beginning the development of skills in using notes in later school years.
6. Guarantee of equal access to classroom materials.
7. An in-class source of information and liaison to resources about hearing loss and support services.

Thus, from perhaps the second grade on, or even earlier if reading skills are present, notetaking is an important, even vital support service for the hearing-impaired or indeed for any language or orthopedically handicapped student. For students in kindergarten or first grade, notes provide information for the teacher of the deaf or for parents who function as tutors.

BRIDGING THE "INFORMATION GAP"

Experience has shown that at the junior high level, hearing-impaired students begin to experience an "information gap"

even greater than before in their school experience. This gap occurs because teachers tend to give less attention to whether or not students have understood instructions, classes are larger, public address systems are used for dissemination of information, and students are expected to be more independent and able to assess their own skills and needs.

In junior high, also, classes may be noisier because of large size with more independence of activity, discussion groups, lab situations, and so forth, so that a hearing-impaired student who depends on residual hearing and lip-reading may not be able to see or hear as much as he or she did in earlier grades. Classes are faster paced, vocabulary is more technical, and students have more homework and are expected to read and understand much more on their own. Teachers begin to lecture and students are expected to listen and retain what they hear. These problems increase exponentially on the high school level.

For a hearing-impaired student, whose language competence can almost invariably be described as *below* grade level simply because of the hearing problem, all of the situations described interact to create a stressful, less than acceptable learning environment. The student begins to experience tensions and constant worry because he or she is afraid of missing something. Behavior problems or acting out are apt to occur, allowing the student to feel more in control of the situation because he or she is the center of attention.

ALLEVIATING ANXIETY

Every hearing-impaired person has a collection of memories about an exam he or she missed because of not knowing about it, the party that was rescheduled (and missed), the assignment that was done incorrectly—all because of an announcement on the PA system or because many teachers have the unfortunate habit of talking to the blackboard or to the departing backs of students leaving the classroom. This means the hearing-impaired student did not see to lipread or did not even know anything was being said. It takes only a few such experiences before a student develops a constant anxiety that he or she is "missing something."

This article was developed in the course of an agreement with the U.S. Department of Education, Office of Special Education.

When students are expected to sit and work at their seats, the hearing-impaired student is again put into an unfavorable situation because he or she cannot look at the book or paper on the desk and, at the same time, maintain vigilance to see if the teacher or others are speaking. A notetaker sitting nearby can cue the hearing-impaired student if necessary, or write down what is being said when the student is unable to watch.

The notes are also useful for students with other handicapping conditions. Students with orthopedic handicaps, cerebral palsy, learning disabilities, brain injuries, or to whom English is a second language can benefit from class notes *if* the notes are written by a trained, competent notetaker. This "if" is a vitally important one, as we shall see.

A dependable notetaker solves many problems. If the notetaker is a member of the class, though this can present some difficulties, he or she is probably taking notes anyway. Such a student could be trained (see "Who Takes the Notes" below) to work as a notetaker. By using the special paper developed at NTID (see "Materials" at the end of the article) one notetaker can make as many as three or four good copies of the notes at the same time—one for the notetaker, one for the hearing-impaired student, and one for the teacher or tutor if tutoring is done by someone else. (At NTID, the same person functions as both tutor and notetaker, in most cases.) Other copies can be mechanically duplicated if necessary.

Some classes may need only minimal notetaking: a listing of the pages in the book to be read before the next class, specific details about homework, points to be covered on the next exam, when it will be, etc. By working with the classroom teacher and taking into account the specific needs of each student, the notetaker and the manager or teacher of the deaf can decide on the level of notetaking desired. The hearing-impaired student can also be included in this decision so that he or she learns to assess his or her own needs, strengths, and weaknesses.

The first sections of *The Manager's Guide* (Osguthorpe, Wilson, Goldmann, & Panara, 1980) are excellent materials for assessing specific needs of the student and classroom and in giving help in deciding the best way to meet these needs.

WHO TAKES THE NOTES?

The notetaker can be either a volunteer, peer or adult, a paraprofessional, or a professional. Table 1, adapted from the *Guide,* briefly delineates the advantages and disadvantages of each.

On the high school or junior high school level, hearing students may act as notetakers (after appropriate training), reporting to the resource room teacher or teacher of the deaf. These student notetakers can be "paid" with academic credit for independent study or community service activities, much as Explorer Scouts receive extra credits. Upperclassmen taking notes for younger students provide excellent role models.

The essential elements in this situation are the presence of adequate management support, and pre- and inservice training. *The Tutor/Notetaker* (Osguthorpe, 1980) and *The Manager's Guide* are excellent companion volumes for information on training activities. The students should be

TABLE 1
Advantages and Disadvantages of Volunteers, Paraprofessionals, and Professionals as Notetakers

	Advantages	Disadvantages
Volunteers	Availability Low cost	High turnover Require training Need monitoring
Paraprofessionals	Availability Moderate cost Control quality Fair communication skills Dependable	High turnover Require moderate management
Professionals	Control quality Dependable Good communication skills Low turnover Management skills	Availability High cost

academically competent and have previous knowledge of course content of the classes in which they will take notes. It is very difficult to take notes on unfamiliar material, particularly where the vocabulary is new or very technical.

QUALIFICATIONS FOR NOTETAKING

Whether a professional, paraprofessional, or volunteer, the following basic qualifications have been identified as vital for anyone taking notes or providing tutoring for hearing-impaired students:

1. *Knowledge of the subject matter of the class.* One obvious way to have attained this is by previous attendance in the class. A professional may well have credentials as a teacher in the subject or at least in the academic level (elementary, secondary, etc.). NTID's experience is that it is difficult to be both a student in the class, for credit, and function as a notetaker at the same time. The roles can be competitive, so this should be kept in mind and carefully monitored if it is necessary to have a student taking notes in his or her own class.

2. *Above average academic achievement.* If students are functioning as notetakers, a place for recruiting notetakers is the local National Honor Society chapter or other organizations reflecting or recognizing academic excellence. Teachers can also be contacted for recommendations of former outstanding students.

3. *Sensitivity to the problems of hearing loss.* Some of this sensitivity is inherent in some individuals, but everyone dealing with academic support services to the hearing impaired should have a good orientation to hearing loss and problems engendered by the loss. Empathy, not sympathy, is the key. A good understanding of why hearing-impaired students exhibit the social and academic behavior they do, the language level of the students, specific learning problems, etc., all are necessary to prepare an appropriate set of notes or to provide information to the classroom teacher on occasion. An individualized approach is necessary to tailor the notes to the specific needs of the students.

4. TEACHING THE HEARING IMPAIRED CHILD

4. *Self-confidence in dealing with classroom teachers.* It is normal and natural for teachers to be hesitant about having hearing-impaired students, or other handicapped students, in class. These students present problems the teacher may not be trained to handle and the teacher may not have had any previous experience teaching or interacting with handicapped students. The notetaker can be a real help to the teacher by alleviating such fears, providing basic information, and acting as a liaison to others in the school or elsewhere who can be of support to the teacher.

5. *Willingness to accept criticism or apparent ill will.* It is also normal and natural for anyone working in a support service function to be criticized—sometimes fairly, sometimes unfairly—and a tutor or notetaker must be prepared to know the difference and to react appropriately. It has been NTID's experience that many times apparent ill will or criticism are symptoms of real fear on the part of the teacher of hearing-impaired students, and the notetaker has been able to calm these fears and be of support to the teacher. An attitude of helpfulness and openness is crucial.

6. *Willingness to accept direction or management.* A notetaker must be able both to work independently in the classroom, dealing with the students and teachers, and at the same time accept guidance and supervision from others who may be more knowledgeable or have more authority. This also implies the necessity for real communication skills, to keep the supervisor informed of day to day happenings, particularly if a potential problem exists.

MANAGEMENT

Consistent, regular management of any notetaking or tutoring service providers can be the key to the success of the program. This management can be done by any one of a variety of persons in the school environment. Some possibilities include the classroom teacher, the resource room teacher, the teacher of the deaf, the speech pathologist, the educational audiologist, the interpreter (if the interpreter also has credentials in education), or someone within the school administration. The manager should be familiar with the techniques, functions, and mechanics of notetaking, and the principles of tutoring, as well as be knowledgeable about the total school environment. The manager should be sensitive to the organization and to the needs of various persons within it.

Ideally, the manager should have good basic background, training, and experience in the educational problems of deafness, and some practicum experience as a *provider* of and training in the tutoring or notetaking services. It is difficult to evaluate a notetaker's work without the evaluator's having experience in providing the service. The manager will also be responsible for recruiting and training the tutor or notetaker. Information on these procedures is included in *The Manager's Guide* (Osguthorpe, et al., 1980). Although the manuals and materials were based on research done on the college level, experience has shown that the basic principles hold true on any educational level.

The manager should keep in close contact with the tutors/notetakers and with the teacher in whose class they are working. Initially, the manager should make sure that everyone involved in the process—the teacher, the tutor/notetaker, and the hearing-impaired student—has, in writing, a clear description of the total program, listing the persons involved and the responsibilities of each. The student and the teacher need an orientation or training session so that each is clear about the process. On the elementary level, or probably through high school, parents should be included in this information sharing.

Clear lines of communication should be established in the beginning, so that appropriate and regular feedback and evaluation of the program can be assured. The manager should bear the primary responsibility for this task. Both the manager and the classroom teacher can share in evaluation of notes and other activities, if this procedure is clarified from the beginning.

SUMMARY

Notetaking and tutoring, particularly notetaking, have been found to be necessary support services for mainstreamed hearing-impaired students. These services can be provided by peers, paraprofessionals, adults, volunteers, or professionals, but the key factors for a successful program are training and management. Notes are useful for teachers, students, and resource personnel and can meet a variety of needs presented by most special needs students.

BIBLIOGRAPHY

Osguthorpe, R.T. *The tutor/notetaker: Providing academic support to mainstreamed deaf students.* Washington DC: Alexander Graham Bell Association for the Deaf, 1980.

Osguthorpe, R.T., Wilson, J.J., Goldmann, W.G., & Panara, J.E. *The manager's guide.* Washington DC: Alexander Graham Bell Association for the Deaf, 1980.

Wilson, J.J. Effective notetaking for hearing-impaired students. *The Volta Review,* 1980, *82*(5), 294-296.

Wilson J.J. A tutor/notetaker program for deaf students that really works. Translated by Heiichi Hamatsu. Tokyo, Japan: *The Journal of the Society of Research on Hearing Impaired Education,* 1980. English reprint available from the author.

Wilson, J.J. *The tutor/notetaker comic book.* Rochester NY: Rochester Institute of Technology, T/N Training Program, 1979.

THERE'S A DEAF CHILD IN MY CLASS

Barry R. Culhane and Richard Curwin

Barry R. Culhane is chairperson of the academic department for general education at the National Technical Institute for the Deaf and a psychology teacher. Richard Curwin, a faculty development specialist at the same institution, has worked with Barry Culhane in presenting workshops about mainstreaming deaf students.

Proponents of mainstreaming make some basic assumptions about the advantages of hearing impaired students being in regular classrooms rather than in special schools. One is that if the hearing impaired student has a chance to interact with the kind of people who will make up the world in which the student will ultimately function, the student's communication skills will be increased, and the basic skills in reading, math and other school subjects will be maintained at a higher level. They further assume that the social skills of hearing impaired students will develop in a way similar to those of hearing students.

There are opponents to mainstreaming, however, who disagree with the assumption that integrating disabled and nondisabled students in the same

classroom has these benefits. Although these educators agree that disabled children should receive the best educational experience possible, they believe that mainstreaming is not the solution because disabled students should have special attention geared to their individual needs. Regular classrooms and teachers, the argument goes, are just not equipped to meet these needs. There is, in addition, a great fear that the disabled student will be misunderstood and possibly ridiculed by the other students. Also, hearing impaired students attain different levels of language development depending upon their age at the onset of hearing loss, the degree of the loss, whether or not the child has deaf parents, the child's communication training and how early the deafness was discovered. Severely inhibited language development can create special problems because one of the major criteria for success in most American classrooms is written or oral fluency in English.

Regardless of Your Beliefs, Prepare for the Situation

Regardless of your beliefs about the pros and cons of mainstreaming hearing impaired students, you might eventually find yourself proclaiming, "There's a deaf child in my class!" The Education for All Handicapped Chil-

dren Act of 1975 (PL 94-142) mandates that all handicapped children have an opportunity to receive free and appropriate educations in the least restrictive environment. The law also provides for due-process safeguards for handicapped individuals and their parents by insisting that states receiving federal aid implement guidelines that guarantee a maximally effective Individual Educational Plan for each handicapped child. We offer the following suggestions for coping with changes that the entry of hearing impaired students will make in your class. In many cases, these suggestions can enhance the education of all students.

1. Do not allow initial awkwardness to develop into lingering, uncomfortable feelings. Acquaint yourself with other hearing impaired individuals before meeting your new students for the first time. Many cities have schools for the deaf that would welcome a visit from an interested teacher. You may meet teachers, many of whom may be hearing impaired themselves, who work with hearing impaired students. Visit their classrooms and interact with their students. A call to your local vocational rehabilitation agency might provide you with another opportunity for meeting hearing impaired individuals. It may even be possible for you to meet with a local deaf club

Reprinted by special permission of LEARNING, The Magazine for Creative Teaching, January 1978. © 1978 by Education Today Company, Inc.

4. TEACHING THE HEARING IMPAIRED CHILD

member who may be willing to accompany you for a visit to a local club. These interactions can help you become familiar with deaf students and adults. Occasionally, one or both parents of a hearing impaired child may be deaf, and these experiences will help you develop positive relationships with both students and parents.

2. Understand that all hearing losses are not the same. They can be mild or profound and involve one or both ears. Different kinds of losses produce different effects on students. Find out the nature of each student's problem and learn the best way to deal with the individual rather than attempt to find general ways of dealing with deafness.

3. Do not assume that deaf students are mute. A large majority of deaf people have no physical problem with their sound-producing mechanisms. But because these individuals cannot monitor their voices, they may sound different with respect to loudness, pitch, tone and discrimination of specific sounds. Many hearing impaired people do not like to use their voices because they lack training or fear embarrassment. Differences in speech and communication modes can create the misconception that deaf persons

---

Encourage the student to ask questions by developing a non-threatening atmosphere in which the hearing impaired student does not feel embarrassed by what she perceives as inappropriate questions.

---

are somehow less intelligent. This, of course, is nonsense—intelligence is distributed normally among deaf students.

4. Do not expect all deaf students to speechread (lipread) well. Not every deaf child learns to be a good speech-reader, and even those who are highly skilled cannot depend on speechreading alone. Good speechreaders can comprehend 25 to 30 percent of the spoken message.

5. Be ready to accept a wide variety of communication skills from deaf students. Those students who come to you from "oral" schools, or schools that stress speech and speechreading, have different skills from those who were trained to use sign language.

6. Do not expect all deaf students to be exceptional readers. And don't think that deaf students will understand a concept by merely reading it. Most deaf children do not read as well as their hearing peers, and just giving a deaf child reading material will not guarantee understanding any more than it will with most children. In fact, deaf youngsters might have difficulty with reading comprehension because of poor vocabulary development and problems with English sentence structure.

7. Reject all the other misconceptions, such as deaf people see better, cannot appreciate music or dance, cannot drive. These give false impressions about deaf students and can limit what might be done to meet their needs and educational requirements.

Some Specific Suggestions

Ideally, before a deaf child enters your classroom, your school system will have provided faculty and administrators with in-service training about the impact of deaf pupils on school programs and the communication processes that will be used in teaching the hearing impaired. In addition, resources for communication training and consultation should be readily available. Finally, the school system should have addressed issues of curriculum modification, adaption of the environment to include visual media as supplements to instruction, and provision of support services including note-taking, tutoring, interpreting and counseling.

This fall, some teachers will find themselves with a hearing impaired child in their classrooms and will need practical suggestions for meeting the challenge of teaching that child. Here are ten:

1. Get the student's attention when you speak. Tapping loudly on a desk or lectern or waving your hand will help. In a group discussion, have the speaker point to the next person to talk. If an interpreter is present, he or she will do this. The main purpose is to ensure that the hearing impaired student knows the visual or auditory source of information. Be aware, however, that continuous visual attention could lead to visual fatigue; allow time for a rest.

2. Using a normal tone of voice, speak clearly at a moderate pace. Exaggerated speech can interfere with lipreading. To facilitate speechreading, look directly at the student as much as possible. Try to maintain eye contact with the student and to avoid moving around the room too quickly.

When you use the chalkboard, wait until you are finished before speaking so that words directed to the board are not lost to the hearing impaired child. Try not to block sight of your lips with a book, pencil or other object when you are speaking.

3. Rephrase a thought or question to make it more understandable to the deaf child. Give test directions, homework assignments, discussion notes and any important instructions *in writing*. You may have to clarify questions and repeat them during fast-moving discussions. If an interpreter is involved, translating may cause a slight time lag that can make it difficult for the hearing impaired student to follow a discussion. If aides are not available for note-taking and tutoring, ask a hearing peer to volunteer. Although the hearing impaired student will need assistance to gain information initially, allow the student to demonstrate independence and creative thinking abilities.

4. Use as many visual aids as possible, including overhead projectors, captioned films, slides, newsprint and the chalkboard. Avoid having the source of information (including yourself) in a poorly lighted area or in an area where bright light is behind it. Pacing around the classroom or changing sources of information rapidly can hinder understanding.

5. Obtain feedback from the student so that you know he understands. Be aware of any vocabulary limitations or difficulties with English idioms. Present new vocabulary in advance. If the student does not seem to understand, repeat or rephrase the information and ask the student to demonstrate his understanding. You may need to slow the pace of communication.

6. Encourage development of communication skills including speech, speechreading, finger spelling and manual communication. Encourage the use of any residual hearing the student may possess. Work with your committee for the handicapped to get needed resources. Encourage the student to ask questions by developing a nonthreatening atmosphere in which the hearing impaired student does not feel embarrassed by what she perceives as inappropriate questions.

7. Seat the student where he will have visual access to the instructor, other students and visual media. Allow the student to change seats to gain this access in all situations.

8. When critical information is presented, be sure the hearing impaired student understands. Be sure someone repeats loudspeaker an-

nouncements, such as early or late bus arrivals. If you know there will be a practice fire alarm, share the information with the hearing impaired student so that he is not thrown into a panic. If critical information is announced or a fire alarm sounds, flicking a light off and on can gain the student's attention.

9. Become knowledgeable about hearing aids. You may be able to replace hearing aid batteries, to reduce certain kinds of noise levels and even to make minor repairs. Be aware of changes in hearing caused by colds, chronic ear infections or other illnesses.

10. Work closely with the support personnel available to you. Provide the interpreter with an outline of the classroom presentation and notify her

If you know there will be a practice fire alarm, share the information with the hearing impaired student so that he is not thrown into a panic.

of any materials requiring special lighting arrangements. Reproductions of charts, graphs and diagrams in the form of hard copies and transparencies can help note-takers, tutors and the hearing impaired students. A profile of the course content, resources and methods of evaluation can help give the student realistic expectations for the class.

These suggestions are merely a start. Your own creative approaches can add to a basic understanding and awareness of the needs of a deaf student as well as diminish the initial apprehension both you and the student may have.

Resource List

• *A Bicentennial Monograph on Hearing Impairment: Trends in the U.S.A.*, edited by R. Frisina. From Alexander Graham Bell Association for the Deaf, Inc., 3417 Volta Pl., N.W., Washington, DC 20007.

• *The Deaf Experience: An Anthology of Literature by and About the Deaf*, edited by T.W. Batson and E. Bergman. From Merriam-Eddy Co., P.O. Box 25, South Waterford, ME 04081. Cost: $7.50.

• *Educating the Deaf* by D.F. Moores. From Houghton Mifflin Co., 1 Beacon St., Boston, MA 02107. Cost: $13.95.

• "An In-Service Program for Integrating Hearing Impaired Children" by L.W. Nober in *The Volta Review* (1975), vol. III, pp. 173–175. From Alexander Graham Bell Association for the Deaf, Inc., 3417 Volta Pl., N.W., Washington, DC 20007.

• *In This Sign* by Joanne Greenberg. From Avon Books, 959 Eighth Ave., New York, NY 10019. Cost: $1.50.

• "Mainstreaming: Issues and a Model Plan" by M. Vernon and H. Prickett in *Audiology and Hearing Education* (1976), vol. II, pp. 5–11. From Audiology and Hearing Education, Inc., 12849 Magnolia Blvd., North Hollywood, CA 91607.

• "Partial Integration of Deaf With Hearing Students: Residential School Perspectives" by W.M. Craig and J.M. Salem in *American Annals of the Deaf* (1975), vol. 120, pp. 28–36. From Convention of American Instructors of the Deaf, Inc., 5034 Wisconsin Ave., N.W., Washington, DC 20016.

• *Sound and Sign: Childhood Deafness and Mental Health* by H.S. Schlesinger and K.P. Meadow. From University of California Press, Berkeley, CA 94720. Cost: $10.00.

• *They Grow in Silence: The Deaf Child and His Family* by E.D. Mindel and M. Vernon. From National Assoc. of the Deaf, 814 Thayer Ave., Silver Spring, MD 20910. Cost: $5.50.

Teaching the Physically Impaired Child

There are so many forms and varied consequences of physical impairments that it is difficult to discuss this area as a singular topic. For example, some forms involve the central nervous system (as in cerebral palsy, epilepsy, spina bifida, and multiple sclerosis). Others take the form of health problems (as in asthma, diabetes, cystic fibrosis, sickle cell anemia, hemophilia, and cancer), musculoskeletal conditions (muscular dystrophy and arthritis), and accidents causing spinal cord injuries. "Integrating the Physically Handicapped Child" describes the various types of impairments and discusses the need for a multidisciplinary approach in educating these children involving physicians, physical and occupational therapists, and teachers. Since so many of these children take medication the guide in the article, "Children on Medication: A Guide for Teachers," provides teachers with information on purposes and types of medication, and alerts them to possible side effects. The authors suggest that teachers work with the medical profession when dealing with children on medication. The problem of epilepsy is addressed specifically in "Is There a Child with Epilepsy in the Classroom?" It offers information about the disease and suggestions for handling seizures in the classroom.

Having a physical impairment does not necessarily result in reduced cognitive ability. If the brain is affected there may be reduced intellectual functioning, speech and language difficulties, and additional physical problems. If there is no brain damage, the intellectual characteristics of physically impaired children will be as varied as in children without physical impairments.

An effective method for integrating handicapped children into the classroom has been facilitated by use of the microcomputer. "Comprehensive Microcomputer Applications for Severely Physically Handicapped Children" discusses the potential uses of microcomputers as teaching tools that break down the barrier of the physical impairment allowing handicapped children to extend their cognitive abilities.

It is often very difficult for nonhandicapped children to accept and understand the physical impairments of their peers. "Learning About Disabilities" discusses the value of setting up a program which will teach students who are not disabled about the special needs of their disabled classmates. The article emphasizes the special problems of the physically impaired child.

Looking Ahead: Challenge Questions

Identify the various forms of physical impairments and describe how each is manifested.

What are the roles of physicians, physical and occupational therapists, and teachers in working with physically impaired children?

What deleterious side effects of medications should teachers look for?

How can microcomputers be put to use by the exceptional child?

How do you acclimate the nonhandicapped child to the special needs of their physically handicapped peers?

What is epilepsy, and how should teachers react to a grand mal seizure?

Unit 5

Integrating the Physically Handicapped Child

Eugene E. Bleck, MD

Eugene E. Bleck, MD, is Professor, Orthopaedic Surgery and Chief, Orthopaedic-Rehabilitation Services, Children's Hospital, Stanford University, Palo Alto, CA 94305.

INTRODUCTION

This paper will serve several purposes: (1) to provide information on the incidence of physically handicapped children (exclusive of the blind and deaf) who are likely to be integrated into schools for normal non-physically impaired children, (2) to describe briefly the major handicapping conditions and their educational implications, (3) to comment on why integration has come about and why it promises to enrich the lives of normal children, (4) to suggest how physicians, physical therapists, and occupational therapists might help to make school programs successful, (5) to comment briefly on financial implications of this program and to suggest ways in which the complexity of the medical management might be simplified, (6) to provide factual knowledge about the handicapped child and his potential to teachers who are already on the firing line to "improve" the academic achievement of the alleged normal child.[1]

DATA BASE

The data from the California Crippled Children's Services, while oriented toward only those requiring such services, is the best available. California, with approximately 21,123,400 persons (1975), is a convenient population model.

Because there is a concern about the "burden" of shifting handicapped children into the regular school program, statistics on the leading handicapping conditions may be helpful. The number of children treated in the special schools by physical and occupational therapists was 8,452 and 7,067 respectively (1974-1975).[1] However, many of these children, especially those with cerebral palsy, were treated by both types of therapists. The in-patient case-load in the special schools in 1978 was 6,213.[3]

In 1974-1975, 1,981 children had cerebral palsy and 1,404 had other forms of paralysis such as muscular dystrophy. Other than spina bifida (222) and juvenile rheumatoid arthritis (244), these are the prevalent types of physically handicapped children that will attend regular school whenever possible. Due to advancements in medicine, the children who were formerly thought to be so physically handicapped that they needed a special school have already been integrated. These are children who have hemophilia, cystic fibrosis, diabetes, congenital heart defects, or orthopedic conditions such as club foot, scoliosis, congenital dislocation of the hip.

In 1974-1975, the estimated number of persons under the age of 21 in California was 7,678,380.[2] If the current handicapped school population is 6,213, the percentage of the potential school population under 21 to be absorbed into the school population is an infinitesimal 0.08%. If every child in a special school were integrated into regular school, the "burden" disappears when the data are considered. We do not appear to be swamped by physically handicapped children; they are a true minority.

Nor are costs exorbitant. The mean expenditure for all Crippled Children's Services cases in 1974-1975 was $3.87 per capita (range of $0.89 to $14.12 depending upon funding in the individual 58 counties). Admittedly, the costs are abnormally low due to the low fee schedules maintained in an era of rampant inflation. Nevertheless, they do indicate the volume of services for children and the expenditure is less than might be presumed. Consequently, additional expenditures in order to up-grade the care of physically handicapped children can be justified.

HANDICAPPING CONDITIONS: EDUCATIONAL IMPLICATIONS
[See Table I]

Cerebral Palsy

This is not a disease, but a term applied to a static (ie, non-progressive) malfunction of the brain that results in spastic paralysis or a motion disorder (athetosis) of the limbs.

In 1977, the majority of children seen (60%) had spastic diplegia — a major involvement of the lower limbs and a very minor involvement of the upper limbs. These children often have associated minor defects, the most frequent of which are crossed eyes (strabismus). Their intelligence is virtually normal, and speech and hearing remain unimpaired. Psychologists and occupational therapists have found a variety of perceptual disorders in many of these children. Remedial methods to overcome these defects have been widely applied, but there is sparse evidence that such methods are superior to compensation for the perceptual problem.

The spastic diplegic child has partly impaired mobility, but the majority walk un-aided. They do fall backward easily; and for this reason, special allowance must be made in physical educational programs. However, these children should not be denied full participation. Most can play basketball, baseball, tennis, and are often good skiers and swimmers. The physical education program should be individualized. The wise program would allow students to choose and concentrate on one or two activities rather than diffuse the effort via a "modified P.E. program" and a doctor's check-list. A knowledgcable physical therapist could be a great help as a consultant for these special sports programs.

Spastic hemiplegia is another type of cerebral palsy and involves only one arm and leg on the same side. If the hemiplegic child has normal intelligence (in contrast to diplegia, many more hemiplegic children have some mental retardation), there is no problem in full participation in learning activities. The involved hand is never more than a helping hand because it usually lacks sufficient sensation. Its use should not be forced.

Total Body Involved Patient

These children have spastic paralysis or involuntary motions of all limbs, trunk, and often the head. Most of these children cannot walk and many lack sitting balance. Their mobility is best provided by manual or powered wheelchairs. Special seating is often indicated in order to stablize the trunk.[7] Frequently, the totally involved child with athetosis has a normal or above-normal intellect. Their speech is apt to be non-existent or unintelligible. Frequently, they cannot write. Compensatory devices, such as special electronically interfaced electric typewriters provide effective written communication. Communication boards in a variety of patterns and symbols are available for making ordinary needs and feelings known.[7] Intensive research is being conducted on synthetic speech devices which are expected to be available in a few years.

These children cannot participate in physical activities, but they can be quite adequate socially due to their interesting personalities and love of people. Social games, such as chess, seem to be the logical choices for out-of-classroom activity.

The Need for Physical and Occupational Therapy

There is a growing concensus that segregation and

TABLE 1*
Children Most Likely in Special Schools in California 1974-75

Paralysis Affecting Trunk, Extremities, Face		3,385
Cerebral Palsy	1981	
Congenital anomalies	501	
Poliomyelitis	354	
Traumatic injury	221	
Other	328	
Impairment of the Central Nervous System		1,199
Seizure disorder	310	
Neoplasms	234	
Spina Bifida	222	
Other diseases of the nervous system	156	
Traumatic injuries (probably head injury - ed.)	134	
Other congenital anomalies	87	
Other	56	
Impairment of the Musculoskeletal System		892
Congenital anomalies	249	
Rheumatoid Arthritis	244	
Traumatic injury	99	
Hereditary neuromuscular disorders	94	
Other diseases of musculoskeletal system	89	
Other arthritis and rheumatism (except rheumatic fever)	33	
Osteomyelitis and other diseases in bone and joints	23	
Other	61	

*Handicapping Conditions by Principal Underlying Cause, State of California Crippled Children's Service, Statistical Report 1971-1975 [13] dehumanization of the physically handicapped, particularly the child with cerebral palsy, begins when the child is "captured for treatment" and then is routed through special centers and schools "forever seeking the chimerical goal of becoming normal enough to be at last integrated into society." [7]

Based upon a few outcome studies with controls, there is doubt about the efficacy of what is called "therapy." [8-11] Surely, "therapy" will not decrease or eliminate spasticity in motion disorders when the locus in the brain is permanently altered.

Infant and pre-school children with cerebral palsy seemed to benefit from organized programs, but in a way that was not directly therapeutic in alleviating the paralysis. [10] The therapist acted as a teacher and trained observer who defined the problem for the parents, encouraged reinforcement of motor development and prepared the way for integration for those children who were intellectually capable. Others needed mental retardation programs, and the very severe physically and mentally handicapped children have been rapidly transferred to community developmental centers with the goal of deinstitutionalization and eventual optimum independence in their home, a foster home, or a small local care facility.

Once the child was walking (and 80% do, depending upon the extent and location of the brain damage [12]) and playing with peers, then "therapy" was unnecessary. Playing with peers, bike riding, and sports *was* the therapy.

In an expanded role, the occupational therapist can be a valuable consultant, particularly for adaptive devices to be used to improve handwriting, typewriting, seating and transfer equipment. Teachers might allay their anxiety about "therapy" and consult the physical and occupational therapist concerning activities for the child.

Muscular Dystrophy

This disease is a steady, irreversible, progressive weakness of all the muscles. It is usually first noted about the age of four, when the child is clumsy and slow in walking. Eventually, children with Duchenne's muscular dystrophy will be in a wheelchair; death occurs in the late teens or early twenties. There is no known treatment. Management programs emphasize mobility provided by powered wheelchairs and living a life of optimum comfort and family participation. Overmedication should be avoided. Regular school is feasible for most, although some children can have a drop in intelligence and the teacher may have to adjust the educational program to this reality. [13]

Speech, although sometimes soft due to weakness of the chest musculature, is unimpaired. There is no problem with hearing or vision. Although their limbs are weak, they can manipulate most hand tools necessary for learning. For some children, an electric typewriter is a boon. For those who are unable to stand or walk even with braces, toileting can be a problem. Usually a urinal is the best solution for boys. Very few girls have muscular dystrophy of the Duchenne's type due to its sex-linked inherited pattern.

Spina Bifida

Spina bifida (meningomyelocele) is a more devastating birth defect. It is a defect in the formation of the spinal cord and overlying bones of the vertebrae. The lower limbs are paralyzed according to the level of spinal cord disruption.

These children need braces for partial walking or wheelchairs for longer distances. To compound their problem, children with spina bifida have bladder paralysis. This means that many boys will need to use a catheter or bag drainage of the urine; the girls will need diapering. The problem in girls can be solved by redirecting the flow of urine from the kidneys to the bladder by diverting the drainage tubes from the kidneys (ureters) to an abdominal opening linked to a piece of small bowel. The urine is then collected in a bag fixed to the abdominal wall opening. Bowel training, so that movements occur before or after school, is feasible in most instances and can be done in the pre-school years.

Hydrocephalus is an enlargement of the fluid compartments (ventricles) of the brain. It is now arrested by shunts before the pressure becomes so great as to compress and damage the brain cells. Shunts are plastic tubes with valves that are surgically placed in the brain ventricle in order to drain the excess fluid into the abdominal cavity (peritoneal shunt) where the fluid is easily absorbed. Children who have hydrocephalus often seem more intelligent than they really are due to their high verbal ability.

Despite their multiple handicaps, children with spina bifida do have some positive aspects: excellent speech, normal hearing and vision, and excellent upper limb use. Consequently, other than participation on the playground, they can do quite well in the regular classroom.

Osteogenesis Imperfecta

Osteogenesis imperfecta is an inherited disease in which all the bones are extremely brittle. Because of multiple fractures, the children have deformed, crooked limbs, a bee-hive chest, and a triangular face. They are often confined to a wheelchair, but some are able to walk short distances with braces and crutches.

To compensate, these little people have charming, out-going personalities, are highly verbal and have almost excess mental energy. They achieve academically and are a joy to the teacher. They have normal hearing, speech and vision. Even though their upper limb bones can be crooked, their hand use is excellent. For this reason they pose no problem in the classroom. As with other children who cannot participate in playground activities, they need social and recreational outlets that do not demand such participation.

Juvenile Rheumatoid Arthritis

Fortunately, juvenile rheumatoid arthritis is not common and the totally disabled child is rather rare. However, all can attend a regular school. They need adaptive equipment for writing, but their speech, hearing and vision are normal so that academic problems are minimal. As with other physically handicapping conditions, individualized playground or recreational programs are necessary. Development of their intellectual and creative talents can be emphasized since their painful stiff joints prevent the ordinary distractions of physical play. Most are self-sufficient in toileting.

Absence of Limbs

No children with absent limbs needed retention in a special school. A boy with three absent limbs who is in a private, highly selective preparatory school was class president in 1977. Children with all four limbs missing can use special wheel devices if insufficient residual limb lengths precludes artificial limbs. Children with absent upper limbs do use their prostheses; but because of the importance of sensory input, most become adept with their toes and feet. They can eat, write and paint with their feet. They may cause some distraction in the classroom initially; but with familiarity, foot activity goes unnoticed by normal children.

Arthrogryposis

Arthrogryposis is a condition of curved, stiff joints involving one or more limbs. These children present no special problems in the classroom and most patients go to regular school. Some can walk and some need wheelchairs. Their hands are often very deformed due to the paralysis and joint stiffness. Even so, they have an amazing use of their hands for almost all necessary activities. Their intelligence is usually quite high, and with unimpaired speech, hearing and vision pose no serious learning problems.

Numerous, even more rare conditions than those already mentioned occur; but with appropriate medical diagnosis, definition of abilities, and goal-orientation, children so affected can cope with a regular school.

REASONS FOR INTEGRATION

Because of society's desire to help, and possibly due to fear engendered by the threat to an intact image, the handicapped child has been segregated early in life into special programs in schools and has remained on the segregation track all of his/her life. As a minority, however, their human desire for community participation is being heeded. Dr. Milani-Comprett of Florence, Italy, felt so strongly about the permanent segregation effects of special schools that all 13 special schools were closed in his community.[14] In San Mateo County, the two special schools were closed in 1978-79. Children have been integrated into the regular high school for at least 10 years.

One other factor in bringing about integration seems to be the changing pattern of the handicapped conditions toward milder forms and more effective treatment. For example, heart surgery has been highly successful in alleviating most congenital heart disorders. Kidney transplantation has permitted children who were born with defective kidneys to live a normal life.

The replacement of the missing factor VIII of the blood in hemophilia has allowed these children to lead almost normal lives. Orthopedic surgery has assisted in overcoming structural deformities in cerebral palsy, and in improving the walking and mobility of children. Orthopedic surgery has made significant advances in the treatment of spinal curvature, club foot, and congenital dislocation of the hip.

Cerebral palsy, as a leading disability, is particularly noteworthy in its changing patterns. Due to the early immunization of the Rh-Negative mother against the Rh-Positive baby she is carrying, the devastating Rh factor baby (erythroblastosis fetalis) has all but disappeared. These babies had severe, total-body-involved cerebral palsy (usually athetosis). Also, obstetrical care has improved enormously, and the number of children born with cerebral palsy due to birth trauma or oxygen deprivation has decreased. Offsetting this progress has been an increasing survivorship of premature infants, 15-40% of whom have had some neurological involvement. Children who have such involvement usually have the milder form of cerebral palsy, eg, spastic diplegia, allowing participation in regular school.

A second factor has been the 30-year experience of organized "therapy programs" in special schools which attempted to remediate permanent defects, teaching us that the promise of various therapeutic approaches has not been fulfilled. Wise and experienced therapists and physicians know this cannot be done. What can be done is alleviation and improvement through surgery, short term physical rehabilitation methods, orthotics, and rehabilitation engineering services.[7] All of these modalities are useful in helping the child cope with and participate in the society of which education is a part.

What can handicapped children do for us and our children? One answer might be that they make us grateful for our own intact bodies. Another is that handicapped persons give us a chance to be truly altruistic — to think of service to others as part of life, and to look at the person behind the handicap. These children are daily reminders that might at least dampen the prevalent "self-involvement" and self-concern evidenced by a large number of popular books.

THE ROLE OF MEDICINE

Although Public Law 94-142 makes little or no provision for medical input, physicians should be consulted to help educators in this task of integration. Careful diagnosis and definition of the child will always be necessary in order to avoid mislabeling and misdirection. Long-term, intensive treatment, such as surgery followed by physical rehabilitation, may be needed by some of the children in the regular school; during such treatment provision will have to be made for short periods of home instruction when the child cannot attend school, or for adequate transportation from the home to the school and back.

The problem with medical services for the handicapped child has been primarily attitudinal as reflected by the financial support for their care. This resulted in handicapped children receiving a disproportionate share of available funds. Most states have Crippled Children's Services to support the care of the handicapped child, but financing of such services has been based upon the absorption of the deficits incurred by low payment schedules to professional providers and institutions. State Crippled Children's programs have been, for the most part, conceived of as a charity. The deficits have been made up in the private sector by the professionals. The case can be made that the patient who has been able to pay for medical care has been charged higher and higher rates in order to finance the deficits incurred in making state programs work.

Overlapping and competing bureaucracies lead to frustration due to delay in determining which agency is indeed responsible. In California, it is not unusual to have several agencies concerned about a particular child — for example, Crippled Children's Services, Medicaid, Regional Centers, and the State Department of Rehabilitation. Some of the children have become eligible for Medicare, adding further complexity.

Because handicapped children have been gradually moving out of institutions and into the community, their needs have become more visible and their demands justifiably greater. However, when confronted with a variety of bureaucracies all claiming to be responsible for planning the best program for a child, the resultant jurisdictional disputes and varieties of perceptions of proper treatment compound and delay prompt access to and delivery of needed services.

In California in the past five years, considerable gains in obtaining funds for communication equipment, mobility devices, and seating have been made.[7] It seems likely that children born with these severe and permanent handicapping conditions really belong in the category of a medical catastrophe and, as such, would be eligible for a catastrophic insurance plan. This, in fact, has been the evolving role of the Crippled Children's Services in California, although its funding is inadequate to this task.

The dilemma of programming for each individual child in a variety of social, cultural and geographic conditions might be resolved if Berkowitz's suggestion would be followed. This experiment would allow handicapped persons the exercise of free choice in choosing the services needed. "It might be easier to define services eligible for voucher payments than to determine who shall be eligible for existing programs." [16]

CONCLUSIONS

The problems of integrating many of the handicapped children into the regular school are largely anticipated — not experienced. Follow-up of integrated handicapped children demonstrates clearly that this is a wise and humane policy. By always keeping the perspective on optimum independence by the mechanism of individual choice and parallel responsibility, the program can be successful and no doubt will become cost-effective because these integrated programs suggested would lead to less dependency on long-term remedial treatment programs and more independence with concomitant responsibility of the handicapped for their own welfare.

No attempt had been made to address the programs and needs of the severely mentally and physically handicapped who are now being deinstitutionalized and are coming into our communities via the developmental centers. These children, too, will need our care and concern in order that they might become optimumly independent and remain as human beings within our communities rather than be hidden away in state institutions.

REFERENCES

1. Quest for better schools. *U.S. News and World Report* Sept 11, 1978.
2. California Department of Health, Crippled Children's Services Statistical Report, 1971-1975 Fiscal Years, 1976.
3. California Department of Health, Center for Health Statistics June 2, 1978.
4. Bell AE, Abrahanson DC, McRae KN: Reading retardation: a 12-year prospective study. *J Pediatr* 91:363-70, 1970.
5. Korsch BM: The answer is no. *Pediatrics* 58:7-9, 1976.
6. Yule W: Issues and problems in remedial education. *Dev Med Child Neurol* 18:674-65, 1976.
7. Bleck EE: Severe orthopedic disability in childhood: solutions provided by rehabilitation engineering. *Orthop Clin North Am* 9:509-28, 1978.
8. Paine RS: On the treatment of cerebral palsy — the outcome of 177 patients. *Pediatrics* 20:605, 1962.
9. Pless BI: On doubt in and certainly. *Pediatrics* 58:7-9, 1976.
10. Scherzer AK, Mike V, Ilson J: Physical therapy as a determinant of change in the cerebral palsied infant. *Pediatrics* 58:47-51, 1976.
11. Wright T, Nicholsen J: Physiotherapy for the spastic child, an evaluation. *Dev Med Child Neurol* 15:146-63, 1971.
12. Bleck EE: Locomotor prognosis in cerebral palsy. *Dev Med Child Neuro* 17:18-25, 1975.
13. Bleck EE, Nagel DA: *Physically Handicapped Children: A Medical Atlas for Teachers*. New York, Grune and Stratton, 1975.
14. Bleck EE: Integrating the care of multiple handicapped children. *Dev Med Child Neuro* 20:10-13, 1978.
15. Fairlie H: *The Seven Deadly Sins Today*. New York, New Republic Books, 1978.
16. Berkowitz M: In Science and Technology in Service of the Physically Handicapped, Vol. II National Research Council, Washington, D.C., 1976.

Children On Medication: A Guide for Teachers

CAROLYN N. LINDSEY,
SUSAN R. LEIBOLD, R.N.,
FRANCES T. LADD, R.N.,
and RALPH OWNBY, Jr., M.D.

Ms. Lindsey is an educational consultant with the Richmond Hospital Education Program, administered under the Virginia State Department of Education, Division of Special Education. She serves the spina bifida and cerebral palsy out-patient clinics located at Crippled Children's Hospital in Richmond, Va. Ms. Lindsey is a member of the Council for Exceptional Children and the Spina Bifida Association of America. She is the author of two booklets entitled Early Learning: PreSchool Activities for the Physically Handicapped Child *and* An Educator's Guide to Spina Bifida.

Ms. Leibold is a pediatric clinic nurse specialist at the Medical College of Virginia, Virginia Commonwealth University. She has also served as a public health nurse and on the staff of the Crippled Children's Hospital in Richmond.

Ms. Ladd is nursing supervisor at Crippled Children's Hospital in Richmond, Va. She is currently serving as vice president of the Richmond Orthopedic Nurse's Association.

Dr. Ownby is the medical director of Crippled Children's Hospital in Richmond. He is the former director of the Consultation and Evaluation Clinic, Virginia Commonwealth University, and the Virginia State Department of Health. Dr. Ownby is also professor in the Department of Pediatrics at the Medical College of Virginia, Virginia Commonwealth University.

A S CHILDREN with physical and emotional disabilities are included in regular classrooms in increasing numbers, teachers and other professionals are facing new problems. Many of these children are on medication, and the teacher must plan an effective program that allows for the effects of the medication, as well as for problems related to the disability.

Teachers who have had years of undergraduate or graduate training in child development, learning behaviors, and in particular subject areas now find they require additional information. What is reasonable to expect from students who are receiving medication?

For example, drugs used for several types of medical problems cause hyperactivity as an undesirable side effect. Children who are taking a theophylline preparation may be restless, unable to concentrate for their usual length of time, and may disturb classmates with an inability to "settle down." Their academic work may suffer also. A concerned but uninformed teacher may look to other causes for the changed behavior. The teacher may feel obligated to exert pressure for better performance and may provide more structure in the classroom. Students may be punished by withholding such classroom privileges as a field trip or membership in a special club; they may even be sent to the counselor or school social worker. Thus, children might not only fail to be helped, but may become embarrassed, and possibly suffer emotional damage.

Other side effects may lead the teacher to believe that the child on medication is ill when he or she is not. Some drugs, especially if the dosage needs correcting, can cause vomiting or loss of appetite. There are drugs that cause such lethargy and fatigue as to interfere with the amount of learning which can take place. The youngsters may not realize that their changed behavior is due to medication; they may feel that they are indeed sick, and worry or think about not exerting enough effort and, therefore, feel guilty.

What are the answers to these questions? Obviously, it is information that should be available to the teacher, coach, therapist, or other professionals working with the child. Sometimes parents will share their information, but sometimes they are unaware of the side effects possible. They may not know that the child is behaving any differently.

The senior author is an educational consultant, working as liaison between medical and educational personnel, with a background in both regular and hospital teaching. As a former classroom instructor teaching children with a number of disabilities, it was difficult not to be aware of the many problems encountered and the often unsure ground on which the teacher walked. As an educational consultant with resources available, it was difficult not to be aware of the many times appar-

Reprinted with permission from REHABILITATION LITERATURE, May/June 1980. Published by National Easter Seal Society, 2023 W. Ogden Avenue, Chicago, IL 60612.

ently insurmountable problems could be solved with information and advice.

An informed teacher can not only avoid misunderstandings such as those mentioned earlier, but can serve as a resource for the health care team, even as they are a resource. The teacher is with the child for a large portion of the child's waking hours, and has an opportunity to observe behavior that may not be seen by parents. The child's total behavior in the learning situation is a primary job. When teachers are aware of the nature of the medication their students are taking, they are prepared as to what to expect. This is where the instructor can most effectively assist the child and can, with the parents' consent, work with them and the therapeutic team in eliminating any unnecessary related problems.

A word of caution concerning use of the accompanying chart is in order here. The chart is designed to assist in understanding the implications of the most commonly utilized medications for school children. The information is in no way intended to be comprehensive, and the teacher or other worker will want to work closely with the parents and health services. While some side effects are to be expected, and present only

Drug	Reason For Use	Problem or Condition	Side Effects That Might Be Noticed by Teachers
Aspirin Ascriptin Bufferin Ecotrin	control joint inflammation	juvenile rheumatoid arthritis	nausea, vomiting, rapid breathing, hearing problems, drowsiness. Should be taken with either milk or some kind of snack
Chemotherapy agents: Vincristin Cytoxan L-asperiginase Methotrexate Adriamycin actinomycin	attacks rapidly growing cancer cells	leukemia solid tumors	hair loss, nausea, vomiting, weight loss, anemia, mouth ulcers
Corticosteroid drugs: (prednisone, cortisone, etc.)	suppress inflammation in diseases of connective tissue - useful in some forms of allergy, kidney diseases, and leukemia	asthma leukemia nephrosis and nephritis childhood arthritis and related diseases	moon-shaped face, increased appetite, euphoria, spontaneous fractures, menstrual irregularities, insomnia, psychic disturbances, sweating, growth retardation, visual disturbances
Cotazym Pancrease	provides enzymes for digestion of food - must be taken with every meal or snack	cystic fibrosis	indigestion
Dantrium	reduces muscle spasticity	cerebral palsy	drowsiness, dizziness, weakness, general malaise and fatigue
digitalis (Lanoxin Digoxin)	increase effectiveness of heart's pumping action	heart conditions (congenital heart disease, rheumatic heart disease)	nausea, vomiting, and slow heart rate
Factor VIII (Factorate, Humafac)	provides missing factor to promote blood clotting and prevention of bleeding	hemophilia	must be given intravenously
insulin	controls blood sugar level	diabetes	too much insulin - not enough food a. change in personality (inappropriate laughing or crying) b. slight to marked confusion c. dizziness, shakiness, "butterflies in stomach" d. headaches e. sleepiness f. sudden hunger g. coma and convulsions can result if not recognized and treated with sugar or orange juice.

(continued on next page)

(continued from preceding page)

Drug	Reason For Use	Problem or Condition	Side Effects That Might Be Noticed by Teachers
Lasix	reduces fluid load of heart; lowers blood pressure, reduces edema	hypertension, congestive heart failure, renal disease	dermatitis, nausea, vomiting, diarrhea, weakness, fatigue, perspiration, muscle cramps, feeling of urinary urgency, dehydration
Motrin	same as aspirin	juvenile rheumatoid arthritis	nausea, epigastric pain, heartburn, diarrhea, indigestion
Phenobarbital and Dilantin	anti-convulsive, seizure control	seizure disorders	drowsiness, ataxia, dizziness, headaches, transient nervousness, nausea, and vomiting
Ritalin Dexedrine	promotes a calming effect and better attention span in children	hyperactivity (minimal brain dysfunction)	nervousness, insomnia, loss of appetite, dizziness, headache, weight loss
Tegretol	anti-convulsive, better seizure control, can be used with dilantin and phenobarbital or alone	seizures—generalized and partial (psychomotor and temporal lobe seizures)	drowsiness, dizziness, unsteadiness, urinary frequency, dry mouth, blurred vision
theophylline preparation: Theo-Dur Tedral Quibron	relaxes bronchial walls to reduce wheezing	asthma	restlessness, nausea, vomiting, headache, dizziness, insomnia, hyperactivity. Should be taken with food
Tofranil	promotes better bladder control	childhood enuresis	nervousness, sleep disorders, tiredness, anxiety, emotional instability, fainting
Tolectin	same as aspirin	juvenile rheumatoid arthritis	epigastric or abdominal pain or discomfort, vomiting
Zarontin	anti-convulsive, prevents lapses of consciousness	seizures - "petit mal"	loss of appetite, nausea, vomiting, drowsiness, headaches, dizziness, lethargy, fatigue, ataxia, inability to concentrate

minor problems, others are serious, and may be alleviated through use of additional drugs. Teachers may wish to augment the information contained in the chart with additional materials. They may find it useful as a format for asking the right questions of the child, the parents, or the physician. They should be able to better understand the behavior observed in their students.

The teacher or other professional can thus be in a better position to report some of the observable results of medication to others working with the child. In addition, he or she will be able to more effectively plan and carry through a positive educational experience.

A student uses the **Computer King Keyboard** to operate an **Apple II Plus** computer. **Large 1¼″ diameter keys are slightly recessed.** (*Photograph provided courtesy of Technical Aids & Systems for the Handicapped, Inc.*)

Comprehensive Microcomputer Applications for Severely Physically Handicapped Children

G. Evan Rushakoff
Linda J. Lombardino

G. Evan Rushakoff *is a member of the faculty in the Department of Speech at New Mexico State University, Las Cruces. His clinical research and teaching have focused on the use of microcomputers for the nonvocal, severely handicapped, and the clinical and administrative applications of microcomputers for the speech-language clinician and audiologist.*

Linda J. Lombardino *is on the faculty in the Department of Speech at the University of Florida. She has published in the area of language programming with developmentally delayed children. She teaches graduate courses in language development; assessment and intervention; parent-child interactions; and nonvocal communication.*

■ Current microcomputer technology will continue to offer increasing benefits for many exceptional populations. Microcomputers have been successfully integrated into special education programs for mentally retarded, autistic, and physically handicapped children (Carman & Kosberg, 1982; Romanczyk, 1982; Sandals, 1979; Thorkildsen, Bickel, & Williams, 1979). Children who are severely physically impaired with uncompromised or minimally compromised intellectual abilities serve to gain significantly from the myriad of benefits that the microcomputer affords. Answers to the following questions will serve to help educators better understand the potential comprehensive uses of microcomputers with severely physically handicapped children.

What are the basic component parts of the microcomputer system?

A basic system for a physically impaired child should include a microcomputer (64K RAM), disk drive, and a monitor (or TV). If the child will be using the machine for writing, a printer is necessary. If the system is to be used as a speech-output communication aid, a speech synthesizer is needed.

In our clinical programs, we have used the Apple II (now Apple IIe) for three reasons. First, the Apple system can interface with most standard televisions when an RF modulator is used to convert the television into a monitor. Second, to date, it appears that the majority of the educational software and programs developed specifically for the physically handicapped are written for the Apple systems. And finally, most devices that allow severely motorically impaired children to control a microcomputer are developed for the Apple.

Can microcomputers be adapted for children who are unable to use a standard keyboard?

While some physically impaired children will be able to use the standard keyboard, others will require keyboard adaptations or modifications. There are five alternatives to standard keyboard use: (a) software-based single and multiple switch control; (b) firmware single and multiple switch control; (c) hardware single switch access; (d) keyguard for the standard Apple keyboard; and (e) expanded keyboards.

Single switches are available for children whose physical limitations preclude them from using the standard keyboard. There are three methods available for implementing single switch operations. The first method is to modify the keyboard entry program with a scanning subroutine. The Florida Scanner (Rushakoff & Steinberg, 1982) and the Special Inputs Disk (Schwejda, 1982) are examples of software which transform some keyboard entry programs into single switch programs. In these programs, all letter or number characters are arranged horizontally on the bottom of the screen. A pointer or marker performs a step-scan process from left to right across the characters until the switch is activated to indicate a desired entry.

The second and more versatile method is to use the Adaptive Firmware Card which, when plugged into the Apple, allows single and multiple switch control of all Apple programs. There are also hardware devices such as the Tetra-Scan II, Zygo 100, Omni, and Express, which will allow single and multiple switch control when hooked to the Apple.

Individuals who are unable to use the keyboard because of erratic motor movements may still have access to all Apple keyboard entry programs. A keyguard will often be sufficient in deterring extraneous keyboard entries. Finally there are expanded keyboards available which would be useful for those children for whom the keyguard is insufficient but for whom a larger keyboard is functional.

What are some of the commonly used applications of the microcomputer for physically handicapped children?

Communication

The microcomputer can be used as an efficient, versatile, and flexible speech output communication aid for nonvocal, severely physically handicapped children. The microcomputer allows for three communication output modes: monitor display, printed material, and synthesized speech.

The specific software chosen determines the degree to which the microcomputer will serve the child's communication needs. While only limited software are presently available, the next few years should witness an increase in the availability of programs which convert the microcomputer into a communication aid. The most comprehensive source of information on communication software is the Trace Center International Software/Hardware Registry (Vanderheiden & Walstead, 1982).

TALK II (Rushakoff, Condon, & Lee, 1982) is an example of a versatile and flexible communication microcomputer program. When an Echo II speech synthesizer is interfaced with the Apple microcomputer, this program automatically converts the microcomputer into a speech-output communication system. TALK II allows for a totally customized vocabulary from 1 to 800 letters, words, and phrases all of which can be accessed from 1–2 key presses. This strategy helps increase message efficiency (the number of key presses needed to produce a message). All of the vocabulary can be deleted, added, and moved around at any time, thus rendering this system readily adaptable to the user's immediate and future communication needs. TALK II can accommodate up to 200 sentences allowing the child to speak any message up to 100 words long with a single key press. The single-key sentence feature greatly increases the speed of spoken conversation. As with the vocabulary, these sentences can be changed at any time. The following are some single-key sentences that have been used in children's communication programs.

"May I have some help please?"
"Hang on . . . it will take me a minute to respond to that."
"I heard this great joke . . . care to hear it?"

5. TEACHING THE PHYSICALLY IMPAIRED CHILD

With TALK II, the message created by the user may be displayed on the monitor, spoken, and printed. Messages of any length (such as stories or jokes) can be stored for use at a later time. Once stored, messages can be spoken or printed with one or two key presses.

Academics

The microcomputer offers several potential benefits for physically impaired children who are unable to meet academic objectives without direct teacher assistance. Once the student can activate the microcomputer via the keyboard or single switch device, computer assisted instruction can provide a mechanism for independent and active learning. Several software packages currently available for academic subjects (Educational Software Directory, 1981) are interactive in nature; that is, they provide the stimulus, prompting, feedback, and reinforcement necessary for independent learning of academic skills. Further, many educational programs possess the capability to maintain ongoing data for immediate and/or future monitoring of the student's work.

Computer assisted instruction should serve to increase the speed of learning when physical rather than cognitive limitations are deterring the student from achieving a normal rate of academic progress. In addition to facilitating student learning directly, computer assisted instruction will allow classroom personnel more time to work with students whose special needs require frequent teacher assistance.

Perhaps most importantly, the microcomputer may function to improve the self-concept of physically impaired students who have not developed a strong sense of autonomy because of their constant dependence on others for even the most basic of needs. In discussing the psychosocial benefits of computer training, Goldenberg (1979) stated that

> Because it [the computer] enables these special children to affect and control their world, and because it is a tool with which they can become proficient and show their creativity, it offers them a powerful chance to develop their own feelings of self-worth and to see themselves as learners and doers. (p. 25)

Writing

Children who use either the keyboard or a single switch device can operate microcomputer word processing programs. Some programs such as the Bank Street Writer are especially appropriate for children. Word processing allows the student to produce written material, make major text changes with relative ease, and store and print that material. These basic functions provide the student with a mechanism for correcting written material before printing a final copy and storing material for continued work at a later time. Word processing programs can reduce greatly the amount of time necessary to complete a writing task.

Creative Arts

In the area of creative arts, mild and moderately physically involved children may be able to use some percussion-like instruments along with recorded music, while severely physically impaired children are often limited to passive participation in music appreciation, i.e., listening. Microcomputers and appropriate music software allow these children to bypass their motor disabilities and generate their own musical creations. They can write music one note at a time, save, edit, and play it through the microcomputer system. For very young children, participation in music might entail merely playing a note-by-note version of "Mary Had a Little Lamb." However, older children can use "music composer" software for creating, editing, and playing more complex music compositions.

In the area of art, many physically impaired children are limited to projects that require direct assistance from the teacher or to activities which require only limited fine motor coordination, such as fingerpainting. Art creation software allows for the production of color artwork and animation. As with music software, the artwork can be saved and changed at a later time.

Recreation

Microcomputers provide severely physically impaired children, including single switch users, access to thousands of recreational programs. In general the most appropriate types of programs are games of strategy, memory, and logic. Several card games such as solitaire, blackjack, and bridge are available and can be played alone or with friends. Board games that are available for two or more players include chess, checkers, cribbage, monopoly, and scrabble.

Generally, games that require fine motor movements and timed responses should be avoided. Most "arcade" games fall into this category and invariably require the use of game paddles. There are a few instances in which such games can be modified to reduce the speed of response; however, typically they are unadaptable for use with severely physically impaired children. Vanloves Software Directory (1983) is one resource available for recreational software.

Vocational

Microcomputer training holds the potential to open up a vast number and variety of employment opportunities for the physically impaired population. The increasing reliance of various sectors of industry on microcomputer technology is spawning numerous career options for physically impaired adolescents and adults who are skilled in the use of computer operations. In reference to the appropriateness of current employment opportunities for the physically impaired, Goldenberg (1979) noted that "jobs exist that depend more on the manipulation of information than on the manipulation of things" (p. 13).

How is the microcomputer currently being used with young severely physically impaired children?

The Speech and Hearing Clinic at the University of Florida has prescribed microcomputer systems for several children between the ages of 5 and 8 years. The rationale varied according to individual needs. Some children required the microcomputer for use as an efficient speech output communication aid. Others used the system primarily for writing and computer assisted instruction. All children used the system for recreational purposes. Two of the children with whom we have worked are described below. These examples were chosen to highlight the diverse communication, academic, and personal needs of this population.

Robbie is a six-year-old non-ambulatory male with cerebral palsy characterized by severe spasticity in all limbs. He is functioning at an intellectual level that is commensurate with his chronological age and is currently attending a Montessori elementary school program. After an evaluation of Robbie's cognitive and motor abilities and a discussion with his family regarding their potential plans for his future educational and vocational needs, we determined that a microcomputer system would be the most appropriate aid for Robbie because of its potential to (a) provide him with a vehicle for independent learning; (b) help improve his writing efficiency; (c) permit his active participation in art and music activities; and (d) begin to prepare him for future career activities.

Within a period of less than a month (eight therapy sessions), Robbie learned to operate independently many academic and leisure programs on his microcomputer. Because he is still learning to read, he often requires assistance with some of the more complex reading programs; however, he has no difficulty operating programs where minimal reading is required. He has learned to input information reliably into the microcomputer by using keyboard control with a single finger.

After minimal training at the clinic, Robbie's parents have assumed primary responsibility for training him to use numerous programs. His parents have indicated that their major difficulty in using the system is finding quality academic and recreational software for his age level. Eventually Robbie's system will be integrated into his classroom activities.

Jasmine is an eight-year-old female with cerebral palsy and severe mixed dysarthria which involves neuromuscular movements necessary for speech production. She is ambulatory and is functioning at an intellectual level that is nearly commensurate with her chronological age. She attends a public school program for the physically impaired.

When first seen at the clinic, Jasmine communicated primarily through vocalizations and unintelligible single-word sign productions. She quickly learned to communicate through a large repertoire of signs and soon combined them into simple telegraphic sentences. However, neither her teacher nor her fellow classmates were able to understand signs, rendering her communication minimally functional outside the home environment. Jasmine's mother and school speech-language clinician agreed that a speech output communication aid would be the most efficient and effective communication mode for classroom use. They also agreed that the other applications of the microcomputer, including writing and computer assisted instruction, would serve to facilitate Jasmine's academic and personal-social development.

Jasmine was funded through Cerebral Palsy Services, Florida Department of Health and Rehabilitative Services for an Apple II microcomputer (48K) with a disk drive, monitor, and speech synthesizer. Within a period of less than two months Jasmine was able to use the microcomputer to construct and speak simple sentences. She was also beginning to use "stock" sentences in appropriate social situations such as *"How are you today?"* and *"Goodbye, it was nice talking to you."* This training is now being accomplished in her classroom where she must contend with more than a dozen communication partners. Jasmine's school speech-language clinician is working with her classroom teacher to integrate the communication system into Jasmine's everyday academic activities.

What are some factors that educators should consider before recommending the microcomputer as an aid for physically impaired children?

A number of performance and environmental factors need to be considered when prescribing a microcomputer as a comprehensive living aid for the physically impaired child. In some cases some degree of reading ability may be necessary for the child to benefit from many of the communication, academic, writing, and leisure activities described above. The level of reading ability varies from program to program. However, some preacademic and communication programs are available which can be used by the nonreader.

An environmental support system is critical if the microcomputer system is to be successfully integrated into the child's daily activities. All persons (family members, teachers, speech-language clinicians, physical therapists, and occupational therapists) who are responsible for the child's academic, social, physical, and communication growth and development should be involved in determining the appropriateness of the microcomputer system as a comprehensive living aid for the child. In addition, the child's primary caregivers need to agree upon goals for the child's immediate and future use of the microcomputer system.

In choosing a system it is important to remember that the microcomputer should be considered a stationary aid. Although it can be moved quite easily from home to school, it does require an electrical outlet. Although a number of portable, battery operated microcomputers have been developed recently they do not have the software needed to accomplish many of the applications described here.

The clinical applications of the microcomputer are far reaching for physically handicapped children who have the potential to achieve academic and non-academic accomplishments when provided with a mode of performance that bypasses their physical limitations. Prescriptions for microcomputer systems require careful consideration of performance and environmental factors to ensure that the individual and comprehensive needs of these children are met.

REFERENCES

Carman, G. O., & Kosberg, B. Educational technology research: Computer technology and the education of emotionally handicapped children. *Educational Technology*, 1982, 22(2).

Educational software directory: Apple II Ed. Austin TX: Sterling Swift, 1981.

Goldenberg, E. P. *Special technology for special children.* Baltimore: University Park Press, 1979.

Romanczyk, R. G. The impact of microcomputers on programming for the autistic child. Paper presented at the annual meeting of The Council for Exceptional Children, Houston, 1982.

Rushakoff, G. E., Condon, J., & Lee, R. TALK II: A speech-output, customized vocabulary microcomputer program. In Vanderheiden & Walstead (Eds.), *Trace Center International Software/Hardware Registry*, 1982.

Rushakoff, G. E., & Steinberg, D. Florida Scanner: Single switch software conversion. In Vanderheiden & Walstead (Eds.), *Trace Center International Software/Hardware Registry*, 1982.

Sandals, L. H. Computer assisted applications for learning with special needs children. Paper presented at the meeting of the American Educational Research Association, San Francisco, 1979.

Schwejda, P. Special inputs disk. In Vanderheiden & Walstead (Eds.), *Trace Center International Software/Hardware Registry*, 1982.

Thorkildsen, R., Bickel, W., & Williams, J. A. Microcomputer/videodisc CAI system for the moderately mentally retarded. *Journal of Special Education Technology*, 1979, 2(3).

Vanderheiden, G., & Walstead, L. (Eds.). *Trace Center International Software/Hardware Registry.* Madison: University of Wisconsin, Trace Center, 1982.

Vanloves 1983 Apple II/III Software Directory, Vol. II. Overland Park KS: Advanced Technology, 1983.

HARDWARE RESOURCES

(*Note:* You will need to specify whether you require equipment for the Apple II Plus or the Apple IIe.)

Adaptive Firmware Card
Adaptive Peripherals
4529 Bagley Ave. N.
Seattle WA 90103

Express III
Apple Keyguard
Prentke-Romich Company
R.D. 2, Box 191
Shreve OH 44676

King Keyboard (expanded keyboard)
Apple Keyguard
Technical Aids and Systems for the Handicapped
2075 Bayview Ave.
Toronto, Ontario
M4N 3M5, Canada

Omni
Communications Research Corp.
1720–130th Ave. N.E.
Bellevue WA 98005

Expanded Keyboard
Cacti Computer Services
130 9th St. S.W.,
Portage la Prairie, Manitoba
R1N 2N4, Canada

Tetra-Scan II
Zygo 100
Zygo Industries
P.O. Box 1008
Portland OR 97207

Learning About Disabilities

Rita Ann Popp

■ It is not uncommon for children in regular education classes to wonder what is going on behind those closed doors where children with special needs are being served. Rarely, if ever, do they see these children engaged in learning, nor do they receive experiences to help them understand and accept those who need special help. As a preschool special education teacher in an elementary school, I found that I could have a tremendous impact on children in regular education classes by helping them get to know our students and participate in activities designed to increase awareness of disabilities.

SETTING UP THE PROGRAM

At the beginning of the school year, each regular education teacher was asked to complete a questionnaire to determine whether they wanted their students to learn more about disabilities and disabled persons. Questionnaire results indicated that all the teachers were interested in participating in the proposed program.

A variety of learning experiences were provided to meet the needs of children in grades K–7. All students were given a tour of the preschool classroom. It was conducted during our free-time period so that visitors could observe and interact with the children and so that the teacher could explain the special materials and equipment being used.

This learning experience was extended for the first graders, who took turns, four at a time, in attending our free-time period three days a week. These children learned to interact with and accept younger children with special needs, and they looked forward to their visits to the preschool class. They were especially proud of themselves when they helped our children during play activities. The handicapped children received excellent modeling of appropriate play behavior, and demonstrated progress by playing properly with a wider variety of materials than they had prior to this experience.

Seventh graders were offered the opportunity to work individually with our children. Each student volunteer was given a short training session. Each day, one of them came to the class to help individual children with specific table-top activities. As a result, the

5. TEACHING THE PHYSICALLY IMPAIRED CHILD

seventh graders received training in working with special needs children, and their teacher observed an increase in responsible behavior on their part. The preschool children received additional training in specific skills and also learned to work for others.

The following sections describe lessons which were presented to regular class students in grades K–6 to help them understand disabilities and disabled persons.

LESSONS FOR CHILDREN IN GRADES K–2

Lesson 1: Individual Differences

Objectives: (1) To understand that all of us are different in some way, and that we do not have to have a disability to be different; (2) To realize that it is okay to be different; (3) To understand that all of us are the same in some way.

Materials Needed: Two house plants of different varieties; paper and crayons; M. Green's book, *Is It Hard? Is It Easy?* (New York: William R. Scott, 1960).

Activities:
1. To demonstrate how things around us are different in some ways and the same in others, place two plants in front of the children and ask them to describe first how they differ and then how they are alike.
2. Ask two children to stand in front of the group. Have their classmates describe how they are different and how they are the same. Discussion focuses on the fact that it is okay to be different and how it would feel if someone teased us about one of our differences.
3. Give each child a piece of paper and a crayon. On one side, ask them to draw a picture of a favorite food, and on the other, a picture of a food they do not like to eat. Ask some of the children to come to the front of the room and describe their pictures. Ask their classmates to hold up their hands if they also like to eat a particular food. Then ask those who dislike that food to hold up their hands. The message is emphasized that it is okay that some of us like the same things, while others do not.
4. The book *Is It Hard? Is It Easy?* is left with the class to be read during story time.

Lesson 2: Wheelchairs and People in Wheelchairs

Objectives: (1) To become familiar with a wheelchair; (2) To determine why people are in wheelchairs and what caused them to be unable to walk; (3) To understand that it is okay to be in a wheelchair.

Materials Needed: Wheelchair; photograph or picture of a child in a wheelchair; bean bags; J. Fassler's book, *Howie Helps Himself* (Chicago: Albert Whitman & Co., 1975).

Activities:
1. Hold up a picture of a child in a wheelchair and ask the children to describe what they see. Have them label the wheelchair and its parts. Discuss what happened to make it necessary for the child to use a wheelchair. Talk about birth defects and accidents so that the children understand that it is not something they can "catch."
2. Have the children take turns moving about the room in a wheelchair. Have them throw bean bags at a target while they are sitting in the wheelchair, making the point that a person in a wheelchair can still have fun.
3. The book *Howie Helps Himself* is left with the class to be read during story time.

Lesson 3: Devices That Help People Walk and People Who Use These Devices

Objectives: (1) To understand that some people have difficulty walking, but this is okay; (2) To become familiar with crutches, braces, and walkers; (3) To realize that people who use these devices are still able to do many things and that they can be our friends.

Materials Needed: Pictures of children using walkers and braces; a pair of braces; a pair of crutches; a walker.

Activities:
1. Show the class pictures of children using walkers and braces, encouraging them to discuss what they see and to talk about why some children need to use these devices.
2. Pass a pair of braces around the room for the children to examine.
3. Have the children take turns walking with a pair of crutches and a walker.

Lesson 4: Amputation, Artificial Limbs, and Amputees

Objectives: (1) To become familiar with amputation, amputees, and artifical limbs; (2) To realize that a person without a limb can be our friend and is capable of doing many things.

Materials Needed: S. Stein's book, *About Handicaps: An Open Family Book for Parents and Children* (New York: Walker, 1974); B. Wolf's book, *Don't Feel Sorry for Paul* (Philadelphia: Lippincott, 1974); a jar of peanut butter; crackers; a plastic knife.

Activities:
1. Use pictures from the two books as the basis for discussion about amputation, amputees, and artificial limbs.
2. Assemble the children in pairs. With one child holding the other's arm behind his or her back, have them take turns trying to unscrew a lid from a pea-

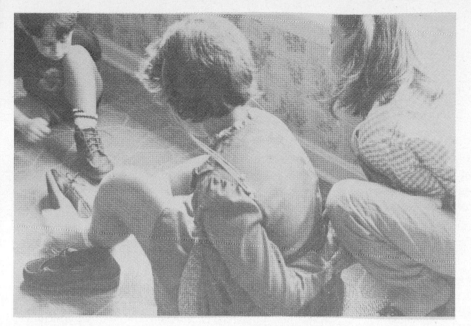

The frustration of trying to tie a shoe with one hand gives students an idea of what it is like to have physical limitations.

nut butter jar and spread peanut butter on a cracker using only one arm. Ask them to try putting on their shoes and socks with one hand. Emphasize that a person without a limb can still do many things, even though it may be more difficult.

Lesson 5: Visual Impairments and People Who Are Visually Impaired

Objectives: (1) To learn about visual impairments, glasses, and canes; (2) To realize that people who are visually impaired can be our friends and can learn many things about the world around them.

Materials Needed: Pictures of children using eyeglasses and canes; an orange; a spoon; a bag of candy; several pieces of paper; a blindfold; a cane.

Activities:
1. Show the class pictures of children using eyeglasses and canes, and encourage them to describe what they see. Talk about the reasons why some people use eyeglasses and canes.
2. Discuss the fact that we use other body parts besides our eyes to learn about the things around us. Have the children close their eyes and smell an orange, identify a spoon by its feel, taste candy, and listen to the sound of paper being torn.
3. Blindfold the children and have them practice using a cane to walk down the hall to get a drink from the water fountain.

Lesson 6: Hearing Impairments and People Who Are Hearing Impaired

Objectives: (1) To become familiar with hearing impairments and hearing aids; (2) To understand that people

who have difficulty hearing may also have difficulty speaking; (3) To realize that people can communicate in many different ways; (4) To realize that it is okay for people to have problems hearing or speaking, and that these people can still be our friends.

Materials Needed: Pictures of children wearing hearing aids; record player and record; tape recorder and tape of speech patterns of children with hearing impairments.

Activities:
1. Show pictures of children wearing hearing aids and encourage the children to describe what they see.
2. Discuss the meaning of a hearing impairment.
3. Turning the volume down low, play a record to show the children what it might be like to have a hearing impairment. Then turn the volume up to illustrate how it would sound with a hearing aid.
4. Have the children practice reading each other's lips. Demonstrate to the class where the speaker should stand when talking to a person with a hearing impairment.
5. Play a tape recording of the speech of children with hearing impairments, discussing the fact that it is hard to learn to speak if you have trouble hearing.
6. Describe alternative ways to communicate, such as the use of facial expressions, gestures, head movements, communication boards, and sign language. Teach the children some simple words in sign language.

LESSONS FOR CHILDREN IN GRADES 3–6

The lessons previously described can be modified and expanded for older children. Discussions may contain more detailed information on the causes and differing degrees of severity of each disability. The feelings

5. TEACHING THE PHYSICALLY IMPAIRED CHILD

of disabled persons may also be emphasized more strongly, exploring such questions as:

1. How would you feel if you were in a wheelchair and couldn't get through the door of the cafeteria?
2. How would you feel if you wore leg braces and everyone stared at you?
3. How would you feel if you did not have an arm and no one would play with you?

At the end of each lesson, answers to questions that nondisabled persons typically ask can be provided, along with answers to any other questions that the students may have. A few of the most commonly asked questions include the following:

1. How does a person in a wheelchair use the bathroom?
2. Can a person without a leg still have fun?
3. Is a person who cannot walk retarded?
4. If I see a blind person, should I help him?

Problem-solving sessions may also be added to these lessons, during which students are encouraged to come up with answers to specific problem situations, usually through direct experience. Sample problems are as follows:

1. How can you help a person in a wheelchair go over a bump?
2. How can you carry your books if you are in a wheelchair?
3. How can you get from your wheelchair to the seat of your car?
4. How can you get something down from a cabinet when you are in a wheelchair?
5. How can you make changes in the game of baseball to include your friend who uses crutches?
6. How can a child using a walker be in a marching band?
7. How can you help run errands for a friend who uses a walker?

Additional activities for older children include walking with their ankles tied together to experience what it would be like to be able to walk yet to have poor muscle control. To simulate the experience of wearing leg braces, the children can tie yardsticks and sand bags to their legs and try moving about the room. To experience what it would be like to have little use of one's hands, students can put socks on their hands and then try to place pennies in a bank or write their names. Drawing a picture without using one's hands is another useful activity.

A short discussion with the aid of pictures can be used to familiarize the students with mental retardation and to point out that mentally retarded children can learn and have fun. Discussions may include ways of helping a person who is mentally retarded.

SUPPLEMENTARY ACTIVITIES

A question box placed outside the special class allows regular class students to submit any questions they may have concerning disabilities. They should be asked to put their names on their questions so that the teacher can contact them with the answer. A hall bulletin board entitled "Can You Name These?" may display drawings or pictures of devices such as a wheelchair, cane, or hearing aid. A "Brag Board" outside the special class can be used to post children's art work or other papers, thus sharing their accomplishments with their nonhandicapped peers.

LOOKING AT THE RESULTS

At the end of the school year, the regular class teachers completed an evaluation form that reflected overwhelmingly positive reactions to the year's experience. Specifically, teachers commented that the experience helped their students (1) to be more accepting of differences in others; (2) to use appropriate terms when discussing disabilities; (3) to have a more positive outlook toward disabled persons; (4) to be more understanding of the feelings of handicapped persons; and (5) to interact more appropriately with the children in special education classes.

The regular class students who participated in these learning experiences related more positively to our handicapped children and showed a greater interest in their progress. Their enthusiasm and excitement as they learned more about disabilities was evident. Future plans include the effort to involve parents and teachers of regular class students to a greater extent. Parents can be provided with detailed information concerning the nature and value of these experiences, and brief lesson descriptions can be given to the regular class teachers. When parents and teachers reinforce and follow up on major points of lessons that are presented, they help contribute to an even wider understanding and acceptance of those who have disabilities.

RESOURCES

Barnes, E., Berrigan, C., & Biklen, D. *What's the difference? Teaching positive attitudes toward people with disabilities*. New York: Human Policy Press, 1978.

Popp, R., & Warrell, S. Helping preschoolers accept the handicapped. *Early Years*, 1980, *10*, 32–33, 66–67.

Ward, M., Arkell, R., Dahl, H., & Wise, J. *Everybody counts! A workshop manual to increase awareness of handicapped people*. Reston VA: The Council for Exceptional Children, 1979.

Is There a Child with Epilepsy in the Classroom?

Hazel Zakariasen

Hazel Zakariasen is a summer volunteer with the Minnesota Epilepsy League. Her home is at 14409 North Calle del Oro, Foundation Hills, Arizona 85268.

Now that you are my teacher for this year, I think you should know that I have epilepsy. Please don't handle me with kid gloves. Just like the other kids, I like to play games, go on field trips — and believe it or not, I'm a good student too. But I want you to know so you and the class can help me if I have a seizure at school, like I did two years ago on the playground.

If you are a teacher, would such a note from a pupil be disconcerting to receive? Quite possibly it might — because many educators are largely ignorant of the physical disorder called epilepsy. Yet epilepsy affects approximately one in every 50 school children.

Teachers particularly need to know the manifestations, since they may be the first to notice the onset of epilepsy. It first occurs during elementary school years in 34 percent of cases, and before age 21 in 75 percent of cases. Parents are often unaware or refuse at first to recognize symptoms.

If your first reaction to the thought of epilepsy or to witnessing an epileptic seizure is revulsion and fright, you need not feel guilty. Epilepsy has been frightening people for centuries.

Even in this modern era of medical breakthrough, when epilepsy need not be so frightening since half of the persons who have it can have their seizures completely controlled through medication, and another 30 percent can be sure of nearly complete control, there still remains a public reaction of panic and revulsion. (The remaining 20 percent as a rule will represent a multiply-handicapped group of children, many of whom will require specialized care outside the public schools in spite of advanced mainstreaming.)

The child with epilepsy is not the only one in need of understanding. All school children need to learn about the disorder so they can be comfortable and natural in their acceptance of a classmate with epilepsy.

What Is Epilepsy?

Epilepsy is not a disease, and it is not infectious. A simplified explanation is that epilepsy is a dysfunction of electrical impulses emitted by the brain.

The cause cannot be identified in 70 percent of cases. There may have been prenatal factors, problems during birth, later a very high fever accompanying an illness, a skull or brain injury caused by a fall or severe blow to the head, injuries sustained in a motorcycle or car accident, toxic factors, a tumor, or other causes.

Epilepsy can happen to anyone — at any period in life. However, it usually occurs in the early years of childhood.

Why the Big Secret?

In this advanced age of teacher education the appalling lack of required training in dealing with the "one-in-50" child who has epilepsy, can only be explained by the aversion to the disorder which the public, including the intellectual community, still feels. Epilepsy needs a public exposure such as the Kennedy and Humphrey families have given to mental retardation.

The fact that great figures of history such as Socrates, Caesar, Alexander the Great, Dostoyevsky, Napoleon, Tschaikovsky, Martin Luther, Lord Byron, Charles Dickens and Van Gogh are believed to have had some form of epilepsy, may not be of too much comfort to the here-and-now school child. Relating to actor John Carridine, or to professional golf superstar Roger Maultbie, may be more helpful. Every young person with epilepsy should know about Patty Wilson, the 17 year old school girl with epilepsy who in 1978 ran a 2000 mile marathon between Minneapolis and Washington D.C. Patty Wilson's achievement — which would be a stupendous one for any school girl — certainly ought to give courage to other school children who share her physical problem of epilepsy.

How Should the Teacher Treat Such a Child?

A child who has epilepsy should not be overprotected either in the classroom or elsewhere. Unless prohibited by a doctor, the student can participate in sports with the possible exception of contact sports. Discipline should be the same as for any other child. Teachers need not fear that singling out the student for needed correction will trigger a seizure any more than will other stresses with which one must learn to live.

Positive Reactions from Teachers Can Help

- Be open and accepting, but do not exhibit pity.
- Call the disorder — once it has been positively diagnosed by the child's physician — what it is: Epilepsy. (However, be aware that not all seizures are epileptic. Some not classified as such are those related only to high fever, imbalance of body fluids and chemicals, alcohol or drug withdrawal, or a single isolated seizure.)
- Teach the class what epilepsy is and is not.

"Is There A Child With Epilepsy in the Classroom?" by Hazel Zakariasen, *Education Unlimited,* September 1979.

- If a seizure occurs in the classroom, assure the children that it does not hurt and that it will pass.
- Look at unique needs of the child with epilepsy as you do the needs of other students.
- Work with the family in a supportive way.
- Minimize stigma by your own matter-of-fact attitude.
- Use your knowledge and experience gained by working with a specific child or children with epilepsy, to become an advocate for better understanding among educators and the general public.
- If you are a high school teacher of a youth with epilepsy, stand ready to vouch for his capabilities to a prospective employer. Company studies where people with epilepsy are employed indicate that they are reliable and conscientious workers who often rate better in job performance, attendance, and safety than do some of their nonhandicapped coworkers.
- If you have the opportunity, be a liaison between persons or families affected by epilepsy. They greatly need support to avoid feeling isolated and overburdened.

What Are the Manifestations of Epilepsy?

Consider the following classroom incidents:

Petit Mal Epilepsy — Jimmy seems to daydream frequently in school. Unlike other daydreamers, however, when the teacher tries to get his attention, Jimmy either continues to stare or acts surprised, as if he didn't realize he had drifted off. The "daydream" incidents last only a few seconds, but they may happen dozens of times in a day. Other children in the class tease Jimmy about them. They — and possibly the teacher — do not realize that Jimmy has petit mal epilepsy (absence seizures).

Jimmy's teacher should confer with the school nurse who, upon verifying the suspicion that the child may have epilepsy, should suggest to his parents that he see a physician, preferably a neurologist.

Psychomotor Epilepsy — Mary may have longer staring spells than Jimmy, perhaps lasting a few minutes. Or in another case, Alice may have involuntary movements of only a part of her body, for example her arm may twitch for a couple of minutes. Or John may roam around the classroom aimlessly, without permission and like a sleepwalker. He may pick at his clothes or smack his lips during such a seizure. Such seizures are also called complex partial seizures.

These children are not aware of their bizarre behavior and cannot be stopped by talking to them or touching them. Although they are not unconscious, they are unable to organize themselves in relation to their environment during such a seizure. In each case, these children have one form or another of psychomotor epilepsy. Unless the teacher is informed and aware, such children may be unjustly accused of bad behavior and deliberate inattention.

Grand Mal Epilepsy — It is difficult not to identify this most dramatic form of a generalized tonic-clonic seizure. In a grand mal seizure the person falls and the whole body convulses. Saliva runs from the mouth and sometimes loss of bladder control can occur.

The teacher should remain calm and reassure the other children. Further suggestions are:

- Do not try to restrain the child.
- Do not put anything into the child's mouth, but do turn the child's head gently to the side so that he will not choke on saliva. A rolled up sweater or something of the kind may be placed under his head.
- Remove any nearby hard or sharp objects which may harm the child.
- It is not necessary to call a doctor except in rare cases when the seizure lasts longer than three or four minutes or is repeated three or more times in succession.
- Do not regard the seizure as any more important than the ordinary illnesses that children are likely to have. Transmit this attitude to the other children.
- Expect that the child may need to rest after the seizure, perhaps in the nurse's office. However, if no evidence of fatigue is noted, the child should be encouraged to resume ordinary activities as soon as possible.
- Notify the parents and school nurse that a seizure has occurred.
- Be willing to assist a young child in remembering to take anticonvulsant medication if this is a problem.

Most children with properly diagnosed and treated epilepsy, even the grand mal form, may have a seizure only if they have missed taking their medication or possibly have encountered really extreme stress. A knowledgable teacher and well informed class will be able to take such an occurrence in stride and continue to treat their classmate normally.

Progress in School Awareness of Epilepsy

More and more school systems are presently doing their part to provide basic instruction on the nature and proper reaction to epilepsy, not only for teachers, school administrators and nurses, but also for school janitors, bus drivers, office personnel, lunch room attendants, and school aides. However, so neglected has public knowledge and acceptance of this disorder been in the past, that even some school nurses have a sketchy grasp of proper procedures. Consequently they may have overprotected or undersupported the child. Adults in the school are of tremendous importance to the child who must learn to live with a disorder of potential traumatic danger as is epilepsy.

Where to Obtain Information and Assistance

The Epilepsy Foundation of America, 1828 L Street N.W., Washington D.C. 20036, provides literature and research reports on every phase of epilepsy. By writing to this national organization, a school system may learn the location of state chapters and what programs and services are available in a particular state. Most Epilepsy Foundation chapters conduct a public education program designed to inform all persons involved in any aspect of a child's educational environment, of the nature of epilepsy and the problems of the child who has seizures. Such programs are conducted in cooperation with the National Education Association, and the ultimate goal is for state education departments to conduct the program. This is currently done in New York and New Hampshire.

Government Programs

State governments are becoming concerned. In the state of Washington, for instance, a state funded inservice training program is offered school personnel, and special education teachers and counselors may take a 10-hour college credit course.

The federal government has been undertaking a wide-scope program of research, prevention, identification, treatment, and rehabilitation on behalf of citizens with epilepsy. Pilot Comprehensive Epilepsy Research and Treatment Centers funded by HEW grants have been established in five locations: Atlanta, GA; Portland, OR; Seattle, WA; Charlottesville, VA; and Minneapolis, MN, in conjunction with universities located in these cities.

CETA funding and HEW grants have also enabled strong state organizations to sponsor inservice training of school personnel, and counseling of children and families affected by epilepsy. In one year, two CETA-paid representatives of the Minnesota Epilepsy League spoke to over 6,000 people in 200 classrooms at 60 different schools in Minneapolis and St. Paul, Minnesota.

Further illustrating what may be available in a single state, Minnesota citizens have the benefit of seizure centers located at St. Paul-Ramsey Hospital in St. Paul, at Hennepin County Medical Center in Minneapolis, and (for veterans) at the Veterans Administration Hospital in Minneapolis. A well known private clinic of Psychiatry and Neurology in Golden Valley, Minnesota serves many persons with epileptic disorders. And TAPS, based in Minneapolis, is an employment training and placement service for persons with epilepsy funded by the U.S. Department of Labor and sponsored by the Epilepsy Foundation of America.

Not every state has such a strong thrust of patient aid and public information, although such notice and acceptance of the problem of epilepsy is long overdue. Since so many school children and their parents are affected, the significance to schools can scarcely be overstressed.

Looking at it in another way, any physical dysfunction experienced by a total of approximately 4,000,000 children and adults combined, as is the case with epilepsy in the United States, cannot continue to be a hidden and neglected problem.

Teaching the Mentally Retarded Child

With the passage of P.L. 94-142, the education of mentally handicapped children has undergone radical changes. Parents no longer have to create and pay for their own ad hoc programs in church basements. Public schools are now required to provide appropriate educational programs at no extra expense to parents of handicapped children. Parents no longer must leave their children in institutions because there are now more alternatives within the parents' own communities for the care and education of mentally retarded children. It is no longer believed that all mentally retarded children need the protection of "asylums" and that they are incapable of leading independent lives. It has been found that separate programs for retarded children often lead to adult lives which are separate from the rest of society. The law clearly is intended to provide mentally retarded children with the same educational opportunities as their nonhandicapped peers. Prior to the law, many of these children were not receiving an educational program even approaching their capabilities. Some were not receiving an educational program at all, but rather custodial care, which only perpetuated the retarded person's dependencies and inabilities to function in society.

To achieve the principles underlying P.L. 94-142, several things must occur. First, expectations cannot be limited, nor can they be generalized, to the entire population of mentally retarded children. "What Is Mental Retardation?" sets forth the history of the concept, presents criteria for identifying children with mental retardation, discusses incidence and prevalence, and addresses problems involving classification. Using the example of Down's Syndrome, one of the most common causes of mental retardation, Merril Harris states that some of these children "are capable of formal learning up to or beyond high school level." Yet, many educators assume that because these children have common physical characteristics, they must also have the same degree of retardation. Since limited expectations tend to produce limited opportunities, it is critical that schools approach each mentally retarded child as an individual with unique traits and learning abilities.

The educable mentally retarded (EMR) child presents many problems in individualizing special needs. Recent-ly a significant change in the population served under the EMR label and, in a sense, a redefinition of the term mild retardation has coincided with decreasing interest in this field. "Changes in Mild Mental Retardation: Population, Programs, and Perspectives" discusses the concept of mild retardation as it relates to the current and future state of affairs in the delivery of educational services. Another problem in handling EMR children is knowing when they are ready for mainstreaming. "An Analysis of EMR Children's Worries About Mainstreaming" examines some of their fears as they await mainstreaming placement.

It is important that schools approach placement in the least restrictive environment with a clear understanding of the concept. For some children, an institution may still be the best and least restrictive environment. Other children may benefit from regular classrooms and activities. "Learning Through Outdoor Adventure Education" describes some activities available to the mentally retarded child which can be integrated into any school's recreational program.

The final article in this section, "Speaking for Themselves: A Bibliography of Writings by Mentally Handicapped Individuals," pulls together several writings by mentally retarded persons that reveal how they feel about their lives and experiences in schools and institutions. It is hoped that they represent only the beginning of a growing positive trend in which mentally retarded people will speak for themselves, rather than have others speak for them.

Looking Ahead: Challenge Questions

What is mental retardation? Why is it important to include adaptive behavior in the definition? What are the major issues in the field?

What is Down's Syndrome? How does it occur? How should these children be educated?

How should one decide when an educable mentally retarded (EMR) child can be mainstreamed?

What sort of programs work for integrating the mentally handicapped child in a school's recreational program?

What can be learned from the writings included in the final article?

What Is Mental Retardation?

Mental retardation presents itself in so many forms, degrees, and conditions, from so many known and unknown causes, with so many questions unanswered, that it is difficult to say clearly: these are the people who are retarded and this is what they can do, and this what we can do for them, and this is how we can eliminate the problem.

To reach into the problem we have to know what it is.

To reach the people who have the problem we have to know who they are, how to understand them and how to help them.

Who Are They?

Mental retardation refers to significantly subaverage general intellectual functioning existing concurrently with deficits in adaptive behavior, and manifested during the developmental period.

This is the formal definition published by the American Association on Mental Deficiency in 1973 and widely accepted today. It identifies mental retardation with subnormality in two behavioral dimensions—intelligence and social adaptation—occurring before age 18. The definition is a culmination of long debate and revision, and may well be modified in the future.

The severely retarded person has an obvious incapacity to exercise the expected controls of reason and of personal management necessary for normal living in any human culture. Left to himself, anyone so impaired cannot easily survive. The great majority of severely retarded individuals also have physical characteristics which suggest a central nervous system defect as the basis of the developmentally retarded behavior.

In many cases no detectable physical pathology accompanies the deficiency of intelligence and adaptation. The limited ability to learn, to reason and to use "com-mon sense" is often unexplainable. Can undetected physical pathology be assumed?

Further questions arise when we discover that milder degrees of intellectual and adaptive deficit are commonly associated with particular families who have serious social and economic problems. Do poor living conditions produce mental retardation, or is it the reverse? Or does each condition compound the other? Still further, members of certain minority groups tend to be highly represented among those identified as having intellectual and adaptive problems, especially in the school-age years. Is such overrepresentation of certain groups a product of racial inferiority or of racial and ethnic discrimination and disadvantage?

For a long time, mental retardation (or its earlier terms idiocy, feeblemindedness and the like), was thought to have much in common with insanity, epilepsy, pauperism and social depravity, all of which were lumped together. And so, a concept of mental deficiency in terms of social deviance developed.

Then, as knowledge advanced, retardation was identified with congenital brain defect or damage, and assigned to heredity. This approach led to redefining mental deficiency in medical terms as an organic defect producing inadequate behavior. Mild forms of intellectual "weakness" became associated with forms of immoral behavior and social disturbance (the "moral imbecile"), and ascribed to more subtle defects of inherited character. Legal definitions in terms of social behavior began to appear.

During the 19th and early 20th century what we now call "mild" retardation was not recognized except as associated with disturbed or delinquent behavior. There was no simple way of diagnosing the more mild or incipient forms of mental retardation until the development of psychometrics around 1910. Then the "IQ" rapidly became a universal means, not only of identifying mental deficiency, but also of measuring its severity.

Goddard, in 1910, in applying the new techniques of Binet and Simon in the public schools, discovered there were ten times as many feebleminded as anyone had suspected, and promptly coined the term "moron" to cover them! Thus a psychometric definition of retardation came into being.

The intelligence test actually measured behavioral performance on tasks assumed to be characteristic of the growth of children's ability at successive ages, but it was interpreted as a measure of capacity for intellectual growth and therefore as a predictor of future mental status. It was assumed to represent an inherent and usually inherited condition of the brain with a fixed developmental potential.

Persistent debate over the nature and composition of intelligence finally led to an operational definition that it is "whatever an intelligence test measures." Since intelligence measurements are scalar, and degrees on the scale were found to correlate rather well with other clinical and social evidences of mental proficiency, low IQ became virtually the sole basis for a diagnosis of mental retardation and for its classification at levels of severity from "borderline" to "idiot."

This measurement was especially important in schools for which, in fact, the first tests were devised by Binet and Simon. IQ tests became the standard means of determining school eligibility and classification. Intelligence tests also were used extensively as sole evidence for determining legal competency and institutional commitment, as well as the subclassifications of institutional populations. The leading authorities, Tredgold, Goddard, Porteus, Penrose, Doll, Clarke and Clarke, all rejected a strictly psychometric definition, but it nevertheless became standard practice in diagnosis and classification.

In the meantime, research in twins, siblings and unrelated children had shown that general intelligence (i.e., measured IQ) is strongly inherited as a polygenic characteristic, following a normal Gaussian curve of frequency distribution in the general population. A slight negative skew was attributable to brain damage or genetic mutation. This deviation led to a theory of mental retardation which divided it into two major groups on the basis of presumed causation. One group consisted of the more severely deficient type with brain damage or gross genetic anomaly characterized by various physical abnormalities and IQ generally of 55 or less. The other group consisted of the lower portion of the negative tail on the normal curve of distribution of polygenic intelligence with IQ between 50 or 55 and 70 or 80 and not otherwise abnormal (Kanner, 1957, Zigler, 1967). This theory could explain the association of milder forms of low intelligence with low socio-economic status and its concomitants. In other words, the less competent tend to sink to the bottom of the social scale in a competitive society. The issue of cultural bias was raised immediately, however, with respect to racial and ethnic groups who scored consistently lower on the standard tests.

Evidence began to accumulate which generated a variety of additional controversial issues. The "constancy of the IQ" was questioned on both statistical and experimental grounds. The pioneering work of Skeels, Skodak, Wellman, and others, in the 1930's (e.g., Skeels, et al., 1938) had indicated that measured intelligence as well as other observable behavior could be substantially modified by drastic changes in the social environment of young children. The quality of the infant's nurture was found to have enduring effects of intellectual functioning, especially in the absence of detectable brain pathology.

Follow-up studies of persons released from institutional care and of those who had been identified in school as retarded showed high rates of social adaptation, upward mobility and even substantial increases in measured intelligence in adult years (Cobb, 1972). Epidemiological studies have consistently shown a "disappearance" of mildly retarded persons in the adult years.

Explanations for these findings could be

offered without abandoning previous assumptions: Improvement in low IQ scores over several repetitions simply exemplifies the statistical regression toward the mean, inherent in errors of measurement: those who improve with stimulation and environmental change were never "really" retarded, but exhibit "pseudo-retardation" which masks true capacity.

Eventually, evidence converged to show that measured intelligence is modifiable within limits, that it is not in any case a measure of fixed capacity, but of the continuity of a developing intellectual and social competence in which "nature" and "nurture" are inseparable components and individual "growth curves" may take a variety of forms and may be influenced by many factors.

A gradual trend developed toward the definition of mental retardation in functional rather than in structural terms and not tied either to specific cause or to unchangeable status. There were those, however, who continued to find a dual view of retardation more credible than a single continuum.

The Stanford-Binet and similar measures of intelligence came to be recognized as primarily predictive of school performance of an academic or abstract nature requiring language skills, and less predictive of other non-verbal types of behavior. Consequently, the need developed to measure other dimensions of behavior. The Army "Beta" test of World War I anticipated this development. New tests, such as the Wechsler series, combined linguistic with non-linguistic performance or quantitative elements and yielded a "profile" of distinguishable mental traits. Factor analysis of measures of intellectual behavior had demonstrated that "intelligence" is not a single trait but a composite of many distinguishable functions.

The measurement of adaptive behavior presented even greater difficulty. Such measures as the Vineland Social Maturity Scale were extensively used but had only a limited validity. The Gesell Infant Development Scale, the Gunzburg Progress Assessment Chart, and subsequently, the AAMD Adaptive Behavior Scale all attempted to measure the non-intellectual dimensions of developmental adaptation but

they lacked the precision and reliability of the intelligence measures. Consequently, there has been a continuing reliance, especially in the schools, on measures of IQ alone as the criterion for mental retardation. This practice is defended by some authorities as legitimate in the absence of better measures of adaptive behavior (Conley, 1973.)

In the meantime the issue of cultural bias became an increasingly serious problem. All measures of either intelligence or of adaptive behavior reflect social learning, hence tend to be culture-bound. Their validity, therefore, is dependent on the cultural population on which the norms have been standardized. No one has succeeded in developing a universally applicable "culture-free" test of behavior. Attempts to devise "culture-fair" tests which employ comparable but culturally different elements have as yet failed to yield valid bases of comparison.

Recent studies by Mercer (1973 and 1974) and others have shown the extent to which cultural bias affects the frequency with which members of minority cultures are labeled "retarded" and assigned to special education classes. This is especially true when only measures of IQ are used; representatives of lower socio-economic and of Black, Mexican-American, Puerto Rican, Indian and other ethnic groups are identified as retarded far out of proportion to their numbers in comparison with middle-class Anglo children. Social evaluations of such children show that a high proportion are not significantly impaired in their adaptation in non-school environments.

This discovery has led to a coining of the term "Six-Hour Retarded Child," meaning a child who is "retarded" during the hours in school, but otherwise functions adequately (PCMR: *The Six-Hour Retarded Child,* 1970).

Mercer has called such persons who are identified in one or two contexts but not in others the "situationally retarded," in contrast to the "comprehensively retarded," who are identified as such in all the contexts in which they are evaluated. "Situational retardation" occurs by far most frequently in school settings, and next most frequently in medical settings, and much less frequently in ratings by families or neighbors or in settings officially responsible for the comprehensively retarded. "We conclude," Mercer says, ". . . that the situational retardate is primarily the product of the labeling process in formal organizations in the community, especially the Public Schools" (Mercer, 1973).

The work of Mercer and others has led to litigation and legislative action, especially in California, limiting the use of IQ tests as the sole criterion for labeling and special class placement, on the ground that such practices systematically penalize minority groups and violate their rights to equal educational opportunity (Mercer, 1974).

The present tendency is to accept the 1973 AAMD formulation by Grossman which requires *both* an IQ of less than 70 *and* substantial failure on a measure of adaptive behavior. The requirement of age of onset prior to 18 is more open to question and not always regarded as critical. The Grossman formulation differed from the AAMD definition of Heber (1961) principally in requiring a criterion of more than two standard deviations below the mean, rather than more than one s.d., as Heber had proposed. This was an extremely important difference because it excluded the "borderline" category which accounted for about 13% of the school age population!

Mental retardation, by any of the proposed criteria, occurs with varying degrees of severity. Many attempts were made in the past to classify differences of severity, usually on the basis of social adaptation or academic learning criteria. Social adaptation criteria distinguished borderline feebleminded, moron, imbecile and idiot. Academic Criteria distinguished slow learner, educable, trainable (with no term suggesting learning capability for the still lower category). Heber (1958) proposed using neutral terms to indicate standard deviation units on the continuum of the IQ and any other scales employed.

This is continued in the Grossman (1973) AAMD system to categorize levels of intellectual functioning, thus:

Level of Function	Upper S.D. Limit	Stanford Binet IQ/ (S.D. = 16)	Wechsler IQ (S.D. = 15)
Mild	−2.0	67–52	69–55
Moderate	−3.0	51–36	54–40
Severe	−4.0	35–20	39–25 (extrap.)
Profound	−5.0	19 and below	24 and below (extrap.)

Note that the borderline category (−1.0 to −2.0 s.d.) is not included under the definition.

Mercer has identified still another variable of a significant sociological nature. A majority of children who rated low on both IQ and adaptive measures by the Grossman criteria, and therefore technically "retarded," came from homes that did not conform to the prevailing cultural pattern of the community (socio-culturally nonmodal). This group appeared to be identified as retarded more because of cultural difference than because of inadequate developmental adaptation. Further evidence showed that members of this group who were identified as retarded children tended more than the socio-cultural modal group to "disappear" as identifiably retarded on leaving school.

Mental retardation, as an inclusive concept, is currently defined in *behavioral* terms involving these essential components: *intellectual functioning, adaptive behavior* and *age of onset.* The causes of retardation are irrelevant to the definition, whether they be organic, genetic, or environmental. What is indicated is that at a given time a person is unable to conform to the intellectual and adaptive expectations which society sets for an individual in relation to his peers. In this sense, mental retardation is a reflection of social perception aided by a variety of clinical and nonclinical techniques of identification.

Within this broad functional definition, the deficits indicated in a diagnosis of mental retardation may or may not be permanent and irreversible. They may or may not be responsive to intervention. They may persist only so long as the person remains in a culturally ambiguous situation, or at the other extreme, they may be of life-long duration. Or perhaps only their consequences may be ameliorated in greater or lesser degree, not the condition itself.

Consequently, it is difficult to estimate how frequently mental retardation occurs and how many retarded people there are.

How Big Is the Problem?

The *incidence* of a disorder refers to the frequency of occurrence within a given period of time. For example, the incidence of smallpox in the United States might be expressed as the number of cases in a specific year per 100,000 population; the incidence of Down's syndrome might be expressed as the average number of cases per year per 1,000 live births. The purpose of determining incidence is to yield information as to the magnitude of the problem with a view to its prevention and to measure the success of preventive programs.

The *prevalence* of a disorder refers to the number of cases existing at a specified time in a specified population and is usually expressed as a percentage of that population or as a whole number. Thus, the prevalence of *diabetes mellitus* in the United States might be expressed either as the percent or as a whole number of the total population known or estimated to have the disease in a designated year. The prevalence of people crippled from poliomyelitis can be expressed as a gradually decreasing figure as the result of the greatly reduced incidence of the disease following the discovery of the vaccines. This shows that prevalence is derived from incidence, but modified by the extent to which cases disappear by death, recovery or inaccessibility. The value of prevalence rates is in determining the magnitude of the need for care, treatment, protection or other services.

Incidence

By definition mental retardation can be diagnosed only after birth when appropriate behavioral indices have developed sufficiently for measurement. During gestation the identification of certain conditions usually or invariably associated with mental retardation may be detected and *potential* retardation inferred.

From the examination of spontaneously aborted fetuses, it is estimated that probably 30 to 50 percent are developmentally abnormal and that if they had survived many would have been mentally deficient; but this information gives us only an incidence of fetal mortality and morbidity, with an estimate of some types of developmental deviation, not an incidence of mental retardation itself.

The mortality rates of the potentially or actually retarded vary with severity of defect, which means that many developmentally impaired infants die before retardation has been, or even can be, determined. Anencephaly, for example, is complete failure of brain cortex to develop; the infant may be born living and exhibit a few responses typical of the neonate, but survival is brief. Is such a case to be counted as an instance of incipient mental retardation or only of anencephaly in particular or birth defect in general?

Since mental retardation manifests itself at different ages and under different conditions, there is no single time—e.g., at birth or at one year of age—when it can be determined of every child that he is or *ever will be* identified as mentally retarded.

Mildly mentally retarded persons are most frequently identified, if at all, during school years, and frequently disappear as recognizably retarded after leaving school.

The methods of identifying retardation are still highly varied; consequently, surveys of incidence or prevalence are frequently not comparable.

The degree of subnormality employed as criterion for identification as retarded greatly affects the count of incidence. For example, the 1961 AAMD definition used a criterion of standard deviation greater than one (S.B. IQ < 85). The 1973 version uses a more restricted criterion of more than two standard deviations (S.B. IQ < 68). This change in criterion reduces the incidence of mild mental retardation automatically by 80%!

A similar problem is created by the use of multiple dimensions rather than a single dimension. If only IQ is employed, say at two standard deviations (IQ < 68 or 70), a global incidence of about 3% of school-age population will be found (cf. Conley 1973). But if a second dimension of impaired adaptive behavior is also required, then some with IQ below 70 will not be classified mentally retarded, and some with low adaptive scores, but IQ above 70, will not be classified as retarded. This reduces the obtained prevalence rate to more nearly 1%. If, following Mercer, a still further determination is made on the basis of "socio-cultural modality" the rate may be still further reduced in some heterogeneous communities.

Taking many such considerations into account, Tarjan and others (1973) estimate that approximately 3 percent of annual births may be expected to "acquire" mental retardation at some time in their lives, of which 1.5% would be profoundly, 3.5% severely, 6.0% moderately and 89% mildly retarded. Currently, however, in view of the problems of arriving at truly meaningful estimates of the incidence of mental retardation on a global basis, emphasis for purposes of prevention is placed on the incidence from specific known causes. Unfortunately, these comprise only a small proportion of the total identified as retarded (Penrose, 1963; Holmes et al, 1965). The following are examples.

One of the earliest success stories in the reduction of the incidence of mental retardation was in the case of endemic cretinism. This condition occurred rather frequently in certain localities, notably some of the Swiss alpine valleys. The problem was attacked in the second half of the 19th century. The first step was to identify the condition with the occurrence of goiter, an enlargement of the thyroid gland. The next step was to relate this condition to the people's diet, and finally to the absence of trace iodine in the soil and water supply. Iodine was found to be necessary to the functioning of the thyroid gland in its production of the hormone thyroxin, the absence of which can cause cretinism.

The addition of iodine to table salt resulted in reducing mental retardation caused by endemic cretinism to near zero. It also led to the preventive and therapeutic use of extract of thyroxin in the treatment of myxoedema or hypothyroidism from other causes (Kanner, 1957).

The incidence of Down's syndrome is well-documented. It has been identified with a specific chromosomal abnormality which occurs most frequently as an unpredictable non-disjunction of autosome 21, but infrequently also as the Mendelian transmission of a translocated portion of autosome 21. The former type is definitely related to maternal age, occurring at about .33 per thousand live births to mothers under age 29 but rising sharply after age 35 to a rate of about 25 per thousand to women over age 45.

Overall, the incidence of Down's syndrome is 1 in 600 to 700 live births, with over half occurring to women over 35 (Begab, 1974). The overall incidence of gross chromosomal malformation of children born to women over 35 is 1 to 2 percent (Lubs and Ruddle, 1970; Begab, 1974). The existence of the condition is detectable by amniocentesis (analysis of a sample of amniotic fluid) during pregnancy.

This knowledge creates the possibility of reducing the incidence of Down's syndrome substantially by: a) limiting pregnancy after age 35; b) detecting the transmissable karyotype of translocation in either the male or female and limiting reproduction; c) identifying the condition early in gestation and terminating pregnancy.

A third example of incidence is more problematic, but nevertheless significant. From prevalence studies, it is known that mild retardation is more frequently found in families of low socio-economic status, especially in families in which the mother is mildly retarded. Heber and others have determined that the incidence of retardation in such families can be reduced by early intervention in providing stimulation to the child and home assistance to the mother.

These examples are sufficient to illustrate the values of pursuing the study of incidence to identifiable causes or correlative conditions as a means of identifying preventive measures (see Stein and Susser, 1974; Begab, 1974). Further discussion of currently known preventive measures appear in later chapters on prevention.

6. TEACHING THE MENTALLY RETARDED CHILD

Prevalence

The principal problems of obtaining reliable prevalence estimates relate to definitions, criteria and administrative procedures on the one hand, and to the absence of uniform and centralized data collection, on the other. The former problems are gradually becoming resolved. The latter requires vigorous and sustained efforts by Federal and State governments to establish an effective data bank.

Prevalence is a product of cumulative incidence modified by loss. Loss may be the result of death or cure or unaccounted disappearance. Whereas measures of incidence are important to the problem of prevention, measures of prevalence are important to the provision of service resources. As prevention requires differential classification by identifiable cause, so service provision requires differential classification by types of need.

Overall estimates of prevalence of mental retardation have been made by two methods: by empirical surveys and by selection of a cut-off point on a Gaussian curve for the distribution of intelligence scores. The latter has led to a widely used estimate of 3%, ambiguously referring to either incidence or prevalence. This would correspond to an IQ level of approximately 70 and is, in fact, an average general prevalence found in some surveys of children (Conley, 1973; Birch et al, 1970).

However, it possible to select a 9% cut-off at about IQ 80 or 16% at IQ 85, the 1961 AAMD criterion. All surveys, however, show that mental retardation does not represent a simple portion of the lower tail on a general Gaussian curve. It is far from being normally distributed, varying widely by age, by socio-economic and ethnic factors. The use of an IQ cut-off alone also assumes a one-dimensional definition of mental retardation, contrary to the AAMD formula and other leading authorities (Tarjan, 1973; Mercer, 1973).

Tarjan (1973, p. 370) points out that the estimate of 3% prevalence, or 6 million persons in the United States, makes four dubious assumptions: "a) the diagnosis of mental retardation is based essentially on an IQ below 70; b) mental retardation is identified in infancy; c) the diagnosis does not change; and d) the mortality of retarded individuals is similar to that of the general population." The first assumption ignores the adaptive behavior component; the second holds only for a small portion, nearly always organically and severely impaired; the third holds only as a generality for those of IQ below 55, and the fourth holds only for the mildly retarded.

As a statement of potential incidence, Tarjan (1973) is probably quite conservative in estimating that 3% of all infants who survive birth will at some time in their lives be identified as mentally retarded in some context—most probably in the public schools.

Epidemiological surveys conducted in various parts of the United States and abroad show comparable prevalence rates for the more seriously retarded—i.e., moderate, severe and profound levels on the AAMD classifications or IQ below 50. Fifteen such studies converge on an average rate of approximately .46% or 4.6 cases per thousand population (Stein and Susser, 1974). These surveys generally covered ages roughly 10 to 20, obscuring the high mortality rate in early childhood. When the surveys are divided between general and rural populations, the three rural studies average at more than double the general rate, or 9.84 per thousand, while the remaining twelve cluster quite closely around 3.6.

Penrose (1963) suggests that prevalence of malformation predictive of profound retardation at birth might be as much as 1 percent, Conley (1973) suggests 1.5 to 1.7 percent, including severe and moderate levels. The rate among prematurely born infants is much higher than among full-term babies. The rate among lower-class nonwhites is higher than among middle-class whites, but the differences are not so striking as is the case in mild retardation levels. Higher rates of prematurity, higher health risk and inferior maternal and child health care could account for the difference at the more severe levels.

In any case, the presumption of actual prevalence of the severe forms of defect predictive of mental retardation would be highest at birth, declining rapidly by mortality to a relatively low rate of .2% in adult life.

Prevalence rates of the severely retarded have been affected by a number of tendencies in the past 20 years. On the one hand, modern medicine has made enormous strides in its ability to preserve life. Infant mortality rates have fallen markedly; survival of prematures at progressively younger ages has become possible, with correspondingly increased risk of developmental damage; recovery from infectious diseases by use of antibiotics has become commonplace. Consequently, along with other infants and young children, severely and profoundly retarded children now have a better chance of prolonged survival.

On the other hand, improved health care, especially for mothers at risk, immunization, protection from radiation exposure, improved obstetrics, control of Rh isoimmunization and other measures have prevented the occurrence of some abnormalities and reduced the complications which formerly added to the incidence and prevalence of retardation. New hazards appear, however, in environmental toxic substances, strains of microorganisms more resistant to antibiotics, new addictive and nonaddictive drugs, new sources of radiation, environmental stress, all of which are potential producers of biological damage and mental retardation (Begab, 1974).

On balance, it is possible that incidence of severe retardation is falling while prevalence is continuing to rise.

The high birth rate of the post World War II period produced a record number of severely retarded children who are surviving longer than ever before. The future, envisioning more control of the causes with a lower birth rate more limited to optimal conditions of reproduction may in time yield lower prevalence rates of the moderate, severely and profound retarded. Currently, a very conservative estimate of their number in the United States is approximately 500,000 (Tarjan, et al, 1973) but may actually be nearer a .3% level or 660,000 surviving beyond the first year of life.

The prevalence of mild retardation is quite a different matter. Where the severely retarded show a declining prevalence by age, based wholly on mortality, the mildly retarded show a sharply peaked prevalence in the school years (6-19) and a rapid falling off in the adult years. This phenomenon cannot be a product of mortality, because the mildly retarded have shown longevity very nearly that of the general population. There are two possible alternatives, both of which may be the case. Large numbers remain retarded but cease to be the objects of attention; or they in fact cease to be retarded. In any case, no survey has yet found prevalence rates of mild retardation remotely approaching a constant across ages, such as would be expected on the assumption of unchanged relative mental status. Tarjan suggests that the rate of 3% traditionally projected as a constant across all ages, actually holds only for the school-age, with rated prevalence in selected age groups of .25% in the 0-5 group, 3.0% from 9-16, .4% from 20 to 24, sinking to .2% in the population over 25; the overall prevalence being approximately 1% (Tarjan, et al, 1973, p. 370). This would yield a total of approximately 2.2 million retarded persons in the United States, as against 6.6 million if an overall 3% is assumed.

In studies of the Riverside, California, population, Mercer (1974) showed that the prevalence and social distribution of mild mental retardation differed markedly according to the definition and methods of identification employed. She compared the application of a "social system" definition ("mental retardate" is an achieved status, and mental retardation is the role associated with the status) with a "clinical" definition (mental retardation is an individual pathology with characteristic symptoms which can be identified by standard diagnostic procedures).

It was found that the use of a one-dimensional clinical definition (IQ less than 69) yielded an overall rate of 2.14% retarded, with Blacks showing a rate 10 times and Mexican-Americans 34 times the rate of Anglos. When a two-dimensional definition is used (IQ less than 69 *plus* deficient adaptive score) the overall rate shrank to .9% which is the "clinical" rate predicted by Tarjan. The distribution now showed Blacks approximately at the same rate as Anglos, but Mexican-Americans still 15 times greater. When pluralistic, culturally adjusted norms were used for both IQ and adaptive behavior, the overall rate reduced still further to .54% but the total shrinkage in this case was accounted for in the Mexican-American group where sociocultural nonmodality (a cultural pattern distinctly different from the predominant mode) and bilingual background were most prominent. Furthermore, when higher criteria for IQ and adaptive behavior were used, the disadvantage to both Blacks and Mexican-Americans, as compared with Anglos, was markedly increased.

The social distribution of mild mental retardation has been found by all investigators to be inversely related to socioeconomic status. It is, according to Conley (1973) 13 times more prevalent among poor than among middle and upper income groups and found most frequently among rural, isolated or ghetto populations. Controversy persists concerning the contribution of constitutional and social learning factors to this distribution, but it is a question of the relative wieght rather than an exclusive alternative. No one doubts the multiple effects of environmental deprivation on both physical and psychological development. Nor is there much doubt that social learning enables the great majority of those with mild intellectual limitations to assume normal social roles in adult life. It is evident that what might appear to be a manifestation of the normal distribution of polygenic general intelligence is really a complex product in which the genetic component is only one among many factors yielding varying degrees and rates of retarded behavior, among varying populations at varying ages.

There is little point, then, in arguing who is "really" retarded. There is great point in determining who is in need of developmental and supportive assistance in achieving a reasonably adequate adult life, in determining the relationships between identifiable characteristics and the kinds of services that will be profitable, and in employing terminology that will aid rather than obscure these relationships. A critical issue is the degree to which cultural pluralism is reflected in the educational process.

The classification suggested by Mercer (1973) involves a four-dimensional matrix in which potentially handicapping conditions, including mental retardation defined in either "clinical" or "social system" terms, may be identified:

a) The dimension of *intellectual functioning,* measurable on a continuous scale represented by IQ. On this scale, following the 1973 AAMD standard, an IQ of 69 or less is regarded as potentially handicapping and is one clinically defining characteristic of mental retardation. Mercer terms the person with *only* this dimension of disability as *quasi-retarded.* Ordinarily this will be reflected in learning difficulties in the school setting and justifies individually prescriptive educational assistance.

b) The dimension of *adaptive behavior,* measurable on a developmental scale of behavioral controls accommodating the person to his environment. On this dimension a person falling substantially below age norms (perhaps in the lowest 3% of a normative distribution) is regarded as potentially handicapped. This constitutes a second clinically defining characteristic of mental retardation of the 1973 AAMD standard. Mercer terms the person who has *only* this dimension of disability as *behaviorally maladjusted,* but she identifies the person with disability in both a) and b) as *clinically mentally retarded,* requiring services in both school and non-school settings.

c) The dimension of *physical constitution,* describable in terms of the health or pathology of the various organ systems of the body. While not a defining characteristic of mental retardation, physical impairment may be in itself potentially handicapping and may be the cause of or magnify the handicapping limitations of a) and b). The probability of organic impairments being present increases with the severity of mental retardation, from 3% at mild retardation levels to 78% at moderate levels and 95% at severe and profound levels (Conley, 1973, pp. 46–7). Individuals characterized by only c) may be termed generically as *physically impaired,* and in combination with a) and b) as *organic mentally retarded.* The term "multiply handicapped" is commonly used, but this would apply equally to persons with more than one substantial physical impairment.

d) *Sociocultural modality* is a fourth dimension which is distinguishable from the other three. It refers to the extent to which sociocultural variables of family background conform or do not conform to the modal culture in which the individual is assessed. When the family background is substantially non-modal, in this sense, the individual may be potentially handicapped in relation to the prevailing cultural expectations because of lack of opportunity for the appropriate learning. Such a person may be termed *culturally disadvantaged.* Mercer found that non-modality yielded effects which, to the dominant culture, appeared as low IQ, low adaptive behavior, or both when measured by the norms of the dominant culture. Utilizing a pluralistic model of mental retardation, sensitive to socio-cultural differences, Mercer found a substantial reduction in the prevalence of mental retardation in the Mexican-American as compared to the Anglo population of Riverside. Throughout the investigation, the Anglo sample yielded a constant rate of 4.4 per thousand identified as mentally retarded (i.e. no Anglos in this sample were judged either quasi-retarded or non-modal culturally). The Mexican-American population yielded the following succession of rates per 1,000:

a) One dimensional—only standard IQ norms, 149.0

b) Two dimensional—standard IQ + standard adaptive behavior norms, 60.0

c) Partial pluralistic two dimensional—standard IQ, pluralistic adaptive behavior norms, 30.4

d) Pluralistic two dimensional—pluralistic norms for both IQ and adaptive behavior, 15.3

(Mercer, 1973, pp. 235-254)

The residual differences between the rate of 4.4 for Anglos and the 15.3 rate for culturally adapted assessment of Mexican-Americans may be attributable to the pervasive effects of their bilingual status.

Granted that Mercer's research is based on a single local population sampling and is a first approach to a "social systems" definition of mental retardation, it suggests the need for much more highly refined procedures in the definition and epidemiology of mental retardation as a basis for the adequate and appropriate delivery of developmental and supportive services where they are needed.

There is complete agreement that it is impossible, at our present state of knowledge, to determine accurately either the incidence or the prevalence of mental retardation. There is far less agreement on what we can do to remedy this situation. Among the most urgent issues in classification:

1. **Definition.** The formulation adopted by the American Association on Mental Deficiency involving two-dimensional deficit in the level of behavioral performance unquestionably is responsive to many problems arising from older definitions. But a number of issues remain:

a) The two dimensions are not independent, but are, in fact, highly correlated, the degree of correlation being related to severity of deficit, suggesting the distinction of intellectual and adaptive measures has not been sufficiently refined. In practice, more reliance is frequently placed on IQ measures than on measures of adaptation or other bases of clinical judgment.

b) The cultural contamination of standardized tests as currently used makes their findings suspect. Mercer and others require a corrective for cultural insensitivity of the instruments employed.

c) The use of a global IQ measure which may be adequate for epidemiological purposes obscures the complexity of intellectual functioning and the variability of individual profiles which is the basis of service provision. Global IQ measures are rapidly losing favor among professional providers of service but are maintained for administrative convenience and ease of determination.

d) Differences in the conditions associated with mild retardation as compared to the more severe forms in terms of organicity, comprehensiveness of impairment, resistance to modification, relatedness to cultural norms, etc., suggest to some that the two types are sufficiently different as to require separate classification, probably based on organic (or presumed organic) versus psychosocial etiology.

2. **Services.** Since the instruments for the measurement of intelligence and adaptive behavior are scalar, with continuous variation on both sides of central norms, the relationship between a specific level of deficit and the need for specific types of service and treatment may be highly artificial. This appears to be the central question underlying the controversy over the criterion level in the AAMD definition which now excludes persons with IQs from 70 to 85 who formerly were included. The fact that relatively few scoring above 69 IQ manifest significant deficits in adaptive behavior may miss the point. Adaptive behavior may be quite specific and situational, especially where culture modality may also be in question. The real issue is to determine individual

need, which cannot be derived from the IQ or adaptive behavior. This issue has been exacerbated by legislation which requires categorical classification as a condition of eligibility for service.

3. **Labeling.** Titles are necessary for any scientific system of classification, and may be useful for certain administrative purposes; but their use in human service systems is a different matter. The attachment of a label to a species of plant or a type of rock makes no difference to the plant or the rock. The label assigned to classify a human being does make a difference. To label a person mentally retarded has consequences of a psychological nature if the person is cognizant of it and can assign a meaning to it; it has consequences of a social nature insofar as other persons assign meaning and respond in terms of that meaning. This is especially the case with the label of "mentally retarded" because all terms associated with deficiency of intelligence are, in our culture, highly charged with negative values.

There have been many attempts to use systems of intellect classification as a means of adapting school and other programs to individual differences without making those differences appear invidious. These have not been entirely successful because value systems, even for children, tend to filter through the most subtle of euphemistic terminology.

This is a difficult issue to resolve. Success is possible only if: a) classification for epidemiological purposes is entirely separated from need-evaluation for purposes of social grouping and prescriptive treatment, b) all treatment is person-centered rather than system-centered, c) cultural value systems are recognized and respected, and d) eligibility for categorical assistance is based, not on global statistical criteria, but on the individual's need.

4. **Recording, Registering and Information Control** (corollary to labeling). Obviously, the best data base for the epidemiologist would be a computerized data bank including all information on every case. This has, in effect, been advocated since Samuel Howe's first attempt to catalogue the "idiotic" population of Massachusetts in 1848, long before modern systems of information storage and retrieval were dreamed of. However, rights of privacy and confidentiality have become a critical issue. The problem is one of reconciling the needs of the service delivery system and the individual recipient, so that he will neither be "lost" as an anonymous number nor stigmatized for having his needs recognized.

5. **"Negativism."** The nature of retardation lends itself to definition and assessment in the negative terms of deficit from desirable norms. The individual person, however, is not made up of deficits but of asset characteristics, however meager or distorted some of them may be. All treatment rests on the positive capacity of the person to respond, whether physiologically or psychologically. The issue of negatively versus positively defined traits and classifications is a basic one between the purposes of epidemiology and the purposes of service assistance.

Who are the people who are mentally retarded? They are individuals whose assets for effective living in their cultural and physical environments are insufficient without assistance. The screen by which they are brought into view to be identified and counted is composed of a mesh of intellectual and adaptive behavior norms. But the screen is a somewhat crude and abrasive instrument and requires to be refined and softened by concern for the individuals it exposes.

How many mentally retarded people are there? The loss of potential for normal development and even survival affects a high proportion of those who are conceived, and probably 3% of those who survive birth. In addition to those hundreds of thousands who are not well-born, there are millions who are not well-nurtured by the world in which they live. How we sort out these millions, how many will be called "mentally retarded" will depend on our definitions and our perceptions of need. The roots of these needs are not yet under control, nor have we sufficiently provided for their assuagement.

REFERENCES

Begab, M.J.: "The Major Dilemma of Mental Retardation: Shall We Prevent It? (Some Social Implications of Research in Mental Retardation)," *American Journal of Mental Deficiency*, 1974, 78:5, 519–529.

Birch H., Richardson, S., Baird, Sir Dugald, Harobin, G., Illsley, R.: *Mental Subnormality in the Community,* Baltimore: The Williams and Wilkins Co., 1970.

Cobb, H.V.: *The Forecast of Fulfillment: A Review of Research on Predictive Assessment of the Adult Retarded for Social and Vocational Adjustment,* Teachers College, Columbia University, N.Y. and London: Teachers College Press, 1972.

Conley, R.W.: *The Economics of Mental Retardation,* Baltimore and London: The Johns Hopkins University Press, 1973.

Heber, R.: *A Manual on Terminology and Classification in Mental Retardation,* A Monograph Supplement to the American Journal of Mental Deficiency, Second Edition, 1961.

Heber, R., Garber, H., Harrington, S., Hoffman, D., Falender, C.: *Rehabilitation of Families at Risk for Mental Retardation,* Rehabilitation Research and Training Center in Mental Retardation, Progress Report, University of Wisconsin, Madison, December 1972.

Holmes, L., Moser, H., Halldorson, S., Mack, C., Pant, F., Matzilevich B. (Eds.): *Mental Retardation: An Atlas of Diseases with Associated Physical Abnormalities,* N.Y.: MacMillan, 1972.

Kanner, Leo: *The History of the Care and Study of the Mentally Retarded,* Springfield Ill,: Charles C. Thomas, 1964.

Lubs, H.A., and Ruddle, F.H.: "Chromosomal Abnormalities in the Human Population: Estimated Rates Based on New Haven Newborns Study," *Science* 1970, 169, 495.

Mercer, J.: *Labeling the Mentally Retarded,* Berkeley: The University of California Press, 1973.

Mercer, J.: "Psychological Assessment and the Rights of Children," *Harvard Educational Review,* February 1974, 44:1, 328 ff.

Penrose, L.: *Biology of Mental Deficiency,* N,Y.: Grune and Stratton, 1963, P. 197.

President's Committee on Mental Retardation: *The Six-Hour Retarded Child, A Report on the Problems of Education of Children in the Inner City,* Washington, D.C.: U.S. Government Printing Office, 1970.

President's Committee on Mental Retardation: *Mental Retardation: The Known and the Unknown, Century of Decision Series,* DHEW Publication No. (OHD) 75–21008, Washington, D.C.: U.S. Government Printing Office, 1975.

Skeels, H.M., Updegraff, R., Wellman, B.L.: "A Study of Environmental Stimulation, An Orphanage Preschool Project," *Studies in Child Welfare,* Iowa University, Published by the University, Iowa City, Iowa: 1938, 15:4.

Stein, Z., and Susser, M.: "The Epidemiology of Mental Retardation," Chapter 31 in *American Handbook of Psychiatry,* Second Edition, Volume Two, N.Y.: Basic Books, 1974.

Tarjan, G., Wright, S.W., Eyman, R.K., and Keernan, C.V.: "Natural History of Mental Retardation: Some Aspects of Epidemiology," *American Journal of Mental Deficiency,* 1973, 77:4, 369–379.

Zigler, E.: "Familial Mental Retardation: A Continuing Dilemma," *Science,* 1967, 155, 292–298.

From *Pictorial Completion Test II,* reprinted from the *Journal of Applied Psychology,* September 1921.

PLATE I

Sketch from the colored illustration of the simplest picture in the series, the demonstration picture, with the inserts which particularly relate to this picture. Of course only one is quite correct, but the others can be inserted with some show of reasonableness.

The Child with Down's Syndrome

MERRIL HARRIS

In cooperation with the effort toward mainstreaming children who have physical and mental handicapping conditions, a large percentage of Head Start and other early education programs are taking mentally retarded children. Many of these are children with Down's syndrome, since this is one of the most common causes of mental retardation.

Down's syndrome is commonly called "mongolism," because one of the distinguishing characteristics of the condition is an oriental-looking slant of the eyes. However, referring to a person with Down's syndrome as a "mongoloid" is offensive, and such usage is discouraged. Down's syndrome has nothing to do with the mongoloid race except that the syndrome appears among orientals as well as blacks and caucasians. It afflicts people of all classes in all parts of the world. The condition is named after the doctor—Langdon Down—who first described this syndrome about a century ago.

Down's syndrome is caused by a chromosome abnormality. Normally, each cell in our body has 46 chromosomes which are arranged in 23 matching pairs. A person with Down's syndrome has an extra chromosome on the 21st pair making it a trio and giving each cell a total of 47 chromosomes. The extra chromosome material somehow causes the characteristics of Down's syndrome. The reasons for the abnormality are not known,

but chromosome damage can be caused by such things as radiations, virus infections, and certain drugs.

Down's syndrome occurs once in every 700 births. It occurs most often in births among women over 35 years of age—half of all "Downs" babies are born to women over 35—but younger women can also bear a child with Down's syndrome. Women under the age of 30 have one chance in 1500 of having a child with Down's syndrome, while women over the age of 45 have one chance in 40.

Physical Characteristics

People with Down's syndrome are usually small in stature and have short arms, legs, fingers and toes. Their eyes have the characteristic exotic slant, while the back of the head and the bridge of the nose are slightly flattened. The inside of the mouth may be very small. This can cause the tongue to protrude and can also cause problems with speech. There is usually a single crease across the palm of the hand. The only positive means of diagnosing Down's syndrome is a chromosome study which will clearly show the presence (or absence) or the extra chromosome. (This can also be done through amniocentesis to determine whether or not a pregnant woman is carrying a fetus with a chromosome abnormality.)

Health

One-fifth of Downs babies have low birth weight, and sometimes they do not feed well as infants. They may cut teeth relatively late. Their physiological systems are generally

quite immature and growth in all areas—physical, motor, cognitive, language, etc.—will probably be slower than that of other babies. Leukemia is 20 times as frequent in Downs children as in other children, about half of them have congenital heart defects, and many are subject to bronchitis, pneumonia, and other respiratory problems. They may also have neurobiological abnormalities which can result in perceptual disorders, and they often have visual or hearing disabilities severe enough to affect learning.

Mental Retardation

This term is arrived at on the basis of an individual's performance on standardized tests. What it actually means is that a child will be at a level of development significantly below the norm for her or his chronological age, particularly in areas of cognitive and intellectual functioning and possibly also in motor, language and social functionings. "Retarded" means slowed or obstructed, *not* stopped. Children who are mentally retarded go through the same developmental stages as do other children, but the duration of each stage may be prolonged, and the acquisition of basic skills will probably take longer.

The greatest area of delay in Downs children is that of speech and language. Physiological differences give their voices a gutteral quality and can cause problems with articulation, while the entire condition of retardation, especially when combined with perceptual disturbances, can cause delays in language development.

There is a great deal of erroneous stereotyping and fallacious opinion regarding children with Down's syndrome. In fact, Downs children CAN learn to walk, talk, toilet train, feed and dress themselves, read, write, count, and socialize. They can NOT be classified as "stubborn" or "friendly." They CAN understand verbal communication, and they ARE capable of responding appropriately. There are rarely problems with violence or sexual activity—children with Down's syndrome CAN be taught socially acceptable deportment as well as any other child can.

Young children with Down's syndrome can be stimulated into following a normal pattern of development at a rate that is not too severely retarded and can progress much faster than one might expect. Many Downs people, even without the benefit of early stimulation, are capable of formal learning up to or beyond high school level, enjoy socializing as young adults, and have the potential to live independently as contributing members of society.

Mainstreaming

Children with Down's syndrome can function quite well in an early childhood program with all types of other children. If they have been stimulated since infancy, they will probably not be much behind other toddlers or preschoolers. Teachers can rest assured that a Downs child who is profoundly retarded will not be placed in the program to begin with. A retarded child who is recommended for mainstreaming will be a child who can function successfully in a normal program on all levels, although she or he will require some extra care in being educated.

As will any child, children with Down's syndrome will become bored if they are not stimulated, and this can be extremely harmful. Boredom and lack of suitable stimulation will result in further developmental retardation and the acquisition of self-stimulating behaviors. Normal children will, even when left to their own devices, seek out stimulation which will contribute to their growth in learning. Downs children must be taught how to do this; they will not do it spontaneously. Because their physiology is in every way conducive to developmental lags (i.e. immaturity, poor motor coordination, perceptual problems), these children must have more than the usual amount of sensory stimulation as well as deliberate structure for learning experiences in order to provide them with enough input and momemtum to progress in all areas of development. If a child with Down's syndrome is not actively stimulated and taught, especially when very young, she or he will probably fulfill all archaic predictions by vegetating.

Because of their general immaturity, Downs children will probably be slower than the average child in motor development. The shortness of their limbs may require more practice in using them to become proficient. They can benefit greatly from gross motor activities with emphasis on balance, coordination, and movement.

Downs children may take longer to process and respond to verbal communications, and because of this, teachers sometimes feel that the child does not understand. These children will respond more readily to instructions that are simple, well-structured, and clearly spoken. It is helpful to the child for the teacher to combine gestures with speech whenever possible, even to the point of pantomiming an activity. If the child appears to be uncertain of what is expected, she or he can be gently manipulated by the teacher through the proper motions or actions. The teacher should be prepared to break down all skills and activities whenever necessary, finding the level where the child is able to perform successfully independently and then, through practice, to build up abilities from that point.

Except for the fact that Downs children will need more active stimulation and more detailed and simplistic direction when involved in learning activities, they should not be treated differently from other children in the program. They are clever enough to quickly realize when they can get away with being a "poor mentally retarded child" and will not hesitate to take advantage where and when they can. They will test the adult in charge the same as any other child will, and they will develop their relationships on the basis of the responses they receive.

Just like other children, Downs children do not all look alike, act alike, learn in the same manner, or have the same temperaments or personalities. Just like other children, they are curious and enjoy exploring and learning. They can participate in all activities offered by an early childhood program—music, art, blocks, water play, trips, etc—and they can be subjected to the same expectations that the teacher has for the other children with regard to behavior and social adjustment.

Children with Down's syndrome are well aware that they are not like other children. Their inclusion in a normal school program will help them to develop a well-balanced self image through involvement in natural situations with other children. It is also healthy for other children to have contact with children who have handicapping conditions; with familiarity comes an end to the disgust that rises out of fear and ignorance, and these children will hopefully grow to be adults who have a greater tolerance for each other and acceptance of individual differences.

Learning through Outdoor Adventure Education

ROGER D. FRANT
CHRISTOPHER C. ROLAND
PAUL SCHEMPP

■ Participation in recreational sports and movement activites, for all children and adults, is an important avenue to developing a richer and fuller understanding of one's own strengths and inner resources. Access to this dimension of growth is no less important for special needs individuals.

Most moderately and severely disabled persons are involved in daily education and rehabilitation programs that do not necessarily include recreation. Recreational sports and movement activities are inherently reinforcing and a physically beneficial means of promoting mobility learning, social interaction, and greater self reliance.

ADDRESSING SPECIAL NEEDS AT CAMP RIVERWOOD

Since 1978, the National Football League Players Association has sponsored a Special Needs Sports and Movement Camp for persons with moderate to severe disabilities at Camp Riverwood in Winchendon, Massachusetts.

Camp Riverwood's conceptual origin was similar to that of the Special Olympics in its intent to train individuals with handicaps for single event competition. As the program evolved, however, its focus was enlarged to include movement and outdoor exploration. This departure from individual event competition toward a more integrated perspective of sports, movement, and outdoor exploration focuses on individual growth in the context of group participation.

The aim of Camp Riverwood is to help disabled persons achieve greater physical, mental, emotional, and social awareness and growth through a well planned, sequenced series of activities. General goals for each camper are the development of self confidence and trust.

More specific goals include improvement in socialization skills, interpersonal relationship skills, and level of independence. Other critical goals include enhancement of verbal and nonverbal communication, physical mobility and coordination, and individual and group initiative. Self reliance and group membership are two key constructs of the camp philosophy.

Enrolled over a 2 week period during the summer of 1980 were 110 campers ranging in age from 9 to 56 years old, with a primary diagnosis of moderate to severe mental retardation. Many exhibited accompanying behavioral problems. Fifty percent of all campers were on medication for a variety of reasons, including seizures, hallucinations, hyperactivity, and aggressive behaviors. Twenty-five percent were subject to seizures. Most were able to feed themselves and were toilet trained; all were ambulatory. Expressive and receptive language skills were highly divergent. Because of the physical limitations of the camp setting, persons in wheelchairs and those with severe visual impairments could not be accepted.

The campers came from a variety of settings, including private homes, group homes, foster homes, and state residential facilities. For most, this was their first overnight camping experience away from their yearly living environment. For all of them, it was their first participation in outdoor exploration and movement activities.

Two camp sessions, each 1 week in length, were conducted. Activities included aerobics, outdoor exploration, New Games, track events, swimming, field events, and quiet recreation activities. Each of the 9 activity instructors had extensive professional training and certification in their area of expertise. In addition, there were 2 head counselors, 18 general counselors, and 2 full-time registered nurses.

ACTIVITY GOALS

The goals of adventure/initiative activities for this special needs population included the following:

1. To enhance gross motor skills.
2. To enhance receptive (listening) skills.
3. To enhance expressive skills (communicating one's thoughts/feelings).
4. To develop analytical problem-solving abilities.
5. To develop cooperation skills within a group setting.
6. To develop an awareness of one's abilities and capabilities.

A primary goal for the camp's staff was that of attitudinal change toward the handicapped. "She can't do that," or "He might get hurt," or "They wouldn't like it, anyway," were frequent staff comments. It was hoped that an adventure program might indeed change camp staff perceptions of the abilities and potential of disabled persons. In addition, because camp staff members participated in activities *along with* the campers, they shared similar experiences, sensations, and perceptions.

Campers were divided into heterogeneous groups loosely based upon age. Each outdoor adventure activity group consisted of 10 to 12 campers, 2 counselors, a registered nurse, and 2 qualified instructors.

ADVENTURE ACTIVITIES

Three phases of adventure activities were conducted in an intentional, progressive order: (a) New Games, (b) Initiative/Problem Solving Tasks and (c) Ropes Course. Although the three areas had similar program goals, each one presented unique challenges to the group members.

New Games

Bolstered by the notion that "winning isn't everything—it's the only thing," the stress of competition discourages many persons from participating in physical activity. Games such as basketball and football are properly referred to as *exclusive* sports or games; only a chosen few "make the team." Those who lack the necessary degree of skill become observers. The result is a sit-and-watch phenomenon, as witnessed by the 86 million fans who attended professional football, baseball, and hockey games in 1977 (Fluegelman, 1977).

New Games are an alternative to the traditionally competitive physical and educational curriculum. They are becoming more and more popular because they emphasize *inclusiveness* rather than exclusiveness. No one is eliminated from these games; everybody wins. Following are two examples of New Games.

The Octopus

Setting: Outside or in a school gym
Materials: None
Preparation: Two parallel lines are drawn, allowing a big enough space for students to run from one line to another and enough lateral movement to run in many directions.
Directions: One student is selected as the OCTOPUS and placed in the center of the open space. The rest of the group lines up on one side behind the line facing the center. The teacher tells the group the following brief story. (Its complexity can vary according to the language comprehension skills of the group.) "The OCTOPUS likes to catch people with its sticky, gooey tentacles. This is the way it grows. When the OCTOPUS says 'Go home,' you must run to the other side and cross the line without getting touched. If the OCTOPUS touches you, hold tentacles with the OCTOPUS and help him grow." Keep the game going until all group members have become part of the dreaded OCTOPUS. Give several different group members a chance to start the game.

Pin Ball

Setting: Outside or in a school gym
Materials: Playground ball (size may vary according to the skills of the group)
Preparation: Students form a large circle, facing away from the center of the circle, with their legs spread wide apart

Getting across the Poison Peanut Butter Pit requires that everyone work together.

and feet touching their neighbors' feet. Teacher or student stands in the middle of the circle holding the ball.

Directions: "You are a human pinball machine. Bend forward at the waist and look at me through your legs." (Teacher models this behavior.) "Try to keep the ball in the circle and do not let it go through your legs. When the ball comes to you, use your hands to hit the ball to someone else." The person in the middle starts the game by rolling the ball toward a player and then joins the circle. The game continues until the score of 5. Give several group members a chance to start the game.

Teachers interested in using New Games in the classroom may wish to consult books by Fluegelman, 1977; Orlick, 1978; Roland & Havens, 1981; and Schneider, 1976.

Initiative/Problem Solving Tasks

These tasks are posed to a group comprised of a minimum of 5 individuals. Solutions are designed to require the combined effort of all group members; no single member can solve the problem alone. Rohnke (1977) commented:

> The outdoor initiative tasks in particular give groups of students a series of clearly defined, physical problems. They are designed so that each group must attempt to work out its own solution....Participants work on the problem in groups in order to take advantage of the combined physical and mental strength of a team. (p. 65)

Following is an example of an Initiative/Problem Solving Task.

Debriefing helps participants get the most out of their experiences.

Poison Peanut Butter Pit

Setting: Outdoors at a large sand pit or indoors at a large marked-off rectangular or square area.

Materials: Planks of wood, wide enough to walk on, but when stretched end to end, not long enough to reach from side to side of the sand pit

Preparation: Group members are standing near the sand pit. The wooden planks lie near the pit in no specific order.

Directions: The teacher tells the following brief story: "You are running away from some lions and tigers. The only way to safety is to cross the Poison Peanut Butter Pit. How can you get across to the other side? Remember, all your friends must go with you." The team members must think of a way to cross the pit and then be able to execute the plan successfully.

Solution: Lay the wooden planks across the pit with enough space between each plank to allow the members to make small skips from plank to plank until they all get across. The length and width of the planks can be modified to accommodate the skills of the group.

The following sources provide an excellent introduction to Initiative Tasks, as well as numerous activities to implement: Darst, 1980; Rohnke, 1977; Roland and Havens, 1981.

With the campers at Riverwood, Initiative Tasks not only brought out the group's problem solving abilities, but also facilitated effective decision making and promoted peer interaction, interdependence, and leadership. Overall, they molded a collection of individuals into a functioning group.

Ropes Course

Once the members had established a cohesive group structure and a mutual support system, they were ready for the

The Ropes Course is an individual challenge, yet group support provides needed encouragement.

third and final activity: the Ropes Course. Here, the tasks were purely individual, yet the need for continued group support was ever-present.

A Ropes Course consists of a series of strong ropes and wire cables that can rise from 4 feet up to 40 feet above the ground. All participants and instructors tie a swiss seat on themselves before the activity begins. The swiss seat is a proven mountaineering harness to which ropes can be attached.

Before climbing, the individual hooks onto a belay system; a goldline rope is attached to the person, then passed over a wire, through two safety hooks, and back to the ground to an instructor who holds it. Once these steps have been completed, the individual can begin climbing on the ropes and cables. Each person is safely guided by staff, two of whom are in the trees and two on the ground. In the rare case of a fall, the person is safely held on the rope by the instructor.

DEBRIEFING

Too often, an adventure activity is immediately followed by another activity, another class, free time, or a bus ride home. The full significance of the activity is not truly realized, and potential benefits are unfortunately lost.

For maximum benefit to occur, a crucial procedure commonly referred to as *debriefing* follows each of the sequential activities. Debriefing can take place at many levels of awareness and expressive skill development in order to accommodate a wide range of disabilities.

The debriefing technique at Camp Riverwood was found to be most effective when conducted in the following sequence:

1. Immediately following an activity, have the group sit in a circle. (If the ground is wet, be sure to bring a covering.) The instructor should be positioned so that the entire group is able to see.
2. Ask the group to identify what they just did.
3. Ask each individual whether they enjoyed the activity, and if not, why not.
4. Ask the group members to describe how they felt about the activity. Was it easy, difficult, scary?
5. Ask the group what person or persons came up with ideas that helped to solve the problem.
6. Ask if there was group support. Did anyone help a friend?
7. Try to bring out students' feelings about their own performance and that of others. Be sure to accept each student's feelings and ideas; this important teacher attitude is sometimes forgotten.
8. Help students summarize the activity by asking them to review the major sequences of events and interactions (a quick review of questions 1 through 7).

A sample dialogue follows between an instructor and a group of campers who have just completed an activity requiring the entire group to climb through a rubber tire suspended above the ground between two trees before they get swept away by an imaginary tidal wave. The tire is too high off the ground for someone to get through without support.

Instructor: "Can someone tell me what you all just did?"
Lillian: "Went through hole."
Instructor: "What was the problem you had to solve?" (Silence)
Instructor: "What did you have to do?"

Peter: "Get through hole."
Instructor: "Why?"
Martin: "Water was coming."
Instructor: "Right! The huge tidal wave was coming. Who came up with an idea?"
Martin: "Billy!" (Billy smiles.)
Instructor: "Well, what was his idea?"
Emily: "Billy found a thing to climb on and get through the hole."
Instructor: "Did it work?"
Group: "Yea!"
Instructor: "Who helped?"
Courtney: "Amy, David, Michael, and Andrea."
Instructor: "Very good. Do you think helping is important?"
Group: "Yes."
Instructor: "Why?"
Peter: "We couldn't do it alone."
Instructor: "That's right; everybody has to help each other to get something done. Kristin, at first you didn't want to go through the tire, did you?"
Kristin: "No."
Instructor: "But you did it, right?"
Kristin: "Uh huh."
Instructor: "Remember, a lot of people are sometimes afraid of things. You're not the only one! Now, before we go to the next activity, let's see if we can all remember the different things we did to solve the problem."
Instructor: "What happened first?"
Loren: "We tried to climb through the hole. But it too high!"
Instructor: "Very good, Loren. What happened next?"
Nick: "We climbed on Martin's back."
Instructor: "Did that work?"
Group: "No. Billy found a box."
Instructor: "Right. What happened next?"
Billy: "Martin climbed in hole and helped Courtney."
Instructor: "Did everyone get through the hole?"
Group: "Yea."
Nina: "Kristin had a hard time."
Instructor: "What happened? Did Kristin make it?"
Group: "Yes. We all helped."
Instructor: "Very good work. You all worked together. Everyone was saved from the tidal wave. Let's do the next activity."

ADAPTING ADVENTURE ACTIVITIES

Elements of the adventure program can be easily duplicated, either in whole or in part. School programs have the distinct advantage of being able to structure a 9 month program for the same group or different groups of students, allowing them to progress at a steady pace throughout a sequence of activities. (For a list and description of the New Games and Initiative/Problem Solving Activities, as well as an explanation and diagram of the Camp Riverwood Ropes Course, write Dr. Roger D. Frant, School of Education, 166 Hills South, University of Massachusetts, Amherst MA 01003.)

New Games and Initiative Tasks lend themselves easily to adaptations based on learner and/or environmental variables. The activities can be adapted as a whole or incorporated into physical education, recess, morning opening exercises, as energizers throughout the day, or as motivators. Most required equipment and materials are either minimal in cost or are already available in schools. Schools have the open space, both indoors and out, that is necessary for most tasks. Others are easily adapted to smaller spaces.

Because the activities are primarily action oriented, verbal directions and story lines can vary from simple to complex. Task difficulty can be geared to the skill level of the group, and activities can be modified for persons with severe physical, visual, and/or hearing impairments.

A school program of this type was designed and implemented in Derry, New Hampshire, for Project TRAILS (Teaching Retarded Adolescents Independent Living Skills) from 1977 to 1979. New Games, Initiative Tasks, and an indoor Ropes Course were all offered. The activities adopted at Camp Riverwood and in Derry are traceable to Project Adventure, developed and implemented at Hamilton-Wenham Junior and Senior High School in Massachusetts (Rohnke, 1977). Project Adventure ideas were also adopted by Project UMPA (Urban Modification of Project Adventure) in Cambridge, Massachusetts.

These programs were implemented with limited funds, yet proved to be successful as well as rewarding for all participants. Starting a program of New Games and Initiative Tasks in a school requires no immediate cost. Materials that are not already a part of the school equipment inventory can be made by teachers and students or donated by families or community groups.

For information about workshops in New Games, contact the New Games Foundation (Fluegelman, 1977). While no formal training is mandatory, teachers should attend New Games workshops or participate in New Games and Initiative Tasks themselves prior to implementing a program in the schools.

A Ropes Course, on the other hand, requires considerable forethought, training, and capital expense. Qualified personnel must be contacted if this third sequence is to be implemented. Teachers interested in training and design of Ropes Courses should contact Carl Rohnke (1977) or Chris Roland (1981).

DIMENSIONS OF PERSONAL GROWTH

For teachers, the most exciting part of using adventure activities and New Games are the tangible results. Among the benefits readily observed at Camp Riverwood were the following:

- *Verbalizations.* Many campers increased the rate and appropriateness of their verbal communications. Responses were encouraged by frequent questioning. "Why? Please explain." Expressive language was further motivated in the context of successfully shared experiences and challenges that were met and completed.
- *Cooperation/Group Membership.* Campers completed problem solving activities in a group setting, and supported

other campers during the Ropes Course activities. Each camper shared responsibility for the safety and well being of others. A feeling of belonging was fostered.
- *Affective Development.* Adventure activities encouraged expression of a wide range of emotions. Elation, fear, anger, wonderment, and satisfaction were all experienced and expressed.
- *Success at Risk Taking.* All campers had the opportunity to take physical and psychological risks. Taking a risk presupposes trust—trust in yourself, trust in your instructor. The level of risk is never an absolute measure. For some, walking on a rope stretched 40 feet over the ground is a risk; for others, walking on a balance beam placed on the floor is an equivalent risk. Positive feelings of accomplishment were assured because all activities could be completed at an individual level of skill readiness.
- *Problem Solving.* All too often, daily decisions are made by others for persons who are moderately or severely retarded. Adventure activities and New Games allow the individual to make independent decisions and solve problems with group support.
- *Nature and Outdoors.* Active outdoor activity has its own reinforcing qualities for most campers. Unlike their yearly living arrangements, this is a relatively new environment. Being outdoors requires different behaviors and fosters the discovery of previously untapped personal resources.
- *Physical Fitness.* Participation in outdoor activities promotes physical fitness through the enhancement of flexibility, strength, and endurance. With sequenced introduction of activities, each camper has the opportunity to proceed on an individually appropriate level.

Outdoor activities and New Games also allow professional staff to view disabled persons in a new setting—a positive, supportive environment with fewer traditional cues that suggest, "No, you can't." Each staff member participated hand-in-hand with the campers. Together they learned, and together they discovered a common ground of respect and success.

REFERENCES

Darst, P. W., & Armstrong, G. P. *Outdoor adventure activities for school and recreation programs.* Minneapolis MN: Burgess, 1980.

Fluegelman, A. *The new games book.* Garden City NY: Doubleday, 1977.

Orlick, T. *The cooperative sports and games book: Challenge without competition.* New York: Pantheon, 1978.

Rohnke, K. *Cowtails and cobras.* Hamilton MA: Project Adventure, 1977.

Roland, C. C., & Havens, M. D. *An introduction to adventure: A sequential approach to challenging activities with persons who are disabled.* Loretto MN: Vinland National Center, 1981.

Schneider, T. *Everybody's a winner: A kid's guide to new sports and fitness.* Boston MA: Little, Brown, 1976.

Changes in Mild Mental Retardation: Population, Programs, and Perspectives

EDWARD A. POLLOWAY
J. DAVID SMITH

EDWARD A. POLLOWAY *is Associate
Professor of Special Education,
Lynchburg College, and J. DAVID SMITH
is Professor of Special Education,
Lynchburg College, Lynchburg, Virginia.*

Abstract: Recent developments in special education have begun to produce a significant change in the population being served under the label of mild retardation. The specific factors influencing this change and the effects of the overall functional levels of students enrolled in EMR programs are examined. Data on decreasing prevalence within programs are presented. Implications are drawn for emerging group characteristics, placement and curricular decisions, and labeling relative to such programs and for concerns about noncategorical grouping. An apparent shift in the conceptualization of mild retardation underscores the discussion of each of these issues.

■ Much of the initial work in the field of special education in this century, and the initial involvement of many professionals, can be traced back to a focus on individuals served under the label educable mental retardation (EMR) or mild retardation. Despite this fact, there has been an accelerating trend away from professional interest in this group. As Bartlett (1979) noted, much of the attraction of the mild retardation field seems to have diminished in recent years. Certainly the formulation of learning disabilities as a separate field and the recognition of severely handicapped as a distinct area have been major factors in this apparent decline.

A significant change in the population served under the EMR label and, in a sense, a redefinition of the term mild retardation has coincided with decreasing interest in this field. The interplay between trends toward reduced professional involvement and enthusiasm and toward changes in population has resulted in a rather dramatic lack of attention to demographic, programmatic, and research concerns for this population as compared to its relative status in special education a decade ago. The purpose of this article is to analyze the concept of mild retardation as it relates to the current and future state of affairs in the delivery of educational services. The article will address four subtopics: factors influencing change in the EMR population, transformations in the characteristics of the population, implications for programming, and the implications of these program modifications for the overall field of special education.

FACTORS INFLUENCING POPULATION CHANGE

An arbitrary distinction could be made in the traditional EMR class between those students identified by Dunn (1973) as "adaptive" and those identified as "nonadaptive" in the sense that the former were more likely to demonstrate the skills associated both with a higher degree of success in part-time mainstream programs and with greater success in terms of postschool adjustment. In considering changes in the EMR constituency, we must recognize the possibility that this adaptive, higher-functioning group will now often fail to meet eligibility criteria as required on national, state, and local levels; that is, they no longer "qualify" as being mentally retarded. At the same time, the efficacy of early intervention programs has prevented some cases of mild retardation. There is also the increasing phenomenon of the "promotion" to EMR placements of individuals previously stereotypically viewed as moderately retarded and placed in trainable classes (e.g., Down's syndrome children).

In considering the first general factor resulting in population transformations, the EMR declassification of adaptive students, an obvious beginning point is the American Association on Mental Deficiency's (AAMD) definition (Grossman, 1973, 1977) that, compared to the previous Heber definition (1959, 1961), resulted in two significant changes. In terms of measured intelligence, the definition, in effect, acknowledged professional reluctance to accept an IQ score of 85 and lowered the ceiling score by an additional standard deviation to 70. However, despite the fact that the AAMD intended that this ceiling score be viewed as a guideline to be subjected to clinical judgment rather than being seen as an absolute requirement (Begab, 1981), in practice the EMR category has been increasingly reserved for those with an IQ of 65 or lower (Gottlieb, 1981). The importance of considering the ceiling IQ of 70 as an approximation subject to clinical judgment has been reaffirmed in the AAMD's most recent definitional revision (Grossman, 1983).

The more significant result of the wide acceptance of Grossman's definition has been increased attention to adaptive behavior (AB). By complementing IQ with this second dimension, the definition clearly decreased the potential number of individuals who could accurately be identified as retarded. Although this shift in public policy has had a direct effect on school procedures, it is surprising to note that a review of research showed no evidence that this change in policy is reflected in any increased use of AB in subject selection and description (Smith & Polloway, 1979).

Litigation has also played a major role in the shift within the EMR population, particularly by calling into question the placement of minority group children. The two most important cases, *Diana v. State Board of Education* (1970) and *Larry P. v. Riles* (1972), were concerned with the educational rights of Mexican-American and Black children, respectively, in the California public school system. The basic assumption in both cases was that the placement of these children in such classes was based on discriminatory procedures and that the outcomes of such placement had a negative effect on their educational progress. Clearly discrimination was the major factor in the court's deliberations. As Reschly (1982) has pointed out, in *Larry P.* and related cases the key issue should have been the effectiveness of the programs, but the focus instead was limited primarily to criteria for placement.

Regardless of focus, the results of the litigation, at least in California, have been clear. MacMillan and colleagues (MacMillan, 1982; MacMillan, Meyers, & Morrison, 1980) summarized the direct implications of these cases for EMR programming. They noted that in the intervening years significant decreases of 11,000 to 14,000 individuals had occurred in the state EMR enrollment largely reflective of the declassifying of minority children in response to the court's mandate. Similar, though less dramatic, results have been noted elsewhere, although substantial variance in prevalence figures between states continues to be the rule (Patrick & Reschly, 1982).

The direct consequences of these cases have been a rethinking of identification procedures and, thus, a reconsideration of the concept of mental retardation. The work of Jane Mercer (e.g., 1970, 1973) and others has stressed a sociological perspective on retardation, which encourages a limited view of retardation as a comprehensive impairment involving permanent incompetence—quite contradictory to the typical picture of persons who have been classified as EMR and to the Grossman (1983, p. 15) manual's specification that retardation is a current life status, which "carries no connotation of chronicity or irreversibility." In lieu of the traditional use of IQ scores, Mercer and Lewis (1977) have offered the System of Multicultural Pluralistic Assessment (SOMPA) toward the goal of unbiased assessment.

The adoption of the SOMPA itself or the acceptance of its rationale even without the use of the tool would have several key effects on identification procedures in EMR programs. By offering a method for the adjustment of IQ scores based on sociocultural status, the instrument yields an Estimated Learning Potential that increases scores for many children. Second, the SOMPA focuses on adaptive behavior *outside* school and, therefore, downplays the real difficulties experienced within school that may have led initially to referral. Assuming that students are referred primarily by teachers for academic and behavioral performance deficits, it should be safe to suggest that IQ tests are not being used by psychologists to "... attempt to catch unwitting victims in their psychometric nets" (Reschly, 1982, p. 23). Thus, a change in identification procedures, though decreasing the number of students *eligible* for services, will clearly not decrease the number who are in *need* of services.

The consequences of such a decrease in population is evident. Reschly (1981) estimated that the use of the measures and criteria built into SOMPA would result in a prevalence figure of less than .5% for mild mental retardation and clearly would have a major effect on children who would no longer be eligible for services. His brief review of research on those found ineligible is not encouraging; of those declassified from EMR programs, one-half were eligible for other special education services, but the others were not despite their continuing intellectual limitations and academic deficiencies. Similar consequences stemming from changes in identification criteria have been reported by Childs (1982) and Mascari and Forgnone (1982). Thus, although a restrictive concept of mild retardation, requiring, for example, an out-of-school focus for adaptive behavior deficits, may reduce the prevalence of identified EMR students, the question remains as to whether this is in their best interest.

Table 1 summarizes federal data on the number of retarded children served on a state-by-state basis between 1976–77 and 1980–81. Although the data does not make a differentiation according to levels of retardation, it can be assumed that the changes are reflective primarily of mild retardation since this group represents the large majority of the overall MR population. Given the fact that these years followed the passage of P.L. 94-142, it is significant to note that *all but eight* states and territories showed a decrease in the number of children served during this five-year period and that six of the eight did show a drop-off between 1979–80 and 1980–81. These changes came in spite of an apparent federal mandate for an increase in the identification of handicapped children. As noted in Table 1, the overall percentage decrease for the nation was 12.9%. Although none of the specific factors discussed earlier can be pinpointed as the critical agent in such a dramatic change, it is reasonable to assume that all were influential to some extent in producing this trend.

A second general factor potentially influencing population change stems from early intervention efforts with poverty level children and their parents. The prevention of mild retardation from psychosocial sources has been well-documented and is fully discussed in volumes edited by Begab, Haywood, and Garber (1981). Clearly the evidence supporting such programs points to the alterability of intellectual levels for children deemed to be at high risk for mild retardation and related learning difficulties in school (e.g., Garber & Heber, 1981; Ramey & Haskins, 1981). The most impressive results have been limited to specific projects, but the evidence suggests that the application of these principles and procedures to poor families in general would reduce the prevalence of EMR students in school programs.

Although recent practices in education have begun to reduce the prevalence of higher functioning, adaptive children identified as EMR in special education programs, there has been an increase in EMR class enrollment of those children traditionally served in programs created for a lower functioning population. As MacMillan, Meyers, and Morrison (1980) accurately pointed out, the openings in such classes due to the reduced prevalence of EMR students have often been filled by children with more serious handicaps who previously would have been placed in trainable classes and labeled moderately retarded.

The most encouraging reason for this change has been the success of early intervention programs with handicapped preschool children. The work of Rynders, Spiker, and Horrobin (1978) is most important in alerting professionals to one aspect in the shift in population in groups from TMR to EMR. After reviewing data on Down's syndrome children who have participated in early intervention programs, they indicated a "temptation" to predict a 30–55% chance that a Down's child would subsequently function in the EMR range. Their review of 29 studies of Down's syndrome children indicated that for all three karyotypes (trisomy 21, translocation, and mosaicism), IQ ranges superseded the current ceiling on IQ scores for MR placement. Similar results have also been reported by other researchers involved in related efforts (e.g., Connolly, 1978).

EMERGING CHARACTERISTICS

Given these shifts in population, the characteristics of students who are labeled EMR are undergoing a metamorphosis that should alter our traditional view of the group. An interesting basis for comparison comes from the list of general characteristics provided by Dunn (1973) as an elaboration on Rothstein (1971). He identified twelve generalizations that were considered to be more accurate for students classified as EMR than for students within the general school population. Mildly retarded students were more likely:

6. TEACHING THE MENTALLY RETARDED CHILD

TABLE 1
Number and Change in Number of Children Ages 3–21 Years Served Under P.L. 89-313 and P.L. 94-142
Annually Since School Year 1976–1977

| State | | | Mentally Retarded | | | | |
State	1976–77	1977–78	1978–79	1979–80	1980–81	1980–81 − 1976–77	% Change 1980–81 − 1976–77
Alabama	31,203	31,990	33,923	35,127	34,840	3,638	+ 11.7
Alaska	1,277	1,294	1,051	906	734	− 543	− 42.5
Arizona	8,608	7,879	7,238	6,879	6,592	− 2,016	− 23.4
Arkansas	14,674	16,489	17,703	17,433	17,449	2,775	+ 18.9
California	42,916	40,768	41,023	39,810	38,947	− 3,969	− 09.2
Colorado	10,077	8,235	8,259	6,808	6,423	− 3,654	− 36.3
Connecticut	10,132	10,330	8,954	8,212	7,940	− 2,192	− 21.6
Delaware	3,199	3,264	2,839	2,629	2,405	− 794	− 24.8
District of Columbia	2,918	1,695	1,882	1,309	1,318	− 1,600	− 54.8
Florida	34,311	33,844	31,990	29,973	27,978	− 6,333	− 18.5
Georgia	31,744	30,478	31,214	30,274	30,021	− 1,723	− 05.4
Hawaii	2,434	2,478	2,465	2,120	1,807	− 627	− 25.8
Idaho	3,567	3,642	3,721	3,021	2,759	− 808	− 22.7
Illinois	48,974	50,022	46,977	50,770	46,058	− 2,916	− 06.0
Indiana	27,784	28,086	28,269	27,165	26,666	− 1,118	− 04.0
Iowa	12,663	12,825	12,786	12,955	12,643	− 20	− 00.2
Kansas	8,665	9,141	7,946	7,780	7,413	− 1,252	− 14.4
Kentucky	22,872	23,138	23,060	23,321	23,193	322	+ 01.4
Louisiana	24,547	24,537	22,661	20,713	19,164	− 5,383	− 22.0
Maine	5,664	5,311	5,467	5,293	5,200	− 464	− 08.2
Maryland	17,523	15,311	12,134	11,870	11,060	− 6,463	− 36.9
Massachusetts	34,972	31,380	26,671	26,822	26,834	− 8,138	− 23.3
Michigan	34,715	34,064	32,921	31,188	29,882	− 4,833	− 14.0
Minnesota	15,140	15,812	14,973	14,894	14,098	− 1,042	− 06.9
Mississippi	15,487	16,365	18,330	18,720	18,593	3,106	+ 20.1
Missouri	25,304	23,539	24,717	23,192	22,076	− 3,228	− 12.8
Montana	2,114	2,167	2,126	1,780	1,615	− 499	− 23.6
Nebraska	7,557	7,837	7,887	7,015	6,610	− 947	− 12.5
Nevada	1,586	1,595	1,780	1,365	1,217	− 369	− 23.3
New Hampshire	2,720	2,859	2,360	2,453	1,787	− 933	− 34.3
New Jersey	22,394	21,612	21,386	18,489	16,537	− 5,857	− 26.2
New Mexico	4,519	4,231	3,930	3,439	3,139	− 1,380	− 30.5
New York	55,582	51,782	48,566	47,960	41,675	− 13,907	− 25.0
North Carolina	46,334	44,662	45,557	43,507	39,986	− 6,348	− 13.7
North Dakota	1,974	2,168	2,050	2,083	1,809	− 165	− 08.4
Ohio	67,626	67,567	66,411	64,422	62,682	− 4,944	− 07.3
Oklahoma	12,753	13,126	14,025	13,781	13,372	620	+ 04.9
Oregon	7,697	7,008	6,195	5,991	5,518	− 2,179	− 28.3
Pennsylvania	56,461	53,221	51,340	49,276	49,202	− 7,259	− 12.9
Puerto Rico	8,132	9,290	13,510	10,539	13,062	4,931	+ 60.6
Rhode Island	2,483	2,200	2,243	1,989	1,974	− 509	− 20.5
South Carolina	29,944	27,260	27,276	26,090	24,941	− 5,003	− 16.7
South Dakota	1,787	2,291	1,374	1,245	1,260	− 527	− 29.5
Tennessee	23,019	26,319	26,510	23,302	21,945	− 1,074	− 04.7
Texas	47,580	42,154	36,259	31,033	28,591	− 18,989	− 40.0
Utah	5,117	5,281	3,532	3,327	3,194	− 1,923	− 37.6
Vermont	2,133	2,069	2,593	3,363	3,095	962	+ 45.1
Virginia	22,359	21,344	19,468	18,950	18,425	− 3,934	− 17.6
Washington	11,684	12,311	11,374	11,063	10,799	− 885	− 07.6
West Virginia	11,963	11,559	11,181	11,552	11,508	− 455	− 03.8
Wisconsin	19,187	17,714	15,792	15,004	14,668	− 4,519	− 23.6
Wyoming	1,197	1,046	1,081	1,044	1,050	− 147	− 12.3
American Samoa	71	94	84	65	69	− 2	− 02.8
Guam	739	907	1,457	921	919	181	+ 24.5
Northern Marianas	-	4	13	9	11	-	-
Trust Territories	526	109	42	19	23	− 503	− 95.6
Virgin Islands	954	619	586	732	792	− 162	− 17.0
Bur. of Indian Affairs	-	672	718	821	612	-	-
U.S. & Territories	969,547	944,980	917,880	882,173	1,844,180	− 125,367	− 12.9

Source: U.S. Department of Education, Office of Special Education, Data Analysis System, November 6, 1981.

(1) to have met defeat, frustration, and rejection in the regular grades where they were first placed; (2) to have exhibited substantial behavior disorders in general education; (3) to be from racial or ethnic minority groups; (4) to have parents who place little value on education; (5) to have inadequate health and nutritional provisions; (6) to be unclean and unkempt; (7) to live in poverty and deprivation; (8) to be boys rather than girls; (9) to come from broken or disorganized homes; (10) to be seriously retarded in school achievement; (11) to have restricted oral language skills in standard English; (12) to have obtained IQ scores ranging between 65 and 78 on individualized tests of verbal intelligence administered in standard English. (p. 131)

Dunn's prediction that dramatic changes would occur in the subsequent decade has been realized and certainly has implications for a number of these characteristics. Although the number of children from poverty backgrounds remains high in EMR classes, the "cultural-familial" stereotype fostered by a number of the listed characteristics (e.g., 3, 4, 5, 6, 7, and 9), faulty as an initial conception, will soon result in an even greater misconception of this population. The designation of mildly retarded children collectively as cultural-familial, indicative of an interplay of genetic and environmental factors in the absence of specific pathological causes (Heber, 1961), is less accurate as the population of children served in EMR classes is increasingly affected by additional etiological agents (e.g., chromosomal anomaly).

The first characteristic listed must be revisited due to the fact that a larger number of EMR children are likely to come into such programs directly from TMR or preschool programs for the handicapped or to have been referred earlier in their school careers. Such a change requires a review of the data on outer-directedness and failure set (e.g., Zigler, 1966), which have been cornerstones in an understanding of the learning styles of mildly retarded children.

The reference to substantial behavior disorders was a reflection of the fact that, given intellectual and academic functioning levels that are roughly consistent with traditional EMR guidelines, the referral of a given child was more likely to have been made when he or she had experienced difficulty with conformity to rules in the regular classroom (Polloway & Patton, 1981). The advent and growth of programs for disturbed or disordered children has likely decreased the prevalence of such behavioral problems in EMR classes, although it is reasonable to assume that concomitant behavioral disorders will continue to increase chances for referral and thus continue to bias identification and the make-up of the population.

The tenth generalization focuses on deficits in school achievement. Given a move to a more handicapped population, this assumption should be of greater concern. The discrepancy between chronological age and achievement level would be expected to be greater, thus presenting a challenge to teachers concerning the possibilities of having students identified as EMR reach at least a level of partial literacy.

In terms of oral language development, the shifting nature of the population should result in more evidence of language delay in this group, as would be common, for example, with Down's syndrome children even after successful early intervention (e.g., Hayden & Dmitriev, 1975; Rynders & Horrobin, 1975) rather than just the dialectical and linguistic differences. Considerations of the interaction between delay and difference will be critical in the educational assessment of the population (Polloway & Smith, 1982).

Clearly the greatest change from Dunn's 1973 list is in intellectual level. The range of IQ scores within EMR programs has been limited significantly by the more widespread adoption of the cut-off established by Grossman. Although in practice this figure has not been universally adopted in eligibility guidelines on a state-by-state basis (Huberty, Koller, & Ten Brink, 1980), the fact remains that cut-offs of 75 or 80 are rarely employed today.

The apparent changes in characteristics as discussed in the foregoing leave the programs serving what MacMillan and Borthwick (1980) termed "a more patently disabled group" (p. 155). This requires a rethinking of EMR programs particularly as related to service delivery and curriculum.

PROGRAMMING IMPLICATIONS

Discussions of the appropriate *placement* for students classified as EMR have been a legacy of special education with efficacy research reviews (e.g., Cegelka & Tyler, 1970; Dunn, 1968; Johnson, 1962). Subsequent to the enactment of P.L. 94-142 much of the "conventional wisdom" was subjugated to the increasing trend toward mainstreaming in the public schools, the Zeitgeist of the times (Meyen & Altman, 1975). Although mainstreaming as the wholesale return of all children to regular classes was not the intent of the legislation, clearly the effects were significant in terms of the placement of many students identified as EMR.

The question that arises at this time is what effect population change will have on the appropriateness of the regular class as the least restrictive environment. Though all placements must be made on an individual basis, some group considerations need to be addressed.

The key issue is that although school practice of the late 1970's featured an increasing emphasis on regular-class-based programs for students classified as EMR, the change operated in a paradoxical fashion. MacMillan and Borthwick (1980) reported that in California very limited integration of EMR students was being achieved and that when this occurred, it was most often in nonacademic areas. They saw this as indicative of the limited potential of this group for success in the regular classroom.

The data generated through efficacy studies, though typically weakened by design limitations, failed to demonstrate significant differences between regular and special classes in achievement. However, as Gottlieb (1982) noted, since the population of students who continue to be classified as EMR occupies the lower-ability levels of the traditional EMR category, past research efforts that analyzed the effectiveness of mainstreaming efforts have limited relevance to the current situation.

In summary, it appears that, where significant population changes have occurred or are occurring, the mainstreaming debate as originally enjoined is now moot. Those students for whom Dunn (1968) urged alternative programming are in many cases simply no longer placed in EMR programs—the original problem has been solved although other problems now must be addressed.

Curriculum is a second major programmatic concern that must be evaluated in light of population change. Despite the general discrediting of the concept of the "watered-down" curriculum, mainstreaming in effect encouraged a dominant emphasis on academic skills in the regular-class curriculum. Simultaneously, the criticism focused on classes for students identified as EMR in the 1970's (e.g., "there's only two things wrong with special education: it's not special and it's not education") began to erode the vigor of the early days of the field of retardation. Bartlett (1979) concluded that a primary outcome of this shift from the efforts of the 1950's and 1960's was a greater emphasis on a purely academic curricular orientation, which he deemed questionable at that time; at the present time it seems even less warranted.

Two factors now dominate curricular concerns. Within special-class settings, a greater degree of "curricular freedom" should accompany the increased recognition of problems in academically integrating the more handicapped EMR population. Such an opportunity should encourage what Kolstoe and Frey (1965) two decades ago referred to as the study of "persistent life problems" and what more recently has been termed as instruction in functional daily living skills and career preparation.

Such an orientation is inconsistent with the cry in regular education for "back-to-the-basics." Smith and Dexter (1980) evaluated this movement for its potential effects on curriculum

for the mentally retarded and concluded that such an emphasis could result in over-attention to the three R's and, thus, possible exclusion of the broad-based curriculum needed for most EMR students.

The question of appropriateness of curriculum is most critical for adolescents and is compounded by the requirement in many states of minimum competency tests (MCT). Whereas secondary programs can be most effective by focusing on vocational and practical considerations, an emphasis on tests with unproven relevance for adult success are likely to have a negative impact on EMR programs by encouraging a more restrictive curriculum (Cohen, Safran, & Polloway, 1980).

The second consideration deals with curricular emphasis as related to part-time regular-class placement. Given the fact that mainstreaming efforts are likely to occur during nonacademic periods (MacMillan & Borthwick, 1980), an increased emphasis on social skills definitely appears warranted (Gottlieb, 1982). Gresham (1982) addressed this particular area of concern in a recent review. He pointed to the past failures of mainstreaming to achieve increased social interaction, social acceptance, and behavioral modeling of nonhandicapped by handicapped students. He concluded that systematic efforts at social-skills training are requisite to student success in these areas.

DISCUSSION

The changes in population, and thus characteristics, and the resultant need for reconsideration of curriculum represent major departures from the former status of EMR programs in public schools. The scope of these trends is such that implications can be drawn for several concerns within special education.

Concept of mild retardation. The most direct implication of these changes is the possible reconceptualization of mild retardation. As the emphasis has shifted toward a more seriously disabled group, the schools have begun the search for the "truly retarded," that is, those demonstrating low competence across all social roles (Reschly, 1981). By thus effecting the removal of those previously misdiagnosed, a positive step toward the elimination of the major discriminatory effects of special education has been achieved. However, continued efforts to eliminate pupils who demonstrate primarily school-based problems ignores the reality of why they were initially referred for services. As Reschly (1981) aptly stated, ". . . the interest of declassification stems from concerns for social equity. The consequences of the methods required in order to achieve this social equity may extend far beyond what was anticipated" (p. 18).

Any radical change in the concept of mild retardation must be carefully evaluated. Although courts or legislatures can encourage such a shift, "...learning problems cannot be mandated or legislated away" (MacMillan, 1982, p. 316). Clearly the population no longer found eligible for EMR programs has a continuing need for assistance beyond regular-class instruction. Any further shift emphasizing the evaluation of adaptive behavior entirely outside the school will accentuate this need.

Noncategorical programming. The rationale for noncategorical efforts in special education in terms of pupil placement must be reevaluated in light of the changes within the EMR group. Areas of categorical overlap that have been noted (e.g., Hallahan & Kauffman, 1977), are based on suppositions that should now be subject to renewed scrutiny. For example, Becker (1978) reported on data from five learning tasks administered to students in California, the state experiencing the most significant changes in population. He questioned the assumed overlap between the mildly handicapped categories and the implications for noncategorical educational programming and teacher training.

The need for a reevaluation of the trend toward noncategorical placement stems directly from the central assumption on which it is based. As Hallahan and Kauffman (1977, p. 147) stated "...grouping according to behavioral characteristics is more advisable than grouping according to traditional categories." The merits of such an orientation are apparent; now, however, we must consider whether behavioral characteristics are more often discrepant across categories than hypothesized previously and, thus, whether there is an increased level of characteristic differences between categorical groupings.

The significant increase in the number of children being served under the LD label (as noted in DOE/OSE figures, 1981) most certainly includes many children previously identified as EMR. Thus many students to whom the noncategorical movement applied have already been subsumed within the LD category. However, there is concern over whether special education services will continue to be available for those who will be declassified in the future. Implicit in much recent work in learning disabilities (e.g., Hammill, Leigh, McNutt, & Larsen, 1981; Poplin, 1981) is an effort to focus that field on the specifically learning disabled and away from the generalized slow learner.

The implication for noncategorical teacher-training programs has more to do with program content than with affiliation with specific as opposed to generic labels. Effective teaching methods selected according to task requirements and individual student responses certainly cut across categories. Curriculum, however, presents the most significant concern. Noncategorical training programs, such as those identified for the mildly handicapped, must reject a narrow focus on academic and remedial concerns in favor of a broader base inclusive of instruction in such areas as personal, social, and vocational development.

Labeling. The continuing concern that underlies trends away from EMR placement is the assumed stigmatizing effects of labeling. Despite the lack of clear-cut support for such an effect (MacMillan, Jones, & Aloia, 1974), this supposition is indeed a powerful one among parents and professionals. In fact, as Lovitt (1982) posited, labels are frequently more upsetting to adults than to the children to whom they are given.

A current investigation into the labeling issue was reported by Reschly and Lamprecht (1979) who questioned the assumptions underlying hypotheses of labels as stigmatizing. They reported that teachers did not retain the initial expectancy if they were presented with an opportunity to observe specific behavioral events that were inconsistent with a given label. They concluded that labels had significant effects only in the absence of other information about an individual child.

Given the acquired power of the label "mentally retarded" and yet mindful of the mixed research data on its effects, an attractive option would be to consider the labeling of services instead of children, in the way that was initially proposed in the field of learning disabilities (Lilly, 1982). Providing programs under a designation such as *academic and adaptive-skills training* would provide a beginning point in serving those students who no longer meet the more stringent EMR identification criteria and yet also fail to qualify as learning disabled. This system of service delivery would facilitate a more intensive instructional arrangement than is typically available, for example, in Title 1 programs. Recognition by federal and state agencies that this approach is an appropriate one for children who have experienced educational retardation would certainly be preferable to the two alternatives: requiring that the label mentally retarded be inappropriately affixed as a condition for eligibility or failing to provide programs.

For those students who remain in EMR programs or who are likely to be destaffed primarily because of professional and parent fear of the label, consideration of a new term may be in order. Consistent with Zigler and Balla's (1981, p. 198) call for "...some term in the area of intelligence that is analogous to the term 'short' when referring to height," we suggest the term *educationally delayed.* It encourages a comprehensive view of the deficits of the population while refraining from the powerful statement that has come to be associated with "mentally retarded."

Research cogent to the topics discussed in this paper is clearly limited at this time. Thus, while calling for public scrutiny of policies tied to the various issues addressed herein, we are calling for empirical study as well. Some of the specific areas of significant need are: comparison of the cognitive and functional levels of the "new" EMR student with "traditional" EMR students; the effectiveness of mainstream procedures with this population; the result of destaffing procedures on former EMR students with attention to where they are placed and how they fare; analysis of changes in the frequency of clinical types (e.g., Down's syndrome) of retardation within EMR classes; and, finally, an analysis of the relative benefits and potential effects of the focus on out-of-school versus in-school adaptive behavior.

After years of abuse and neglect by policymakers and professional educators, special classes for students classified as EMR have often become, either intentionally or inadvertently, the "whipping boys" of education. However, to permit court decisions to convince us that such programs are educational anachronisms and "dead-end" classes (as in *Larry P.*, 1972) essentially allows us to be convinced that we are unable to regulate our own profession. There remains a sizable population of school-age children who, without appropriate special education services, will fail to reach their academic and personal potential. Educational concerns demand educational solutions.

REFERENCES

Bartlett, R. H. Mental retardation—Where does the future lie? *Education and Training of the Mentally Retarded*, 1979, 14, 3–4.

Becker, L. D. Learning characteristics of educationally handicapped and retarded children. *Exceptional Children*, 1978, 44, 502–511.

Begab, M. J. Issues in the prevention of psychosocial retardation. In M. J. Begab, H. C. Haywood, and H. L. Garber (Eds.), *Psychosocial influences in retarded performance: Issues and theories in development* (Vol. 1). Baltimore: University Park Press, 1981.

Begab, M. J., Haywood, H. C., & Garber, H. L. (Eds.), *Psychosocial influences in retarded performance: Issues and theories in development* (Vols. 1 & 2). Baltimore: University Park Press, 1981.

Cegelka, W. M., & Tyler, J. L. The efficacy of special class placement for the mentally retarded in proper perspective. *Training School Bulletin*, 1970, 67(1), 33–37.

Childs, R.E. A study of the adaptive behavior of retarded children and the resultant effects of this use in the diagnosis of mental retardation. *Education and Training of the Mentally Retarded*, 1982, 17, 109–113.

Cohen, S. B., Safran, J., & Polloway, E. A. Minimum competency testing and its implications for retarded students. *Education and Training of the Mentally Retarded*, 1980, 15, 250–255.

Connolly, A. Intelligence levels in Down's syndrome children. *American Journal of Mental Deficiency*, 1978, 83, 193–196.

Diana v. State Board of Education. C-70-37 (RFP, District Court for Northern California), 1970.

Dunn, L. M. Children with mild general learning disabilities. In L. M. Dunn (Ed.), *Exceptional children in the schools*. New York: Holt, Rinehart, and Winston, 1973.

Dunn, L. M. Special education for the mildly retarded: Is much of it justifiable? *Exceptional Children*, 1968, 35, 5–22.

Garber, H. L., & Heber, R. The efficacy of early intervention with family rehabilitation. In M. J. Begab, H. C. Haywood, and H. L. Garber (Eds.), *Psychosocial influences in retarded performance: Strategies for improving competence* (Vol. 2). Baltimore: University Park Press, 1981.

Gottlieb, J. Mainstreaming. *Education and Training of the Mentally Retarded*, 1982, 17, 79–82.

Gottlieb, J. Mainstreaming: Fulfilling the promise? *American Journal of Mental Deficiency*, 1981, 86, 115–126.

Gresham, F. M. Misguided mainstreaming: The case for social skills training with handicapped children. *Exceptional Children*, 1982, 48, 422–433.

Grossman, H. J. *Classification in mental retardation*. Washington DC: American Association on Mental Deficiency, 1983.

Grossman, H. J. *Manual on terminology and classification in mental retardation*. Washington DC: American Association on Mental Deficiency, Special Publication (No. 2), 1973, 1977.

Hallahan, D. P., & Kauffman, J. M. Labels, categories, behaviors: ED, LD, and EMR reconsidered. *Journal of Special Education*, 1977, 11, 139–149.

Hammill, D. D., Leigh, J. E., McNutt, G., & Larsen, S. C. A new definition of learning disabilities. *Learning Disabilities Quarterly*, 1981, 4, 336–342.

Hayden, A. H., & Dmitriev, V. The multi-disciplinary program for Down's syndrome at the University of Washington preschool center. In B. Z. Friedlander, G. M., Sterritt, G. E. Kirk (Eds.), *Exceptional infant: Assessment and intervention* (Vol. 3). New York: Brunner/Mazel, 1975.

Heber, R. A manual on terminology and classification in mental retardation. *American Journal of Mental Deficiency*, 1959, 1961. (Monograph supplement)

Huberty, T. J., Koller, J. R., & Ten Brink, T. D. Adaptive behavior in the definition of the mentally retarded. *Exeptional Children*, 1980, 46, 256–261.

Johnson, G. O. Special education for the mentally handicapped—A paradox. *Exceptional Children*, 1962, 29, 62–69.

Kolstoe, O. P., & Frey, R. M. *A high school work-study program for mentally subnormal children*. Carbondale IL: Southern Illinois Press, 1965.

Larry P. v. Riles. C-71-2270 (RFP District Court for Northern California), 1972.

Lilly, M. S. *Divestiture in special education: A personal point of view*. Paper presented at the 60th International CEC Convention, Houston TX, April, 1982.

Lovitt, T. *Because of my persistence, I've learned from children.* Columbus OH: Charles E. Merrill Publishing Co., 1982.

MacMillan, D. L. *Mental retardation in school and society* (2nd ed.). Boston: Little, Brown, & Co., 1982.

MacMillan, D. L., & Borthwick, S. The new educable mentally retarded population: Can they be mainstreamed? *Mental Retardation,* 1980, *18,* 155–158.

MacMillan, D. L., Jones, R. L., & Aloia, G. F. The mentally retarded label: A theoretical analysis and review of research. *American Journal of Mental Deficiency,* 1974, *79,* 241–261.

MacMillan, D. L., Jones, R. L., & Meyers, E. C. Mainstreaming the mildly retarded. *Mental Retardation,* 1976, *14,* 3–10.

MacMillan, D. L., Meyers, C. E., & Morrison, G. M. System-identification of mildly mentally retarded children: Implications for interpreting and conducting research. *American Journal of Mental Deficiency,* 1980, *85,* 108–115.

Mascari, B. G., & Forgnone, C. A follow-up study of EMR students four years after dismissal from the program. *Education and Training of the Mentally Retarded,* 1982, *17,* 288 – 292.

Mercer, J. R. Sociological aspects of mild mental retardation. In H. C. Haywood (Ed.), *Socio-cultural aspects of mental retardation.* New York: Appleton-Century-Crofts, 1970.

Mercer, J. R. *Labeling the mentally retarded.* Berkeley: University of California Press, 1973.

Mercer, J. R., & Lewis, J. P. *System of multicultural pluralistic assessment: Parent interview manual.* New York: Psychological Corporation, 1977.

Meyen, E. L., & Altman, R. Research implications. *Education and Training of the Mentally Retarded,* 1975, *15,* 526–530.

Patrick, J. L., & Reschly, D. J. Relationship of state educational criteria and demographic variables to school-system prevalence of mental retardation. *American Journal of Mental Deficiency,* 1982, *86,* 351 – 360.

Polloway, E. A., & Patton, J. R. Biological causes. In J. S. Payne & J. R. Patton, *Mental retardation.* Columbus OH: Charles E. Merrill Publishing Co., 1981.

Polloway, E. A., & Smith, J. E. *Teaching language skills to exceptional learners.* Denver: Love Publishing, 1982.

Poplin, M. S. The severely learning disabled: Neglected or forgotten? *Learning Disability Quarterly,* 1981, *4,* 330–335.

Ramey, C. T., & Haskins, R. The causes and treatment of school failures: Insights from the Carolina Abecedarian project. In M. J. Begab, H. C. Haywood, and H. L. Garber (Eds.), *Psychosocial influences in retarded performance: Strategies for improving competence* (Vol. II). Baltimore: University Park Press, 1981.

Reschly, D. J. Evaluation of the effects of SOMPA measures on classification of students as mildly mentally retarded. *American Journal of Mental Deficiency,* 1981, *86,* 16 – 20.

Reschly, D. J. Assessing mild retardation: The influence of adaptive behavior, sociocultural status, and prospects for non-biased assessment. In C. R. Reynolds and T. B. Gutkin (Eds.), *A handbook for school psychology.* New York: John Wiley, 1982.

Reschly, D. J., & Lamprecht, M. M. Expectancy effects of labels: Fact or artifact? *Exceptional Children,* 1979, *46,* 55–58.

Rothstein, J. H. (Ed.) *Mental retardation: Readings and resources* (2nd ed.). New York: Holt, Rinehart, & Winston, 1971.

Rynders, J. E., & Horrobin, J. M. Project EDGE: The University of Minnesota's communication stimulation program for Down's syndrome infants. In Friedlander, B. Z., Sterritt, G. M., & Kirk, G. E. (Eds.), *Exceptional infant: Assessment and intervention* (Vol. 3). New York: Brunner/Mazel, 1975.

Rynders, J. E., Spiker, D., & Horrobin, J. M. Underestimating the educability of Down's Syndrome children: Examination of methodological problems in recent literature. *American Journal of Mental Deficiency,* 1978, *82,* 440–558.

Smith, J. D., & Dexter, B. L. The basics movement: What does it mean for the education of mentally retarded students? *Education and Training of the Mentally Retarded,* 1980, *15,* 72–79.

Smith, J. D., & Polloway, E. A. The dimension of adaptive behavior in mental retardation research: An analysis of recent practices. *American Journal of Mental Deficiency,* 1979, *84,* 203–206.

U.S. Department of Education, Office of Special Education, Data Analysis System. Numbers and change in number of children ages 3–21 years served under P.L. 89-313 and P.L. 94-142 annually since school year 1976–1977. November 6, 1981.

Zigler, E. Research on personality structure in the retarded. In N. R. Ellis (Ed.), *International Review of Research in Mental Retardation* (Vol. 1). New York: Academic Press, 1966.

Zigler, E., & Balla, D. Issues in personality and motivation in mentally retarded persons. In M. J. Begab, H. C. Haywood, & H. L. Garber (Eds.), *Psychosocial influences in retarded performance: Issues and theories of development* (Vol. 1). Baltimore: University Park Press, 1981.

An Analysis of EMR Children's Worries About Mainstreaming

Abstract: The decision to mainstream an EMR child from a self-contained special education setting constitutes a significant change in the child's academic and social environment. This study attempted to identify areas of concern that EMR children describe as they await the change to a mainstream placement. Responses of EMR students awaiting placement were compared to responses offered by EMR students already assigned part-time to regular classrooms. Data indicate that EMR students express a range of worries related to academic performance, social interactions and the transitions inherent in split placement. Significant differences between the groups were reported in all three areas of concern with transition worries most prevalent. Implications for further research on intervention strategies are discussed.

Barbara Tymitz-Wolf
Indiana University

Most special education teachers recognize the difficulty in making decisions about mainstreaming a child into a regular education classroom. Certainly this action is no less serious or complex than the initial placement decision. Despite the fact that a paucity of conclusive empirical evidence exists on mainstreaming effectiveness, some scholars in the field conclude that the movement to mainstream handicapped children will likely continue and probably accelerate (Gottlieb, 1982; Johnson, Johnson, & Maruyama, 1983; Wang, 1981). With this trend toward mainstreaming, educators must decide when a child, who has been primarily in a self-contained special education setting, is ready to spend time in regular education. As Gottlieb (1981) suggests, for many EMR children, mainstreaming constitutes placement in the regular classroom for at least half of their school day.

In this context, deciding when a child is ready for mainstreaming requires considerable insight. Part of the difficulty is that no stable or clear cut measures exist to determine with any degree of precision a child's readiness for mainstreaming (Barton, Brulle, & Repp, 1982; Masat & Schack, 1981). Recently, however, special education researchers have focused their attention on the issue of exit criteria and competencies in an effort to identify levels of behavior that would predict success in the mainstream setting (Algozzine, Whorton, & Reid, 1979; Hundert, 1982).

Traditionally, assessment of readiness has been accomplished through use of standardized measures of intellectual ability and academic performance. But in-depth analyses have revealed the need for more complete assessment strategies particularly in the domain of psychosocial development. Gresham's (1982) review of the literature on social performance in mainstreamed classrooms clearly indicates that mentally retarded children do not fare well in the social climate of regular education programs. Multifactored assessment in *both* academic and social areas, therefore, will provide a better understanding of a child's readiness for mainstreaming. Likewise, an analysis of all contextual and environmental variables within special and regular education classrooms appears quite helpful in predicting mainstreaming success as some research on exit competencies has already suggested (Barton et al., 1982; Brown, 1982; Heron & Skinner, 1981; Palmer, 1983).

In developing a comprehensive view of readiness for mainstreaming, particularly in light of the need for knowledge regarding social/emotional adjustment, it would seem extremely useful to understand children's own perceptions of whether they are ready to enter mainstreamed settings. A review of existing research has not uncovered any empirical analyses of children's reactions to mainstreaming decisions, although Gillet (1982) recently underscored the importance of assessing children's feelings regarding mainstreaming placement. Because the mainstream setting represents a psychological threat and stressful circumstance for many handicapped children (Gallent, 1981; Hannah & Parker, 1980; Morris, Davis, & Hutchings, 1981; Tennant, Smith, Bebbington, & Hurry, 1979), inquiry into children's worries and concerns might

Reprinted by permission, *Educating and Training of the Mentally Retarded*, October 1984, pp. 158-168.

reveal aspects of readiness that current assessment of exit competencies or readiness intervention programs presently do not address.

Stress, Worry and Mainstreaming

Even though much has been written in the popular literature on stress, attention has primarily focused on adults. However, the processes of stress appear to operate similarly in adults and children (Izard, 1982; Rutter, 1981). Negative events (i.e., poor performance, rejection, inappropriate behavior) create psychological stress which manifests itself in a variety of anxiety related behaviors such as anticipating failure (Schultz, 1980), fear (Tanner, 1976), forgetfulness, distractibility, depression and worry (Cotler & Guerva, 1976). Worry, as the cognitive aspect of anxiety, is inversely related to academic performance (Chandler, 1982; Morris et al., 1981; Morris, Finkelstein, & Fisher, 1976; Morris, Kellaway, & Smith, 1978; Morris & Liebert, 1970). In other words, feelings of worry are associated with lowered performance. Diminished social performance has also been noted in high anxiety children (O'Connor & Cuevas, 1982).

Little is known about the types of stress children are exposed to and the worries those stresses create. Research conducted thus far has involved non-handicapped students. Morris et al. (1976) found no significant differences in the amount of worrying between third through eighth grade males and females. Kovacs and Beck (1977) concluded that seventh and eighth grade students who received high teacher performance ratings scored low on a test of depression. More recently, Crowley (1981) corroborated the findings of Morris et al. (1976) and also reported no significant differences in the types of worries when urban, suburban, and private school students were compared. Crowley did note that some worries change with grade level, although for all students in his sample (third through eighth grade) the predominant worry concerned grades.

In discussing the need for research on stress and worry in children Rutter (1981) noted that there is "increasing interest in the phenomenon of resilience, as shown by the young people who 'do well' in some sense in spite of having experienced a form of 'stress' " (p. 323). He further suggested that intellectually able children may be "constitutionally more resilient." Thus, there is an intuitive appeal to the hypothesis that mentally retarded children are limited in their ability to cope with the stresses of mainstreaming. Correspondingly, numerous mainstreaming intervention approaches have been based on this assumption. Among them are programs for assertiveness training (Cotler & Guerva, 1976), social skill training (Bates, 1980; Fleming & Fleming, 1982; Palomares & Bull, 1974; Powell & Lindeman, 1983), and relaxation training (Lupin, 1977; Seiler & Renshaw, 1978). Continued development of intervention programs is likely.

The decision to mainstream a child from a self-contained special education setting constitutes a significant change in the child's academic and social environment. Theorists posit that change brings stress and that one's response may be negative or positive. Thus, how individual children respond to potential change appears to be a function of the perceived threat and the personal characteristics (e.g., I.Q., age, sex) the individual brings to the stress situation.

This study was exploratory in nature and attempted to identify areas of concern that mentally retarded children describe as they await the change to a mainstreamed placement. The intent was to delineate aspects of programming for preparing and ultimately assessing the exit competencies of mildly retarded students. Because assessment devices in this area of inquiry are unavailable, a description of instrumentation procedures follows.

Procedures

Phase I

The purpose of Phase I was to determine if EMR students could define the concept of "worry." A pool of 40 EMR students assigned to self-contained special education classrooms was identified. Students were dispersed among two urban school corporations and ranged in age from 8.5 years to 12.2 years of age. Parents were apprised of the intent of the interviews and provided needed consent. Using present performance levels from the most recent IEP and WISC-R verbal IQ scores, teachers categorized students into "high" verbal IQ EMR (WISC-R verbal IQ 84-70) and "low" verbal IQ EMR (WISC-R verbal IQ 69-51). Two doctoral interns with former elementary level teaching experience were trained to employ naturalistic interview procedures (Wolf, 1979), and each was randomly assigned to 20 students. Interviewers were not aware of the designated IQ group rating of the children interviewed.

Using a series of semi-structured questions (see Kazdin & Petti, 1982; Selman, 1981), subjects were first asked to describe what was meant by the word "worry." Subjects were then asked to provide an example of "something you worry about at home" and "something you worry about at school." Interviewers were trained to present selected probes for those children initially unable to describe the term or provide an example (Rich, 1968). Responses that fell within the broad categories of worry as previously described by Crowley (1981) and Rutter (1982) were rated as acceptable. From this subject pool, seven students (18%) were unable to respond to either of the interview tasks, e.g., gave inappropriate responses after three prompts. Post hoc analysis revealed that all seven were low verbal EMR and five of the seven had the lowest verbal IQ ratings (range 51–55) of the Phase I sample population.

Phase II

The purposes of Phase II were two-fold: (a) to determine if EMR students could articulate their concerns about potential assignment to a regular classroom; (b) to generate protocol items for an interview instrument on student concerns regarding mainstreaming. A second sample of 57 intermediate level EMR students (ages 9.0–12.5) attending self-contained education classrooms in 11 urban schools was identified. Based on WISC-R verbal IQ scores, all subjects were within the 84-55 WISC-R verbal IQ range. All students attended classrooms that were in close physical proximity to regular classrooms (McDaniel, Sullivan, & Goldbaum, 1982) and were judged by their teachers as having had frequent opportunity to observe and occasionally interact in the regular classrooms at the fourth, fifth and sixth grade levels. None of the subjects had been formally assigned to a regular classroom for any percentage of the day since their initial placement in self-contained special education. However, 27 students (47%) had attended regular education classroom prior to special education placement.

Parental consent for interviews was obtained and individual interviews were conducted in a nearby empty classroom. Interviewers repeated the process of asking respondents to describe and then provide an example of a worrisome school situation. Two subjects were unable to provide an acceptable response to the interview task and were terminated at this phase of the study.

Students were then asked to describe their reactions to possible assignment to a regular classroom for some portion of the school day. The standard introductory probe was stated as follows: "What would you think about it if (teacher's name) decided to have you spend time every day in a class like (name of regular teacher in physical proximity)?" "Could you tell me what kinds of things would make you happy about being in that classroom for part of the time?" [Subject response(s)] "Could you tell me what kinds of things would make you worry about being in that classroom for part of the time?" (See Morris et al. [1981] for validation of the term "worry" in self-report inventories on worry and emotionality.) Using recapitulation strategies (Payne, 1951; Wolf, 1979) interviewers asked EMR subjects to verify the interpretation of their comments. The mean length of interview was 11.45 minutes. Interviews were tape recorded and subsequently transcribed.

Transcripts were then analyzed for category (happy vs. worry statement); theme (content of statement within category); elaboration (degree of detailed description of content); and verification rating (agreement, unsure, disagree). From this analytical scheme items were generated that represented agreement in high and low frequency concerns within category and across subjects. Ninety-two percent of the sample expressed more statements categorized as "worry" compared to statements categorized as "happy." When compared to students with no regular class experience, students with prior educational experience in regular classrooms tended to express a higher number of worries although these differences were not statistically significant.

Analysis of content by independent raters suggested three emergent themes:

I. Academic— concerns which related to classroom achievement in the mainstream setting. Statements are characterized primarily by concerns about performance, evaluation or being the recipient of differentiated treatment by the teacher.

II. Social— concerns which relate to social and peer interactions which are independent of the teacher or curriculum. Statements are characterized primarily by concerns about being chosen or being the recipient of a negative social encounter.

III. Transition—concerns which relate to comparisons between the regular and special education settings. Statements are characterized primarily by concerns about control and authority.

Within this framework, concerns regarding social and transition issues were approximately equal while academic performance concerns were less prevalent.

A pilot version of 39 protocol items was then presented to a randomly selected subset of Phase II subjects. Interviewers were assigned only to students they had interviewed previously. As interviewers read each item, subjects were asked to place colored stickers under appropriate columns of a response sheet scaled as follows: (1) No, I don't worry about this (Red), (2) Yes, I do worry about this (Yellow). To further interpret separate items for respondents, interviewers consulted a prepared script which identified additional probes and examples in simplified language. Comparison of these responses with interview comments recorded seven weeks previously supported reliability over time and between measures (.82). Internal consistency coefficients for the no worry/worry items were reported at .74 and .71 respectively.

Phase III

The purpose of Phase III was to compare responses of EMR students awaiting placement in a mainstream setting with EMR students already assigned part-time to regular classrooms. During the late spring of 1982, 40 EMR students participated in the final phase of the study. Students were randomly selected from a larger pool of subjects meeting the characteristics of the two comparison groups. Students represented schools in both urban and suburban districts. Sex of the sample population reflected the percentage distributions of the school district's mildly retarded population with 13 females and 27 males participating as subjects. Twenty students between the ages of 8.5 and 13.1 and scoring within the WISC-R verbal IQ range of 84-55 had completed annual review procedures and were aware that they would be attending a regular classroom for some portion of the schoolday beginning in September, 1983. All had been participants in a minimum of five hours of non-academic classroom activities with their prospective regular classroom teacher. The remaining 20 students ranging in age from 8.7 to 13.0 and demonstrating WISC-R verbal IQ scores between 84-55 had been assigned to a regular classroom for at least six months.

Interviewers repeated the process of eliciting a definition of worry and then an example of a worrisome situation. During individual sessions, students completed the response sheet as the interviewers read items following the protocol format and prepared script. Subjects were encouraged to comment throughout the interview session. Interviewers terminated individual sessions with a portable computer game and rewarded each student's participation.

Results

Two main questions were posed by this research: (a) What are EMR students worried about in relationship to mainstreaming?; and (b) Are there differences in the amount and type of mainstreaming worries between EMR students awaiting mainstream placement and those already in mainstreamed classrooms? The type of mainstreaming worries refers to the themes of academic, social and transition concerns that emerged from the content analysis of Phase II interviews. The results are presented in response to each question.

Worries About Mainstreaming

As shown in Table 1, the percent tabulations demonstrate that at least 50% of all EMR students perceived 29 out of the 39 items on the inventory as being worrisome. The items that were most worrisome (selected by 75% or more of the subjects) tended to be in the transition category with social and academic concerns following respectively. The single most prevalent concern related to having a same sex friend from the regular education class to sit with at lunch (97.5%), followed by concern for getting good grades on daily work (92.5%) and concern about having to answer out loud in the regular class (92.5%). The most frequently cited transition worries were: being the only child from special education (82.5%); being sent back to special education as a punishment (82.5%); being sent back to special education full-time (82.5%); still being liked as much by the special education teacher (77.5%); knowing which teacher is boss (77.5%); and still being liked by the kids in special education (75%). Other prevalent social worries included: being chosen to play on the playground (80%); being called names (77.5%); and being asked to parties (75%).

EMR students do not appear to be very worried about: having clothes as nice as the regular education kids (32.5%); whether regular education kids will visit them at home (22.5%); getting different directions from both teachers (17.5%); getting lost in the building (16%); having messy papers (15%); and having to sit next to the regular education teacher (12%).

Based on the review of research in the areas of exit competencies and social and educational adjustment in mainstreamed settings, it was anticipated that social and academic worries would

TABLE 1

Distribution of Percent Responses by Item in Descending Rank Order

Item #		Academic	Social	Transition
32	I worry about having a (girl) (boy) from the new class to sit with at lunch/on the bus. [*same sex choice*]	97.5		•	
13	I worry about getting good grades on my daily work in the new class.	92.5	•	
31	I worry about having to answer out loud.	92.5	•	
27	I worry about being the only one from (SET name) in my new class.	82.5			•
17	I worry about being sent back to (SET name) when I get punished.	82.5			•
14	I worry about the new teacher sending me back to special education. [*full-time*]	82.5			•
24	I worry about being chosen to play on the playground/at recess.	80		•	
6	I worry about still being liked as much by (SET name).	77.5			•
33	I worry about which teacher is the boss.	77.5			•
9	I worry about being called names.	77.5		•	
12	I worry about being asked to go to parties.	75		•	
8	I worry about still being liked as much by the kids in my old class.	75			•
39	I worry about being liked by the new teacher.	74.5	•	
30	I worry about being made fun of [*imitated*] by the other kids.	72.5		•	
22	I worry about having to ask for a lot of help. [*in the new class*]	72.5			•
21	I worry about having a (girl) (boy) friend. [*opposite sex choice*]	72.5		•	
26	I worry about finishing my work on time.	72.5	•	
37	I worry about making my parent(s) sad/mad with how I'm doing.	72.5	•	
18	I worry about being picked by the other kids to play on a team in P.E.	70		•	
5	I worry about being picked by the other kids to work with them on things in my new class.	69.2	•	
23	I worry about missing work in (SET name) when I'm in the other class.	67.5			•
36	I worry about when the other kids use words I don't know—ones they make up for special things.	60		•	
2	I worry about remembering all the rules in my new class and my old class.	55	•	
29	I worry about missing work in my new class when I'm in (SET name) room.	55			•
28	I worry about having tricks played on me.	55		•	
4	I worry about being able to do special classroom projects with the kids in my new class.	55	•	
3	I worry about being asked to do something after school with a classmate.	55		•	
7	I worry about having my name on the board (*in the new class*) for being bad.	52	•	
25	I worry about having to use books and things that are different from the other kids'. [*in my new class*]	50	•	
34	I worry about having different work than the other kids. [*in my new class*]	47.5	•	
19	I worry about having to pay attention all the time. [*in my new class*]	45	•	
35	I worry about getting into fights.	42.5		•	
10	I worry about getting good grades on my report card.	35	•	
15	I worry about if my clothes are as nice as the other kids. [*in the new class*]	32.5		•	
38	I worry about whether the kids in my new class would come to visit me at my house.	22.5		•	
20	I worry about the teachers telling me to do things differently.	17.5			•
11	I worry about getting lost in the building when I change rooms.	16			•
16	I worry about having messy papers.	15	•	
1	I worry about having to have my desk next to the new teacher.	12.5	•	

* SET = Special Education teacher in self-contained setting.

dominate. But as the above data suggest, concerns over transition are the most worrisome category of the three.

Differences Between EMR Student Prior to and During Mainstreaming

Table 2 reports the differences between students awaiting mainstream placement and those already in mainstream settings for each item on the Worry Inventory. To establish the significance of these differences a test of proportion was accomplished. Bivariate contingency tables were constructed for each item and a chi-square was calculated for each contingency table.

In comparing percent differences across the two groups it appears that EMR students tend to be more worried about academic, social and transition concerns *after* being exposed to a mainstreamed classroom than they are while they await mainstream placement. This is particularly true in the transition and academic categories. The differences between the two groups are statistically significant on nine worry issues. Again, transition worries dominate.

TABLE 2

Percent Responses of Students Prior to Mainstreaming and Students Already Mainstreamed

	Prior to Mainstreaming	Already Mainstreamed	$\chi^2(1)$
SOCIAL			
I worry about having tricks played on me.	85	25	14.5***
I worry about whether the kids in my new class would come to visit me at my house.	25	20	0.14
I worry about being made fun of [imitated] by the other kids.	80	60	3.13*
I worry about if my clothes are as nice as the other kids. [in the new class]	20	45	2.85
I worry about being called names.	80	75	0.14
I worry about having a (girl) (boy) from the new class to sit with at lunch/on the bus. [same sex choice]	95	100	1.03
I worry about when the other kids use words I don't know—ones they make up for special things.	50	60	0.40
I worry about being picked by the other kids to work with them on things in my new class.	55	65	0.42
I worry about having a girl/boy friend. [opposite sex choice]	65	80	1.13
I worry about being asked to do something after school with a classmate.	60	50	0.40
I worry about being picked by the other kids to play on a team in P.E.	80	60	1.90
I worry about being asked to go to parties.	65	85	2.13
I worry about getting into fights.	55	30	2.56
I worry about being chosen to play on the playground/at recess.	70	90	2.50
TRANSITION			
I worry about having to ask for a lot of help [in the new class].	55	90	6.14**
I worry about still being liked as much by the kids in my old class.	80	70	0.53
I worry about being the only one from (SET name) in my new class.	75	90	1.56
I worry about still being liked as much by (SET name).	70	85	1.29
I worry about which teacher is the boss.	60	95	7.03**
I worry about being sent back to (SET name) when I get punished.	90	75	1.56
I worry about missing my work in my new class when I'm in (SET name) room.	55	80	2.85*
I worry about remembering all the rules in the new class and my old class.	45	65	1.62
I worry about getting lost in the building when I change rooms.	20	10	0.79
I worry about missing work in (SET name) when I'm in the other class.	40	70	3.64*
I worry about the new teacher sending me back to special education. [full time]	70	95	4.33*
I worry about the teachers telling me to do things differently.	15	20	0.17
ACADEMIC			
I worry about having messy papers.	10	20	0.78
I worry about being able to do special classroom projects with the kids in my new class.	75	60	0.64
I worry about finishing my work on time.	85	60	3.13*
I worry about getting good grades on my report card.	50	20	3.96*
I worry about getting good grades on my daily work in the new class.	95	95	0.36
I worry about making my parent(s) sad/mad with how I'm doing.	70	75	0.13
I worry about having to answer out loud.	90	95	0.36
I worry about having to pay attention all the time. [in my new class]	50	40	0.40
I worry about having to have my desk next to the new teacher.	10	15	0.23
I worry about having to use books and things that are different from the other kids'. [in my new class]	45	55	0.40
I worry about having different work than the other kids. [in my new class]	45	50	0.10
I worry about having my name on the board [in the new class] for being bad.	45	60	0.90
I worry about being liked by the new teacher.	70	75	0.41

*** $p < .001$
** $p < .01$
* $p < .05$

In social concerns, EMR students awaiting placement into a mainstreamed setting are more worried about having tricks played on them and being made fun of than are EMR students who have already spent time in a mainstreamed classroom ($\chi^2(1) = 14.5***, \chi^2(1) = 3.13*$). Likewise, in the area of academic concerns, students awaiting placement are more worried about finishing work on time and getting good grades on report cards than are students already mainstreamed ($\chi^2(1) = 3.13*; \chi^2(1) = 3.96*$). With transition concerns, however, the pattern is reversed. EMR students already mainstreamed are more worried than their counterparts awaiting placement about having to ask for help ($\chi^2(1) = 6.14**0$, determining which teacher is boss ($\chi^2(1) = 7.03**$), missing their work in special education ($^2(1) = 2.85*$), missing work in regular education ($\chi^2(1) = 3.64*$), and being sent back to special education full time ($\chi^2(1) = 4.33*$).

These findings contrast with predictions in the research literature which imply that children are likely to perceive more threat in unknown situations. The fact that children are more worried about transition issues after being in mainstreamed settings appears educationally significant.[1]

Discussion

The results of this study suggest that for this sample of children, worries surrounding the mainstreaming decision are prevalent. Worries exist among EMR children who are awaiting a change in placement and they continue to exist in children several months after placement. A clear limitation of the present study is that information on whether mainstreamed students had received any intervention training is not known. If they did, then the intervention(s) did not seem to allay the many concerns expressed by these children. If they did not receive training, the findings suggest that assessment of concerns prior to and during the mainstreaming placement is warranted. This is true for both the frequency of worry as well as concerns about the changing environmental/situational demands placed upon the child. The findings also imply a revision of training protocols so as to better respond to children's perceived needs in the mainstreaming process.

Children in this sample had fewer worries about academic stresses than either social or transitional concerns. One explanation for this trend in responses might be explained by developmental changes in the child's concept of ability (Nicholls, 1978). At ages 7 and 8, children believe that, regardless of ability, amount of effort will result in an outcome equal to the effort. Children aged 9–11 believe that those who work harder are smarter. Finally, at approximately 11 years of age, the child understands that ability can place limits on outcomes, irrespective of how hard the individual works. These stages describe the perceptions of nonhandicapped children and it is not known whether perceptions among the mentally retarded proceed at the same rate. It is suggested, however, that with age, EMR children begin to accept their limited capacity. A common observation, for example, is that of the EMR child saying, "I can't do that because I'm in special education." While it is true that some use this as an avoidance strategy, many of the students in this study appeared clearly matter-of-fact about their abilities.

The fact that social concerns are expressed by both groups reflects students' perceptions of the interactional demands of the mainstreaming placement. That finding is also indicative of the increased salience of peer evaluation at pre-adolescent and adolescent stages. Students at this age level are particularly conscious of being negatively judged as different. Rosenweig and Vacca (1983) found that regular education students observing special needs students receiving help created fears regarding their own abilities and that one strategy for dealing with those fears was to isolate or reject the mainstreamed student.

The accumulated research on limited peer group acceptance among nonhandicapped students supports the social concerns of EMR students. Correspondingly, that research also suggests that continued efforts to train handicapped students in social competence skills are needed. It should be noted, however, that *all* children experience some rejection or isolation. Putallaz and Gottman (1981) found, for example, that popular children were rejected or ignored 26% of the time. This finding should give pause to intervention strategies predicated on goals which do not reflect the contemporary social community of children. In fact, one of the subjects in the sample plainly remarked to the interviewer, "It's a jungle out there."

The transition between classes places a unique set of demands upon the EMR child. Requiring the child to move back and forth between classroom settings presents numerous situations for the child to make comparisons to a standard which can be external (i.e., teacher directed, peer directed) or to a standard which is internal to the child. Children beyond the second grade typically use normative or group standards for comparisons. Thus, the child in a mainstream placement is frequently presented with norms for comparison which are likely to be quite different between regular and special education classrooms, teachers, and students that populate each respective setting. For children with limited social and academic resources, functioning under shifting norms can create confusion and apprehension. Moreover, Chandler (1962) notes that when normative standards are subtle or covert, children experience increased anxiety and concomitant stress responses (i.e., worry). Researchers have further linked increased anxiety levels to lowered self-concept (Coopersmith, 1967) and to perceptions of limited locus of control (Lawrence & Winschel, 1975).

Concerns about transition suggest a need for a clear role definition within the two classroom environments. Perhaps mainstreamed students experience anxiety in the self-contained classroom because they no longer maintain continuity or even choose to identify with that class. Neither do the scheduling realities of part-time mainstream placements allow students to maintain complete continuity with the regular classroom population. Assuming a role in either situation proves to be a difficult adjustment given differing group dynamics and disruptions in group membership.

Implications

Public Law 94-142 sets out the mechanics whereby a child, when deemed appropriate, may legally participate in selected educational decisions that concern him/her. This is, in fact, the only educational legislation that provides such opportunity to children. How often this option is actually used in placement decisions has not been documented. The option implies, however, that the child has an important perspective to consider.

Solicitation of direct subjective input is not prevalent in reported research on mainstreaming. Researchers have primarily focused on the assessment of observed behavior employing objectively based instruments. Perhaps, in the case of EMR subjects, methodological difficulties in obtaining reliable verbal expressions of feeling, insight or preference have been viewed as difficult to obtain. There is some merit to this point of view as shown in the present study, since, in Phase II of instrumentation, low verbal EMR students (WISC-verbal IQ 51–55) were generally unable to participate in the interview task as designed. This does not, of course, preclude further experimentation to determine successful and reliable techniques to elicit self-report data on lower functioning children.

Because the "science" of mainstreaming decisions is inchoate, professionals cannot assume to know fully what is best for the child without understanding his or her self-perceived needs, perceptions and concerns. This does not suggest that the child knows what is best but rather that the child's perceptions should be valued and included as exit criteria and competencies are assessed.

It might also be postulated that assessment and programming which are grounded in the individual child's perception could contribute to more pervasive generalization of skills which are introduced in various intervention strategies. Although numerous studies have reported success in the social training of handicapped children, transfer and maintenance of skills are limited (Asher & Taylor, 1981; Fleming & Fleming, 1982; Powell & Lindeman, 1983; Schloss & Sedlak, 1982). Training which is more closely aligned to the child's perceived needs and concerns may extend the benefits of intervention programs and facilitate the positive transfer of acquired social skills and social attitudes.

Growing interest in socio-emotional assessment in relation to mainstreaming has produced a variety of useful intervention strategies. At present, most of these strategies are aimed at providing: (a) social skill acquisition; (b) modification of the social environment; or (c) psychosocial support. All have the express intent of enabling a child to better cope with the mainstreaming situation. In general, research on coping with stressful circumstances indicates that individuals respond differently to coping strategies. Some strategies are more effective for one person than they are for another.

Given that EMR students display a range of concerns regarding mainstreaming as evidenced by this investigation, it appears that the selection of any intervention to help a child cope with the stress inherent in mainstreaming must be based on that child's individual needs. Content of an intervention program can be technologically sound and accurate, yet not in concert with the child's sense of perceived threat or level of concern.

Perhaps a more important implication of this analysis of EMR students' worries and concerns is not on the specific items that emerged as significant. Rather, the issue of children's worries suggests that over the long term, meaningful intervention might prove to be more successful if it takes children's own sense of apprehension into account.

A perusal of research on intervention for socio-emotional adjustment in the context of mainstreaming reveals intensified efforts which include sociometric groupings, role playing, psychological counseling, behavioral analysis, shaping, coaching, peer modeling, cognitive behavior therapy, relaxation therapy, and video tape self-analysis. Each strategy is reported to be successful in some instances and not successful in others. Methodologically, researchers have employed single isolated techniques such as social validation procedures, naturalistic observation, teacher rating scales, paired comparisons, situational testing, peer nominations, and the analysis of social climate, social distance and social competence, using sociometric protocols. Little work has been done in combining these strategies to collect more comprehensive information. Correspondingly, an empirically based battery of interventions to test whether combined approaches create a greater probability for success has yet to be tested. Research efforts to find the *match* between the current intervention technology available and an individual child's self-perceived needs, worries and concerns could then be explored.

The present study has demonstrated that EMR students in this sample worry about a variety of issues. In fact, their concerns over transition items had not been revealed through conventional assessment. The findings suggest that intervention in this domain might not only prove fruitful in reducing stress in mainstreaming, but they also suggest that identifying children's own perceptions about what worries them can generate insights which are often obfuscated by behavioral analysis or sociometric techniques alone. Children, even handicapped ones, can offer a rich source of critical information that might lead to more effective intervention and ultimately to more effective policy in areas such as mainstreaming. Discussing their concerns, fears, hopes and dreams with them is a significant research process yet untapped.

References

Algozzine, R., Whorton, J. E., & Reid, W. R. (1979). Special class exit criteria: A modest beginning. *The Journal of Special Education, 13,* 131–135.

Asher, S. R., & Taylor, A. R. (1981). Social outcomes of mainstreaming: Sociometric assessment and beyond. *Exceptional Education Quarterly, 1* (1), 13–30.

Barton, L. E., Brulle, A. R., & Repp, A. C. (1982). The social validation of programs for mentally retarded children. *Mental Retardation, 20,* 260–265.

Bates, P. (1980). The effectiveness of interpersonal skills training on the social skill acquisition of moderately and mildly retarded adults. *Journal of Applied Behavior Analysis, 13,* 237–248.

Brown, W. (1982). Classroom climate: Possible effects of special needs on the mainstream. *Journal for Special Educators, 19*(2), 20–27.

Chandler, L. A. (1982). *Children under stress.* Springfield, IL: Charles C. Thomas.

Coopersmith, S. (1967). *The antecedents of self-esteem.* San Francisco: Freeman.

Cotler, S. B., & Guerva, J. J. (1976). *Assertion training.* Champaign, IL: Research Press.

Crowley, J. A. (1981). Worries of elementary school students. *Elementary School Guidance Counseling, 16,* 98–102.

Fleming, E. R., & Fleming, D. C. (1982). Social skill training for educable mentally retarded children. *Education and Training of the Mentally Retarded, 17,* 44–50.

Gallent, B. L. (1981). Out of the frying pan, into the fire: A teacher's view. *The Clearing House, 54,* 345–348.

Gillet, P. (1982). Models for mainstreaming. *Journal for Special Educators. 19*(11), 1–12.

Gottlieb, J. A. (1981). Mainstreaming: Fulfilling the promise? *American Journal of Mental Deficiency, 86,* 215–226.

Gottlieb, J. A. (1982). Point of View—Mainstreaming. *Education and Training of the Mentally Retarded, 17,* 79–82.

Gresham, F. M. (1982). Misguided mainstreaming. The case for social skills training with handicapped children. *Exceptional Children, 48,* 422–433.

Hannah, E. P., & Parker, R. M. (1980). Mainstreaming vs. the special setting. *Academic Therapy, 15,* 271–278.

Heron, R. E., & Skinner, M. E. (1981). Criteria for defining the regular classroom as the least restrictive environment for LD students. *Learning Disability Quarterly, 4,* 115–121.

Hundert, J. (1982). Some considerations of planning the integration of handicapped children into the mainstream. *Journal of Learning Disabilities, 15,* 73–80.

Izard, C. E. (1982). *Measuring emotions in infants and children.* New York: Cambridge University Press.

Johnson, D. W., Johnson, R. T., & Maruyama, G. (1983). Interdependence and interpersonal attraction among heterogeneous and homogeneous individuals: A theoretical formulation and a meta-analysis of the research. *Review of Educational Research, 53,* 5–54.

Kazdin, A. E., & Petti, T. A. (1982). Self-report and interview measures of childhood and adolescent depression. *Journal of Child Psychology and Psychiatry, 23,* 437–457.

Kovacs, M., & Beck, A. T. (1977). An empirical clinical approach towards a definition of childhood depression. In J. G. Schulterbrandt, & A. Rasking (Eds.) *Depression in children: Diagnosis, treatment and conceptual models* (pp. 121–163). New York: Raven Press.

Lawrence, E. A., & Winschel, J. P. (1975). Locus of control: Implications for special education. *Exceptional Children, 41,* 483–490.

Lupin, M. (1977). *Peace, harmony awareness: A relaxation program for children.* Austin, TX: Learning Concepts.

McDaniel, E. A., Sullivan, P. D., & Goldbaum, J. L. (1982). Physical proximity of special education classrooms to regular classrooms. *Exceptional Children, 49,* 73–75.

Masat, L. J., & Schack, F. K. (1981). Mainstreaming: Training is not enough. *Principal, 61*(2), 28–30.

Morris, L. W., Davis, M. S., & Hutchings, C. H. (1981). Cognitive and emotional components of anxiety: Literature review and a revised worry-emotionality scale. *Journal of Educational Psychology, 73,* 541–555.

Morris, L. W., Finkelstein, C. S., & Fisher, W. R. (1976). Components of school anxiety. Developmental trends and sex differences. *Journal of Genetic Psychology, 128,* 49–57.

Morris, L. W., Kellaway, D. S., & Smith, D. H. (1978). Predicting anxiety experiences and academic performance in two groups of students. *Journal of Educational Psychology, 70*(5), 589–594.

Morris, L. W., & Liebert, R. M. (1970). The relationship of cognitive and emotional components of test anxiety to psychological arousal and academic performance. *Journal of Consulting and Clinical Psychology, 35*, 322–337.

Nicholls, J. G. (1978). The development of the concepts of effort and ability, perception of academic attainment and the understanding that difficult tasks require more ability. *Child Development, 49*, 800–814.

O'Connor, M., & Cuevas, J. (1982). The relationship of children's prosocial behavior to social responsibility, prosocial reasoning and personality. *The Journal of Genetic Psychology, 140*, 33–45.

Palmer, D. J. (1983). An attributional perspective on labeling. *Exceptional Children, 49*, 423–429.

Palomares, V., & Ball, G. (1974). *An overview of the human development program.* La Mesa, CA: Human Development Training Institute.

Payne, S. L. (1951). *The art of asking questions.* Princeton, NJ: Princeton University Press.

Powell, T. H., & Lindeman, D. P. (1983). Developing a social-interaction teaching program for young handicapped children. *Exceptional Children, 50*, 72–75.

Putallaz, M., & Gottman, J. M. (1981). An interactional model of children's entry into peer groups. *Child Development, 52*, 986–994.

Rich, J. (1968). *Interviewing children and adolescents.* London: Macmillan & Co.

Rosenweig, J., & Vacca, D. (1983). The L. D. student and social integration: Getting it to work. *Academic Therapy, 18*, 267–283.

Rutter, M. (1981). Stress, coping and development: Some issues and some questions. *Journal of Child Psychology and Psychiatry, 22*, 323–356.

Schloss, P. J., & Sedlack, R. A. (1982). Behavioral features of the mentally retarded adolescent: Implications for mainstream educators. *Psychology in the Schools, 19*, 98–105.

Schultz, E. (1980). Teaching coping skills for stress and anxiety. *Teaching Exceptional Children, 13*(3), 12–15.

Seiler, G., & Renshaw, K. (1978). Yoga for kids. *Elementary School Guidance and Counseling, 12*, 228–238.

Selman, R. L. (1981). The child as a friendship philosopher. In Steven R. Asher & John M. Gottman (Eds.). *The development of children's friendships* (pp. 82–138). New York: Cambridge University Press.

Tanner, O. (1976). *Stress.* New York: Time/Life Books.

Tennant, C., Smith, A., Bebbington, P., & Hurry, J. (1979). The contextual threat of life events; the concept and its reliability. *Psychological Medicine, 9*, 525–528.

Wang, M. C. (1981). Mainstreaming exceptional children: Some instructional design and implementation considerations. *The Elementary School Journal, 81*, 195–221.

Wolf, R. L. (1979). *Strategies for Conducting Naturalistic Interviews.* Indiana Center for Evaluation. Monograph Series: Indiana University, Bloomington, IN.

Speaking for Themselves: A Bibliography of Writings by Mentally Handicapped Individuals

Keith E. Stanovich and Paula J. Stanovich

Authors: Dr. Keith E. Stanovich, Assistant Professor of Psychology, Oakland University, Rochester, Michigan 48063. Ms. Paula J. Stanovich, Teacher, Hawthorne Learning Center, Pontiac, Michigan.

Abstract: Society is increasingly becoming aware that it is important that communication with mentally retarded individuals become a truly two-way street. One barrier to the two-way flow of information is the fact that there exists no large body of literature authored by mentally retarded persons. There are isolated examples of such written work, however, and these provide valuable insights into the thinking and feelings of mentally retarded individuals. It is our purpose to bring these scattered writings into a bibliography so that they will become more readily available to parents, professionals, and advocates.

It is not uncommon to hear parents, professionals, and advocates say, "We speak for the retarded because they cannot speak for themselves." Unfortunately, like most cliches, this assertion encourages stereotyped thinking. Taken in the extreme, the statement is manifestly untrue. Most retarded people *can* speak for themselves. The problem is that until the recent development of increased concern for the rights of mentally handicapped people, no one seemed to be listening. Hopefully, in the future, when a history of the treatment of mentally retarded people is written, our era will be viewed as a time when society began to open its ears to these individuals.

Why is it important that we let retarded individuals speak for themselves? Why is it important that we listen? Clearly, a complete and fully adequate answer to these questions would involve a lengthier response than can be given here. However, we will attempt to point out the directions that such an answer might take. In this era of mainstreaming and the normalization principle a concerted effort is being made to deemphasize the difference between people labeled mentally retarded and the rest of society. However, programs of mainstreaming and integration are subverted by an excessive emphasis on the "specialness" of this group of people. Community acceptance will never come as long as we in the profession inculcate society with the belief that retarded individuals differ qualitatively from nonretarded human beings. The sense of "specialness" is emphasized by the fact that retarded individuals are always placed in a subordinate position in every social exchange in which they participate. This includes their interactions with the professionals who are supposed to have their interests at heart. *We* are always writing about *them*. *We* make documentaries about *them*, on and on, *ad nauseum*. Of course, all of this is necessary for professional communication. On the other hand, it does serve, at least implicitly, to accentuate the differences between *them* and us. At a simple level, our desire to encourage society to listen to retarded individuals is simply a desire to strike more of a balance and treat these individuals as equal partners in the human family. Let's let *them* talk about *us* for a change. At this point in our profession's ethical development, who could possibly object? And if there are objections, one can only speculate that some of us must be afraid of what we would hear.

On another level, it is easy to see that there may be immediate practical advantages in allowing retarded individuals to speak for themselves and publicizing what they say. For example, there reside in almost every institution, individuals who are capable of giving authorities accurate information regarding abusive practices in the facility. This has been clearly demonstrated in the Willowbrook controversy (Rivera, 1972), to a limited extent in a paper by Biklen (1977), and in other similar situations in which the authors of the present paper have been involved. One can also envision imaginative uses of the writings and opinions of retarded individuals as pedagogical aids in programs designed to change negative attitudes and expectancies. These materials might be of particular use when

From *Mental Retardation*, Vol. 17, No. 2, April 1979. pp. 83-86. Reprinted with the permission of the American Association on Mental Deficiency, Washington, D.C.

incorporated within programs designed for human services personnel. For example, they might be included in programs for attendants of residential institutions for mentally retarded individuals, since the negative attitudes of the attendants toward the residents have been amply documented (Bogdan, Taylor, de Grandpere, & Haynes, 1974).

There remain, however, several obstacles to making communication with mentally retarded individuals a truly two-way street. For example, although many parents have written of the lives of their retarded children, there exists no large body of literature authored by mentally handicapped individuals available to parents, advocates and retardation workers. Articles by parents are valuable, but they are not enough. We must have the story from the retarded person's point of view. There are isolated examples of such written work and these vividly illustrate the insights to be gained from letting mentally handicapped people speak for themselves. These works are important for several reasons, not the least of which is that they caution us against holding restricted views of human potential.

It is our purpose here to bring together these scattered writings into a bibliography so that they will become more readily available to parents, professionals, and advocates. Some of the articles are written works authored by mentally handicapped individuals, while others are transcripts of conversations in which retarded individuals took part. Short descriptions of some of the most important works are provided. It is hoped that these articles represent only the beginning of a growing positive trend—mentally handicapped people speaking for themselves, rather than having others speak for them.

Hunt, N. *The world of Nigel Hunt.* Beaconsfield, England: Darwen Finlayson, Ltd., 1967, available from the Exceptional Parent Bookstore.

Nigel Hunt is an Englishman who was born with Down's syndrome. Shortly after his birth, his parents were informed of this condition and were told that their son was ineducable. Refusing to accept this empirically unfounded conclusion, Nigel's parents worked from the very beginning to develop his educational abilities. His mother would sound out words to him and play games with plastic letters. Nigel learned to recognize the letters by name, gradually progressed to whole words, and was finally introduced to books. In later years, he requested a book of poems and a dictionary and taught himself to type on his father's typewriter. Nigel's book which is entirely the product of his own efforts, is a fitting monument to his and his parents' determination. The book contains a foreward by L.S. Penrose and a preface by Nigel's father. The main text is part autobiography and part description of Nigel's travels abroad with his parents. As a whole, *The World of Nigel Hunt* is full of humor, beautiful descriptions, and the excitement of life, which Nigel so enjoys.

Deacon, J.J. *Joey.* New York: Charles Scribner's Sons, 1974.

Joey is the autobiography of Joseph John Deacon, a man who has severe spastic cerebral palsy affecting all four limbs. It chronicles his life from birth to age 53, following the young Joey through various hospitals, including St. Lawrence's in Caterham, England where he resides today. Joey tells of his struggles to make himself understood, his speech being completely unintelligible due to the cerebral palsy. His struggles ended in his twenty-first year, however, when he met Ernie Roberts. Miraculous though it may seem, Ernie could understand Joey.

The story of how the book was written is itself fascinating. Joey would relate the tale to Ernie who would then tell it to another friend, Michael Sangster, who would write it down. This draft was given to the charge nurses for corrections of errors in spelling and punctuation. The rewritten script was then reread by Joey, letter by letter, to Ernie. Ernie relayed it to Tom Blackburn, the fourth member of this group of friends, who then typed it, using a special code for the alphabet which he had devised. Working for a couple of hours each night, the men completed about four lines a day and the entire book required approximately fourteen months to complete. Joey ends the book with a tribute to all the friends who made it possible, most especially his friend, Ernie, of whom he says, "I'm just coming up to my fifty-third year. Half of those were silent, half were not, thanks to you. You gave me the chance to talk to the outside world."

Deacon, J., & Roberts, E.I will. *Special Children,* 1977, 3(2), 44-68.

On a visit to St. Lawrence's we were happy to find that Joey and Ernie were continuing to write. While we were there, they entrusted us with a manuscript of a short story entitled "I Will." We were extremely pleased when *Special Children* agreed to publish the manuscript in its entirety. Although the work is fiction, it provides a rare window into the inner conflicts and emotions which thousands of other handicapped individuals must share with Joey and Ernie.

"I Will" is the story of two people who both have cerebral palsy. They meet at the hospital where they both reside and they fall in love. The theme running throughout the story is one of two people striving to be "normal," to be like the rest of us. As one of the nurses says in the text, "They want to live a normal life like us. They want to settle down like two normal people." Alfred and Mary are determined to learn to walk, to talk, and to get married. It is our feeling that this work of fiction can at times be more revealing than nonfictional studies of the personality dynamics of handicapped individuals. Certain aspects of the story hit home with particular force. For example, the excessive concern of Alfred and Mary that their child be "normal" and "not like them" should make us all, as a society, ashamed that the negative valuation we attach to handicapping conditions has had such a deleterious effect on the self-images of handicapped individuals.

Nirje, B. The right to self determination. In W. Wolfensberger, (Ed.), *The principle of normalization in human services.* Toronto: National Institute on Mental Retardation, 1972.

As part of this chapter, Bengt Nirje tells of a three day conference held in Malmo, Sweden during May, 1970. It was attended by 50 delegates from all over Sweden who were mildly or moderately retarded men and women, age 20-35. Their conference (in which intervention by nonretarded observers was negligible) culminated in a full report which was presented to the Swedish National Association for Retarded Children by three elected representatives of the group. The full report contained conclusions and demands, some of them eye openers to the nonretarded readers of the report. The topics covered were leisure time activities, vacations, living conditions, education, work, and final comments from the last day of the conference. The following examples give some of the flavor of their demands.
—under no circumstances do we want to walk in large groups in town
—we have all agreed that summer camps for adults should be banished
—we want the right to move together with members of the opposite sex when we feel ready for it, and we also want the right to marry when we ourselves find the time is right
—we want to have more personal freedom
—there should be student councils
—freedom of choice in determining our vocations
—we demand that our capacity for work should not be underestimated
The report is concluded with the establishment of a committee to inform the authorities and the public of conditions needing correction. The document is a compelling demonstration that retarded individuals can clearly articulate their needs and demand their rights when given a forum.

Bogdan, R., & Taylor, S. The judged, not the judges. *American Psychologist,* 1976, **31,** 47-52.

This article contains the edited transcripts of discussions with a marvelously insightful 26-year-old man (called Ed Murphy) who is a former resident of a state institution for retarded individuals. The transcript deals with many topics of importance to both parents and professionals. For example, Ed discusses the overprotectiveness of his mother and his treatment by psychologists. His discussion of the state school gives a unique insider's view. The transcript ends with Ed's analysis of the concept of retardation, must reading for all professionals.

Edgerton, R.B. *The cloak of competence.* Berkeley: University of California Press, 1967.

Edgerton's classic follow-up study of 48 individuals who were discharged from Pacific State Hospital between 1949 and 1958 contains many transcripts of interviews. One particularly striking aspect of the interviews is the vehemence with which many of the individuals deny the label "retarded." One wonders why we, as supposedly concerned professionals, have insisted on applying a label that we know is negatively valued by society. After reading the interviews, one cannot help but feel that they rightly reject it.

MR 74: A Friend in Washington, The Eighth Annual Report of the President's Committee on Mental Retardation, 1974, 6-8.

Excerpted in this publication are speeches to the committee by two men, Peter Smith and James Kinney, both of whom had been in institutions for 20 or more years of their lives. Peter Smith recounts life in an institution before and after intervention by the National Association for Retarded Citizens and its state organization in Minnesota, listing the positive changes which have occurred. He describes his attempts to rehabilitate himself (he is physically handicapped) and his eventual move out of the institution into an apartment with James Kinney. He concludes with his belief that a lot of improvements still need to take place. James Kinney's excerpt reminds the President's Committee of the importance of education (which he found lacking in the three institutions in which he lived) when he says, "But cake and ice cream were not learning. I had cake and ice cream. That's all I saw. If I had an education book I could learn."

After reading the articles summarized above, one cannot help but come away with the feeling that there is an unrealized potential in these works. Of the many potential uses of these articles, two seem particularly salient. First, it would be of value to compare what mentally retarded individuals say about themselves to what is said about them by parents, professionals, and the general public. From this comparison, it might be possible to get a firmer grip on the mechanisms by which expectancies and stereotypes operate, as well as uncovering areas where there is a particular discrepancy between the perceptions of retarded and nonretarded individuals. These discrepancies could then be dealt with by programs directed at both retarded individuals and the public. Secondly, these articles could be well used as pedagogical aids both in programs to change societal attitudes and in programs for direct-care workers (including for example, hospital attendants and special education teachers).

Finally, we must relay one emotional reaction that we came away with after reading this literature. Many of these retarded individuals *clearly* perceive the negative valuation of the label that we have attached to them and many actively reject its application. One leaves these readings with a lingering, haunting question. Is the psychological damage done to these individuals outweighted by the administrative convenience of the label?

Bibliography

Braginsky, D.D., & Braginsky, B.M. *Hansels and Gretals: Studies of children in institutions for the mentally retarded.* New York: Holt, Rinehart and Winston, Inc., 1971.

Conversation. *The Retarded Adult,* 1977, 3(3), 9-13.

Meyers, R. Retarded newlyweds seek new life. *The Washington Post,* August 21, 1977.

Nitzberg, J. Talk—felt and meaningful. *The Retarded Adult,* 1976, 3(1), 48-65.

Nitzberg, J. Who will tie my shoe? *The Retarded Adult,* 1977, 3(3), 46-68 (Part I): 1977, 4(1), 30-60 (Part II).

Schenkein, Mr. and Mrs. W. Happy the day. *The Exceptional Parent,* 1972. 1(6), 5.

Seagoe, M.V. *Yesterday was Tuesday all day and all night.* Boston: Little Brown, 1964.

Stern, K., & Horowitz, I. Growing up retarded: An interview. *The Exceptional Parent,* 1977, 7(6), Y8-Y12.

Tegtmeier, W. Sex education with retarded adults. *The Retarded Tegtmeier, W. Sex education with retarded adults. The Retarded Adult,* 1977, 3(3), 19-36.

What the shop means to me. *The Retarded Adult,* 1975, 2(1), 59-62.

Yore, B. Something he had to say. *Mental Retardation News,* 24(6), 1975.

References

Biklen, D. The politics of institutions. In B. Blatt, D. Biklen & R. Bogdan (Eds.), *An alternative textbook in special education.* Denver: Love Publishing Company, 1977.

Bogdan, R., Taylor, S., de Grandpere, B., & Haynes, S. Attendants' perspectives and programming on wards in state schools. *Journal of Health & Social Behavior,* 1974, 15(2), 141-151.

Rivera, G. *Willowbrook,* New York: Vintage Books, 1972.

Teaching the Learning Disabled Child

Learning disabilities are among the most difficult of handicaps to understand. These children are of average and above average intelligence, yet their academic performance is far below their ability. Their visual and auditory acuity is fine, yet they often have problems with visual or auditory perception. Many show the same symptoms as known brain-damaged children (i.e., hyperactivity, coordination problems, perceptual-motor impairments), yet there is no hard evidence of brain damage. They are usually motivated to learn, yet their disability prevents them from learning many school-related concepts quickly and easily, thus leading to extreme frustration and resistance to new learning situations.

It is not surprising that teachers faced with teaching these children are confused about what to do. There continue to be so many theories about causes and treatment of learning disabilities that teachers are left with several myths and unfounded concepts on which to base their instruction.

The lead article, "Recognizing Special Talents in Learning Disabled Students," underlines the importance of defining a program that can develop and support a learning disabled student's special strengths and talents. The difficulty in diagnosing the particular learning disability of a child is examined in "How Do We Help the Learning Disabled?" The article offers guidelines for parents and instructors to help them define and cope with learning disability problems.

Often establishing and running an individual program for the learning disabled child is difficult and counterproductive due to the ongoing needs required by these special children. "Teaching Learning Disabled Children to Help Themselves" provides suggestions for instituting a self-instructional training program.

There are many problems involved in mainstreaming learning disabled students, including integrating them into the academic program, controlling instructional variables, and modifying curricular materials. "Mainstreaming: How Teachers Can Make It Work," while not focusing entirely on the learning disabled child, offers many innovative ideas relevant to mainstreaming learning disabled children.

Looking Ahead: Challenge Questions

What is a learning disability?

Why is it difficult to define learning disabilities?

How can exams and other written work be modified for the learning disabled student?

How can teachers help these children become truly integrated into a mainstreamed setting?

Recognizing Special Talents in Learning Disabled Students

Susan Baum
Robert Kirschenbaum

Susan Baum *is a teaching assistant and doctoral candidate in educational psychology at the University of Connecticut, with a specialization in education of the gifted. She is presently working with the West Hartford Public Schools in developing and piloting an enrichment program for learning disabled/gifted students in grades 4–6.*

Robert J. Kirschenbaum *is a school psychologist and coordinator of special education in Coronado, Arizona. He received his doctorate in special education from the University of Connecticut at Storrs.*

■ *Riddle:* How can a child learn and not learn at the same time? This is the dilemma of a child who demonstrates above-average ability on standardized tests of mental ability, but who performs considerably more poorly on school tasks. Students like this are often diagnosed as learning disabled.

Over the last two decades, much research has been conducted into the nature and needs of the learning disabled child. Numerous diagnostic and remedial techniques have been developed, and curriculum materials have flooded the market. Indeed, once properly identified, these children are bombarded throughout the school day with the best remedial techniques so far developed.

Yet some children diagnosed as learning disabled also exhibit superior abilities in one or more areas. Not only do learning disabled gifted and talented students need remediation activities, but they also require op-portunities to develop their own special strengths and talents. Emotional support is also necessary to help them cope with the self-perception of inconsistency of abilities and the consequent effect on self-image (Meisgeier, Meisgeier, & Werblo, 1978).

NURTURING THE WHOLE CHILD

What happens when all the needs of the child are not addressed, due to a preoccupation with academic deficits? Neil, a junior in high school, was failing all of his subjects. He was disgusted with school and was exhibiting symptoms of depression requiring weekly visits to a psychologist. His teachers described him as lazy, claiming that he could do better if only he would apply himself. A typical comment was, "When I talk to Neil, he has so much to offer. However, he just doesn't produce."

On the Detroit Tests of Learning Aptitude, Neil scored extremely well on the subtests of Likenesses and Differences, Disarranged Pictures, and Verbal Opposites, indicating strengths in use of spoken language, verbal conceptualization, and spatial organization. His weakness was exhibited on tests requiring short-term memory of symbols. Overall, his derived IQ was in the above-average range.

Problems also arose in the area of written expression. Pulling out main ideas and organizing them into a well written paragraph was extremely difficult for Neil. This deficit did not generalize to visual material, however, as suggested by the test results on the Detroit.

The school adjusted Neil's curriculum in light of the test findings. He was given short-answer tests and individualized math instruction. Staff made special efforts to provide the structure and emotional support he needed to complete his assignments. Even though Neil began to do better in school, he became more and more angry. He explained that he was only succeeding because the school was making concessions for him. He continuously complained that the school was not interested in his ideas or in what he knew.

On his own, Neil had acquired a wealth of knowledge about music, religion, psychology, and photography. He pursued his extracurricular interests with enthusiasm and persistence. His major interest during this time was photography. Following is an excerpt from a conversation concerning his pictures:

I don't like posed pictures. I often carry my camera with me. I am a people watcher, and sometimes I can predict a mood. I feel it inside. I really can't put it into words. I seem to know internally when to snap the picture. I know when I see it; it's a feeling that lasts but a moment.

Neil, do you feel that you are creative?

I feel I am different. I suppose I may be creative. My schoolmates see me as being different. I am not acting this way to be a rebel, but my classmates' views on life irritate me. They think I am funny—the class clown.

What do you think creativity is?

Creativity is taking what you know and taking it a step further. When I am taking a picture, it becomes a very personal thing. It's an unexplainable feeling, hard to explain even to myself.

Do you think you will choose photography as your career?

No. I see it as a hobby, where I am my own critic, just like the piano player in Salinger's *Catcher in the Rye*, who performs for his own enjoyment.

Neil's photographs and related comments speak for themselves. He had not received much praise for his creativity. Instead, he had been regularly criticized for poor academic work. Neil finished high school, but decided not to go on to college. Four months after graduation, he said, "Now that school is out, I finally have time to learn." He talked about several contemporary history books he was reading, even though he had hated history in school.

Neil's experiences dramatically illustrate the importance of considering the whole child. It can be profoundly destructive to a student's self-esteem to be labeled and treated only in terms of a learning disability when, in addition, a student may be exhibiting gifted behaviors that are equally worthy of attention.

Neil's learning disability existed primarily in the context of the school, and once out of that setting, it seemed to diminish.

IDENTIFYING TALENT: THE NEED FOR INFORMATION

How do we recognize gifted, talented, or creative behavior in learning disabled students? Children who demonstrate above-average ability, task commitment, and creativity brought to bear upon a specific area of knowledge can be considered to be exhibiting gifted behavior (Renzulli, 1978). Within the school setting, with its fixed time periods, predetermined curricula, isolated subject areas, and teacher accountability with regard to students' minimal competencies, gifted behaviors often go unrecognized.

What is needed, then, is *information* about the talents and strengths of these children. Usually, the folders of learning disabled students are filled with notations concerning the things they *can't* do in school. Their strengths are overshadowed by problematic weaknesses that consume the school's well intentioned energies and attention.

Neil's strengths became more apparent when identified in a systematic way. One such construct categorizes the components of information necessary for screening students for above-average ability, task commitment, and creativity (Renzulli, Reis, & Smith, 1981). Neil exhibited characteristics in each of the three clusters (see Figure 1). The process of screening children specifically for these groups of characteristics will increase the likelihood that learning disabled students with superior abilities can be identified.

CURRICULUM AND PROGRAMMING

Learning disabled gifted children "need very special enrichment experiences to ensure that [their] special abilities . . . are made to serve [them] and society well" (Meisgeier et al., 1978, p. 7). Where can the special type of enrichment be found which will encompass both interests and strengths?

Renzulli's Enrichment Triad Model (1977) bridges the gap between in-school and out-of-school behavior. Children are encouraged to identify an area of interest and then focus on a real problem to be investigated and possibly solved. The model consists of three types of activities: general exploratory; group training; and individual and small group investigation.

General exploratory activities entail exposure to potential areas of interest not necessarily found in the regular curriculum. For learning disabled students, they may be introduced through lectures, demonstrations, movies, interest centers, or other approaches that bypass weaknesses in reading. These no-fail entry activities expose students to new ideas in a nonthreat-

FIGURE 1
Indications of Talent Along Three Dimensions

	Psychometric	Developmental	Performance	Sociometric
Above Average Ability	Subtest scores on the Detroit Tests of Learning Aptitude are superior.	Teachers describe Neil as very bright, but does not produce. Parents report advanced reading.	Photograph wins first prize! Intelligent analysis of work	
Creative Ability		Perception of self: Neil has sensitivity to beauty, sense of humor; sees things from many viewpoints	Photographic essay	Peers see him as being different, call him the class clown
Task Commitment		Parents report that Neil has taught himself to play guitar as well as take and develop pictures	Number of hours spent perfecting photographic ability; attends to minute details	

ening atmosphere where they are given the opportunity to explore freely.

Type II enrichment activities provide training in such areas as critical thinking, creativity, and problem solving. Since learning disabled children often perform better on activities using higher-level thinking skills as opposed to memory and perceptual capacities (Maker, 1977), these types of activities are quite appropriate. In general, these children will often invent original responses to avoid doing a task. On several occasions, the authors have observed students combining many pairs of lines into a composite figure on the Parallel Lines subtest of the figural Form of the Torrance Tests of Creative Thinking. When questioned, they responded that their main reason for doing so was to avoid making so many pictures. When highly verbal learning disabled students were placed with their gifted peers in a simulation activity requiring problem solving, the two groups could not be distinguished from each other either by students or by teachers who observed the activity on videotape (Maker, 1981).

In Type III activities, the student becomes an investigator of a real problem—one that has not been contrived as a classroom assignment—and is guided in the development of a problem that will have an authentic impact on an audience, preferably outside the school setting. The student focuses on an original idea for study and proceeds as a "practicing professional," using appropriate methods of inquiry to solve a chosen problem. Of course, the student needs to be assisted in the development of skills in the use of a specific methodology.

WHEN THE PROBLEM IS REAL

The solution is not as simple as tailoring curriculum to the interests of learning disabled gifted and talented students. Attention needs to be given to strengths (in their own right) as well as weaknesses, rather than simply working *through* strengths to get to weaknesses. When Neil's school tried to incorporate his interest in photography into academic assignments, he rebelled to the extent of temporarily abandoning photography. Instead of attracting him to academics, Neil was "turned off" to photography for months. He wanted to enjoy his photographic ability unfettered by the expectations of the school.

One day Neil was in an irritable mood, complaining about the demands the school was making on him. He angrily remarked, "I will not learn this. School is just like a basketball game, totally irrelevant to life. Schools should care about kids. Schools should be made to know how they are not meeting the needs of some kids." We asked him how this could be done, and together we listed ideas about how Neil could express his feelings in a way that would have an impact on others. He finally decided to compose a photographic essay to be titled "How I Feel About School."

Once Neil had defined a personally chosen task, he became alive and motivated. He became an investigator of a problem real to him, and the product that resulted has indeed had an impact on others. This photographic essay has been displayed in his school and shown to teachers at workshops and conferences in many locations in the United States and Canada. Perhaps it will make a difference.

Just prior to completing this article, Neil called to inform us that he was now attending a four-year college. He was also excited about a new project—producing a record album! We happily wish Neil luck,

and hope that his story will encourage other students to pursue their creative interests.

REFERENCES

Maker, C. J. *Providing programs for the gifted handicapped.* Reston VA: The Council for Exceptional Children, 1977.

Maker, C. J. Personal communication, August 4, 1981.

Meisgeier, C., Meisgeier, C., & Werblo, D. Factors compounding the handicapping of some gifted children. *Gifted Child Quarterly*, 1978, 22, 325–331.

Renzulli, J. S. *The Enrichment Triad Model: A guide for developing defensible programs for the gifted and talented.* Mansfield Center CT: Creative Learning Press, 1977.

Renzulli, J. S., Reis, S., & Smith, L. H. *The Revolving Door Identification Model.* Mansfield Center CT: Creative Learning Press, 1981.

TEACHING LEARNING DISABLED CHILDREN TO HELP THEMSELVES

Glen Carlton
Terry Hummer
Southwestern City Schools
Grove City, OH 43123
David Rainey
The College of Wooster
Wooster, OH 44691

Teachers frequently criticized traditional behavior management techniques for a number of reasons. For instance, many feel it is inappropriate that teachers should bear the responsiblity for creating and maintaining behavior change. Further, they point out accurately that much of the change accomplished through traditional techniques does not generalize to other situations. One non-traditional technique that successfully counters these criticisms is self-instructional training. This approach has been used to improve a number of classroom behaviors, including reducing aggressive behavior (Camp, Blom, Hebert, & Van Doornick, 1977) and increasing on-task behavior (Bornstein & Quevillion, 1976). One purpose of this article is to present a step by step outline that teachers might use to implement self-instructional training. A second purpose is to report briefly on one such effort that helped learning disabilities teachers improve their students' selective attention deficits.

Self-instructional Training

At the core of self-instructional training is the notion that children who are successful in the classroom guide their own behavior with their thinking. Children experience academic and/or social difficulties may be deficient in these cognitive skills. Some common problems apparent in such children are inattentiveness and impulsiveness. The first step in improving their cognitive skills is to teach these students to deal with problems and tasks by thinking them through in four stages (Kendall & Finch, 1979). The four stages are as follows:

1. Students think *preparation statements*, which tell them what must be done prior to confronting a task (i.e., "I must do ____ and ____ and ____ to get ready for this assignment.").
2. Students then think *confrontation statements*, which help them analyze the task they are about to execute (i.e., "If I am to finish this task, I must do ____ and ____ and ____.").
3. Students then use *coping statements* to guide them throught task subcomponents and to provide self-correction if a problem is encountered (i.e., "I've finished ____, and now I must do ____." "That's not quite right; I need to go back and do ____.").
4. Finally, students think *reinforcing statements* to praise themselves after they have completed the task or task subcomponents (i.e., "That really looks good." "I'm doing a super job.").

While it might appear that students would have difficulty learning to use these statements, the following five step process has been used successfully to guide that learning (Meichenbaum & Goodman, 1971):

1. Initially the teacher performs the task himself/herself while saying the desired self-instructional statements. These teacher verbalizations should reflect each of the four types of statements detailed above (preparation, confrontation, coping, and reinforcement).
2. The teacher and student perform the entire process together, with the teacher verbalizing while the student carries out the task.
3. The student performs the task while instructing himself/herself aloud (overt self-guidance.) Thus, responsibility for executing the task and internalizing the instructional statements begins to shift from the teacher to the student.
4. Students then start to fade the overt self-guidance by whispering the instructions to themselves while performing the task. The teacher continues to monitor the process, but direct involvement is minimal.
5. Finally, the student begins to perform the task while guiding that performance via private (silent) speech. Covert self-instruction has now developed, and the student is in control of the process. Teacher involvement is no longer required.

Reprinted from *THE DIRECTIVE TEACHER*, Vol. 6, No. 1, (Winter/Spring 1984), pp. 8-9, NCEMMH, The Ohio State University.

Two Case Examples

We used these procedures with two first grade boys. These were students from primary learning disabilities classrooms, with average to above average ability, but with severe selective attention deficits. The two teachers involved had expressed an interest in self-instructional techniques and had studied some of the relevant research.

The two students were observed twice prior to the intervention. The first observation revealed that both engaged in many non-work behaviors focused specifically on their independent handwriting assignments, and a second observation obtained baseline data of their on-task and off-task behaviors during these assignments. The teachers developed appropriate preparation, confrontation, coping and reinforcement statements for the handwriting activities of each student and taught them to use these self-instructions via the five step training process. This training required approximately five hours to complete during ten 30 minute sessions over a period of two weeks.

Observations of the two students following this intevention revealed that both had dramatically and significantly increased on-task behaviors and decreased off-task behaviors during their writing assignments.[1] Both teachers also observed these students overtly applying preparation, confrontation, coping, and reinforcement statements to other classroom tasks not associated with this study. While data was not collected to measure the extent of this generalization, this observation is very encouraging.

The usefulness of self-instructional training is well established. This technique effectively deals with two of their fundamental criticisms of traditional behavioral interventions. First, this approach clearly transfers the repsonsibility for behavior change to students, as students come to guide and reinforce their own behaviors. Second, this technique promotes generalization. Students' thoughts are portable, and once they have learned these cognitive skills, they can apply them to new problems and tasks. This approach, then, does seem to be one that is worthy of teachers' attention.

Related References

Bornstein, P.H. & Quevillion, R.P. The effects of a self-instructional package on overactive preschool boys. *Journal of Applied Behavior Analysis*, 1976, 9, 179-188.

Camp, B.W., Blom, G.E., Hebert, F. & Van Doornick, W.J. Think aloud; A program for developing self-control in young aggressive boys. *Journal of Abnormal Child Psychology*, 1977, 5, 157-169.

Kendall, P.B. & Finch, A. Developing non-impulsive behavior in children: Cognitive-behavior strategies for self-control. In P.C. Kendall & S.D. Hollons (Eds.), *Cognitive-behavioral interventions: Theory, research and procedures.* New York: Academic Press, 1979.

Meichembaum, D.H. & Goodman, J. Training impulsive children to talk to themselves: A means of developing self-control. *Journal of Abnormal Psychology*, 1971, 77, 115-126.

---

[1]Data and statistical analyses of these results can be obtained from Dr. Carlton upon request, as can a list of the specific behaviors delineated as on-task and off-task for the pre- and post-intervention observations.

How Do We Help the Learning Disabled?

Judith Dolgins,
Marcee Myers,
Patricia A. Flynn,
and Jossie Moore

A portion of this article was written by **Judith Dolgins,** who has a master's degree in special education with a specialization in learning disabilities. She teaches skills development at Hunter College Elementary School in New York City. Other contributions are from **Marcee Myers,** associate professor of education, University of North Carolina, Wilmington; **Patricia A. Flynn,** educational consultant for learning disabled children in New York City; and **Jossie Moore,** State Technical Institute, Memphis, Tennessee.

Teachers who have been successful in working with these puzzle children share their diagnostic observations and teaching strategies

Probably every teacher has known some of these puzzle children. They are bright enough, perhaps even gifted in many ways, yet they have problems learning to read, write, spell, or calculate. Some also have behavior problems; they interrupt, jump out of their seats, do not listen or follow directions, lose everything, rarely finish their work. These learning disabled children lack some of the essential skills they need to receive, store, organize, retrieve, and utilize information.

The term *learning disabilities* came into use in the 1960s as specialists recognized that many children with learning problems have deficits in more than one skill area and require remedial methods gleaned from several disciplines. Newly formed organizations began disseminating information about learning disabilities, and the media created a burst of interest in the problems of children who did not learn. Several cities established diagnostic centers, and universities began training special education teachers. Private special education schools proliferated, and many public schools instituted special programs.

In 1975, Congress passed Public Law 94-142, requiring states to provide a free, appropriate public school education for all children with educationally handicapping conditions, *including learning disabilities.* The act mandates that each handicapped child be educated in the least restrictive environment, appropriate for his or her needs. Most schools have interpreted a "least restrictive" environment as placement in the regular classroom, with special class or resource room help as needed. Thus, the major responsibility for LD children lies with you, the classroom teacher, for even if a child succeeds in a resource room but does not in the classroom, he or she fails to learn for a great portion of the day.

All this means that *you,* the classroom teacher, will often be the first to identify and refer a child for help. *You* will be part of a team to evaluate and develop an educational program for this child. *You* will also be the person who must develop a classroom strategy so he or she can achieve success.

What is a learning disability?

A learning disability is not easy to pin down or define. It can include a wide assortment of deficits and characteristics, ranging from the specific skills necessary for reading or spelling or calculating to a collection of maladaptive behaviors such as hyperactivity, impulsivity, distractibility, and poor concentration. Few children present all the symptoms associated with learning disabilities, and some who are not learning disabled will exhibit these same characteristics from time to time. And, in the end, *a learning or behavior pattern,* no matter how it may deviate from the ideal, *is not a disability unless it interferes with the child's capacity to learn.*

As generally used, the term *learning disability* excludes children who have learning problems as a result of poor vision or hearing, motor handicaps, mental retardation, emotional disturbance, or environmental disadvantage. By definition, it includes children with average or better intelligence (IQ of 90 or above), and presumes a significant discrepancy between a child's potential and his or her actual academic achievement. A bright child over the age of six or seven who is struggling with reading may have a learning disability. A bright child who is capable of getting A's but only makes B's does not.

Children who are truly learning disabled tend to exhibit a great variability in their performance from task to task, or in the way they handle the same task from day to day. They excel at some activities and fail miserably at others. Often a skill that seems solid one day is gone the next. It is this inconsistency, and the uneven, high-low pattern of their performance that confounds teachers and parents.

Some children with learning disabilities appear to progress quite normally through their early development. While they have difficulties with academic work, they usually function well in other areas. Other children show early signs of lacking the readiness to perform the tasks required in kindergarten. They may have slowly developing language, excessively high or low level of activity, a short attention span. Later, along with having academic problems, they seem to be less mature than other children their age, and are often observed to be distractible, impulsive, and disorganized. Some of the processing problems that make reading words troublesome also appear to interfere with their ability to "read" people and size up situations. Consequently, they experience difficulty interacting with peers.

How can we diagnose a disability?

While we still don't know much about the causes of LD and have not discovered any miracle cures, educators have come a long way in diagnosing and remediating them. A first step is to try to determine where the learning process breaks down for each child. Children who are poor at putting puzzles together, identifying shapes, doing block designs, and remembering what letters and words look like may have weak visual skills even though their visual acuity is adequate. Learning to read by the whole-word method is difficult for them. Children who find it hard to rhyme, follow spoken directions, answer oral questions, and remember the sequence of things heard, such as telephone numbers, may have auditory channel deficits even though their hearing acuity is not impaired. Children who have difficulty learning phonics are often found to have poor auditory processing skills.

Some children appear intact in both visual and auditory skills when each modality is assessed alone, but cannot integrate the two systems. Children who are disorganized, work very slowly, rarely finish assignments, and seem confused much of the time may be presenting signs of integrative problems. While they possess the skills needed for a task, they have trouble organizing them into a coherent and useful whole.

Some researchers attribute many learning disabilities to a defect in the way information received through the senses is perceived and interpreted. Children with faulty visual discrimination do not observe the fine distinctions

between letters such as *b/d* or *n/h* and so may read *big* as *dig* or *snare* as *share*. Those with auditory discrimination problems have trouble hearing differences between such letters as *f/v, p/b,* or word pairs like *mat/map, sat/set*. They tend to omit the second letter in initial blends (*sep* for *step*), the first letter in final blends (*pat* for *past*), and have difficulty distinguishing between short vowel sounds.

Children deficient in visual figure-ground perception skip lines and words when they read, lose their place easily, and inadvertently omit questions on written tests. Those with auditory figure-ground problems are poor listeners and find it hard to read and concentrate when someone is talking nearby.

Closure permits us to synthesize sounds or visual symbols, to use the parts to make a whole. Auditory closure is needed for blending single sounds into words so that *c-a-t* is perceived and read as *cat*. Visual closure tells us that an *A* is a particular uppercase letter, not merely three unrelated lines.

Memory plays an essential role in learning. Recollections of past experience must be stored, related, and then retrieved and utilized in new situations. Many children with learning problems have difficulty recalling what things looked or sounded like, where, when, or how something occurred. They forget a math concept they knew yesterday because it is presented in a different format. They read a word correctly, then fail to recognize it three lines later.

Learning disabled children often have language disorders as well. They may exhibit lags in the comprehension of word meanings, vocabulary usage, and sentence formulation. Their speech is heavy with nonspecific terms *(thing)*, near-miss synonyms *(shoe* instead of *sneaker)*, descriptions of class *(the thing you cut with* for *knife)*, and circumlocutions *(a story you say with clues to make people guess* instead of *riddle)*.

One or two of these behaviors are rarely enough to decide who is or who isn't a learning disabled child. In fact, a child may exhibit several of these behaviors, but if he or she is learning, he or she is not disabled. On the other hand, the child who exhibits them over a long period of time and whose symptoms impair the learning process is

probably an LD child and should have a formal evaluation.

Referral guidelines

The following guidelines and procedures from the AFT's booklet *What Are Learning Disabilities?* will assist you in determining whether or not to pursue a formal evaluation.

1. Gather pertinent information. This includes the family background, developmental history, medical and health information, results of sensory screenings, report card grades, and scores on standardized tests.

2. Collate and interpret data concerning the child's present performance in academic, motor, verbal, and social areas. (Assistance from a counselor or medical or special education personnel may be required.)

3. Analyze the child's learning style and note strengths and weaknesses in both academic and nonacademic areas.

4. Review the teaching approaches and the techniques that have been successful or unsuccessful in resolving or remediating the deficit areas.

5. Confer with the learning disabilities specialist from your school or central office, if available.

6. Summarize and analyze information. If a significant educational discrepancy exists, that is, if the child is not functioning at a level commensurate with age, grade, mental capacity, physical abilities, and educational opportunity, then ask your principal, learning disabilities teacher, or central office special educational personnel for information concerning your district's referral procedures.

7. Arrange for the appropriate school official to contact the child's parents. Parental notification and permission for evaluation are mandated by law.

8. Complete the forms or procedures enabling the child to receive further screening or formal evaluation.

9. Contact your local teacher union for assistance if procedural problems arise that cannot be handled through normal administrative channels. Once a student has been referred and evaluated, the school's special services committee will develop an individual educational program (IEP), consisting of long-term goals, short-term objectives, and evaluation procedures.

Teaching strategies that work

Because learning disabled children vary according to age, achievement level, learning style, type of disorder, degree of impairment, and emotional and social behavior, it is not possible to specify teaching techniques and instructional materials suitable for all learners. Teachers have found the following strategies, however, to be helpful when working with the LD child.

1. Identify the child's strong learning channel. Children who have difficulty processing what they hear benefit from seeing information written on the board. Those with visual problems need to have it told to them.

2. Provide structure. Help them approach tasks in an organized, sequential way. The learning disabled need predictability, consistency, the security of limits, and clearly stated expectations to function at their best.

3. Teach children to monitor their work. Encourage proofreading of all written work; use materials that they can check themselves.

4. Help children focus on the problem. Seat distractible children in a quiet spot, or have them work in small groups. Make directions simple and short, and deliver them two or three steps at a time. Before speaking, grab a child's attention by saying "Listen!" first. Give warnings ("I want you to listen for two important points"). Have children repeat what was said to them.

5. Give children concrete objects to count and measure, and pictures and toys to help them identify and remember letters and sounds. Children who cannot draw forms such as circles and squares need to first produce them with sticks or string or clay. Teach concepts of size, direction, and cause and effect by having children move their bodies and objects around in space.

6. Keep it simple. Break a task down and teach it step by step. Avoid overloading children with too much information at one time. If 20 spelling words are too many for a child, start him or her out with fewer. Simplify your language and speak slowly.

7. Build self-esteem. Keep samples of work folders so children can see their progress. Help children who are behind their classmates save face by giving them different and "special" materials so their lag is not as obvious. Remind children that everyone has problems and tell them about a few of the things that are hard for you. It is reassuring for a child to learn that even adults have trouble getting it together.

8. Give frequent reinforcement. Use social reinforcers such as *good, great, super, fantastic, wow, dynamite,* and

POINTERS FOR PARENTS

These ideas will help the parents of an LD child modify the home situation so he or she can function more successfully in the family. Duplicate a copy for each family, and keep one for yourself. Many of the ideas will also be useful in the classroom.

A structured environment

1. Too few cues and too many changes perplex the LD child. He or she feels secure when there is one way of doing things and the tasks accomplished in the family are performed in a routine manner. When activities change, the child should be prepared for the shift. "Herb, we will take the dishes off the table. After this is finished, we will all have ice cream outside." Whenever possible, explain any abrupt changes in the normal family routine before they actually occur.

2. Provide a nondistracting, quiet place where the LD child can work or be alone when he or she feels ill at ease. Belongings should be stored here, in specific places, so the child will know where to find items needed. These storage places should be ample in size so items can be manipulated in them.

3. When approaching any task, clear the area of as many materials as possible. During meals, the table should be uncluttered. When doing homework, the child should have only the paper, pencil, and book with which he or she is working on the table or desk.

4. Keep large amounts of unstructured time to a minimum, but plan for some time during the day for the child to be free and unoccupied. He or she needs to play. If the child has had some failure and frustration at school, suggest he or she do something active.

Completion of tasks

5. Homework assignments and household tasks should be short enough so that the child can complete them before his or her interest and concentration span are lost. "Do three problems now. Watch television until the timer sounds. Then we will finish the last four problems."

If the child lacks long-term memory or confuses perceptions, schedule teaching sessions close together so the child is less likely to forget what was taught. Keep sessions short, no longer than 20 to 30 minutes in length.

6. Give only one direction at a time. Have the child complete it; then give the next. Giving direct and concise instructions verbally and then demonstrating them will often help the child internalize these directions. Or, give a pictorial representation of directions.

7. Give reinforcement at each step so the child can correct errors before he or she makes a long series of mistakes.

Without meaningful correction at frequent intervals, the child becomes confused and cannot trace his or her steps back to the original error. If there is too much to correct, he or she becomes discouraged.

8. Checklists are helpful for household chores. Make the steps small. For the nonreader, use pictorial language to depict the task. Set aside specific work periods so the child will know that "now" is the time to perform this task.

Explanation of new learning

9. Demonstrate a new learning task while explaining it; then have the child verbally interpret the task and then imitate it. This method presents the new material through several modalities (auditory, visual, tactile).

10. When the new task involves several skills, present one skill at a time, then allow sufficient practice. Practicing simple steps will help the child improve his or her memory, sequencing, and whole-part relationships.

11. When the child makes an error, show explicitly what was done wrong. To only say it's wrong does not give the child the necessary information to make the correction.

Discipline

12. Be consistent in what you ask of the child. There must be a close time rela-

so on. Nonverbal reinforcers such as a smile, nod, wink, OK, or a thumbs-up sign are also effective.

Modify the requirements

The chances for success in the classroom often involve modifying some aspects of the school requirements.

9. If a pupil has major difficulties in handwriting, consider the following.

● Allow assignments to be typed.

● Allow reports to be taped or dictated to others to write.

● Have material to be copied or directions for an assignment on the child's desk rather than on the board.

● Ask a nondisabled child who is a good writer to carbon copy any lecture notes or board work for the LD child.

● Increase the time allowed to complete written assignments.

● Decrease amount of writing for a given assignment.

● Allow work to be completed in either manuscript or cursive styles.

● Omit handwriting as a criterion for evaluating reports.

● Construct tests that require minimal writing, such as multiple-choice, matching, true-false, fill-in-the-blank.

10. When a child has major deficits in reading skills, make adjustments:

● Tape selections that the child cannot read, but can comprehend.

● Use filmstrips, movies, and other visual aids to present or reinforce concepts in the books.

● Provide opportunities for group projects with different assignments for each group member.

● Allow peer tutoring with reading assignments.

● Provide alternative reading materials on the appropriate level (old textbooks, library books, newspapers).

● Write summaries of reading assignments; laminate them.

● Underline key concepts in science or social studies texts.

● Use contracts or learning centers.

11. For the pupil experiencing a severe difficulty in spelling, the following suggestions could enhance the possibilities for success.

● Decrease the number of spelling words required at one time.

● In severe cases, allow the student to write only the first letter of each word for the spelling test.

● Use words that are also required in reading, science, or social studies lessons, to increase exposure.

● Avoid spelling as a criterion for evaluating assignments.

12. The LD student who is primarily deficient in math skills would probably benefit from these options.

● Require fewer problems for an assignment.

● Place fewer problems on one sheet of paper or use heavy lines to separate one problem from another.

---

tionship between the action and the punishment. Do not punish the child for behavior he cannot control.

13. While parents need to structure tasks and activities, the child should have a choice within this structure. Do not, however, give him or her a choice unless you intend to abide by the choice. When you really want him or her to obey, state instructions firmly.

14. The child may use many methods to avoid a task. Learn to anticipate his or her resistive moves.

Many kinds of drill

15. Vary drill activities. Instead of reviewing quantitative words through endless workbook pages, for example, utilize the kitchen: compare *big* soap bubbles and *smaller* ones; hear, feel, and see the difference between an *empty* coffee pot and a *full* one.

16. Let LD children respond to a task differently than their siblings do. A child who has difficulty in writing, for example, might tape-record a message to a favorite aunt instead of writing a thank-you note.

17. Ask the child who resents reading "baby" books to read to younger siblings or to conduct a reading hour for neighborhood toddlers.

18. Start a library of high interest, low vocabulary level books. Many of the classics have been adapted. Through these books the child will be exposed to the same characters and events that peers and siblings are reading about.

19. Asking a child to locate a specific product in the grocery store requires him or her to think in categories. Organizing cupboard or drawers and sorting laundry, buttons, and groceries help the child to think about similarities and differences in items.

Handling frustrations

20. Provide an acceptable way to release frustrations. Young children can hit a tandem ball or punch a bag. Older children can retreat to a "quiet place" to cool off, compose themselves, and then reappear. They need to feel they will be listened to when expressing feelings about the problem situation. Parents should talk freely to make their child aware that they want to help him or her through these times of conflict.

21. Retrace the events leading to an outburst. Often it will give the child clues he or she has misunderstood or missed. Later he or she may be able to think through these actions and resolve problems without the need for release of physical activity, seclusion, or parental assistance.

22. Do not try to correct all behaviors at the same time. Concentrate on the essential one and forget about others for the present. Parents and teachers

should select the same behavior so both can approach the remediation in a similar manner.

23. Use short, one-concept phrases supplemented with gestures and facial expressions when asking questions. Avoid figurative language, eliminate pronouns, and get attention before starting (touch, call the child's name, and so on). Give ample time to respond. He or she may need multiple-choice answers from which to select a response.

Self-comparisons

24. Compare newly acquired skills and present performance with the child's previous performance, not with the ability of others in the family or neighborhood. The LD child should not feel that he or she must catch up to others.

25. Select an activity that the LD child does well, and let him or her have that as his or her special area of expertise.

26. Inconsistency of performance is a characteristic of many LD children. Give support, not punishment, during these periods of frustration.

27. Help the LD child learn several of the games played by peers and siblings. As a family, often play games together, selecting those where the LD child can compete on an equal basis.

Pamela Gillet is superintendent of the Northwest Suburban Special Education Organization in Palatine, Illinois.

● Allow the use of calculators or other manipulative aids for calculations.
● Provide concrete examples for procedures and problems.
● Encourage estimation skills to check the likelihood that answers are correct.

Decipher language

Language is the essential means of "making it" in our very verbal society. Because LD children often are very literal-minded, help them decipher multimeaning words and the connotations of words.

13. Provide clues to those children who have trouble identifying what to do in a particular situation. For instance, because fourth-grader Teddy was having severe difficulties with word problems in math, he was given small cards with key words for each of the four math operations. Addition words included *add, sum, together, altogether, total, joined, increased.* Subtraction words were *difference, remains, decrease, remainder, subtract, left.*

Teddy would then read a problem, begin to look for the clue, and underline the word or group of words that he thought made up the signal for the operation. If he was in doubt, he would check back on the cards. Gradually he no longer needed the cards.

14. Be specific and precise in giving directions. Teddy, for instance, once worked out a problem to find the total number of boys in a school and came up with the correct answer— 237—but failed to write the word "boys" next to the total. When the teacher asked where the boys were, Teddy proceeded to draw all 237 boys in a two-inch space reserved for the answer. Always use the words exactly as you want them to be interpreted.

15. Give directions in two or three different ways. Greg, in grade seven, exhibited a difficulty in locating adverbs in sentences. He said the exercise was really easy, but all his answers were wrong. He had underlined the words *how, when, where,* not realizing that one asked oneself those questions and the answers were the adverbs. Again it was a problem in processing what was and wasn't literal.

16. Give a child additional language experience. A student in grade three always seemed to have at least 50 percent of his reading answers wrong. An analysis of the type of error revealed it involved words with multiple meanings and the need to make inferences. Due

to his limited experience with words, Steve could not mentally picture the appropriate meaning indicated in the story. He would picture the inappropriate one, and it would strike him so funny that he would laugh hilariously, disturb the class, and get scolded as well.

"Language is the essential means of succeeding in our very verbal society."

When a sentence said that the dog's coat was yellow, he pictured a little mutt with a yellow raincoat. The teacher saw nothing funny and began to think of Steve as the class clown. But when she understood what Steve's problem was, she made small index cards with pictures of a word's different meanings. Later she created other index cards that had two or three sentences with a blank to complete with a 1 (first meaning on a picture card) or a 2 (second meaning). Gradually Steve

learned to visualize both possibilities and choose the one that made sense.

Provide motivation

17. Finally, a most important thing to do is to motivate learning disabled students. The following story by teacher Jossie Moore illustrates what motivation did for seventh and eighth grade students whose reading ability was at the primary level and whose self-confidence had been very low.

"It all began when I took my class to see a play in the school's Little Theatre. The players, a group of accelerated students, were not well rehearsed and read from their scripts, but their expression was good and they obviously relished performing. My students were impressed and pleaded for permission to put on a play in our theatre. Although I refused at first, thinking the task too difficult for children who couldn't read very well, their persistence changed my mind.

"After searching the library for a play, I at last found 'The Three Sons,' a story in *Grimm's Fairy Tales.*

Resources

Organizations
Association for Children with Learning Disabilities
  4156 Library Rd.
  Pittsburgh, PA 15234
Closer Look
  1201 16th St., N.W.
  Washington, D.C. 20036
Council for Exceptional Children
  1920 Association Dr.
  Reston, VA 22091
National Easter Seal Society
  2023 W. Ogden Ave.
  Chicago, IL 60612
The Orton Society, Inc.
  724 York Rd.
  Baltimore, MD 21204

Periodicals
Exceptional Children
Teaching Exceptional Children
  Council for Exceptional Children
The Journal of Learning Disabilities
  101 East Ontario St.
  Chicago, IL 60611
The Journal of Special Education
  1950 Street Rd., Suite 408
  Bensalem Heights, PA 19020

Books and Pamphlets
Banbury, Mary M. *What Are Learning Disabilities?,* Item #438 (American Federation of Teachers, Educational Issues Dept., 11 Dupont Circle, N.W., Washington, D.C. 20036).

Gearheart, B. R., and Weishahn, M. W. *The Handicapped Student in the Regular Classroom* (2nd Ed.). The C. V. Mosby Co., 1980.

Hammill, D.D., and Bartel, N. R. *Teaching Children with Learning and Behavior Problems.* Allyn & Bacon, Inc., 1978.

Kaluger, George, and Kolson, Clifford J. *Reading and Learning Disabilities.* Charles E. Merrill, 1978.

Lerner, Janet W. *Children with Learning Disabilities* (2nd Ed.). Houghton Mifflin, 1976.

Mangle, Charles, Brutten, Milton, and Richardson, Sylvia O. *Something's Wrong with My Child: A Parent's Book About Children with Learning Disabilities.* Harcourt Brace Jovanovich, 1973.

Mann, P. H., and Suiter, P. *Handbook in Diagnostic Teaching: A Learning Disabilities Approach.* Allyn & Bacon, Inc., 1974.

Smith, Sally L. *No Easy Answers: Teaching the Learning Disabled Child.* Little, Brown, 1979.

Smith, Sally L. *Plain Talk about Children with Learning Disabilities* (Consumer Information Center, Dept. 513L, Pueblo, CO 81009, single copies free).

Yahraes, Herbert. *Learning Disabilities: Problems and Progress,* Public Affairs Pamphlet No. 578 (The Public Affairs Committee, Inc., 381 Park Ave. South, New York, NY 10016, $1 per copy).

"Attempting to show rather than tell my students what was involved in putting on a play, I duplicated scripts for students to follow along as I read. They did, identifying with the characters who they felt were losers like themselves. I then teased them by collecting the scripts, which they wanted to keep, and by presenting the vocabulary as I would any directed reading lesson. To ensure their eventual success, I didn't want to rush them, for I had learned that step-by-step learning had the best results. So they divided words into syllables, found definitions, and used each word in a sentence. They were impatient and wanted to begin rehearsals, but I was adamant in demanding they be prepared prior to reading.

"After a few days, they knew the vocabulary well enough to begin *phase two,* silent reading and discussion. I distributed the scripts again, along with comprehension questions. They had to read silently to find and write answers to the questions. When completed, they discussed their answers, often reading excerpts that provided proof and support for them.

"It was now time to begin *phase three,* oral reading. They arranged their chairs in a semicircle, sat down, and waited in silence for someone else to begin the reading. They were reluctant to tackle the lengthy first paragraph, for they knew the person who chose it would have to memorize it.

"I had hoped that Sam, my most astute student and a 16-year-old third grade level reader, would give it a try. To give him a little encouragement, I painted a lavish picture of the lead character and told Sam he was perfect for the part. He read and the sequence began. Their reading was smoother than expected. After making a few minor changes, they read the play again. For the third reading, they strove for a little more expression.

"After only one day of reading and rereading, they were ready for *phase four,* memorization. Sam was asked to read and then to recite his part from memory. He read well but panicked when I took away his copy. I prompted him with the first two or three words, and he responded by completing the first sentence. As his awestruck classmates looked on, he continued reciting. At his slightest hesitation, I quickly supplied missing words. After two more times, he had it.

"By now the others insisted I prompt them, too. What they didn't realize at first was that my help was minor, and they were proving they were quite capable of reading, memorizing, and reciting words with real feeling and understanding.

"They were now begging to rehearse in the Little Theatre. To slow them down long enough to polish their act, I suggested they make costumes and a backdrop.

"It was now time for *phase five,* dress rehearsal. Adorned in tunic outfits and scarf headdresses (made after they had read and followed the directions), they rehearsed on stage. As the final phase drew near, they made invitations to send to the different classes.

"The day before the final day had come. Students hung the backdrop and opened the curtains of the theater so that passing spectators could admire it. The three-dimensional trees, the wooded forest, the little hut—all depicted great, but for so long hidden, artistic talent.

"*Phase six,* the presentation, had arrived. After the first performance, the word traveled fast. The seventh and eighth grade regular classroom teachers, who had declined their first invitations, asked to be rescheduled. Thus, the 'retarded students' (the name that so often gets attached to learning disabled students) had to give six performances (each better than the one before) in order to accommodate all classes. This, however, worked in their favor since their peers saw them during the final, most polished performances. In fact, their performances, scene design, and costumes far surpassed those in all other student plays previously given in the Little Theatre. What was the best part was that the LD students and other students alike knew it.

"So, what was thought impossible turned out to be very possible, indeed. My only regret was not doing it sooner and not inviting the parents, who are usually denied the privilege of seeing their children perform on stage. All too often, these parents, like teachers, have little or no real expectations of learning disabled children. And, as a result, they give us exactly what we expect—nothing."

Mainstreaming: How Teachers Can Make It Work

Libby Goodman and Hinda Miller
School District of Philadelphia

The LRE requirement of PL 94-142 which mandates normalization of education for the handicapped has had a far reaching effect. Daily, increasing numbers of students and teachers from the ranks of special and regular education are becoming participants in the mainstreaming experience.

The educational community has, for the most part, accepted the fact that mildly to moderately impaired children will receive some if not all of their educational programming in regular classrooms in the company of their nonhandicapped peers.* However, as teachers try to cope with new educational priorities the absence of a clear definition of what mainstreaming is to be and the lack of definitive guidelines for the implementation of nonrestrictive educational programs creates obstacles to the mainstreaming endeavor. Many regular education teachers find few resources to assist in the management of the learning and behavioral problems of the handicapped student. Their colleagues in special education share these same concerns and often are reluctant to relinquish their youngsters to the uncertainties of the regular education program—the mainstream. While this attitude may appear overly protective, there is ample justification for it.

Regarding the current trend toward mainstreaming, *Kaufman, Gottlieb, Agard & Kubic. (1975)* stress that "the emphasis to date has been on administrative arrangements more than on instructional or curricular matters." As a consequence, we find that mainstreaming is a philosophical concept based upon legal and social values but with little practical value (Keogh and Levitt, 1976). If the ideal of mainstreaming is to be achieved for those students and teachers who are already part of the mainstreaming experiment and for those who will follow in the future, we must begin to address the practical day-to-day educational concerns of the classroom teacher. Therefore, in the remainder of this article we will tread lightly on the theoretical issues and instead will emphasize some of the realistic and practical factors involved in the development of integrated educational programs for mild to moderately handicapped students.

Mainstreaming: A Starting Point

The development of successful mainstreaming programs for the handicapped requires the commitment of both the regular education and the special education teacher who jointly share responsibility for the child in question. Because of their different backgrounds and expertise, both of these professionals have an important contribution to make to the educational plan for the child. The special education teacher will have knowledge of methodologies in the areas of differential diagnosis of learning and behavioral problems and individualized learning materials and instructional strategies. The regular education teacher must be recognized as a subject matter specialist, particularly at the secondary level, and of the foundational subjects at the elementary level. And it may be that the regular education teacher has the better understanding of the educational environment which the handicapped child will enter—particularly if special education services are provided on a consultative or itinerant basis. The lines between special and regular education teachers are not drawn with indelible ink, the professional roles do overlap. There are many special educators with considerable expertise in content subjects just as there are regular educators who are adept at diagnosis and individualization. Unfortunately, professionals with dual credentials in both regular and special education are still a rarity—and it may be that the job to be done is more than one person can do. We need to recognize that the professional roles of teachers are expanding and changing and that a "basic negotiation of the relations between regular and special education is underway (Reynolds, 1978)." We need to strive for the working partnership which will bring maximum benefits to children and a sense of professional satisfaction to their teachers.

The remainder of this chapter is devoted to a discussion of the academic and social integration of handicapped children. No distinction is made between regular and special educators; our remarks and suggestions apply equally to both.

*The severely impaired and sensorily or physically handicapped are not to be excluded; and such youngsters are also being mainstreamed to the extent possible, often with remarkable results.

 Reprinted from "Mainstreaming: How Teachers Can Make it Work," by Libby Goodman and Hinda Miller, *Journal of Research and Development Education*, Vol. 13, No. 4, Summer 1980, pages 45-57, with permission.

Social Integration

An important point to consider in the planning of mainstream programs is the importance of social integration. Too often teachers and administrators pay attention to the academic aspect of education to the exclusion of attitudes, values, and social skills. Such skills and attitudes are so important that Cartledge and Milburn (1978) have labeled them the "hidden curriculum" of the classroom. We know from experience that success in the classroom is often more dependent upon social and behavioral skills than academic achievements. Therefore, the mainstreaming plan must address both the social and behavioral variables as well as academic skills if the student is to have a fair chance for success in the regular classroom.

Admittedly, the foremost component of the mainstreaming plan is the amount of time that the youngster will spend in regular education environments and the types of programs in which the student will participate (e.g., non-academic subjects such as gym or academic classes such as English or math). The amount of time to be spent by the student in regular versus special classes, scheduling and other logistical matters are legitimate concerns. But we would argue that a mainstreaming plan which focuses mainly or exclusively upon such considerations is insufficient. Such logistics merely entail temporal adjustments and physical accommodations and in and of themselves will not guarantee the child's success. A minimal plan of this sort, measured by the amount of time spent with the nonhandicapped versus the handicapped will not achieve the real goals of mainstreaming which are social integration and academic success. In the long run, if mainstreaming achieves no more than the superficial co-mingling of the handicapped and nonhandicapped, all who are concerned about the success of the mainstreaming effort will be dissatisfied; and the students, disabled or non-disabled, will be cheated of a valuable learning experience.

Social integration should strive for meaningful interaction between the disabled and non-disabled in which there is an opportunity for the nonhandicapped to acquire positive attitudes about disabilities and for the disabled individual to increase his or her personal feelings of competence and self-worth. There are two sets of attitudes in the classroom—the attitude of the nonhandicapped toward the disabled and the attitudes of the handicapped toward themselves (Johnson and Johnson, in press)—ideally the mainstreaming experience will impact positively on both sets of attitudes.

Attitudes Toward the Handicapped

A major force behind the mainstreaming movement has been the wide spread belief, held by lay persons and professionals alike, that closer contact between the handicapped and the nonhandicapped, particularly within the classroom, would dispel negative attitudes and help to foster positive attitudes and acceptance of the handicapped (Christopholos and Renz, 1969). But despite our beliefs or desires in the matter, research reports on this critical point have yielded mixed results. While some researchers have found that the "contact hypothesis" is viable, others have found that contact between the handicapped and nonhandicapped does not increase social acceptance. In some instances, physical proximity between the groups actually resulted in an increase in prejudice and rejection (Goodman, Gottlieb & Harrison, 1972; Gottlieb & Budoff, 1973; Iano et al., 1974). The conflicting research findings underscore the complexity of attitudes and the difficulty involved in attempting to change attitudes.

Changing Attitudes About the Handicapped

Towner (in press) has recently reviewed the research literature on modifying attitudes toward the disabled. He found that most research studies involved attitudes toward mildly handicapped though other handicapped groups were studied. The participants in attitude change studies included students, (elementary, secondary, college), teachers and administrators, related professionals, and community groups. Though many different strategies were used, the two basic approaches to attitude change were (a) increased contact with the handicapped and (b) increased knowledge about the handicapped. Towner reports that attempts, to date, to alter attitudes have been minimally effective with scant attention to long term effects or to observed changes in teacher behavior when teachers were the target group. Despite such disappointing results, the importance of the task demands continued efforts. A final judgement on the question of attitude change is premature at this time. The research literature must be sifted to identify positive effects and to glean insight even from negative outcomes which will provide the direction for better empirical investigations that will rest upon firmer theoretical and methodological foundations.

Attitudes and Classroom Interaction

Johnson and Johnson (in press) have described the social judging of the handicapped as a process evolving from negative attitudes and stereotypes to attitude change or confirmation - eight stages in all. On the basis of their research they suggest that the outcome of the process—acceptance or rejection—is tied to the pattern of interaction between the handicapped and the nonhandicapped which prevails in the classroom. Johnson and Johnson maintain that one finds three patterns of classroom interaction: competitive, cooperative or individualistic and that "these three types of goal interdependence create different patterns of interaction among students which in turn creates positive attitudes toward and acceptance of classmates regardless of their handicap or negative attitudes toward and rejection of handicapped peers."

A competitive atmosphere prevails in most classrooms, yet research has shown that competition interaction has a negative effect on interpersonal relations among students. In contrast research findings suggest that cooperative learning situations fostered positive attitudes, mutual liking, and respect as well as other benefits such as an improved learning climate in which students who tended toward anxiety and/or tension felt more comfortable (Johnson and Johnson, in press). There are clear implications for the teacher—cooperation should be the preferred mode of interaction in the classroom, competitive learning situations should be employed sparingly and only in those situations in which the introduction of competition clearly produces some benefit.

Finally, there is relatively little research available on individualistic learning; however, Johnson and Johnson suggest that the lack of interpersonal contact argues against its use. Individualistic learning, i.e. a student interacting primarily with materials or equipment rather than other students, is quite prominent in many special education classrooms. On the basis of Johnson and Johnson's work one ought to reevaluate this instructional strategy in special education and guard against its overuse in regular classroom settings. The essence of individualization is not "learning by one's self" but rather learning as one learns best.

Johnson and Johnson also categorize approaches to attitude changes as behavioristic, cognitive, social, and structural. They offer suggestions aimed at fostering positive attitudes among the nonhandicapped and improvement of self attitudes of the handicapped individual. Many of the specific strategies are consistent with Towner's observation that primary strategies for attitude change involve increased contact and information. Johnson and Johnson have also added the element of confrontation between attitudes toward self and perceptions of others as a strategy to bring about changes in the self evaluation of the disabled. It may be, and research tends to support the notion, that a combination of information and contact is a powerful attitude change agent.

Improving Attitudes Through Social Skills

Contact between individuals focuses attention on the social skills; the increasing contact brought about by mainstreaming emphasizes the importance of social and interpersonal skills of the handicapped. Yet research has shown that the handicapped individual is frequently rejected, and more importantly, that the rejection is due to personal or behavioral characteristics and not the handicap per se (MacMillan and Morrison, in press). In the classroom social skills are related to

peer and teacher acceptance of the handicapped and academic achievement (Cartledge and Milburn, 1978); and, yet, the acquisition of social skills is left to chance. Rarely are social skills incorporated into the fabric of the curriculum.

Cartledge and Milburn (1978) have defined social skills as "those social behaviors, interpersonal and task related, that produce positive consequences in the school classroom setting." The types of behaviors which teachers value and which will stand students in good stead are smiling or nodding, taking notes, eye contact, asking questions, volunteering responses, completing assignments, paying attention, helping, sharing, greeting others, controlling aggression, following directions, etc. Social skills, sometimes referred to as survival skills, can and should be taught (Oden and Asher, 1977; Hops and Cobb, 1974). Positive reinforcement strategies and modeling are successful approaches to the inculcation of social skills be they interpersonal or task related. Research studies have also demonstrated a reciprocal relationship between student and teacher behaviors—students can alter teacher behaviors by altering their own (Klein, 1971; Noble and Nolan, 1976).

Published resources are available to help the teacher build a social skills curriculum and impart social skills to students (Sheppard, Shank and Wilson; 1973; Swift and Spivack, 1975; Stephens, 1977)—but the starting point is to recognize to need to do so.

Academic Integration

Academic integration involves the inclusion of the handicapped student into the instructional activity of the regular classroom. Placement of the handicapped student should be made with great care and foresight so that the student will be introduced into a situation which permits him or her to blend academically with his or her peers. Ideally the handicapped students' standing in the classroom should be such that their academic handicaps are relatively inconspicuous. If the discrepancy between academic levels of the student and the class is too great, the mainstreaming experience may consist only of a superficial involvement in which the students are present in class but not profiting from or contributing to the on going instructional activity. For lack of adequate skills, students may find themselves unable to contribute to the academic life of the class and socially isolated as well.

Therefore, a critical consideration in the mainstreaming plan is the degree of academic discrepancy between the handicapped students and the group(s) in which they are placed. It is essential to determine the degree of difference between the academic functioning of the handicapped and the nonhandicapped students and to gauge the degree of pupil variance to which a particular teacher can accommodate. The accommodative skills of teachers do vary. For the student who is too far removed from the norm of the class, successful integration is not likely. Keogh and Levitt (1976) have suggested that "successful mainstreaming occurs when there is congruence in educational competence." This point has been given too little attention by proponents of mainstreaming. However, our own experience with mainstreaming corroborates the importance of this consideration. The School District of Philadelphia, via a federally funded grant, recently completed a three-year study of one of the obstacles to mainstreaming frequently mentioned in the literature—lack of specific skills among regular education personnel needed to teach handicapped students in the regular class. The primary goal was to equip regular education, secondary teachers with the skills they would need to provide instruction to the special education students to be placed in their classrooms. Assessment of teacher attitudes toward mainstreaming at the beginning of the study indicated that the teachers felt handicapped students should be mainstreamed but that their willingness to accept handicapped pupils in their classrooms was dependent upon their acquisition of the skills to teach these students. Three years later at the conclusion of the study, the teachers still expressed positive attitudes toward the concept of mainstreaming and, moreover, felt that they had received excellent information and knowledge about special students, as well as specific skills regarding how to teach them. However, the teachers now expressed an unwillingness to accept the students into their classes if the handicapped students were too far below their nonhandicapped students in skill development. Of the students who were slated for mainstreaming some were functioning as much as four, five, and, in some cases, six years below their regular education classmates. Apparently these teachers were cognizant of a critical factor which has not been given sufficient consideration by educators and administrators at large. The results of the Philadelphia study corroborated the thesis proposed by Keogh and Levitt—the greater the discrepancy of the academic skills development between the special student in the regular class the greater the chances of mainstreaming failure.

Individualization: A Critical Consideration

To maximize the probability of mainstreaming success, regular class placements for handicapped students must be carefully chosen. In addition, teachers must give consideration to the modifications or accommodations that will enable handicapped students to participate meaningfully and successfully among his peers. "Good teaching and good learning take place when the education processes are varied according to interests, abilities, achievement, learning styles and student preferences." (Turnbull and Schulz, 1979). Teachers who share these sentiments will be anxious to learn techniques for the individualization of instruction.

Assessment

An essential factor to effective individualization of instruction is the gathering of accurate information regarding what each student knows, what he does not know and what he needs to learn. The handicapped student generally comes to the regular education class laden with assessment information from previous evaluations, anecdotal records, pupil files, etc. The pupil's file will also contain the Individualized Education Plan, the "blue print" of the handicapped student's instructional program. The I E P may be the most helpful document to the teacher in the planning of instructional activities. The seven components of the I E P fulfill three basic purposes:

1. establishing where the student is (determining present levels of educational performance);
2. identifying how much and what one can reasonably expect him/her to learn by the end of a year (*writing annual goals*);
3. determining the steps to be taken in achieving annual goals and the means to measure the student's progress (specifying short-term objectives and terming the means of evaluating progress).

The present education levels will be especially helpful to the regular education teacher receiving the handicapped student as it roughly indicates where the child should begin in the regular curricular programs. If further testing is required, appropriate tests can be chosen from the large selection of standardized or informal tests, or the teachers can design tests which are better suited to getting accurate information about the student's strengths and weaknesses. But, when testing the handicapped it is often necessary to consider the mode of presentation and response to the test instrument, e.g., whether to use a paper and pencil test, whether to put a test on tape to bypass a student's reading problems, whether to ask a student to respond orally or into a tape recorder to avoid fine motor problems, whether to allow more time for the particular student to complete the test, whether to score content only, etc.

Assessment is primarily for the purpose of determining what a student knows and does not know. This information must be linked to what the teachers want the student to learn; what the school system, via its curricular requirements, wants the student to learn and to what the student wants to learn. These, in turn, must be tied to teaching strategies that have been identified as successful in enabling a student to learn.

Controlling Instructional Variables

Our suggested approach to instructional planning stresses that the teacher controls the learning environment and can manipulate curricular and instructional factors (Goodman, 1978).

The teacher controls the time a learning activity will take place; the place where the learning will occur, e.g. whether the student will be taught individually or as a part of a small group, a large group or by a peer. Teaching a student individually, in a small group or as a part of the whole, large group is generally done by the teacher. Peer teaching can be a great help to both the teacher and the handicapped student if the teacher finds that the student needs just a bit more individual instruction than the teacher can give. Peer tutoring can also contribute to the learning process. For one thing, students often find great satisfaction in working with each other. For another, it is extremely valuable for students to learn that knowledge and skills can be shared and that handicapped students may have something to teach to the nonhandicapped students.

The teacher has control over external motivators and can use techniques such as behavior modification, student self-monitoring, student contracting, etc., to actively involve students in the learning process. Contracts, are particularly useful because they remove the time variable from learning by permitting students to work at their own pace. They also promote independence on the part of the learner and help students to take responsibility for their own learning. In addition, and perhaps most importantly, contracts emphasize analysis of individual needs and the preparation of lessons and materials suited to a specific child—the essence of individualization.

The teacher has control over the amount and the type of homework required of students. An indirect benefit of homework is that it often brings parents into the learning situation which gives the teacher an opportunity to make parents feel that they can be a part of the instructional environment if they so desire.

The teacher controls his own teaching style. A predominantly lecture approach can be used or techniques which encourage discussion and discovery. Individual instruction may be stressed using learning stations, interest centers, media corners, learning activity packets, etc. Such techniques cast the teacher in the role of instructional manager of the learning environment and instructional activities. As a manager the teacher has greater freedom to observe what is happening to the student, to intervene, when needed or to allow students to work alone.

Learning centers are particularly helpful if they are constructed properly. Learning centers should have multilevel activities and materials that allow for various modes of learning to meet individual needs and learning styles. Learning centers should offer activities that range from easy to difficult, from concrete to abstract, from manipulative materials to paper and pencil tasks; in this way centers can be used by both handicapped and nonhandicapped students. Learning centers provide a setting that is related to the ability and the learning style of each of its users and can be used for independent study, follow-up for concepts taught by the teacher, enrichment, etc. (Turnbull and Schulz, 1979).

Learning activity packets are yet another instructional strategy that take individual differences into account. They are somewhat different from a learning center in that a learning packet is intended for use as a self-instructional unit designed to assist students in learning a basic concept. It is difficult to construct a packet that "teaches." Therefore, teachers might want to contruct "Practice Activity Packets," which are also useful instructional aids but which stress practice, not the initial teaching, of concepts. Learning activity packets should be prepared to meet a specific instructional needs. One of the misuses of learning (or practice) activity packets is that of assigning them to every student whether needed or not.

There are many resources available which provide instruction on the development of learning and practice packets, but perhaps one of the clearest is *Mainstreaming Handicapped Students: A Guide for the Classroom Teacher* by Turnbull and Schulz, (1979). These authors indicate the following essential components of a learning activity packet:

1. a specific objective or set of objectives;
2. a pretest designed to assess the student's level of achievement relevant to the objective or objectives appropriate to the instructional experience;
3. a series of instructional activities designed to help the student meet the objective or objectives;
4. a posttest designed to assess the student's level of mastery relevant to the objective or objectives;
5. remediation procedures for those students who do not demonstrate mastery on the posttest.

Specific Learner Problems

Teachers will often seek strategies for specific learner problems—one of these is the problem of inattention. Many handicapped students, especially those who have had difficulty acquiring reading skills, have acquired little information from what they hear. (Few of us realize that 57.5% of class time is spent listening [Taylor, 1973]). Therefore, an essential teaching strategy to be employed for both the handicapped and nonhandicapped student must be to teach students how to listen. Too much of listening activity is without purpose, and, therefore, it is done inefficiently and with limited learning. According to Barbe & Myers (1971), students in general should do more talking and listening to each other instead of the teacher to combat the problem of inattention.

Turnbull and Schulz (1979) have the following strategies to suggest to counteract problems that center around attention:

1. seat an inattentive student close to the teacher or attentive peers (use as role models);
2. be sure that assigned tasks are commensurate with the student's achievement and ability level;
3. make directions clear and easily understood by using
   - consistent language
   - as few "Jargon" terms as possible
   - routine formats for seatwork assignments
   - a peer tutor to explain directions
   - a tape recorder for more detailed directions
4. limit distractors on the printed page;
5. adjust the length of time the student is required to stay on a task;
6. intersperse work activities with games in between;
7. capitalize on student's interest - even if what the student is interested in learning is out of the planned sequence;
8. use mechanical, manipulative devices more often— paper and pencil less often.

Another common and difficult problem is that of concept development. A common misconception among too many teachers is that the handicapped cannot learn abstract concepts and problem solving skills. But, there are teaching strategies to overcome the problems that many handicapped students display in the acquisition of higher order concepts and problem solving skills. According to Turnbull and Schulz (1979), the teacher's fundamental approach to instruction of concepts and problem solving should be via the same sound pedagogical procedures that are used with non-handicapped students:

1. teach from the concrete to the abstract,
2. teach from the known to the unknown,
3. teach from manipulative objects to paper and pencil tasks, etc.

The complicated, higher level, abstract concept development skills will follow. Just bear in mind that these basic teaching principles must be paced to the handicapped student's rate of learning.

Difficulties in remembering that which is taught is often another problem that special students present to the teacher. Though memory problems are not as responsive to remediation as discrete academic skills, Cawley and Vitello (1972) suggest the following strategies:

1. attach some meaning to the material so that it can be remembered more easily;
2. be sure to teach the concept behind any facts that you want a student to memorize, before asking the student to memorize the facts;
3. determine, via a pre-test, which facts the student already knows;
4. determine what is absolutely essential to be committed to memory and eliminate that which is irrelevant;

5. identify preferred learning style and method of practice;
6. document effective strategies (i.e., clustering, associating, rehearsing);
7. establish the amount of information or the number of facts a student can memorize at a given time, so that the amount assigned to be learned is realistic;
8. permit students to chart their own learning;
9. work toward over-learning.

Despite such efforts there are students who simply will not be able to memorize. For such students it will be necessary to develop a system that they can use quickly and unobtrusively, that is also socially acceptable, to help them with certain essential information and skills. For example, a student who is never going to be able to master basic arithmetic facts could be taught to use and to carry a small pocket calculator. Kramer and Krug (1973) and Kokaska (1973) developed a system for students who cannot seem to memorize arithmetic facts that uses fixed reference points on numbers to help students count.

The strategies discussed are but a few of the many ways teachers can adjust and adapt to the needs of the handicapped youngster who come to the regular education class. It is impossible to include more than a few suggestions in the confines of a single chapter. In fact, many authors have written extensively on the topics we have briefly touched. But our purpose is to make teachers more sensitive to the problems of the handicapped and more aware of the resources available to them. And, of course, the regular education teacher's greatest resource may be his/her special education colleague. In addition, strategies that regular education teachers have employed simply as a matter of course as they adjust to the individual differences and needs of the students they already have will come to mind as helpful to the handicapped youngsters as well. Conversely, as teachers identify new strategies that seem to work particularly well with handicapped students, they may find some of these techniques to be helpful to the nonhandicapped student in the class as well.

Using Existing Curricular Materials

Whenever possible the handicapped student should be placed in the curricular programs in the classroom. However, the conceptual load, linguistic complexity and the readability level of the curricular materials must be considered.

One of the simplest ways to determine if a student will be able to read a particular text is to apply Botel's "Rule of Thumb." Select a short passage of approximately 100 words. Ask the student to read it aloud. If 5 or more words are missed the selection will be too difficult. Students can be taught to do this for themselves. This is a helpful technique because many times textbooks are written at much higher reading levels than the grade for which they were intended. Knowing that the handicapped student is reading on a fourth-grade level and having a fourth-grade social studies text book will not always yield a match.

One it is established that a youngster can read a particular text, a quick pre-test on content of each chapter or section that the student will be required to read, is in order. The teacher must assure that the content will provide some new information but that the student will not be without any information at all on the topic. While there are some procedures and criteria that a teacher can use to decide if a student has been placed properly in a given set of materials, in the final analysis, the teacher's judgment will prevail. To help teachers evaluate materials the reader is directed to the work of Boland (1976) in *Teaching Exceptional Children* in which she indicated fifteen specific criteria to help the teacher select materials that are suited to the students, the teacher and the classroom environment. Wiederholt and McNutt (1977) offer suggestions to help teachers initially select materials and once in use, help the teachers determine if the materials were effective.

Modification or Adaptation of Curricular Materials

If curricular materials can be used as they are, so much the better. It is more likely that some adaptations or modifications will have to be made to accommodate the handicapped student.

A major problem encountered in presenting the regular curriculum to the handicapped student is readability. In these instances, a tape recorder is often one of the simplest ways of modifying or adapting existing materials. Lessons requiring extensive reading can be taped. The teacher may be surprised to find many of the nonhandicapped students in the class will also very much appreciate the change in presentation of printed material that the tape recorder affords. Content areas such as science, social studies and language arts lend themselves well to tape recording. While tape recording is time consuming for the teacher, it would not be considered so by volunteers such as other students, grandparents, parents, college students, etc., who are frequently available and willing to help.

The teacher may also wish to rewrite textual material at a lower cognitive and vocabulary level. Older, more capable students, parents, other teachers in the building such as reading specialists and special education teachers could be asked to help with this time consuming task. Once it is done, the rewritten chapters could be catalogued, laminated and filed to be ready for use with other students with similar problems and needs. Further, a regular education student or two may be having difficulty with the same concept and the rewritten chapter will help them as well.

Another adaptation that can be made to existing materials to simplify them for the student is to reorder the sequence of the content as the chapter is being rewritten. For some handicapped students, the impediment to the acquisition of abstract concepts is a lack of prerequisite skills and knowledge in the hierarchy of a particular content area, not poor thinking skills.

It may also be helpful to the student to limit the required content to that which is essential rather than requiring mastery of excessive text. In addition, the amount of time allotted to acquire the information may have to be lengthened, and the mode of presentation may have to be altered.

During class discussion of content area materials, the teacher should guard against limiting questions to the handicapped student to only low level queries. This habit may be due to a sincere concern for the child but may seriously hamper the student's opportunities to develop higher order thinking skills.

For the student who has difficulty writing or spelling, the tape recorder is again a valuable tool. The tape recorder permits the student to record his answers instead of writing them, thus removing unnecessary pressure. This technique can be extended to writing activities in general for the student who is resistant to writing for other reasons. If a peer tutor, teacher, or volunteer could write out that which the handicapped student has put into the tape (or tells the tutor directly), the student may appreciate the value of his own thoughts and responses and be more willing to write for himself.

If it is a question of the student lacking the fine motor coordination needed for legible penmanship a typewriter is in order. For those students with milder motor skills problems, who may simply find it difficult to hold onto the pencil, a commercial pencil grip or a ball of clay or sponge molded around the pencil will be of great value.

When modifying or adapting materials, a few general suggestions always apply. Initiate as few alterations as possible to achieve the desired results. Experiment with one variable at a time and assess its effectiveness before making another change or any multiple changes. Try the simplest and most obvious solutions first. Give any change a reasonable period of trial. Maintain records of student's performance during each change so that objective decisions can be made.

Monitoring of the instructional program is the final critical step in individualization. As teaching takes place, the teacher should be engaged in continuous assessment of student progress and documentation of the techniques and materials that were most successful. Otherwise, the teacher has no way of knowing whether or not instruction, no matter how carefully constructed, has been effective (i.e., the student has learned what was taught).

Monitoring instruction will provide important information regarding the instruction process (i.e., when to speed up, slow down, drill review, change the mode of presentation, etc.). However, all of the information regarding the various interventions will fall short if the teacher has not documented what works and what does not. Documentation is such a critical step in the instruction process, that it is a requirement of the Individualized Education Plan. As the handicapped student progresses through the regular class program, it is necessary to document the level of instruction the student achieves, the instructional objectives that are met and the evaluation criteria that was used to judge the student's performance and progress. As the exceptional student achieves the annual goals and short term objectives on the IEP, new goals, objectives and evaluation criteria will be generated. Writing the new IEP will be so much easier if the teacher has kept good records, and has documented student performance and growth.

Conclusion

Our discussion of mainstreaming has revolved about three critical considerations: the importance of social integration, the importance of academic discrepancy between the handicapped and nonhandicapped as a factor in the decision to mainstream and the importance of individualization of instruction to success of the mainstream program. There are other considerations which also contribute to the eventual success or failure of mainstreaming, e.g. administrative concerns. However, our focus has been the classroom and the classroom teacher.

This brief, limited exposure to some of the requirements for the development of mainstreamed educational programs was not intended to discourage teachers. The job to be done indeed may appear Herculean. Yes, but the needs of the student cannot be denied. The key to accomplishment of the many tasks may lie in the cooperation and collaboration of the regular and special education staff which can maximize the invaluable resources of professional time and expertise.

References

Barbe, W.B. and Myers, R.M. Developing listening ability in children. S. Ducker, (Ed.), *Teaching listening in the elementary school: Readings.* Metuchen, N.J.: Scarecrow Press, 1971.

Bloom, B.S., Englehart, M.D., Furst, E., Hill, W., & Krathwahl, D.R. *Taxonomy of educational objectives, handbook I: Cognitive domain.* New York: David McKay, 1950.

Boland, S.K. Instructional materialism—or how to select what you need. *Teaching Exceptional Children,* 1976, *8*, 156-158.

Cartledge, G., Milburn, J.F. The case for teaching social skills in the classroom: A review. *Review of Educational Research,* 1978, *48*, 133-156.

Cawley, J.E., and Vitello, S.J. Model for arithmetic programming for handicapped children. *Exceptional Children,* 1972, 39, 101-110.

Christopholos, F., & Renz, C. A critical examination of special education programs. *Journal of Special Education,* 1969, *3,* 371-379.

Goodman, L. Meeting children's needs through materials modification. In June B. Jordan (ed.), *Teaching Exceptional Children: Progress by Partners in Step.* Reston, Va.: Council for Exceptional Students, 1978, *10*(3), 92-94.

Goodman, H. Gottlieb, J., and Harrison, R.H. Social acceptance of EMR's integrated into a nongraded elementary school. *American Journal of Mental Deficiency,* 1972, *76,* 412-417.

Gottlieb, H. and Budoff, M. Social acceptability of retarded children in nongraded schools differing in architecture. *American Journal of Mental Deficiency,* 1973, *78,* 15-19.

Hops, H. and Cobb, J.A. Initial investigations into academic survival-skill training, direct instruction, and first grade achievement. *Journal of Educational Psychology,* 1974, *66,* 548-553.

Iano, R.P., Ayers, D., Heller, H.B., McGettigan, J. and Walker, V.S. Sociometric status of retarded children in an integrative program. *Exceptional Children,* 1974, *40,* 267-271.

Johnson, D.W. and Johnson, R. *Translating attitude change principles for use in educational settings.* Reston, Va.: Council for Exceptional Children publication, in press.

Kaufman, M.J., Gottlieb, J., Agard, J.A., and Kubic, M.B. Mainstreaming: Toward an explication of the construct. Intramural Research Program, Bureau of Education for the Handicapped, U.S. Office of Education, March, 1975.

Keogh, B.K., Levitt, M.L. Special education in the mainstream: A confrontation of limitations. *Focus on Exceptional Children,* 1976, *8*(1), 1-10.

Klein, S.S. Student influence on teacher behavior. *American Educational Research Journal.* 1971, *8,* 403-4.

Kokaska, S.M. A notation system in arithmetic. *Education and Training of the Mentally Retarded.* 1973, *8,* 211-216.

Kramer, T., and Krug, I.A. A rationale and procedure for teaching addition. *Education and Training of the Mentally Retarded.* 1973, *8,* 140-144.

MacMillan, D.L. and Morrison, G.M. *Sociometric research in special education.* Reston, Va.: Council for Exceptional Children publication, in press.

Noble, C.G. and Nolan, J.D. Effect of student verbal behavior on classroom teacher behavior. *Journal of Educational Psychology,* 1976, *68,* 342-346.

Oden, S. and Asher, S.R. Coaching children in social skills for friendship making. *Child Development,* 1977, *48,* 495-506.

Reynolds, M.C. Staying out of jail. *Teaching Exceptional Children,* 1978, *10,* 60-62.

Sheppard, W.C., Shank, W.W., and Wilson, D. *Teaching social behavior to young children.* Champaign, Ill.: Research Press, 1973.

Stephens, T.M. *Teaching skills to children with learning and behavior disorders.* Columbus, Ohio: Merrill Publishing Co., 1977.

Swift, M.S. and Spivack, G. *Alternative teaching strategies: Helping behaviorally troubled children achieve.* Champaign, Ill.: Research Press, 1975.

Taylor, S.E. *Listening.* Washington, D.C.: National Educational Association of the United States. 1973.

Turnbull, A.P., and Schulz, J.B. *Mainstreaming handicapped students: A guide for the classroom teacher.* Boston: Allyn and Bacon, Inc., 1979.

Towner, A.G. *Modifying attitudes toward the disabled: A review of literature and methodological considerations.* Reston, Va.: Council for Exceptional Children publication, in press.

Wiederholt, J.L. & McNutt, G. Evaluating materials for handicapped adolescents. *Journal of Learning Disabilities,* 1977, *10,* 132-140.

Teaching the Emotionally Disturbed and Behaviorally Disordered Child

Children with social and emotional difficulties are a diverse group, yet they are all problematic in how they learn and how they choose to interact with their environment. They often have difficulty carrying out the usual daily routine without disruption, and their emotional problems can interfere with their learning and academic performance. Often they cause others in their environment to feel frustrated or distressed. Some show lower intelligence test scores, while others are far above the norm. Some have a serious academic achievement deficiency, while others perform well above grade level. Some externalize their problems by acting out, while others become withdrawn. Some evidence relatively minor difficulties resulting from situational problems in the environment (i.e., severe family disruption), and have a positive prognosis, while others evidence severe psychotic or autistic behaviors, and have a less positive prognosis.

These children, no matter what the seriousness of their label implies, are being mainstreamed, and teachers are being asked to develop skills in managing their behavior in a group classroom setting. While the task is challenging, there are many things a teacher can do to ease the transition for all students. The articles in this section describe strategies for teachers for coping with many different situations they are likely to encounter.

There are many critical dimensions in mainstreaming the emotionally disturbed or behaviorally disordered child. In "The Psychology of Mainstreaming Socio-emotionally Disturbed Children," William Morse considers some of the factors that are important to the success of the children's education, and identifies the psychological elements to be considered in reintegrating the children into their peer group.

Developing social skills is of great importance for emotionally disturbed students, not only in school but in their overall social assimilation as well. "Skill-Streaming: Teaching Social Skills to Children" emphasizes the importance of social skills training and discusses methods for developing a flexible and prescriptive teaching program.

The problems faced by educators and their students in a classroom that includes behaviorally disordered children are compounded when teachers are not adequately equipped to teach the diversity of students found in that setting. "Educator Perceptions of Behavior Problems of Mainstreamed Students" discusses the necessity of having teachers develop attitudes and skills for behavior management in the mainstreamed environment.

The conflicts that arise in the classroom when emotionally disturbed students are mainstreamed result in many stressful situations. "Reducing Stress of Students in Conflict" presents eight concrete strategies for reducing stress so that teachers are not overwhelmed by the magnitude of the problem.

Some children display behavioral disorders as a result of abuse and neglect. "Child Abuse and Neglect" addresses family problems which influence a child's behavior in the classroom, and outlines the teacher's role and responsibilities in reporting abuse and providing education for the prevention of child neglect and abuse.

Looking Ahead: Challenge Questions

Why are children with socio-emotional problems considered difficult to mainstream?

What strategies can teachers use to cope with the emotionally and behaviorally disturbed child in the classroom?

Why is child abuse and neglect on the rise, and how can teachers help to prevent it?

The Psychology of Mainstreaming Socio-emotionally Disturbed Children

William C. Morse

The concept and promise of mainstreaming for the socio-emotionally disturbed can be considered from diverse viewpoints. Historically it is nothing new: old style mainstreaming was once the total program and still is all that has been provided for many special education pupils. Politically, mainstreaming has been a popular approach and is envisioned as a way to serve more with less during this period of acute financial stress. A pupil is hardly special except for brief encounters and this has already led to the idea that reimbursement should be on a piecework basis—the child being special only when not in the mainstream. Administratively, mainstreaming might look simple at first glance, and consultation avoids the accountability and responsibility which accompany direct service to children. In many districts the teachers and their unions are not yet aware of the meaning of the new design. Regular teachers themselves frequently express dismay when they learn of the new obligations and extended accountability they have inherited.

Mainstreaming is usually combined with mandatory legislation giving parents and advocates a new power base for participation in getting service for children in need. Special education professionals range in opinion about mainstreaming from seeing it as a loss of financial and operational control to helping children to the dawn of the new day when special education is about to direct and reform the total educational establishment. Whether the specialists will actually increase or decrease their influence is still an interesting speculation. Philosophically we cannot forget that whatever actually happens in given circumstances, mainstreaming is the hope for a more humane and concerned special educa-

tion. The guilt for our past sins and the cultural revolution leads us to know we must learn to do better.

But attention to these matters does not allow us to avoid the central purpose of it all. The psychological study of mainstreaming focuses on one issue: how well does this process provide the actual experiences which the socio-emotionally deviant pupil needs? This psychological examination starts with the definition of our special education pupils. The socio-emotionally disturbed pupils are those, who by virtue of the dissonance pervading their inner and outer life space, have a need for more intense and more sophisticated professional investment than do their normal peers. The simple fact is, if there is no need for this special input, the youngster should not be considered a special education pupil. The unsimple fact is, if he has special needs, we have not yet begun the proper examination of how we can actually provide the help. The preoccupation with the various mechanics of the delivery of service is better suited to milk distribution than to providing mental health. It puts emphasis more on the efficiency of a system than on the profound complications inherent in re-raising a child who is in the midst of his own unique constellation of stress. This is a psychological problem.

Exploring the Psychological Nature of our Task

We may begin our psychological exploration by reminding ourselves of an assumption. This assumption is that most of our subset population of special education, in contrast to other areas, can be restored and made whole. This goal of normality or recoverability sets off a chain of accountability expectations seldom recognized. Some have a goal of more than normality for these deviant pupils: they anticipate a high level of self-actualization. There is also the confounding aspect that

Reprinted from *Mainstreaming Emotionally Disturbed Children*, Edited by A.J. Papanikou and James L. Paul (Syracuse, N.Y.: Syracuse University Press, 1977), pp. 18-30. Used with permission.

the child's normal developmental growth is destined to produce periods of relative stress and relief within and without. This flux must be separated from long-term directional change. Since in many states special education resources are not legally available for prevention or crisis, the problem has to reach a proven "bad" level before it is "good" enough to be serviced. Without the continua of mental health service, the uncategorized child or adolescent is left to his own devices since he is not ours. We speak of alternative plans for such special program mismatches, but we forget that the intensity of help required may be equal, though presumably for a shorter time span.

But there are other matters: From the ecological point of view espoused by Rhodes (1970), we know we must be equally concerned with the child's nature and milieu factors. This expands the universe of both assessment and interventions. Again, since socio-emotional problems are seldom found in a pristine state, we should be involved with the welfare of special pupils who may "belong" to some other label, though they may have an overlay of emotional difficulty. Finally, we are given to ignore the fact that many of the socio-emotional problems are not born of the educational enterprise (though some are and others may be exacerbated by the school). But the necessary interventions may not be primarily educational in the usual school sense. It is not uncommon to see special programs for socio-emotionally impaired pupils which do not have even a remote mental health component.

It is necessary to devote brief attention to the children included before moving to specific psychological aspects of mainstreaming. Though special education has persisted in picking and choosing what it would consider, there are three syndromes which are included. Since these have been described in detail (Morse in Cruickshank and Johnson 1975 and Morse 1975), we need only to make it clear that we are not speaking of minor or temporary defections of behavior where cures are simple and even instant. While the fact is that the individual profile overrides any general pattern, the meaning of the child's specific symptoms rests in the pattern. Regardless of how the impairments were generated or the theories about recovery, there are three general states of serious impairment. The first overall pattern stems from an incapacitating struggle between impulse and control. At a conscious or unconscious level there will be evidence of subjective distress, anxiety, and guilt. Such children may act out or be depressed and are usually plagued by severely damaged self-esteem. A second category, which has often been ignored by special education, consists of children and youth who are growing up with serious defects in socialization. These are the value-deficient (as contrasted with value-different) children who are growing up without acquiring an age-appropriate concern for others. This pattern is probably the most rapidly growing group; we also see an increasing

number of girls who evidence this dilemma. As the primary socialization factors in society have become less effective, there are more and more desperate children with no trust and no caring, who live on their impulses. They are damaged both by blunted feelings for others and by their limitations in using symbols, or reading (King 1975 and 1976). Third, special education is responsible for the severely disabled children who have profound communication difficulties, acute relationship distortions, and difficulty coping with even a simplified environment. They seem to have no interest in others and live immersed in their own preoccupations; their play produces neither the normal exploration nor the satisfaction found in the normal youngster. While many hold that both psychotic and autistic children have a limited future, we must increase our efforts to help.

Mainstreaming must be put in the context of the psychological nature of those children in the above syndromes. This raises two central considerations. One is that the idiosyncratic nature of each child determines the specific intervention of choice. The behavior patterns which help us think and plan cannot be a substitute for individualization of the work. Just as each child is individual, conversely, there is no mainstream entity. We made that mistake when we created the fiction of a hypothetical special class. We even talked about special classes as if the name delineated a given psychological substance. Let us not make the mistake again. There are as many mainstreams as there are youngsters mainstreamed. Each has a unique set of intervention resources and strictures.

We turn now to a brief examination of the two parts of the puzzle—the children and the mainstream place. What is in the search for the degree of match? At best, we know very little about the children we would serve. Our lack of skill in understanding them has driven us to tests and devices, to meetings and consultations. Anything but the child! It is of much concern to find psychological tests now being given and interpreted by untrained personnel. It is of equal concern to find new unproven devices spawned at every turn. If we have enough scales to depend upon, there is no need to test our human understanding, which is what clinical skill was all about. It would be refreshing to ask, in the midst of the reports of data collected about the child, if the real child would please stand up. Of course he usually could not stand up because he is not really here. We are all busy trying to reconstruct him from examining his artifacts which we have collected. He has become an archeological discovery, known from his remains and not his person. And if he did stand up, would we recognize him? Diagnosis has become the blind foursome who, as the story goes, described their knowledge of the elephant. When we look at the evidence from discussions about disturbed children, we learn as much about the perceiver as the perceived.

8. TEACHING THE EMOTIONALLY DISTURBED

The crux of the issue of mainstreaming lies in differential knowledge about the needs of a pupil. There seems to be an illusion that severity is the index of placement. "Mild cases" (whatever they are) can be mainstreamed, while severe ones never can be, or so we are told. Anyone who has tried to work with an ego-intact, value-deviant delinquent in a classroom might decide to try very different and more seriously impaired in the classroom the next time. We have as yet worked out no system for determining who can be helped where.

Since anyone's behavior is always a consequence of a given ratio of the internal and external condition, we can no longer focus on either just the child or just the environment. The diagnostic search is conducted to discover (Morse 1974) which intervention is relevant in the particular child-environment ratio. There is also the danger of the "greenhouse" phenomenon: an environment which exactly meets the needs of the deviant child may create an instant elimination of his reactive behavior, but is this a cure? Some believe that, if the environment is unprovoking, the given child will heal himself. Other times we anticipate that any correctional influence will take time to prepare for the later transplanting out of the greenhouse. Developmental growth counts for something, but we often wonder how much.

On the other hand, mainstreaming might result in a necessary confrontation revealing the child's inability to cope successfully. The problem can then be dealt with realistically. Teaching socio-emotionally impaired children presents a unique and continual challenge whether the pupil is in a special setting or in the mainstream. We want him to work up to his ability, but we do not want to push him beyond his coping capacity. We try to work at the very cutting edge of his cognitive and affective potential. This requires that teachers neither over- nor undersupport the youngster. This is a continual clinical judgment. If we require too little, the child is robbed of his ability to function on his own. If we give too little, we undersupport the need. If we give too much, the child remains dependent on the "helper."

Probably the most significant thing we can hope for in mainstreaming is innovation in the ability to infuse school with interventions (new and old) rather than the illusion of an automatic great stride forward based on the geography of where we put the problem. Often the old classes for the emotionally disturbed did very little for the "statistical average" pupil, but did help some a great deal. It was also clear that special classes so called were often really not special at all. . . . At other times and for particular pupils and their families the special class added insult to original injury. Then the task became one of getting the child to quit fighting the delivery system, never getting to his basic problem for which the placement was made. We have yet to study the persons for whom the class is useful versus those for whom it is not. Mainstreaming does not eliminate intervention problems; it just presents a new set of variables—a set, we hope, that can be better managed if we use it for the right youngsters.

Partly because of our educational myopia, we have had a tendency to overlook the psychological needs of a child. As it is put, the diagnosis must be educationally relevant. It can be that and still not relevant to the child we are trying to help. It may be heretical to say that every socio-emotionally disturbed child may not be a special education problem. Of course they must have schooling, and to say that rescue will not come from special education does not mean we should not provide special education. Many of the easy educationally based cures written about are children whose behavior was a consequence of direct educational insult. These are reversible through educational interventions alone if caught soon enough. Not so with the many children who are casualties of massive family and societal destructiveness. The potential for restoration and compensatory support for these children is a matter of a life support system and not a class or a regular classroom alone. The educator who advocates going it alone in such instances will find the well-meaning effort of excellent teachers consumed in the too little which is provided.

With the diminution of multi-disciplined involvement and the ascendance of educational responsibility, we have unwittingly boxed ourselves in. The socio-emotionally disturbed child may not respond to special education. While the school often generates or acerbates a condition, education may be the *major* intervention channel, *one* of the channels, or it may be a *low power* involvement.

Educational Programs in Perspective

As we examine what is necessary to help a youngster toward a reasonable personal and social life, we have to ask to what degree the total milieu must be controlled and what specialization must be infused in the milieu if we are to be successful. We have to ask what must happen to give the child a new lease on life.

Will changes be necessary in the family and community, or will a change in how the child perceives and responds to the conditions be sufficient? Will minor changes in the child's behavior heal an interactive pattern (Henry 1971)? The work of Love (1974) suggests non-traditional, school-related methods for altering families on the ego level, which may be enough. If one can adjust the curriculum and method and by this end the child's problem, that is one thing. Experience with severe value deviancy raises questions about even a total milieu (unless it is highly sophisticated) ever providing what is needed.

When the change is made from providing a program to providing a sufficient program, the situation will be vastly different. To some of us educational accountability has become an excuse by the community for providing for the needs of emotionally and socially deviant children. A school program takes over just a part of life, but it can be made to look as though it cares for all of the child's needs so we can avoid the programs required for a total effort.

The generic problem of providing for the real psychological needs of the child does not change with a special provision or mainstreaming. We never mastered meeting the needs in special classes which is one reason for the mainstream mania. Sometimes, related to the special class, the most incisive experiences were on the bus trips and not in the actual classes at all—so little did we attend to the psychological realities. There are public school programs which have incorporated group therapy, individual therapy, and family interventions. There are those for adolescents which engage in work "therapy" but these are the exception to the rule. Even when resources of the work experience type are available to mainstream adolescents, members of our group are frequently rejected as misfits.

In planning interventions we have been very naive, ignoring the complexity of socio-emotional disturbance. Always we look for a short cut. There are three generalizations which have emerged in my own thinking with regard to this. The first generalization is that the child is a dynamic organism who fortunately often remolds what is done to him to fit his problem even if it is a poor choice. It follows then that there is no one magic way to assist a child. This lack of specificity results in the sometimes success by a wide variety of interventions and, at the same time, the never perfect success by any one mode—be it curriculum or psychotherapy, neither or both. Finkel (1976) lists twenty-two currently practiced approaches to psychotherapy along with six principal group therapies. This listing is really a restricted classical listing of therapy and those of us who have followed Redl see the therapeutic *potential* of many, many more approaches (Morse and Cheney 1972), most of which can be incorporated into the school experience. Many are emphasized in this volume. Can we professionals live long enough to get over focusing on the delivery mechanic rather than the pupil's problem? If we do begin to appreciate the wide variety of interventions which may be effective, we next realize that our ability to predict which one is appropriate for which youngster is often low. In a way this is because "help" is in the eyes of the helpee, not the helper. It is often indirect rather than direct, and has a quality of the consumer's perception about it.

A second generalization comes from the observation that pilot programs often cannot be considered as pilots at all. The successful model in many cases simply does not transfer. This may be because what is effective in obtaining positive results may not be the thing to which people attribute the change. The Hawthorne effect, zest, deeper human commitment, the hope engendered and caring (expressed in diverse ways to be sure), the emotion of initial surge vs. the grinding long term

hauls—things of this nature may be involved. Thus it seems that the covert psychological conditions underlying help may override the overt elements described.

Third, the impatience for instant change looms large. It is possible that this violates the essential nature of child growth, development, and especially remediation. One could almost say if there is instant or rapid change there was either no real problem in the first place or else the new behavior is superficial. Yet impatience about change makes for much false expectation. What we should be concerned with is life stream as a psychological process and what we talk about is mainstreaming as an educational process. The degree to which the mainstreaming mode of instant pressing out of plastic objects in this society has been embraced by the child raisers is an indication of the shallow understanding of children which pervades our work.

The goal then should be to assess (we can no longer talk much about diagnosis) the dissonance in the person and place system as Rhodes has said and then apply the best possible psychological interventions.

Analyzing the Psychological Resources in the Mainstream

Kendall (1971) was one of the first to discuss the psychological realities of mainstreaming, and he based much of his point of view on the fact that "school systems are notoriously resistant to fundamental change." The questions he raises have to do with the nature of mainstream resources for the special child. These range from curriculum to attitudes, and not one of them is subject to easy control. We can focus on this matter by examining the three main sources of psychological input in the mainstream: the adults, the peers, and the tasks. The utility of mainstreaming has to do with what these immediate sources produce and what the child requires for both maintenance and improvement. The impact must not only be hygienic; it must be restorative. . . .

The Teacher's Input

It is well known that training and ability have only a low correlation. There are regular teachers who are able to interact usefully with socio-emotionally disturbed children though they never took a course, do not know the terms, and could not describe what they do. But there are also limits (of the initiated and uninitiated as well) in capacity to be psychologically helpful. In mainstreaming we had better seek out the natural human resources in teachers rather than take on the task of making over the whole profession. For example, children who need structure and an adult with a sense of authority should not be put in a classroom where the native style of that teacher does not embody such resources. The consequence of expecting the mainstream agents to generate a scarce or absent psychological input will lead only to defeat. Of course the fact that a pupil is sustained by a teacher does not always mean that there will be any automatic growth to absorb the problem which the child has. When we expect that the teacher or some resource adult will have to help the youngster with profound distortions of feelings, additional skills are needed in the mainstream. Can the teacher counsel in depth with the pupil? Does the teacher have the ability to dissociate counter transference responses? We know that trained and untrained alike falter (King 1976) in handling aggressive behavior which is a major component. Can the teacher referee the psychological games and avoid the traps children play with adults and peers (Newman 1974)? By any stretch of the imagination, can the teacher be a figure to fill the void in the child's identification pattern? From this viewpoint, we must consider the proper use of the native adult resources in the mainstream for the necessary psychological input. Sometimes there will be resources enough and other times not enough.

The Peer Climate

Classroom groups differ significantly in their mental health resource index. There are stable, resilient groups which absorb and diminish the output of a deviant child. Some go further and reach out in an empathic way to help a troubled child. Other groups have such a low margin or are already saturated with problems, whether designated as special education or not, that a precarious, marginal balance can be destroyed with an addition in the mainstream. There are groups with a frustration quotient so high that scapegoating is the order of the day. Other groups have so little reservoir of peer liking that there is no relationship to offer a new pupil. Fearful groups may be traumatized by the behavior of some youngsters. The dynamics of class size in itself are little considered in mainstreaming. The huge class sizes invoked to solve budget problems determine the time teachers have to invest in each pupil. What one pupil gets extra another pupil misses, and sooner or later the majority of the children (or the parents) are going to catch on and object. The "value of learning to live with different children" may not be adequate compensation. At present, the movement to employ aides, get and train volunteers, and other modes to add to the ratio of adult investment is in need of a great deal of study.

It is our observation that the current social disorganization is producing a significant group of children without a primary group experience needed to establish basic trust and a sense of self identity. The usual classroom secondary group will not be enough: in fact such a child will attempt to use the classroom in ways destined to failure. Or to take another problem, current role identification problems of girls are producing an increasing number of failures which will need a more intensive relationship than is possible in many classrooms. If we are going to provide what is needed, we will have to find ways of breaking down the group size without putting expectations on regular classroom teachers which will drive them to further distraction. Let alone solving this problem, a good many in special education do not even recognize it. Behavior repression is not the solution for such deprived children.

While the school is a group work agency our own studies suggest that even in special classes there is little group work done. Since we know the group is often a more powerful agent than the adult, it is axiomatic that we must either select groups with the necessary qualities to provide what the mainstreamed special child needs or work through the group conditions which are counterindicated. This is seldom accomplished by consultation since group work itself is a very complicated process.

The research on how normal children in general respond to deviance has only begun—to say nothing of what might happen in any given classroom due to the idiosyncratic conditions. In a replication of earlier work by Kalter and Marsden, Hoffman (1976) has found that elementary age children can distinguish levels of pathology in described peers but their liking and disliking are independent of the level. Degree of disturbance does not always signify the degree of rejection. It is the disruptive or threatening character of the behavior which upsets the normal peer group. Regressive and immature behavior is often the most threatening. Gold (1958) has found four main dimensions in positive peer evaluation: expertness, physical attractiveness and prowess, social-emotional sensitivity, and skill and interests which are similar to peers. The very lack of these behaviors could be used to describe disturbed children. It is no wonder we have programs for these children which virtually "individualize out" any group involvement. The stark reality is that the peer culture can be a mainstream resource or disaster.

The Curricular Experience

To learn a fact or a skill can be therapeutic in itself. To see yourself as the slowest and lowest can be negative self-fulfillment. In an achievement-mad society—without special education protection—there are psychological messages all about. We have a right to ask, regarding mainstreaming, not only how much is the learning situation individualized but how much is the individualization accepted as a natural and inevitable condition. The careful scrutiny of many so-called open conditions indicates that to each his own is the way things are organized but if your "own" is to be low man on the totem pole, you have the curse. Providing psychological support for the child's state of accomplishment within the ethos of the typical classroom is the task.

There is a second part of the task factor in addition to the management of traditional curriculum elements.

This is the affective educational enterprise. Since our special children are by definition having difficulty in the affective area, the utilization of affective education methodology becomes necessary. There are as many definitions of affective education as there are advocates, and as much confusion as direction in this field. Nonetheless, in mainstreaming a youngster, we need to attend to the breadth of the curriculum. In matter of fact, those few who appear to have the most impressive impact on the distraught child have moved so far from what a traditional classroom does that one has misgivings about finding the remedial environment in the typical regular or special education classroom. The bridge from the flexible special classroom to the typical regular classroom is a long one. The distance from the school-defined educational format to life-relevant programs for disturbed children may be too long to span. The few successful alternative schools may point the way. The degree to which these approaches have permeated the mainstream is also a question. One open elementary school (look—no inside walls at all!) absorbed all the problem kids who were able to just drift around in the low-pressure setting, but that is not special education accountability.

Conclusion

This book deals directly with the complications required to maximize the resources which can be generated in the mainstream. It is a truism that the very same generic elements constitute the conditions which create, acerbate, or restore. There are these adults, these peers, and these task experiences to consider. The psychological analysis of mainstreaming requires painstaking examination of what these elements produce relative to our best understanding of what is needed. It is necessary that we leave the fantasy world of decreeing arbitrary attributes and relevance to conditions whether they be the mainstream, the special class, or individual therapy. There should be many studies of "one special education boy's day" so that we begin to face up to the actual psychological transactions *vis-a-vis* the diagnostic prescription. Accountability is in the psychological substance of the experience. What must the socio-emotionally distraught child learn and where and how can it be provided? To speak of mainstreaming out of the psychological context can lead us astray.

References

Cruickshank, W.M., and Johnson, G.O., eds. *Education of Exceptional Children and Youth.* 3d ed. Englewood Cliffs, N.J.: Prentice-Hall, 1975.

Finkel, N.J. *Mental Illness and Health: Its Legacy, Tensions, and Changes.* New York: Macmillan, 1976.

Gold, M. "Power in the Classroom." *Sociometry* 21 (1958): 50-60.

Henry, J. *Pathways to Madness.* New York: Random House, 1971.

Hoffman, E. "Children's Perceptions of their Emotionally Disturbed Peers." Unpublished Ph.D. dissertation, University of Michigan, 1976.

Kendall, D. "Towards Integration." *Special Education in Canada* (November 1971): 3-16.

King, C. "The Ego and the Integration of Violence in Homicidal Youth." *American Journal of Orthopsychiatry* 45 (1975): 134-45.

_____. "Counter-Transference and Counter-Experience in the Treatment of Violence Prone Youth." *American Journal of Orthopsychiatry* 46 (1) (1976).

Love, L.R., and Kaswan, J.W. *Troubled Children: Their Families, Schools, and Treatments.* New York: Wiley-Interscience, 1974.

Morse, W.C. "Concepts Related to Diagnosis of Emotionally Impaired." In *State of the Art: Diagnosis and Treatment.* Monograph, Office of Education, U.S. Dept. of HEW, Bureau of Education for Handicapped, Cont. No. OEC-0-9-25290-4539(608), 1974.

_____. "The Education of Socially Maladjusted and Emotionally Disturbed Children." In *Education of Exceptional Children and Youth,* edited by W.M. Cruickshank and G.O. Johnson, 3d ed. Englewood Cliffs, N.J.: Prentice-Hall, 1975.

_____. *The Seriously Disturbed: Psycho-Social Disorders of Childhood and Youth.* Report to Hawaii Special Education Department, 1975.

_____, and Cheney, C. "Psychodynamic Interventions in Emotional Disturbance." In *A Study of Child Variance,* edited by W.C. Rhodes. Vol. 2: *Interventions.* Conceptual Project in Emotional Disturbance. Ann Arbor, Michigan: University of Michigan, Institute for the Study of Mental Retardation and Related Disabilities, 1972.

Newman, R.G. *Groups in Schools. A Book about Teachers, Parents, and Children.* New York: Simon and Schuster, 1974.

Rhodes, W.C. "A Community Participation Analysis of Emotional Disturbance." *Exceptional Children* 36 (1970): 309-14.

Skill-Streaming:
Teaching Social Skills to Children with Behavioral Disorders

Ellen McGinnis
Laurie Sauerbry
Polly Nichols

Ellen McGinnis *is an education consultant in the Child Psychiatry Unit at the University of Iowa, Iowa City.* **Laurie Sauerbry** *is a special education teacher in the Cedar Rapids Community Schools, Cedar Rapids, Iowa.* **Polly Nichols** *is an education consultant in the Child Psychiatry Unit at the University of Iowa, Iowa City.*

■ Educating children with behavior disorders means more than meeting the traditional goals of enforcing limits on behavior and teaching academic competencies. These students also need to have direct attention paid to their interpersonal and social needs. These areas are suggested for inclusion in a student's educational program by the federal definition of emotional disturbance (Public Law 94-142), and special educators are increasingly aware that attention must be given to these areas if students are to return to their regular school environments successfully.

In special classrooms for children with behavioral disorders, emphasis is often placed on telling the students what they should *not* do. After all, deviant behavior is the primary reason they are placed in this type of program. Such strategies as logical consequences (Dreikurs & Cassel, 1974) can teach Mary that responding with physical aggression when she is teased on the playground will result in the loss of this playground privilege. However, when Mary's response of physical aggression is taken away from her, what is put in its place? We believe that in addition to teaching students that certain responses are unacceptable, we must teach the prosocial alternatives to these antisocial behaviors.

Students who have been removed from the mainstream of education and placed into a special class due to their behavior disorders either have not picked up socially acceptable alternatives through incidental learning or have not received sufficient practice for these prosocial choices to be a consistent part of their behavioral repertoire. How often have we heard students say, "I should have ignored him!" Yet, although the students promise to ignore their tormentors the next time, they just cannot seem to do it. Such students will likely recite positive alternatives to dealing with conflicts and other social problems. However, merely being able to verbalize these choices is very different from actually being able to carry out the actions.

BACKGROUND

Goldstein, Sprafkin, Gershaw, and Klein (1980) have described a method of teaching prosocial skills to adolescent students. Based on the behavioral technique of structured learning, Goldstein's method, called "skill-streaming," promotes positive social behaviors by systematically providing:

1. Specific steps that are learned to a mastery level, with actual examples to illustrate these steps (modeling).
2. Practice with the steps in simulated problem situations (role playing).
3. Information as to how the student has performed the steps (feedback).
4. Practice in real-life situations (transfer of training).
5. Approval for successful use of the skill (reinforcement).

We shall describe a modification of skill-streaming for elementary-age students that focuses on the maintenance and generalization of learned social skills. (A more comprehensive explanation of this program can be found in *Skillstreaming the Elementary School Child* [McGinnis & Goldstein, 1984]). This method of deliberate teaching enables behaviorally disordered youngsters to become proficient in socially acceptable ways of meeting their needs.

SOCIAL SKILLS STEPS

Key social skills, such as the skill of How to Deal with Wanting Something That Isn't Mine, are task analyzed into a sequence of steps, as in the example shown in Figure 1. Other examples of this type of skill can be

FIGURE 1
When I Want Something That Isn't Mine

1. Say to yourself, "I want this, but I can't just take it."
2. Say, "It belongs to _____ ."
3. Think of your choices:
   a. You could ask the person to loan (or share) it.
   b. You could earn the money to buy it.
   c. You could ask the person to trade.
4. Act out your best choice.

found in Goldstein et al.'s *Skillstreaming the Adolescent* (1980) and Stephens' *Social Skills in the Classroom* (1978).

PREREQUISITE SKILLS

Entry level skills will need to be assessed and, where necessary, instruction provided as part of the actual teaching of a specific social skill. For example, many of the skill steps in this approach for elementary-age students incorporate self-control techniques such as conscious relaxation (Fagen, Long, & Stevens, 1975). Students may also need practice with key cognitive skills such as reading social cues, verbal mediation, identifying and labeling feelings (see Cartledge & Milburn, 1980), consequential thinking (see Bash & Camp 1982), and problem solving (see Spivak & Shure, 1974). The example shown in Figure 2, Dealing with Own Anger, includes two alternatives that will require specific teaching as choices for the student.

CHOOSING THE SKILLS

Many social skills chosen for instruction are those that research has suggested are related to peer acceptance. Examples of such skills are sharing and having a conversation (Mesibov & La Greca, 1981), positive teacher attention (e.g., asking about work assignments) and academic success (e.g., following directions) (Cartledge & Milburn, 1980), and those likely to elicit reinforcement in the natural environment. It is important to note, however, that the goal of this program is not simply to teach the students to conform, but rather to teach them positive ways of dealing with social conventions, with their own feelings and the feelings of others, and with stressful or conflict situations. Skills such as Making a Complaint and Dealing with Group Pressure (Goldstein et al., 1980) are also included.

Identifying Needs

Before actually beginning the social skills group, a Social Skills Checklist (found in *Skillstreaming the Elementary School Child*) is completed for each student. This helps to identify the student's specific needs and is a method of recording the social difficulties the teacher has observed.

The skills needed by each student are then recorded on the Group Chart. This procedure not only serves as a record of individual needs, but also guides the teacher in the selection of target skills. The Group Chart is used by teachers to group students according to specific skills needed (Goldstein et al., 1980).

BEGINNING INSTRUCTION IN SOCIAL SKILLS

The setting in which the training occurs must resemble as closely as possible the actual setting in which the skill will be applied (Goldstein, 1981). For example, if

FIGURE 2
Dealing with Own Anger

Steps:
1. Stop and count to 10.
2. Think of your choices:
   a. You could tell the person in words why you are angry.
   b. You could walk away for now.
   c. You could do a relaxation exercise.
3. Act out your best choice.

Teacher Notes for Discussion: This is an example of teaching the person in a way that will not make that person angry too. Students practice by asking the teacher if they can leave the room and run an errand for her, run outside for 2 or 3 minutes, and so forth. Discuss these choices, which could be part of "walking away."

Suggested Situations:
These techniques could be used when you do not think the teacher or your parents have been fair to you or when you are having a day "where everything seems to go wrong" (e.g., you are late for the bus).

The skill steps are written to include the student reactions, and they are displayed where students can easily refer to them.

the skills are needed in the classroom, the training should occur in the classroom. If the skills are needed on the playground or in the school hallways, the training should happen in these settings whenever possible. As stated by Walker, *"The rule to remember is what you teach is what you get, and where you teach it is where you get it!"* (1979, p. 298).

Following the completion of the Social Skills Checklist and the Group Chart, the purpose for the group is explained to the students, for example, "We will be learning skills for getting along with other people," and "We'll be practicing ways to stay out of trouble" (Goldstein et al., 1980).

Rules will have to be agreed upon by the entire group prior to implementing the social skills teaching sessions (McGinnis & Goldstein, 1984). Such rules may include "Wait until another person has finished talking before you begin to speak"; "Remember to leave toys and other objects at your desk"; "Remember to let others know that you are listening"; and so forth. Rules such as these are needed in the early stages of group work and can prevent many behavior difficulties. Allowing the group itself to establish these rules, with guidance from the teacher, encourages student commitment to abide by these rules.

Time for Instruction

Students should be instructed in social skills for 20 to 30 minutes, 3 times per week, with the group time on the remaining 2 days set aside for work on related skills such as relaxation training, communication skills, and identification of feelings. At the end of each session, an additional 10 minutes should be allowed for students to record the skills they have practiced throughout the day.

A new skill, if it is one of the less complicated ones such as Listening or How to Ask a Question, can be introduced every week or two. However, because overlearning is crucial in this technique (Goldstein et al., 1980), a new skill should be introduced *only when the students can recall the steps of the skill and have shown some generalization outside of the group teaching setting.* When a more complicated skill is introduced (such as dealing with own anger), 3 weeks or longer can be spent on it. While teaching this new skill, group sessions can also include periodic review of previously taught skills. This review will reinforce these skills and encourage their use in new situations, provide systematic fading of the training to promote generalization (Walker & Buckley, 1972), and prevent students from becoming bored from concentrating on only one skill at a time.

Introducing the Problem

The problem situation and inappropriate ways of dealing with it are described by the group leaders. Two leaders are recommended and can be any adult trained in this technique (i.e., teacher, aide, social worker, consultant, psychologist, or counselor). Discussing the problem sets the stage for learning, secures the students' attention, and helps to establish the need for learning the skill. The discussion can also include the likely consequences of dealing with the problem in an ineffective manner.

The group is then encouraged to explore alternative ways to handle the difficulty. Finally, the skill steps are written to include the student reactions, and they are displayed where students can easily refer to them.

SKILL-STREAMING

Modeling

The first phase of skill-streaming is modeling the skill steps by the group leaders for the group. This shows the students *what* to do. The participants identify the steps after they have been modeled. It is important, at least initially, that the adults carry out the modeling displays, because it is necessary to *show* the students how to perform the skill steps proficiently. Because a same age peer may actually be a more effective model, a student proficient in the specific skill may also rehearse the skill with the teacher and then act as a model for the social skills group.

For modeling to be most effective, the skills should be those actually needed by the students, at least two examples should be provided, and the steps should be shown in sequence (Goldstein et al., 1980). As the modeling of actions occurs, self-talk—or verbal mediation—should also occur. In modeling the skill of How to Handle Teasing, for example, the model recites the steps of the social skill, saying something like "Okay, first I count to five. 1 . . . 2 . . . 3 . . . 4 . . . 5. Then I think of my choices." This procedure is followed for the remaining skill steps. Self-talk models the cognitive process or verbal mediation, helps to curb impulsivity (Meichenbaum & Goodman, 1971), and calls attention to following the specific steps.

Modeling has been shown to be more effective when the model (a) is of the same age, sex, and social status;

FIGURE 3
Skill-Streaming Homework Worksheet

STUDENT _____ DATE _____

SKILL _____

STEPS:

WITH WHOM WILL I TRY THIS? _____

WHEN? _____

WHAT HAPPENED? _____

_____

_____

HOW DID I DO?

(b) is helpful and friendly; (c) appears to be highly skilled; and (d) is rewarded for the behavior (Goldstein et al., 1980). It is also important that the teacher, in the course of the school day, be conscious of modeling appropriate social behavior. For example, when the teacher

A student proficient in the specific skill may rehearse the skill with the teacher and then act as a model for the social skills group.

becomes angry or frustrated at the students' behavior, it has a powerful effect if the teacher, too, recalls the steps of Dealing with Own Anger and models them clearly and deliberately.

FIGURE 4
"Red Flag" Evaluation Form

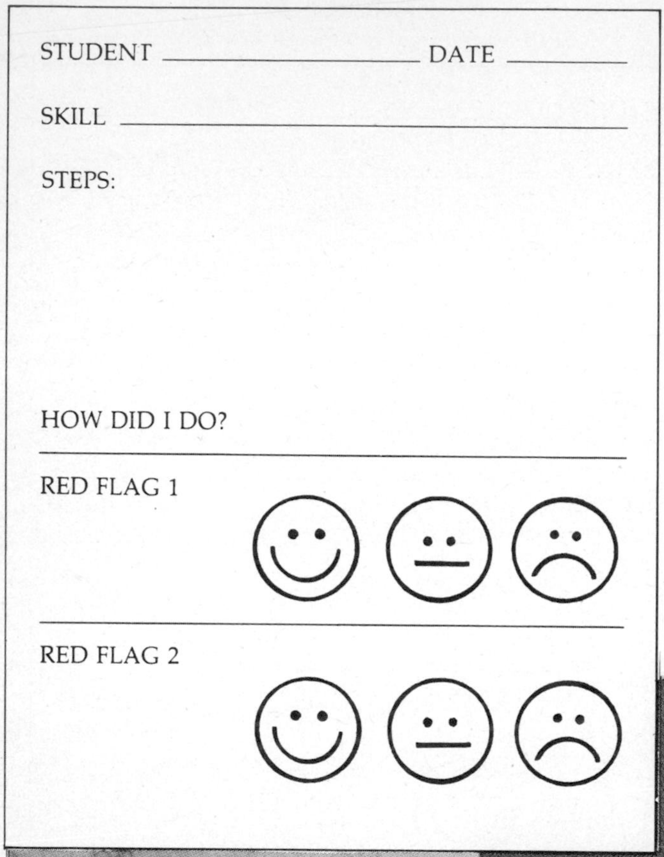

STUDENT _____ DATE _____

SKILL _____

STEPS:

HOW DID I DO?
_____

RED FLAG 1

☺ 😐 ☹

_____

RED FLAG 2

☺ 😐 ☹

Role Playing

The students next identify situations in which they could use the skill and practice the behaviors that have been modeled. This second phase of skill-streaming helps the students learn *how* to perform the skill.

A student identifies a specific situation in which he or she has experienced this problem and role plays the situation. The student then chooses another role player, one who reminds him or her most of the person with whom the problem occurs (Goldstein et al., 1980). Role playing the skill a number of times, with different people and in a variety of settings and situations, will facilitate generalization of this skill (Stokes & Baer, 1977).

The students are also encouraged to practice self-talk statements during their role playing. The verbal mediation helps to restrain impulsivity and assists their organization of skill steps in sequence (Meichenbaun & Goodman, 1971).

Feedback

Approval is given by teacher and peers as the role playing becomes increasingly like the behavior of the models (Goldstein et al., 1980). If the role player does

Role playing the skill a number of times, with different people and in a variety of settings and situations, will facilitate generalization of this skill.

not follow the skill steps, then feedback can be given by discussing what could be done differently, reteaching, or prompting the student through the skill steps. It is necessary for the role player to be successful before proceeding to the transfer of training. The main role player evaluates his or her own performance. Group participants may also provide feedback to the role players, but this must be done in a positive manner. Suggestions for what the role player could do to become more successful, constructive reminders to include a specific skill step, and comments pertaining to the feelings of the role players are examples of acceptable feedback.

Transfer of Training

This approach is not a "train . . . and hope" one (Stokes & Baer, 1977); instead, it plans for the generalization of learned social skills through a structured sequence of homework assignments.

These assignments begin with the teacher and students together deciding when and how the students will practice and progress to the stage where the students themselves record the skills they have used.

Homework assignments are given to several students each day. Four stages of homework are used, depending on the level of the student's mastery of the skill. For the younger student or a child who has difficulty with the mechanics of writing, the written portions of these assignments should be completed by the teacher. Picture cues can also be used to assist the student with reading difficulties.

Stage 1: Homework. The students think of situations (either at home or school) in which they want to practice the skill. Each student and the teacher agree to the skill steps, with whom they will be tried, and when the plans will be carried out (see Figure 3).

Stage 2: Red Flag. The student is told that he or she will be "set up." For example, if the skill is dealing with teasing, the student is told: "During math this morning, I will tease you. I want you to remember the steps; they are on your homework sheet. Remember, I will be setting you up. It's a red flag!" When the teacher has teased the student and the student has reacted, the teacher calls, "Red Flag." Then, together, they evaluate the student's response (see Figure 4). (Credit for the "Red Flag" concept and term goes to Wes Hawkins of Ottumwa, Iowa.)

Stage 3: Self-Recording. The child who has almost achieved mastery of a skill (knowing the steps well and showing success with the other two stages of homework) writes the steps onto the self-recording sheet. Then, throughout the course of the day, the student writes when the steps of the skill were practiced, and self-evaluation is completed (see Figure 5). This homework sheet can be taken with the younger student into the regular class, thereby assisting in the transfer of learning to the setting to which the student is slated eventually to return.

Stage 4: Keeping a Tally. Several skills are listed on a 3 × 5 note card, and the student tallies each time he or she practices the skill. This self-recording method also gives the older student an inconspicuous way to chart skills used in regular education classes and settings such as the playground and school cafeteria.

Self-Recording and Self-Evaluation

In addition to self-evaluation during role playing, the student evaluates his or her own performance in each stage of the homework assignments. Assignments are shared with the group, with reinforcement given for completing the homework assignment and for self-evaluation of the performance.

This sequence of homework, self-evaluation, and self-recording procedures promotes maintenance and generalization of critical social skills in the child's total milieu. In addition, the Group Chart can be modified as a means of daily recording of social skills. The student simply reports when the skills were used. This provides for peer support and the monitoring of skills

FIGURE 5
Self-Recording Sheet

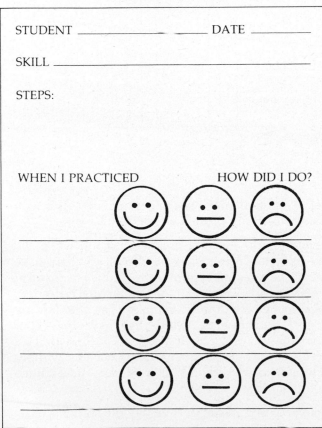

FIGURE 6
IEP Example

ANNUAL GOALS/SHORT-TERM OBJECTIVES

STUDENT

FROM _____ TO _____
FROM _____ TO _____ INDIVIDUALIZED EDUCATION PROGRAM

GRADE | BIRTHDATE | AUTHOR | REVIEWER | DATE

PRESENT LEVEL

(See pre-post checklist)

ANNUAL GOAL FOR _____ Social Skills _____
(CONTENT AREA)

Brian will demonstrate his mastery (evaluation of
No. 4 on Elementary Social Skills Checklist) of 80%
of Group I social skills as demonstrated in "natural"
settings as measured by the classroom teacher.

OUTCOME ABOVE ☐ EXPECTED ☐ BELOW ☐

Outcome columns: Other: | Accepting a Compliment | Giving a Compliment | Joining In | Following Instructions | Asking a Favor | Asking A Question | Beginning a Conversation | Saying Thank You | Asking for Help | Listening

SHORT TERM OBJECTIVES (STATE WHAT THE STUDENT WILL DO, HOW WELL) | STRATEGIES/MATERIALS

Brian will identify the skill steps. | Modeling, feedback

Brian will recall the skill steps.

Brian will role play the specific steps. | Feedback, role playing, Mastery Record Card

Brian will identify situations where the skill is appropriate. | Homework Assignments

Brian will plan the use of the skill (When-Where-How-With Whom) | Homework 1

Brian will act out the specific steps in a simulated situation. | Homework 2 (Red flag)

Brian will record the practice of the skill: | Homework 3, Homework 4
Settings: | Daily Recording Sheet
_____
_____
_____

Brian will evaluate his success in using the skill. | Homework 1 through 3 Discussion of accuracy of this self-evaluation.

---

actually used, and it suggests periodic review of the skills that are not used as frequently.

Reinforcement System

Tokens, always paired with verbal praise, are given on an intermittent basis. The tokens used are SCAMOs (Showing Caring About Myself and Others). They are earned for following general group rules, role playing and participation, practicing previously learned skills in the group setting and throughout the school day, and completing homework assignments.

In the initial stages of learning, a critical rule is to give lots of positive reinforcement (Bornstein & Quevillon, 1976). The reinforcement schedule is thinned once the students have become more successful with the skill-streaming process.

Reinforcement Phase I. Following group work, the students write their names on the tokens they have earned. These tokens are put into a "raffle box," and at the end of each week, or more frequently if needed, several names are drawn for prizes. The students are told that the more SCAMOs they have the better chance they have for their name to be drawn. This procedure provides frequent reinforcement without much monetary cost and builds interest and enthusiasm for learning social skills.

Reinforcement Phase II. Each day the students chart the number of tokens earned for practicing the social skills and for group participation. Each student is then able to "spend" these points on a variety of privileges that are assigned a particular point value. Students are allowed to choose the specific privilege they will earn. This system provides frequent or delayed reinforcement, depending on the needs of each student.

The privileges that can be earned are ones that encourage social acceptance (such as ordering a film for the entire class to view) and allow for the practice of the social skills they have learned (such as playing checkers with a friend or eating lunch in the classroom with a friend). Tokens are given less frequently during Reinforcement Phase II, but social praise is continued on a random schedule even when not combined with tokens.

Documentation of Progress

Documentation of student progress in mastering the selected social skills is carried out by the teacher through completion of the Social Skills Checklist (pre- and posttraining) and by charting objectives achieved on the student's individualized education program (IEP). (See Figure 6.) The student provides additional progress documentation through the means of self-report (daily record of skills and homework assignments).

CONCLUSION

The entire school can be informed of this technique through inservice education or working with individual teachers on reinforcing the skills individual students will be practicing. We found that regular education teachers, recognizing the social needs of their students, will incorporate skill-streaming into their curricula. The training of mainstream teachers and peers increases the likelihood that the target students will generalize these skills into mainstream settings (Walker & Buckley, 1972).

With the skill-streaming approach, potential problems are changed into successful situations. When the need arises—the teachable moment—the student is prompted through the steps of the needed skill. The teacher elicits an appropriate response from the student by suggesting that the skill steps be used and then gives approval when the steps are taken. Each time this happens, the teacher is reminding the student of *what to do*, rather than *what not to do*. More positive interaction than criticism from teachers is

assured; more social competence than frustration from students is likely; more generative than repressive training is inevitable.

REFERENCES

Bash, M. A., & Camp, B. W. (1982). *Think aloud.* Champaign IL: Research Press.

Bornstein, P. H., & Quevillon, R. P. (1976). The effects of a self-instructional package on overactive preschool boys. *Journal of Applied Behavioral Analysis, 9,* 179–188.

Cartledge, G., & Milburn, J. F. (1980). *Teaching social skills to children.* New York: Pergamon Press.

Dreikurs, K., & Cassel, P. (1974). *Discipline without tears.* New York: Hawthorn Books.

Fagen, S. A., Long, N. J., & Stevens, D. J. (1975). *Teaching children self-control: Preventing emotional and learning problems in the elementary school.* Columbus OH: Charles E. Merrill.

Goldstein, A. (1981). *Psychological skill training.* New York: Pergamon Press.

Goldstein, A. P., Sprafkin, R. P., Gershaw, N. J., & Klein, P. (1980). *Skillstreaming the adolescent: A structured learning approach to teaching prosocial skills.* Champaign IL: Research Press.

McGinnis, E., & Goldstein, A. P. (1984). *Skillstreaming the elementary school child.* Champaign IL: Research Press.

Meichenbaum, D. H., & Goodman, J. (1971). Training impulsive children to talk to themselves: A means of developing self-control. *Journal of Abnormal Psychology, 77,* 115–126.

Mesibov, G. B., & LaGreca, A. M. (Winter/Spring, 1981). A social skills instructional module. *The Directive Teacher,* 6–7.

Spivak, G., & Shure, M. B. (1974). *Social adjustment of young children: A cognitive approach to solving real-life problems.* San Francisco: Jossey-Bass.

Stephens, T. (1978). *Social skills in the classroom.* Columbus OH: Cedars Press.

Stokes, T. F., & Baer, D. M. (1977). An implicit technology of generalization. *Journal of Applied Behavioral Analysis, 10,* 349–367.

Walker, H. M. (1979). *The acting out child: Coping with classroom disruption.* Boston: Allyn & Bacon.

Walker, H. M., & Buckley, N. K. (1972). Programming generalization and maintenance of treatment effects across time and across settings. *Journal of Applied Behavioral Analysis, 5,* 209–224.

Educator Perceptions of Behavior Problems of Mainstreamed Students

Abstract: The behavior problems of students in mainstreamed classrooms may be due in part to the expectations of educators who have not internalized information on teaching the diversity of students found in that setting. The educators involved in this study were predominantly regular classroom teachers but also included counselors, librarians, special educators, administrators, etc. They appeared to perceive student behavior problems as more serious when displayed by nonhandicapped or physically handicapped students than when displayed by mentally handicapped students. The same educators recommended more behavioral treatments having an authoritarian orientation for nonhandicapped than for physically handicapped students. This study indicates educators need to develop attitudes and skills necessary for behavior management in the mainstreamed school environment.

N. JO CAMPBELL,

JUDITH E. DOBSON,

JANE M. BOST

N. JO CAMPBELL *is Associate Professor, and* JUDITH E. DOBSON *is Professor, Oklahoma State University, Stillwater, Oklahoma;* JANE M. BOST *is Counseling Pychologist, Southwestern University, Georgetown, Texas.*

■ As one result of the 1975 Education for All Handicapped Children Act, increased numbers of educators are directly involved with handicapped students even though regular educators have received little training in teaching special students in the mainstreamed classroom. Lakin and Reynolds (1983) reported that 70% of all students who have been identified as having some form of handicapping condition spend at least a part of each school day with a regular classroom teacher. While agreement exists among educators about the impact of the teacher's intellect and personality upon learning, little is known about the effects of students' handicapping conditions upon teachers' perceptions of students' behavior problems. Teachers' inequitable perceptions and treatments of students' behaviors in the mainstreamed classroom have the potential to produce more serious discipline problems which can limit the value of carefully planned lessons. While managing student behaviors in the mainstreamed classroom is a relatively new concern for educators, discipline in the schools has been a highly ranked concern for

years. The results of the 15th Annual Gallup Poll of the Public's Attitudes Toward the Public Schools (Gallup, 1983), as in 12 out of 13 previous years, indicate that the number one concern regarding education is discipline in the schools.

There are many opinions as to the causes of student misbehaviors. Some researchers have suggested teachers may be inadvertently responsible for students' behavior problems. In a review of research on student misbehaviors, Duke (1978) reported several situations in which the biases and expectations of educators were contributory factors to student misbehavior. The results of research by Algozzine (1976) and Larsen (1975) indicate that teachers who are not special educators may have lower tolerance for certain student behaviors than teachers educated to work with exceptional students. Algozzine (1976) suggested that this lower tolerance may actually contribute to the behavior problems occurring in the classroom.

The impetus for this investigation was provided by the lack of research on how teachers interact with the diversity of students in a mainstreamed classroom. Jackson (1968) reported that some students invoke apathy or, at the other extreme, animosity in their teachers. Research that supports Jackson's assertion has demonstrated that a variety of student characteristics, both physical and intellectual, are related to differing teacher expectations. These characteristics include achievement level (Brophy & Good, 1970), racial and ethnic identity (Jackson & Cosca, 1974; Rubovitz & Maehr,

1973), diagnostic category label, i.e., emotionally disturbed and learning disabled (Algozzine & Sutherland, 1977; Foster, Schmidt, & Sabatino, 1976), and sex (Schlosser & Algozzine, 1979). Regular classroom teachers are now expected and required to teach students who 10 years ago would have been taught by teachers educated to work with handicapped students in a restricted situation, i.e., a special education class.

The purpose of this research was to compare public school educators' perceptions regarding the seriousness and recommended treatments for behavior problems of six hypothetical students who might be found in a mainstreamed classroom. The hypothetical male and female students are described as being nonhandicapped, mentally handicapped, or physically handicapped.

METHOD

Subjects

A total of 105 currently employed educators enrolled in five evening graduate courses in the College of Education of a large land-grant university were subjects in this study. A total of 70 educators indicated that they were either regular elementary (n = 39) or secondary teachers (n = 31). Of the remaining 35 educators, 7 were special education teachers, 5 were school counselors, and 23 indicated they held various other positions in the schools (i.e., librarian, media consultant, administrator, etc.). The subjects' length of employment as educators varied from 1 to 28 years with a mode of 3 years and a median of 4.8 years. Only 53% of the educators reported having taken one or more college courses focusing on handicapped children, while 62% reported having an acquaintance who was handicapped.

Instrument

For use in this study, six forms of an instrument designed to collect educators' perceptions of the seriousness and recommended treatments of specified behavior problems of students were developed. Each form contained a stimulus paragraph presenting a different hypothetical student. The six paragraphs were of the following format. Each sex was crossed with each handicap type:

> J.P. is a (male, female) student. (He, She) (has an I.Q. of 70; is crippled as a result of birth defects and confined to a wheelchair; has an I.Q. of 110). (His, Her) last year teacher describes (him, her) as (an educable mentally retarded student; having impaired fine motor skill development; an average, normal student).

To avoid confounding the results, the age of J.P. was not specified in the descriptions. Specifying a particular student age would have required educators to rate the seriousness of behavior problems at age levels with which they may have not had teaching experience.

The remainder of the instrument was consistent across forms and included adapted versions of the Behavioral Problems Inventory (BPI) (Dobson, 1966), the Behavioral Treatment Response Sheet (BTRS) (Dobson, 1966), and items requesting selected demographic data. The BPI and BTRS were selected for adaptation and use in this study because the form and content of the two instruments more closely met the requirements imposed by the research design than did other more frequently used instruments.

The original BPI consists of a list of 37 acts of behavior on which teachers are requested to indicate their perceptions of the seriousness of each act by ranking it as high, medium, or low in seriousness. Because the list of behaviors on the BPI was developed over 15 years previous to this study, the researchers asked a panel of 11 educators, 8 employed in public schools and 3 College of Education faculty members, to review the list of behaviors and to identify any which they felt were not behavior problems in the schools of the 1980s. The responses of the panel indicate that over 75% of the behaviors are considered to be the problem behaviors in today's schools. Only 2 of the behaviors, slovenly appearance and sissy or tomboy, were identified as not being current behavior problems by as many as four of the panel members. The researchers believe these results indicate the validity of classifying the behaviors on the BPI as current problem behaviors of students. These behaviors are listed in Table 1. The BPI was adapted by increasing the 3-point response scale to a 5-point scale in order to maximize the reliability of the responses (Ferguson, 1941).

The original BTRS lists 22 possible actions a teacher might adopt in responding to students' behavior problems. Of the 22 treatments listed (see Table 1), 11 are generally considered nonauthoritarian or positive methods of teaching self-discipline and 11 are more often viewed as coercive or authoritarian in nature (Dobson, 1966). The BTRS was adapted for this study by requesting educators to select 1 or 2, if 2 were considered equally effective, of the 22 treatments they felt would be most effective in responding to each of the 37 behavior problems acted out by the described hypothetical student. The original BTRS directed the respondent to select only 1 treatment for each behavior problem. The directions for complet-

TABLE 1
Behavior Problems and Treatments Listed on the BPI and BTRS

Behavior Problems		Treatments	
Running in the hall	Willful disobedience	Give pupil opportunity to make contribution to class[a]	Send child to principal's office[b]
Rudeness to class member	Cruelty, bullying	Pupil apologizes[b]	Role playing[a]
Cheating	Quarrelsomeness	Teacher uses simple control (a look, nod of head, etc.)[a]	Isolate the pupil[a]
Defacing property	Tattling on others		Emphasize good qualities of child's behavior
Habitual tardiness	Stubbornness, contrariness	Parent-teacher conference[a]	Accept misbehavior as normal for child and attempt to change through a positive approach[a]
Petty thievery	Rages, temper tantrums	Teacher lowers grade[b]	
Lying, untruthfulness	Rudeness to teachers	Detention after school[b]	
Masturbation	Shyness, withdrawal	Pupil-teacher conference[a]	
Truancy	Acting smart	Pupil temporarily suspended from room[b]	Physical control of student[b]
Swearing	Unhappiness, depression	Pupil temporarily suspended from school[b]	Require additional assignment[b]
Smoking	Daydreaming	Pupil loses some privileges[a]	Some action by fellow students[b]
Obscene notes, talk	Slovenly appearance		
Playing with genitalia	Sissy or tomboy		
Disorderliness in class	No interest in class work	Pupil referred to special service personnel[a]	Behavior called to attention of other class members[b]
Whispering, writing notes	Sex offense	Corporal punishment is used[b]	Assess and improve through group discussions[a]
Interrupting	Eating candy		
Does not pay attention	"Horseplay"		
Carelessness in work	Physical attack on teacher		
Physical laziness			

[a] Generally considered positive methods of teaching self-discipline.
[b] Generally considered coercive methods of teaching self-discipline.

ing the BTRS were altered to increase the probability that educators' responses were actually indicative of their true philosophical orientation, coercive or positive, toward the treatment of behavior problems of the described student. Allowing the choice of 2 responses results in the identification of educators who do not hold a clearly defined orientation regarding the treatment of a particular behavior problem and permits the omission of their responses for that behavior problem from the data analysis. This results in a more reliable and valid measure of the educators' philosophical orientations toward dealing with the described students' behaviors.

Procedures

The six forms of the instrument were randomly ordered and then delivered to the professors teaching the graduate classes involved in the study. The professors administered the instruments during regular class time. The data collection was completed within a 2-week period because one of the professors had an exam scheduled on the evening the other four professors wished to administer the instruments. Data were collected from that professor's class the following week. Educators who were en-

rolled in more than one of the classes involved in the study were requested by the professors not to complete the instrument more than once.

Total scores on the adapted BPI were created by summing the 37 responses of each subject. The Coefficient Alpha subprogram from the

TABLE 2
Means and Standard Deviations of Perceptions of Seriousness of 37 Behavior Problems of Different Types of Students[a]

Student Stimulus	N	Mean	SD
Nonhandicapped	38	119.06	14.42
Male	17	121.31	14.71
Female	21	117.24	17.45
Mentally Handicapped	33	105.32	21.77
Male	16	102.65	19.58
Female	17	107.84	23.97
Physically Handicapped	34	118.51	23.39
Male	20	121.00	24.28
Female	14	114.95	20.97

[a] Perceptions were indicated on a 5-point scale.

SPSS *Update 7-9* (Hull & Nie, 1981) was used to obtain estimates of reliability (internal consistency) of the total scores on the six forms of the instrument. The six estimates of coefficient alpha vary from .88 to .95 with a mean of .92.

In scoring the adapted BTRS, 2 treatments of a nonauthoritarian nature, 2 of a coercive nature or 1 treatment recommended for any behavior problem of the hypothetical student were coded "positive" or "negative," depending on the nature of the educator's recommended treatment. If nonauthoritarian and coercive treatments were both recommended for the same behavior problem by an educator, the responses were coded as undecided and not used in the data analysis. The 105 educators coded 2 such noncongruent responses on less than 8% of the 3,885 items. The Analysis of Variance (ANOVA) and Crosstabs subprograms from the *Statistical Package for the Social Sciences* (Nie, Hull, Jenkins, Steinbrenner, & Brent, 1975) were used to analyze the data collected using the adapted BPI and BTRS, respectively.

RESULTS

The means and standard deviations of the total responses to the adapted BPI and the number of subjects responding to each student stimulus are presented in Table 2.

The results of a 2 × 3 (student sex by student handicap) analysis of variance calculated using responses to the adapted BPI as the dependent variable reveal one significant effect, type of student handicap ($F = 5.88$, $df = 2/99$, $p < .01$). Using the formula for η^2 (Linton & Gallo, 1975), it was determined that 11% of the variance in the perceived levels of seriousness of the behavior problems can be accounted for by differences in the type of student handicap. A post hoc analysis using Tukey's Honestly Significant Differences (HSD) test indicated that the various types of educators rated the behavior problems of the nonhandicapped and the physically handicapped students as being significantly ($p < .05$) more serious than the same behavior problems of the student described as mentally handicapped. The difference between the mean ratings of the seriousness of the behavior problems of the nonhandicapped student and of the physically handicapped student was nonsignificant.

The differences between frequencies of the 2 types of treatment for the behavior problems of the 6 hypothetical students recommended by the educators were investigated using a 2 × 2 (type of treatment, authoritarian versus nonauthoritarian, by sex of student) chi-square analysis and a 2 × 3 (type of treatment by student handicap) chi-square analysis. No difference in type of treatment recommended due to sex of student was found. The results of the second chi-square analysis indicated a significant difference ($\chi^2 = 6.69$, $df = 2$, $p < .05$) between the types of recommended treatments for the 3 types of students. Ryan's procedure (Linton & Gallo, 1975), used as a post hoc analysis, revealed a significant ($p < .05$) difference between the types of treatments recommended for the nonhandicapped student and the physically handicapped student. More behavioral treatments of an authoritarian nature were recommended for the nonhandicapped student than for the physically handicapped student. The frequency of authoritarian or coercive treatment recommendations was approximately 6 times greater than the frequency of nonauthoritarian treatment recommendations across all 6 groups of subjects.

DISCUSSION

The conclusions which can be made based on the results of this study do not apply only to regular classroom teachers since the subjects included a variety of types of educators. The results of this investigation indicate educators' perceptions of the seriousness of students' behavior problems do differ according to the type of student handicap. These educators perceived the behavior problems of the mentally handicapped student as being less serious than the same misbehavior of either the physically handicapped or the nonhandicapped student. It appears that the discrepancies among the educators' perceptions of the seriousness of behavior problems may be based, in part, on the judgment of whether the student has the capacity to "know better."

Another explanation for the educators judging the behavior problems of the mentally handicapped student as less serious might be that educators expect those students to exhibit more behavior problems than other students and thus do not view the expected misbehaviors as serious in nature. Finn (1972) wrote that teacher expectations are powerful forces in shaping children's behaviors and these expectations, along with other factors such as the physical environment and the curriculum, form a network which makes up an important component of each student's educational environment. This network plays a significant role in the process through which students develop their self-expectations which become determinants of their personal behaviors. One might hypothesize that inappropriate behaviors of mentally handicapped students in the mainstreamed environment is perpetuated by educators who have not internalized information for working with handicapped children.

A significant difference between the nature of treatments recommended for the behavior problems of students having different types of handicaps was also found. Educators tended to recommend more coercive types of treatments for the misbehaviors of nonhandicapped students than for the misbehaviors of physically handicapped students. It was somewhat alarming to note that a 6:1 ratio was found between the frequency of authoritarian types of recommended treatments to the frequency of nonauthoritarian types of recommended treatments. This finding is a cause for concern because research findings such as those reported by Meacham and Wiesen (1974) indicate that punishment is generally ineffective and may even lead to further behavioral problems.

The results of this study indicate that the diversity of educators who work with children in the school setting need to acquire skills relative to dealing with behavior problems of both handicapped and nonhandicapped students in an equitable and appropriate manner. Teacher training institutions must prepare educators to effectively deal with the behavior problems of handicapped and nonhandicapped students. Colleges and universities cannot continue to prepare educators as though they will encounter a homogeneous group of students. Preparing all types of educators to function effectively in mainstreamed environments necessitates providing information and opportunities for internalization of techniques in managing the behavior of all students, both those with identified special needs and the so-called "normal" students. Educators may then be able to provide a learning environment conducive to increasing student achievement and self-discipline.

REFERENCES

Algozzine, B. (1976). The disturbing child: What you see is what you get? *The Alberta Journal of Educational Research, 22,* 330–333.

Algozzine, B., & Sutherland, J. (1977). The LD Label: An experimental analysis. *Contemporary Educational Psychology, 2,* 292–297.

Brophy, J., & Good, T. (1970). Teachers' communication of differential expectations for children's classroom performance: Some behavioral data. *Journal of Educational Psychology, 61,* 365–374.

Dobson, R. L. (1966). *The perceptions and treatment by teachers of the behavioral problems of elementary school children in culturally deprived and middle-class neighborhoods.* Unpublished doctoral dissertation, University of Oklahoma.

Duke, D. L. (1978). Why don't girls misbehave more than boys in school? *Journal of Youth and Adolescence, 7,* 141–158.

Ferguson, L. W. (1941). A study of the Likert technique of attitude scale construction. *Journal of Social Psychology, 13,* 51–57.

Finn, J. D. (1972). Expectations and the educational environment. *Review of Educational Research, 42*(3), 387–410.

Foster, G., Schmidt, C., & Sabatino, D. (1976). Teacher expectations and the label "Learning Disabilities." *Journal of Learning Disabilities, 9,* 58–61.

Gallup, G. H. (1983). The 15th Annual Gallup poll of the public's attitudes toward the public schools. *Phi Delta Kappa, 65*(1), 33–51.

Hull, C. H., & Nie, N. (1981). *SPSS Update 7-9.* New York: McGraw-Hill.

Jackson, G., & Cosca, C. (1974). The inequality of educational opportunity in the southwest: An observational study of ethnically mixed classrooms. *American Educational Research Journal, 11,* 219–229.

Jackson, P. (1968). *Life in the Classroom.* New York: Holt, Rinehart, & Winston.

Lakin, K. C., & Reynolds, M. C. (1983). Curricular implications of Public Law 94–142 for teacher education. *Journal of Teacher Education, 34*(2), 13–18.

Larsen, S. C. (1975). The influence of teacher expectations on the school performance of handicapped children. *Focus on Exceptional Children, 6*(8), 2–16.

Linton, M., & Gallo, P. S., Jr. (1975). *The practical statistician: Simplified handbook of statistics.* Monterey CA: Brooks/Cole.

Meacham, M. R., & Wiesen, A. E. (1974). *Changing classroom behavior.* New York: Intext Educational Publishers.

Nie, N., Hull, C. H., Jenkins, J. G., Steinbrenner, K., & Brent, D. H. (1975). *Statistical package for the social sciences* (2nd ed.). New York: McGraw-Hill.

Rubovitz, P., & Maehr, M. (1973). Pygmalion black and white. *Journal of Personality and Social Psychology, 25,* 210–218.

Schlosser, L., & Algozzine, B. (1979). The disturbing child: Is it a he or she? *Alberta Journal of Educational Research, 25,* 30–36.

Reducing Stress of Students in Conflict

Elizabeth Duffner, Nicholas J. Long and Stanley A. Fagen

Elizabeth Duffner is assistant professor of special education at Loretta Heights College in Denver, Colorado. Nicholas J. Long is professor of special education at The American University of Washington, D.C. Stanley A. Fagen is staff development consultant and director of the supplementary education trainer development program for Montgomery County Public Schools in Rockville, Maryland.

Editorial Comment: All children experience stress in school at various times. For most, this stress is mild and relatively infrequent and is incorporated into the course of growth. For some, however, this stress is intense and recurrent and precipitates serious disruption in performance and conflict in relationships. With awareness, teachers can help to reduce stress, when necessary, to prevent damage to a child's achievement, interpersonal relations, or self-esteem.

Teachers and parents of children with emotional problems often feel overwhelmed by the magnitude of such problems. One teacher expressed this concern openly, "I am willing to help Carl but I feel it's like building sand castles that are washed away by the nightly tide of home and community struggles. What I do doesn't seem to make a difference. He needs much more than the schools or I can provide. After all, I have only a limited amount of time and skill" (Long & Fagen, 1979).

While this attitude is understandable, it does an injustice to the real value of helping-teacher relationships for troubled children (Hobbs, 1969; Jones, 1968; Morse, 1976). Through a helping relationship, teachers can adjust levels of classroom stress to prevent emotional breakdowns, while they gradually promote skills for coping with stress (Fagen, 1977).

In developing a helping relationship, the following significant factors should be kept in mind:

- **A student in stress needs to believe there is hope to his life situation.** Even if the hope is temporary, the student can experience some personal acceptance by someone who does not blame him for his circumstances or intensify his problems.
- **Every successful experience a student has with an adult is important, no matter how small it may appear.** While a teacher's assistance may not be enough to "turn the student around," it may create a basis for trust in adults. It is an experience that cannot be denied or erased. Perhaps next semester or next year another adult will find it possible to build on this foundation, resulting in significant gains.
- **Psychological conditions change with time.** Nothing remains static or fixed. Crises in the family or school or peer group often become resolved or at least tolerable. When a student can be helped *not* to complicate situations by adding new problems, he can be more easily helped to overcome a primary source of stress as that stress diminishes.

Once a teacher becomes willing to risk dealing with the emotional stresses faced by their students several strategies are available. The risk to the teacher, of course, is failure and self-blame. As William James (1890) put it, "with no attempt there can be no failure; with no failure no humiliation." Fortunately, many educators are motivated to help their students master difficulty and are looking for strategies to promote better coping.

TEACHER STRATEGY ONE: Reducing Stress by Decoding, Labelling, and Accepting Feelings

The more we observe students in stress, the more we listen to what they tell us without words. We learn to respond to their body language. We become acutely aware of the messages they send with their eyes, muscles, breathing pattern, and body movement. Many students learn early in life that if they express negative feelings and words, adults react in anger. They also learn that the spoken word can be held against them as self-incriminating evidence.

When a student is under stress, language is often used to mislead, hide, and protect real feelings. Consequently, teachers must learn to pay as much attention to *how* a student is speaking as to *what* he is saying. By listening to the flow and tone of his words, a teacher can "hear" them in terms of feelings such as anger, fear, sadness, ambivalence, or happiness. For example, a student may say, "Get out of here and leave me alone!" while trying to communicate, "Please don't go; I need your help, but I'm afraid to ask because you might reject me."

Once the teacher learns to trust and decode nonverbal communication, it is possible to label the student's feelings. Based on what the teacher perceives and feels, she can say to a student in stress, "You look *sad* today. Can I help you?" or "You look really *upset.* Can you talk to me about it?" or "I have a feeling that you are *worried* about something. Did anything happen?" At times, the child will deny or reject the teacher's labelling. That is to be expected. The issue is not whether the teacher is right or wrong but whether communication channels are opened. More often, the student will begin to verbalize some genuine feelings.

The next step is accepting the student's feelings. Here the teacher needs to support the student's feelings as an honest and healthy expression of his interpersonal struggles. The teacher should indicate that the feelings the student has toward school, home, society, and the world are real for him. A common mistake is to argue with their existence by saying things like, "Oh, you don't hate her" or "You shouldn't be upset." In accepting feelings the teacher can say, "It's okay to feel sad when you flunk an exam" or "I can see why you're so excited today" or "I know you're angry with Larry, but I can't let you hit him back." In many cases, the teacher can drain off the student's feelings by allowing him to express them through words as in the following exchange between a student and teacher:

Billy: "I would like to punch him out!"
Teacher: "I know you're really angry. You really hate his teasing."
Billy: "Boy, he makes me mad."

During this process of decoding, labelling, and accepting feelings the student can discharge his pent-up emotions in a safe, nondestructive manner. As these feelings are expressed and are accepted by the adult, the student begins to experience physical and psychological relief, as well as a sense of normalcy and a relationship trust.

TEACHER STRATEGY TWO: Reducing Stress by Redirecting Feelings into Acceptable Behavior

Just as man can channel the potentially destructive force of a rapidly flowing river into electrical power that increases personal comfort and productivity, so a student can be taught new ways of expressing intense, explosive thoughts and feelings in socially approved behavior. This strategy for coping with stress not only reduces tensions, but also develops personal and social skills. Aggressive, sexual, fearful, and sad feelings can be directed into school activities such as art, sports, dance, manual arts, literature, drama, and creative writing.

Through this strategy, feelings are used as a source of motivation and power. For example, "Okay team, now that you are mad, let's go out and show them what we can do."

For teachers, there are many ways of redirecting feelings into acceptable behaviors. A few examples are: (1) "You know, Cathy, maybe it would help you to spend some time in the art room on the kickwheel. You might feel better if you could put some of your energy into throwing a few pots." (2) "I think Mr. Donnelli needs some help in the auditorium with the light fixtures. Maybe if you would work with him for some time this morning you'd feel like you've accomplished something. I know when I feel confused, helping someone else always makes me feel like I have a little more control over things." (3) "It's hard to feel so alone. Maybe you'd like to join Sarah and Joyce—they're just getting started on a project about different kinds of transportation."

TEACHER STRATEGY THREE: Reducing Stress by Lowering School Pressure

While the teacher cannot control what happens to the student in other environments, she can control what happens in the classroom. One significant way teachers can reduce student stress is by lowering academic requirements, standards, and deadlines temporarily. She can tell the student, "You have enough on your mind right now, so don't worry about the book report this Friday. Once we work this problem out, I'll help you catch up."

This strategy is like providing the student with a mental aspirin that will temporarily relieve excessive academic pressures. However, it is important not to eliminate the student's responsibility for learning and classroom assignments. The student is expected to keep up with as many assignments as possible during the crisis but not to feel—"You will fail if the assignment is late or at a lower level of competence." This strategy is an obvious one but one used too reluctantly by classroom teachers.

TEACHER STRATEGY FOUR: Reducing Stress by Completing One Task at a Time

When too many stresses and responsibilities build up, the collective view becomes gigantic, and many students panic, lapsing into a state of helplessness and frozen behavior. The experience is like being handed a ball of string tangled in a hundred knots and told to straighten it out in sixty seconds. Where do you begin? The task seems impossible! After a few attempts, it changes from impossible to totally hopeless. A helpful strategy is to assist the student to reduce the task to a manageable unit of work, for example, by selecting one concrete task to complete within a day. This single action can generate new energy and hope. It reflects a basic law of nature: A body in motion stays in motion, while a body at rest stays at rest.

In carrying out this strategy, the teacher might say, "Right now it seems like you have a lot of problems that you're dealing with. Sometimes when you have so many things to think about it's hard to know where to start. Or you might feel like it's just too much—they all can't be solved at once. And you're right! It helps to start with one area and work on that one for awhile until it's cleared up. So for this period, let's just concentrate on getting some multiplication done."

TEACHER STRATEGY FIVE: Reducing Stress by Accepting Disappointment and Failure

Disappointment and failure are a natural and inevitable condition of interpersonal and family life, and little can be done by others to prevent students from experiencing frustration. However, it is important for teachers to help students learn that their stress is not due to their *badness* or *wrongdoing* (Fagen, Long & Stevens, 1975). Many times the focus is to help students develop a greater capacity for enduring upsetting or disappointing life events without falling apart. This can be promoted by teaching students to accept a normal amount of hostility from others.

Unfortunately, many middle-class students have an unrealistic expectation that people should always be nice, kind, sympathetic, courteous, and fair. When they experience any criticism or rejection or a blast of verbal abuse, they often perceive it as a personal attack instead of accepting it as a reasonable amount of hostility. If the student does not overreact to this behavior, the stress cycle can be stopped. As teachers we can help our students accept some negative feelings from all relationships, including their closest friends.

Another meaningful way of coping with stress is to accept defeat. "I know it's really hard to lose something after you've worked so hard for it. You've been practicing that speech every afternoon and we all thought you were excellent at the contest on Saturday. But I also know how much you wanted to win. I know you feel bad. It takes courage to try and to risk losing."

Disappointment or defeat can be more easily accepted when the student can see some value or benefit from the experience. For example, "I also know you learned a lot about contests, and you'll never have to go through your first one ever again. Next time you'll be a veteran and not so afraid of the unknown. You really did get something from that experience."

The teacher can also let the student know she has faith that he is strong enough to endure the frustration. "You have done everything possible to improve your situation, but right now you are going to have to live with it. You are a good person and can be proud of your skills. It will be difficult at times, but I believe you have the strength to tolerate it."

TEACHER STRATEGY SIX: Reducing Stress by Separating from the Setting

A basic survival mechanism is flight. When stress becomes a huge red alarm, one way of coping is to leave the stressful environment temporarily. To withdraw to a more supportive environment to rest, play, and think by oneself or with others is a useful technique. The phrase "too close to the trees to see the forest" is applicable. Inserting some physical distance between the stressful setting and the student frequently provides the needed psychological conditions for problem solving. Free from the pressures of the situation, the student may be better able to think through the situation. "Sometimes, Sherry, it makes good sense to get some time away from a problem to regain a little strength. Didn't you tell me your Girl Scout Troop was planning a backpacking trip? Maybe a few days away from all the concerns you have, would be good for you. You might even have a better picture of the situation at home when you come back." Or, "You know, Andy, maybe it's a good time for you to visit your grandfather for the weekend. You've been talking about how long its been since you two visited together. I bet a few days at the lake would not only give you a chance to visit with him but would also give you some energy to deal with these problems here. I think everyone needs time away from what seems like overwhelming problems to restore himself a little."

In supporting brief separations from the stressful situation, the teacher can convey a quiet confidence that an alternative way of coping will be worked out on return. It is also helpful to emphasize positive aspects of the student so self-esteem can be maintained as the student leaves the situation. For example, "OK, Tony, so we'll let this go for now. Let's think of something you can do well—painting pictures, that's one. How about spending the rest of the afternoon down at the art center. We'll pick this stuff up again tomorrow."

TEACHER STRATEGY SEVEN: Reducing Stress by Helping Less Fortunate Students

The opportunity to wallow in feelings of self-pity, grief, and anger is available to everyone. Many students have little experience of the multiple pains of life and can react to normal developmental stress (e.g., failing an exam, being rejected by a girl-boyfriend, not being selected for a team) as though it were a disaster rather than a disappointment. For these students, there are many benefits in helping less fortunate or younger students:

- The helping experience promotes the realization that there are other students whose problems are more complex and stressful than their own. When they observe the coping skills of these students, our target students may see their problem shrink in size and importance
- The process of helping others enhances the helper's feelings of self-worth while concurrently lowering his need for self-depreciation
- The process of helping pushes the helper to focus on the present and future rather than analyzing the past

"You know, Richard, I think it's sort of hard for you to understand that life isn't always exactly the way you'd like it to be. I know you'd like everything to work out and be pleasant. I think it would be an interesting experience for you to get to know Peter in Mrs. Kellogg's classroom. He's younger than you and needs some help in reading. Since his illness, he is a month behind in his English assignment. Maybe you could spend a half hour a couple of times a week with him. I know he will appreciate it. Maybe you can help him catch up if I give you a few teaching techniques."

TEACHER STRATEGY EIGHT: Reducing Stress by Helping the Student Seek Professional Help

When stress becomes chronic and overwhelming, teachers are in the right position to refer a student for psychological services or to encourage a parent to seek professional mental health assistance for their child. All too often, parents and children, who are unhappy and dissatisfied with life, perceive a request for professional help as an obvious sign of personal weakness and inferiority. They become ashamed and spend their time denying and avoiding the reality of the situation. Teachers can be helpful by reflecting the view that, while the decision to call the local community mental health center or a private psychotherapist is painful, it takes personal courage, maturity and insight, and a conviction their child should feel more comfortable with himself and the world around him.

Initially, students are anxious about going to therapy, but, once they learn that therapy sessions are confidential, the fear subsides and the student begins the process of discovering the value of therapeutic support and self-acceptance.

REFERENCES

1. Fagen, S.A. Minimizing emotional wear and tear through adaptive frustration management. Proceedings of a Conference on Preparing Teachers to Foster Personal Growth in Emotionally Disturbed Students, University of Minnesota: Department of Psychoeducational Studies, May 29-31, 1977, 67-78.
2. Fagen, S.A., Long, N.J., & Stevens, D.J. *Teaching children self-control: Preventing emotional and learning problems in the elementary school.* Columbus, Ohio: Charles Merrill, 1975.
3. Hobbs, N. Helping disturbed children: Psychological and ecological strategies, In H. Dupont (ed.), *Educating emotionally disturbed children.* New York: Holt, Rinehart & Winston, 1969.
4. James, W. *Principles of Psychology.* New York: Holt, 1890.
5. Jones, R.M. *Fantasy and feeling in education.* New York: New York University Press, 1968.
6. Long, N.J. & Fagen, S.A. Therapeutic management: A psychoeducational approach. In G. Brown, R. McDowell & J. Smith (eds.), *Educating adolescents with behavior disorders.* Columbus, Ohio: Charles Merrill (in press).
7. Morse, W.C. The helping teacher/crisis teacher concept. *Focus on Exceptional Children,* 1976, *8* (4), 1-10.

Child Abuse and Neglect

CHILD ABUSE and neglect continue to be a major problem in our country, with reported incidents still on the increase. The HEISNER REPORT *in the February, 1978,* INSTRUCTOR, *informed teachers of what they could do to help. Here, in the latest update on this vital topic, is an* INSTRUCTOR *Special Report by* **Jerome E. Leavitt,** *professor at California State University at Fresno, and Coordinator of the Central California Child Abuse Project. Leavitt summarizes his recent conversation with* **Jolly K.,** *who, along with Leonard L. Lieber, founded Parents Anonymous in 1970.*

Q. How serious is child abuse and neglect in the United States?
A. Deadly serious. More than 2,000 children a year die as a result of child abuse and neglect, and an additional estimated two million or more children suffer pain and anguish because of it. We seem to have many persons in our society who are so troubled that they behave in ways that kill or injure the bodies and minds of their children. In addition, latest estimates are that for every incident reported, some 300 cases are ignored. So I am afraid the full magnitude of the problem may never be known.

Q. Why is child abuse and neglect on the increase?
A. Some increase is due to the greater percent of reported cases—abuse has always been with us, but now a greater number of incidents become public. Another critical factor, I believe, is the large unemployment situation that still exists. Unemployment puts those who are prone to abusive behavior back into the home with the child. It can also create stresses

not found while employed: loss of relationships with former employees, loss of income, frustration in adapting to lower incomes, and loss of one's "working person" dignity. Often, parents take out these frustrations on the most convenient and vulnerable objects—their children.

Q. What are the different types of child abuse and neglect?
A. *Physical abuse* is the most obvious type—often very severe and not uncommon. It might be a beating with the hand or an instrument, shaking (which can result in brain damage), or burning with a lighted cigarette or hot water. *Sexual abuse* involves either harassment, fondling, sodomy, or intercourse between adult and child, usually within the same family.

Physical neglect accounts for the largest number of cases: abandoning children, leaving them without supervision for long periods of time, or failing to properly house, feed, clothe, or provide needed medical assistance.

Emotional abuse or neglect is not talked about very much but can be the most harmful of all. This involves parents verbally harassing children or refusing to speak to them, shifting between massive affection and mistreatment, putting unrealistic pressure on children to achieve, or in some other way upsetting their emotional balance.

Q. Who are the child abusers? How can we tell them from other people?
A. There are absolutely no stereotypes. I have not found a single significant characteristic that can be used to tell a child abuser from someone else—he or she may be a churchgoer, a grandmother, an attorney. Not

so terribly long ago, I used to swear that I'd know if I were talking with an abusive parent, in the same fashion as one might say, "I can always spot an out-of-uniform cop." I cannot "spot" an abusive parent. However, during a conversation one can usually identify a troubled person. If you listen between the lines, guide conversation, and ask delicate, sensitive questions, you can sometimes tell when a person is prone to use violence to cope with his or her problems and frustrations.

Q. What signs can a teacher watch for that suggest a child is being abused or neglected?
A. Watch children for the obvious signs—bruises, burns, unusual injuries. Also watch for not-so-obvious signs—frequent hunger, chronic absenteeism, unusual docility or aggressiveness, scant clothing, or unusual expressions of fear. Watch parents for aggressive behavior at conferences, or parents' meetings.

None of these clues individually, unless extremely severe, indicates abuse. Collectively, however, they indicate that a child needs the assistance of a responsible adult to look into his case.

I recommend that educators take a course or workshop in child abuse offered by a local college or school district. If this is not practical, then read one of the many books available and learn to spot the signs of abuse or neglect.

Q. What should a teacher do who suspects a student is being abused or neglected?
A. Become involved. In most states, teachers are required by law to re-

port suspected cases. All persons making such a report are protected from civil liability. The principal is a good person to contact first.

There are also state and county agencies which will help, along with numerous private agencies such as Parents Anonymous. A list of community resources can usually be obtained from your local Department of Welfare, Mental Health Association, or Chamber of Commerce. Only by involving these groups can the causes be treated along with the symptoms.

Q. How can teachers help abusive or neglectful parents who request assistance or information?
A. Few parents know where they can turn when they feel that they might abuse their child. Even fewer know where they can turn without fear of reprisal. Teachers can offer the following suggestions. Ask if the parents have relatives, neighbors, or friends they can turn to when in stress. Give parents the addresses and phone numbers of local social service agencies which can be contacted for help. Usually the larger towns and cities have crisis or intervention lines, many with toll-free numbers. Some of these are listed in the telephone directories under headings such as HELP, HET, or LIFE LINE. And, of course, teachers should tell parents about PA.

Q. What is Parents Anonymous and how does it work?
A. Parents Anonymous (PA) is a national self-help group with a twist. We are similar to the well-known Alcoholics Anonymous model for self-help, except we include a mental health professional as an active member of each chapter. Each local chapter meets weekly with an average of eight to ten members attending, on a no-cost, no-fee basis. Leadership for the chapter comes from the chairperson, who is a parent member. The sponsor (professional) is an auxiliary support to the chairperson and to chapter members.

Discussions at the meetings usually pertain to what's happening in one's life—stress-creating circumstances, alternative positive ways of coping with stress, and general sharing of the ups and downs of members' lives. Telephone numbers and addresses are exchanged with encouragement to contact other members and discuss problems between meetings. Most chapters seek help from other community resources such as county mental health clinics, protective services, housing authorities, legal aid, and parent aid programs.

More detailed information can be obtained by writing Parents Anonymous, 22330 Hawthorne Blvd., #208, Torrance, CA 90505. The PA also maintains a national toll-free number, 1-800-421-0353, which you can call for referral to local chapters or for advice 24 hours a day.

Q. What can teachers do to help children keep from becoming abusive parents in the future?
A. First and foremost, teachers can become thoroughly knowledgeable about abuse and neglect—how to spot them, where to report, and how to get help for parents who want it.

I hope, too, that someday this topic will be included in teacher education courses. With such study and increased awareness, school personnel would be better equipped to identify abused and neglected children, to assist parents, and to make referrals.

The school system should also identify children experiencing severe emotional or mental problems. With early identification, the school can be a coordinator for the family in securing confirmed diagnosis and necessary assistance that could prevent the dysfunction from surfacing later as abusive or neglectful parental behavior.

Some schools have already begun programs of parenting education. It is too soon to know the long-range results, but there is every reason to believe that if elementary and secondary school students develop a better understanding of family life, and have desirable first-hand experiences with young children, they will become better parents themselves. And they will have a better chance to break the cycle of the abused child who becomes an abusing parent.

One last comment. If, after reading this, you believe you know of a child who is abused, or you know a parent who might be abusive or neglectful, don't ignore that feeling— support the right of human beings to assistance when life's problems hit them and their kids in the face. They need and deserve our help!

WE WANT YOUR ADVICE

Any anthology can be improved. This one will be regularly. But we need your help.

Annual Editions revisions depend on two major opinion sources: one is the academic advisers who work with us in scanning the thousands of articles published in the public press each year; the other is you—the person actually using the book.

Please help us and the users of the next edition by completing the prepaid article rating form on the last page of this book and returning it to us. Thank you.

Teaching the Gifted and Talented Child

Although gifted and talented children are not covered under P.L. 94-142, and though they are not considered to be "handicapped," they are children with special needs and are generally included in textbooks on special education. The articles in this section explore the nature of giftedness and the various forms in which giftedness can be expressed. While it is estimated that there are two and a half million gifted children in this country, many of these children go unrecognized as gifted. Of those that are recognized as gifted, many are not involved in any organized program to enhance their exceptional abilities.

Accelerated programs for the gifted are important to the student and school alike. However, many gifted children suffer the fate of undeveloped potential by being forced to conform to the normal pace of the average classroom. Although there have been many impressive advances made in serving these children, only a minority of this population is receiving services that challenge them. Universities have begun instituting programs which prepare specialized teachers for this group of children, however, and state funding, though still inadequate, has increased. The first article in this section, "Our Most Neglected Natural Resource," identifies four myths commonly associated with the gifted which tend to present obstacles for further advances in gifted education.

Although establishing an academic program for the gifted and talented is a primary objective, equally important is the need to address their affective development. "The Teacher as Counselor for the Gifted" discusses ways that the teacher can encourage the total development of gifted students. This theme is further developed in the article, "A 'Social' Social Studies Model for Gifted Students." The article considers the value of establishing a social studies model that enables gifted children to further utilize their abilities to confront the "real" problems of life.

A large percentage of gifted and talented children are also physically and emotionally handicapped. Often the handicap detracts from the special talent. It is important to recognize this portion of the gifted population so that they can be challenged academically. "Special Children . . . Special Gifts" examines this problem and discusses a recently developed model called the Retrieval and Acceleration of Promising Young Handicapped and Talented (RAPYHT) which was designed to nurture their abilities.

The final article, "Will the Gifted Child Movement Be Alive and Well in 1990?" addresses the future of programs for the gifted and talented. The author considers four areas that need to be strengthened to ensure their continued development.

Looking Ahead: Challenge Questions

Why have gifted children been neglected by our educational system?

What are gifted children really like?

How can teachers nurture the abilities of gifted children who are also handicapped?

What is the future of the gifted child movement?

Unit 9

Our Most Neglected Natural Resource

Harold C. Lyon, Jr.

Director, Office for the Gifted and Talented, U.S. Department of Education; Author of Learning to Feel—Feeling to Learn, It's Me and I'm Here, *and* Tenderness Is Strength; *Coauthor of* On Becoming a Teacher.

In recent years, the American educational system has recognized cultural, physical, and social differences among students. Indeed, the average student—once the focal point of American education—is fast becoming an endangered species. And rightfully so. The ideal of an average student was at best a myth and at worst a destroyer of human potential. Yet, despite this new-found sensitivity to individual needs, many schools still ignore the unique qualities and characteristics of many students. One group, the gifted and talented, suffers—ironically—the neglect of a system and a society that could reap inestimable benefits from the development of its potential.

The gifted and talented is a minority distinguished not by race, socioeconomic background, ethnic origin, or impaired powers, but by its exceptional ability. Its members come from all levels of society, from all races and nationalities, and from both sexes in about equal numbers.

The children in this group have an unusual endowment of talent—analytical or creative in an intellectual, artistic, or social way or even in some ways that neither schools nor society yet understands. Whatever their special talent, their ranks will produce that small percentage of humans whose work will greatly affect the disciplines they specialize in, the societies they live in, and perhaps all humankind. They are the future Albert Einsteins, Ludwig von Beethovens, Pablo Picassos, and Martin Luther Kings.

The gifted and talented constitute approximately 5 percent of the school-age population or about 2.5 million children. These statistics may appear low to those who, in an effort to remove the stigma of elitism from education for the gifted, would label as many as 15 percent of the school-age population gifted. Bloating the estimate in this way might make gifted education more palatable politically, and it is compatible with my belief that schools need to search for the gifts in every child. I believe, however, that as arbitrary as the 5 percent figure may be, we need to begin with a population that is noticeably different from the majority in order to establish public acceptance of gifted education.

In spite of the significant number and vast potential of gifted children, our government and our society have taken only occasional interest in them. The federal government began its wavering commitment to the gifted in 1957, when it was faced with what it perceived to be a national crisis, the launching of Sputnik. This event triggered some hysteria over the Soviet Union's superiority in space technology and in science education. The uproar produced the National Defense Education Act (NDEA) of 1958, a massive aid-to-education program originally designed to help the schools improve instruction in chemistry, physics, mathematics, biology, and economics for the most academically able students.

During the 1960's, as we matched and later exceeded the Soviets in quality of space exploration, the national panic about the caliber of our best schools ebbed. Other concerns—most notably, civil rights—moved into the educational spotlight. American educational priorities shifted from the most able students to the least fortunate, and interest in educating the gifted waned. Promising programs vanished, and the number of articles on the subject in educational journals dropped sharply.

It was not until 1969, 12 years after Sputnik, that the gifted again came under federal scrutiny. In that year, Congress mandated a study of gifted education—the so-called Marland Report—that produced a startling and disturbing portrait of neglect. This landmark document revealed that—

• The schools were adequately serving fewer than 4 percent of the 2.5 million gifted and talented population.

• Only 10 states had full-time directors of gifted education, despite a high correlation between full-time effort at the state level and excellence in programming.

• Only 10 universities had graduate-level programs specializing in gifted education.

• Fifty-seven percent of school administrators were unaware of any special needs of the gifted and talented population.

• A high percentage of dropouts were actually gifted children who left school because of boredom with a lockstep system geared to the average child.

The report concluded its analysis by asserting that gifted and talented children reached their potential not because of our schools, but in spite of them.

The education community responded to the Marland Report with shock and dismay. In line with many of the Report's recommendations, the federal government established, in early 1972, the Office for the Gifted and Talented (OGT) within the U.S. Office of Education.

Today, 10 years after the Marland Report and despite public apathy, bureaucratic obstacles, and severe budget restraints, a recent Office for Civil Rights survey of school districts indicates that our schools are serving approximately 35 percent of the gifted population. In addition, 40 states have full-time directors of gifted education; the remaining states and territories maintain at least part-time consultants. The number of universities with graduate-level programs specifically in gifted education has expanded to approximately 26. Perhaps most important, many educators and parents are now aware of the special needs of gifted children.

Indeed, gifted education has never before stood on such firm ground. Currently, 17 states have laws mandating appropriate education for all gifted children. Another 33 states have established guidelines for gifted programs.

Moreover, state funding has increased sevenfold in less than 10 years. When the Marland Report came out, total state expenditures for gifted education stood at approximately $15 million. Today, that figure has grown to about $117 million.

As we begin a new decade, the future of gifted education appears promising. But we must always temper our optimism with the knowledge of past regressions and frustrations. Many fundamental challenges and issues remain unsolved, and we cannot count the current moratorium on public apathy as permanent.

In a policy paper presented to the U.S. Congress, James Gallagher, author of *Teaching the Gifted Child,* points out that federal expenditures for the handicapped are 200 times greater than for the gifted:

> Are these the appropriate expenditure proportions for exceptional children in our society? Probably not. The situation does reflect the political realities that attend our present system of crisis decision making in government. Gifted children suffer because they are a "cool," or long-range problem. Budget and legislative decisions are made not on the basis of what might be of ultimate benefit to society but on what is the greatest immediate crisis. Gifted children may be our best long-range investment in education, but they do not create problems of immediate significance; nor have they had a vocal constituency capable of extracting attention and dollars from public policymakers.

Other, specific obstacles to gifted education exist. These include the powerful myths—which must be destroyed—surrounding gifted children and programs for the gifted.

• Myth 1: "The gifted and talented will do fine on their own. They do not need special help."

Unfortunately, this statement is far from true. Just as children of less-than-average mental ability frequently have trouble keeping up with their classmates, so children of above-average ability have trouble staying behind with their classmates. Prevented from moving ahead by the rigidity of normal school procedures and assigned to classes with others of the same age but not necessarily of the same ability, gifted youngsters typically take one of three tacks: They drift into a state of lethargy and apathy; they conceal their ability, anxious not to embarrass others or to draw their ridicule; or they become discipline problems.

• Myth 2: "Teachers love gifted children. These children already receive all the extra attention they need."

In addition to identifying widespread teacher indifference to gifted and talented children, the Marland Report identified some teacher and administrator hostility toward them. Some educators resent the gifted for quite human reasons, including impatience with any unusual child and an assumption that the gifted are a favored elite who deserve less than normal consideration.

• Myth 3: "Gifted education is an elitist and racist concept and is inappropriate in our egalitarian society."

In the past, minority and ethnically different groups did not fare well in selection procedures for admission to programs for the gifted. This situation is changing for the better. Federal programs for the gifted have consistently sought to eliminate bias. Most gifted education programs now use a variety of criteria to identify the gifted. Many have reduced their reliance on culturally slanted IQ tests and increased their reliance on more subjective criteria. Peer, parent, and teacher evaluations are becoming as important as IQ tests in identifying the gifted and talented. The commitment to minority participation in gifted programs is strong and will remain so.

• Myth 4: "A massive federal program is the answer to our problems in educating the gifted and talented."

Constitutionally, in the United States the education system is characterized by federal concern, state responsibility, and local control. Accordingly, the real future of gifted education rests primarily with the states, individual school systems, and the teachers who deal directly with gifted children.

Once a school system has identified and assessed its gifted population, it can pursue any of a host of strategies. Following are categories of gifted and talented students and some of the programs available to them.

The academically gifted. These students may possess high IQ's and generally high achievement levels in all areas, or they may be "single shot" achievers with outstanding ability in a single academic field. Most often schools provide advanced placement courses, enrichment, independent study, or mentorships for these students. Mentorships make use of community resources, pairing students with individuals who are willing to share their expertise in a particular field. (As part of the 1968 White House Task Force on the Gifted, I participated in interviews with some of this country's most brilliant people to find out what had made the biggest difference in their development. Almost all pointed to a mentor as the single most important factor for success.)

Creative and productive thinkers. These children may benefit from being in classes where they have opportunities to explore, to ask questions, to express themselves, to experiment, to react to different stimuli, and to use a variety of materials. Affective education and development of skills in problem solving are important to these students.

The artistically talented. While some schools offer courses in art and music, children talented in the arts have traditionally had to find their instruction outside the school system. This pattern is slowly being changed, however, with some states (New York, North Carolina, Texas, Louisiana, and others) offering high school programs for those talented in the

OGT Works for the Gifted

The Department of Education's Office for the Gifted and Talented (OGT) addresses four primary objectives:

• Strengthening the capacity of state education agencies (SEA's) to deliver services to gifted and talented children through local education agencies (LEA's) and by other indirect modes.

• Strengthening the capacity of LEA's to deliver direct services to gifted and talented children.

• Strengthening leadership through professional development and training programs (only 1 of every 6 teachers of the gifted has had any formal training for this special work).

• Finding through research and distributing widely some answers to key questions concerning education for the gifted and talented.

Under legislation (PL 95-561) enacted in 1978, OGT initiated the State-Administered Grant Program. This program allows states to apply for two types of federal funds: a basic minimum grant award open to all states and additional grant awards distributed to about half the states on a competitive basis. This seed money, 75 percent of OGT's meager but highly leveraged $6.28* million budget for fiscal year 1980, is designed to stimulate the investment of approximately 20 state dollars and 80 local dollars for every federal dollar invested. A full 90 percent of these state awards must flow through to local schools that compete successfully in a state-wide competition. Fifty percent of these projects must have a component for the gifted who are economically disadvantaged.

The remaining 25 percent of OGT's budget is for discretionary grant awards, including national model projects, professional development and leadership training in gifted education, statewide activities grants for further assistance to less developed SEA's, and research and information products.

States may also obtain funds for gifted education from a variety of other sources in the federal government, including the Office of Indian Education, the Office of Bilingual Education, Title IV C, Title I, and the National Institute of Education.

Despite the slowly increasing federal commitment to gifted education, the responsibility for providing adequate programming rests primarily with SEA's. In addition to running their own programs, SEA's support and stimulate LEA's.

Perhaps the most significant result of the growing state leadership role is a new three-way relationship of cooperation and understanding among the federal government, the SEA's, and the LEA's. Only a few years ago, this relationship hardly existed. State and local agencies operated independently of one another without coordination. From time to time the federal government gave them assistance. Today, many state and local agencies are beginning to work in harmony, and the federal government supplies them with timely information, funds, and technical assistance. Perhaps more than any other single factor, this new relationship accounts for the remarkable progress in gifted education that has been made in such a short time.

---

*In fiscal year 1981, the federal government authorized $35 million for the level of funding for gifted and talented education; in fiscal year 1982, $40 million; in fiscal year 1983, $50 million. In the 1981 budget year, however, the federal government provided only $6.28 million—only 18 percent of the authorized level of funding.

arts. Some of these schools offer a full-day program in academics in addition to special instruction in dance and other art forms.

Leaders. Some students demonstrate leadership ability by winning offices; others are still "emerging" leaders. Schools should provide special programs for these categories of students as well as for those who show leadership ability in negative ways—the gang leaders and con artists. The development of leadership skills could take place in any class where students engage in discussion or debate or practice group-process skills. Schools may also set up separate classes to develop leadership abilities. For example, in 1979-80 OGT funded the Leadership/Social Giftedness/ Decision-Making Project in North Chelmsford, Massachusetts, which has attempted to teach potential leaders to base future decisions on sound moral and ethical values. In this program, the teacher would introduce an issue or problem, and students would discuss it and evaluate the lesson.

Beyond these practical teaching strategies, we are now on the verge of some incredible breakthroughs in scientific discovery and levels of awareness and consciousness about the gifted and talented.

Carl R. Rogers has done significant research in the last couple of decades in determining traits of the successful therapist. Over the last 14 years, Rogers' colleagues David Aspy and Flora Roebuck have conducted empirical studies that apply Rogers' findings to teachers. Rogers found three traits present in the successful therapist, and Aspy and Roebuck corrobo-

rated that the very same traits exist in the successful teacher. The first one is *genuineness:* the ability to be a human being with strengths and weaknesses, to be genuine with students. The second trait is *empathic understanding:* the ability of the teacher to put herself or himself in a student's shoes. The third trait is *prizing:* the opposite of apathy. It's caring enough about the uniqueness of an individual to celebrate that uniqueness. Aspy and Roebuck found that the governing trait of these three is empathic understanding. Teachers with high empathy tend to have the other traits as well.

Aspy and Roebuck studied the high-empathy teachers and found that their students had significantly higher achievement scores than students whose teachers were not highly empathetic. High-empathy teachers also smiled 200 percent more than low-empathy ones—and so did their students. High-empathy teachers tended to have greater influence on students the earlier the students were exposed to them.

In a forthcoming book, *On Becoming a Teacher,* Dr. Rogers and I give a more detailed analysis of the Aspy and Roebuck study.

For every gifted child who is not allowed to reach his or her potential, there is a lost opportunity. That child might have eventually composed a concerto, found the cure for a hitherto terminal disease, or developed a formula for world peace. Wasting the potential of a gifted mind is reckless for a society in desperate need of creativity and inventiveness.

The Teacher as Counselor for the Gifted

Joyce VanTassel-Baska

■ Special counseling for gifted students should be an essential part of their school program from the time they enter school as Kindergarteners until they leave as graduated seniors. While some progress has been made in addressing cognitive areas of development in an appropriate manner, little has been done for gifted students in the arena of affective development. Yet we know that the gifted possess differential affective characteristics that demand nurturance (Clark, 1980). A good program philosophy and goal structure has always included the concept of integration of self as a basis for a gifted student's development in other areas (VanTassel-Baska, 1981). And yet the use of counseling in special programs for the gifted is quite limited.

One reason that this situation exists relates to the perception by many educators that counseling is only for "problem" students. Thus the categories of gifted underachiever or gifted handicapped may have been the only ones considered for intervention. It is important to realize that all gifted students require special counseling, not because they are "problems," but rather, because they have unique abilities and needs that require attention. In this context, the definition of counseling for the gifted is seen as the provision of guidance for the personal, social, and educational development of an individual based on the nature and extent of his or her giftedness.

Another reason that counseling tends to be ignored in the education of the gifted is the lack of trained personnel who feel adequately prepared to deal with the counseling domain for gifted students. Trained counselors are in short supply in most educational institutions. When available, they tend to work exclusively at the 7–12 grade levels. Their job responsibilities for all students will also necessarily limit the services they are able to render to gifted students. In addition, few counselors have been trained in the special characteristics and needs of a gifted population, and therefore may not perceive the necessity of providing special services to this group. All of these reasons obviate against the likelihood that gifted students will receive appropriate counseling intervention from a counseling specialist.

THE UNIQUE ROLE OF THE TEACHER

Who then can provide for the gifted in the counseling domain? Perhaps it is the teacher of the gifted who is uniquely able to meet such needs. When the teacher fulfills the role of counselor, there are multiple advantages to the student:

1. The gifted student can receive counseling assistance in the context of the classroom, rather than being "taken out" for one more type of activity.
2. The gifted student can begin to perceive his program as holistic, not segmented by concerns for affective issues separate from cognitive ones.
3. The gifted student can discuss common interests and problems in a small group of gifted peers with an adult who knows the student in another context, rather than be dealt with as an individual oddity by an outside specialist.
4. The gifted student can receive reinforcement and encouragement on an ongoing basis rather than postponing it until a special appointment has been made.

In reality, the teacher of the gifted spends more time with such students and therefore presumably knows

From *Teaching Exceptional Children*, Spring 1983, pp. 145-151. Copyright 1983 The Council for Exceptional Children. Reprinted with permission of The Council for Exceptional Children.

them better than other educational personnel. Furthermore, the teacher of the gifted is trained in understanding and responding to the special characteristics and needs of this population. Thus, providing a counseling service to them merely extends and broadens the nature of services already being offered. Benefits to the student also benefit the teacher, especially in the case of "problem" students whose behavior needs some form of modification. The teacher, then, is a natural facilitator to implement small group activities that address the unique counseling needs of the gifted.

COPING WITH GIFTEDNESS

The gifted child has many counseling needs that can be met successfully if the classroom teacher is aware of some basic strategies to use in addressing the special kinds of affective needs of such children. In fact, these needs in general tend to adapt rather easily to the situational context of a classroom for remedy. In the domain of personal-social counseling, for example, there emerges the strong set of needs related to coping with the exceptionality of giftedness, coping skills that may best be developed and nurtured in the larger society of the classroom.

What are the issues involved in coping with giftedness? They include, but are not limited to, the following:

- Understanding one's differentness, yet recognizing one's similarities to others.
- Understanding how to accept and give criticism.
- Being tolerant of oneself and others.
- Developing an understanding of one's strengths and weaknesses.
- Developing skills in areas that will nurture both cognitive and affective development.

These needs and others can be addressed through strategies that can be used or at least developed in the regular classroom context. Among such strategies are the following: roleplaying, tutorials, mentorships, internships, bibliotherapy, discussion groups, special projects, simulation, gaming, special interest clubs, skill development seminars, and career exploration.

The following sections present sample activities that illustrate the linkage between the affective needs of gifted students and the various strategies that can be employed to meet them. The activities that are highlighted reflect motivational lead-ins to small group counseling opportunities. As such, some of them could be seen as affective educational activities. Others clearly represent a guidance or advisement perspective. Still others constitute predominantly intellectual activities. *Counseling*, then, is being used as the umbrella term to encompass all aspects of the teacher's role in aiding the affective development of gifted students.

UNDERSTANDING SELF AND OTHERS

Counseling the gifted must begin with the issue of *perception* with respect to how each gifted student frames his or her world. Development of healthy self-concept and self-esteem is predicated on such self-understanding. The teacher of the gifted can use small group activities to help foster in them a better sense of who they are in relation to others. Requisite to the use of such activities, however, is the opportunity for discussion among gifted students with the teacher acting as facilitator. The sample activities that follow address this issue of understanding.

Activity: The Value Card

Objectives: To encourage examination of a personal value system. To promote an understanding among gifted students of how they are both alike and different from others.

Level: K–12

Procedure:

1. Have each student make an 8½″ × 11″ cardboard tag and write his or her name in the center. Individualistic approaches to designing the name tag should be encouraged. Then give the following set of instructions to the students:
2. Above your name, write the name of the person from history or current events whom you *most* admire.
3. Below your name, write the name of the person from history or current events whom you *least* admire.
4. In the upper left corner, write the three things you *do* best.
5. In the upper right corner, write three things you *like* to do.
6. In the lower left corner, order the following processes according to your personal sense of priority: thinking, feeling, doing.
7. In the lower right corner, write one word you hope a friend would use in describing you.

Students then put on their name tags and gather in small groups of 3 to 5 to discuss what the items on their tags might mean about their way of perceiving the world. Each group reflects on the following questions as they discuss their name tags:

1. What similarities are there among the students in the group? How can these be accounted for?
2. What differences are there among the group? How can these be accounted for?
3. What was the rationale behind each student's choice of most admired and least admired person?
4. What does the name tag tell you about yourself? What does it tell you about your group?

9. TEACHING THE GIFTED AND TALENTED CHILD

The teacher of the gifted can use small group activities to help foster in them a better sense of who they are in relation to others. Opportunity for discussion, with the teacher acting as facilitator, is particularly important.

Extension Activities

1. Interview ten adults by asking them to complete a personal name tag. Tally the results and report your findings.
2. Keep a log on a person you know well. Hypothesize this person's value preferences. Interview to confirm.
3. Start a discussion group on values clarification.

Activity: Photosearch

Objective: To provide gifted students with an understanding of human value systems.

Level: 4–12

Procedure:

1. Show students a set of slides, each one depicting a human episode related to an important event in history. (Old magazine pictures or reproduced photographs can be made into slides.)
2. Have each student choose one slide on which to concentrate research efforts which explore (a) the place, time, and major historical event occurring; (b) the significance of the episode; (c) the human condition that is depicted; (d) the value conflict that is involved; (e) the resolution of the episode and its effect on the human condition.

Extension Activities:

1. Prepare a set of slides that portray human beings in conflict with their surroundings. Do a taped commentary that reveals the issues involved.
2. Explore the community in which you live in order to evaluate concern for human values:
   a. Interview a city official to discuss ordinances that protect citizens.

b. Discover what agencies and service groups exist to help people.

c. Discuss what institutions in the community exist to help people. Prepare a chart to show how these institutions function. Rate your community with respect to its "people" orientation. Share your findings with classmates.

3. Read a book about a culture other than your own. Write down what you perceive to be differences in viewing the world. Interview someone from that cultural background to discuss your perception of "difference." Describe your findings in an essay entitled "What Accounts for Cultural Differences."

MODELING

Gifted students, particularly females and individuals from a disadvantaged background, can profit from exposure to good role models that provide impetus for mirroring gifted behaviors (Fox, Brody, & Tobin, 1980; Frazier, 1980). The teacher of the gifted has various avenues for providing students with such models. Although mentorships and internships offer one context for modeling, time constraints often make it difficult for the teacher to set up such experiences. Alternative kinds of experiences may then be more appropriate.

Since gifted students enjoy reading and can easily become absorbed in the lives of characters, the use of bibliotherapy is a natural approach to try for the purposes of establishing role model behavior. Bibliotherapy can also be used successfully as a strategy for working with gifted students in other areas of counseling. Excellent annotated book lists for such purposes are readily available (Baskin & Harris, 1980; National Council of Teachers of English, 1979).

The following sample activity focuses on the genre of biography to address role model needs. A cluster group of gifted students is necessary to carry out the activity. An independent study unit on biography could be developed for extended use, and the cluster of students could be formalized into a "biography club" for additional activities.

Activity: The Eminence Game

Objectives: To highlight role models for gifted students. To encourage identification with an adult who has achieved eminence.

Level: 4–12

Procedure:

Have gifted students read biographies of Frank Lloyd Wright, architect; Pablo Casals, musician; Marie Curie, scientist; Albert Einstein, physicist. In a small group discussion, concentrate on the following questions:
1. Did each of the eminent individuals you read about become famous because of innate abilities, a nurturing environment, or just plain luck?
2. What similarities and differences do you perceive among the four individuals?
3. What personal qualities enhanced their work?
4. How did they cope with being different, being "loners," being laughed at or scorned?
5. In your opinion, what made these individuals able to create at high levels?
6. What can we learn from them about the pursuit of excellence?

Extension Activities:

1. Participate in a mentorship or internship with a living architect, musician, scientist, etc., to research current career issues in each field.
2. Read three more biographies of other eminent persons and select an area of interest for investigation.
3. Study the works and/or discoveries of these individuals.
4. Research the background cultural influences on each individual.

SOLVING UNFAMILIAR PROBLEMS

The gifted student is frequently seen as one who takes tests well and has mastery over the kinds of content material they contain. While it is reasonable to assume that gifted students can do well with tests that are beneath their cognitive level, such as most in-grade standardized achievement tests, it cannot be assumed that they have good skills for coping with the more difficult tests that provide an appropriate challenge to which they will be exposed as early as junior high age.

In fact, many gifted students are *not* good test takers for several reasons, not the least of which is a lack of interest in or concern for what particular tests measure or what purpose they serve in a student's life (Renzulli, Reis, & Smith, 1981). Yet if gifted students can begin to perceive tests as "problems to be solved" and as indicators of areas in which they excel, perhaps test score information would more accurately reflect potential.

The following set of activities reflects a skill mastery approach to test-taking that involves practice with problem-solving techniques as well as types of test items that are rooted in verbal and mathematical aptitudes. Students need to sense that taking a test represents a new learning experience that engages them in problem-solving.

Activity: Solving the Test

Objectives: To acquaint gifted students with skills in test-taking. To teach problem-solving strategies needed to take tests effectively.

Acting as an informal advisor to gifted students is another important function for the teacher. Only if teachers involve themselves in this way can gifted students get the "longer view" from someone who knows and understands their needs.

Level: 6–12

Materials: Practice tests in math and verbal areas (e.g., *How to Take the SAT,* the School College and Abilities Test (SCAT), or old test forms); *Techniques of Problem Solving,* Dale Seymour Press, P.O. Box 10888, Palo Alto CA 94303.

Procedure:

1. Have students work through test items trying the following approaches:

   a. Try some hypothetical answers.
   b. Make-a-list.
   c. Draw a picture.
   d. Break the test item into parts.
2. Discuss how each strategy can work on a given test item.
3. Review with students the following types of test items and provide practice with each type: analogies; sentence completion; antonyms; synonyms; reading comprehension; algebraic topics; geometry topics; comparison problems.

INDIRECT INTERVENTIONS

While the activities just described reflect a "direct intervention" approach to counseling gifted students, the role of the teacher can be extremely effective in more indirect ways as well. Acting as an advocate for gifted students with other educational personnel and with parents is one way of helping others understand specific behaviors of gifted students.

Parents, for example, often express concern when their gifted child shows a clear preference for reading over more conventional "play" activities. Even educational personnel can become concerned about such a pattern of behavior. A teacher advocate can assure parents and others that this behavior is rather typical and indeed even "normal" for a gifted child, even though it may seem unusual when viewed against the background of the preferences of normal children.

Acting as a good listener can also serve a worthwhile function. Too frequently, gifted students feel there is no one with whom they can share their feelings, particularly those that reflect negatively upon themselves, such as feelings of inadequacy and imperfection. When entering a gifted program for the first time, for example, gifted students frequently feel inadequate. Suddenly they are no longer the brightest in the class, and the "getting by" behavior they have cultivated through their earlier years of schooling no longer works. Owning up to these feelings is an important part of a student's development and is necessary to shed old, inappropriate behaviors. The teacher can provide a setting for revealing these feelings without fear of being exposed, thus providing an important outlet for expression and ultimate growth.

Acting as an informal advisor to gifted students is another important function for the teacher. Many gifted students of junior high age, for example, have little idea of appropriate coursework to take as they enter secondary school, particularly as the decision relates to later college and career choices. The teacher can help them plan ahead in their educational experiences in order to maximize potential long-range benefits from taking certain types of courses for which they may be especially well suited, and can point out the importance of such courses, perhaps even based on personal experience. Only if teachers involve themselves in this way can gifted students get the "longer view" from someone who knows and understands their needs.

MEETING DIVERSE NEEDS

Certainly not all the counseling needs of gifted students can be met through the teacher in a classroom context, nor can individual and group activities meet every diverse and complex need. A knowledgeable and sensitive teacher working with the gifted in a group setting can, however, successfully address some of the significant affective needs of gifted students. In this way, counseling provisions for the gifted can become a part of standard program practice rather than a wished-for ideal.

REFERENCES

Baskin, B., & Harris, K. *Books for the gifted child*. New York: R. R. Bowker, 1980.

Clark, B. *Growing up gifted*. Columbus OH: Charles E. Merrill, 1979.

Fox, L., Brody, L., & Tobin, D. (Eds.). *Women and the mathematical mystique*. Baltimore: Johns Hopkins Press, 1980.

Frazier, M. Programming for the culturally diverse. In J. Jordan & J. Grossi (Eds.), *An administrator's handbook on designing programs for the gifted and talented*. Reston VA: The Council for Exceptional Children, 1980.

National Council of Teachers of English. *Language Arts*, January, 1979.

Renzulli, J., Reis, S., & Smith, L. *The Revolving Door Identification Model*. Mansfield Center CT: Creative Learning Press, 1981.

VanTassel-Baska, J. A comprehensive model of career education for gifted and talented. *Journal of Career Education*, June 1981, 325–31.

Special Children ....Special Gifts

Merle B. Karnes

Merle B. Karnes, Ed.D., is professor of Special Education, Early Childhood/Elementary Education and Educational Psychology in the Institute for Child Behavior and Development, University of Illinois at Urbana-Champaign.

There is probably as large a percentage of gifted/ talented children among the handicapped as among the non-handicapped. In the past, however, little or no effort was made to identify these children, much less to design programs for them in their areas of strength. If handicapped children did develop their gifts or talents, it was almost in spite of the educational program, not because of it. As a rule, special educators have focused on children's handicaps in developing programs and ancillary services and have failed to program for areas of unusual strength. On the other hand, educators in the field of the gifted have seldom turned to the handicapped population to identify children with special gifts or talents. Lack of training and experience in working with the handicapped explains why the latter was—and to a large extent still is—the case. By the same token, lack of formal training in what gifted children are like and in their special needs for differentiated curricula has often kept special educators from identifying the gifted or talented and providing them with a program that challenges and nourishes them.

Since my interest in the gifted dates back farther in my career than does my interest in the handicapped, it is understandable that I should have become concerned over the failure to identify potentially or functionally gifted/talented children among the handicapped population. In 1970, my associates and I were funded by the Bureau of Education for the Handicapped, now the Office of Special Education Programs in the Department of Education, to develop a model program for mildly and moderately handicapped childred aged three to five. During its development we became aware of characteristics among some of these children which led us to believe they might prove gifted or talented if properly motivated. In addition, we visited other programs and noted among the preschool handicapped a small percentage who demonstrated unusual abilities. These observations reinforced our belief that there are gifted/talented children among the handicapped preschoolers and that we should take steps to serve them more appropriately.

We first sought funding for a research project in 1973 from the State of Illinois, Department of Public Instruction, Office of the Gifted. The project was approved, but the legislators did not appropriate funds for research. We sought funding elsewhere and in 1975 received a grant from the Bureau of Education for the Handicapped to develop a model project for identifying and designing a program for gifted/ talented handicapped children at the preschool level. The project—Retrieval and Acceleration of Promising Young Handicapped and Talented (RAPYHT) —was developed over three years and we subsequently received grants to disseminate the project nationwide. At present the model has been replicated at 57 sites in 18 states,[1] and we anticipate adding 25 more sites during 1984-85. Recently, we received a grant from the Administration for Children, Youth and Families, OHDS, to adapt the model to identify gifted handicapped children in Head Start programs.

From the outset, it has been difficult to convince professionals in special education that some handicapped children can also be gifted and talented.[2] In fact, some have even laughed at the idea. I quickly point out that many notable persons who have made outstanding contributions to society have also had handicaps—Beethoven, Franklin D. Roosevelt, Helen Keller, Edison, Van Gogh, and so on. How many handicapped persons who were potentially gifted or talented have

Reprinted from *Children Today*, Vol. 13, No. 5 (September-October 1984), pp. 18-23. Published by the Office of Human Development Services, Department of Health and Human Services six times a year.

gone unidentified and under-developed because people working with this population did not believe the handicapped could be gifted or talented?

As we continue to work with our replication sites and to interpret our model at conferences and in articles in professional journals, we have been encouraged by the increasing numbers of professionals in both special and gifted education who are becoming committed to improving the educational lot of this segment of our population. In fact, administrators, teachers and others who have replicated the RAPYHT model tell us consistently that doing so has tended to upgrade programs for all the handicapped children in the program. They explain that they now attend to the strengths of all the children more than they formerly did. Moreover, they find that many strategies effective with the gifted/talented handicapped can be adapted to children with lesser abilities. Teachers also report that parents become much more optimistic and accepting of their child's handicap when they learn about his or her strength, especially if the strength is so unusual as to qualify as a gift or a talent.

The Program

RAPYHT is designed to serve mildly and moderately handicapped children (diagnosed for physical, sensory and/or emotional handicaps or exhibiting behaviors markedly associated with learning disabilities) who have been identified as potentially or functionally gifted in one or more of the six following areas: intellectual, academic (with the subcategories of science, reading, math), leadership, creativity, visual and performing arts (with the subcategories of music and art) and psychomotor.

Typical of the children served are three we shall call Tom, Amy and Peter. Tom has cerebral palsy, is quadriplegic, and at the time he entered a special preschool program, he could not produce speech sounds. He is also an intellectually superior child, with a demonstrated IQ within the "very gifted" range. Amy demonstrates a talent for leadership in her interactions with other children at school. They choose her as a playmate and come to her for help or advice. She also has a severe language delay due to poor sound discrimination and poor auditory memory. Peter has a problem with sensory-motor integration; as a result, his fine and gross motor development are delayed. But he has an unusual memory and an exceptional vocabulary for his age. He developed reading skills very early and has been reading words on signs since the age of two. These children have two things in common: They demonstrate potential giftedness or talent and they have handicapping conditions.

Handicapping conditions often do obscure or mask gifts and talents. It follows that teachers of the handicapped need training and guidelines to assist them in observing children and determining whether there are signs of gifts or talents, potential or functional. One error an untrained teacher may make is to compare the handicapped children in her or his room with nonhandicapped children already considered gifted/talented. Experts concur that such a comparison is unjustified.[3] The comparison must instead be made with other children who have comparable handicaps.

The RAPYHT model embraces seven components: general programming, talent screening, talent identification, in-depth talent assessment, linking talent assessment with talent programming, parent involvement and evaluation.

General Programming

Over the years, these components have been modified, expanded and rearranged in response to feedback from teachers who have replicated the model. One major change has been the timing of screening and identification. Formerly, screening was scheduled in the first few weeks of school, after training sessions. Currently, teachers are trained during the first half of the year to foster creativity, higher-level thinking, problem solving and talent in all the handicapped children in their classrooms. Activities are provided in a *General Programming Manual* and in the Nurturing Talent guides, for the six areas of talent.[4] This approach gives the teacher an opportunity to acquire and practice strategies that encourage the emergence of gifts and talents. It also reduces the risk of overlooking the potentially talented—a danger when screening and identification are introduced too soon.

Concurrently with their general training, teachers learn the characteristics associated with various talents so that they will be prepared to identify the gifted/talented in the six areas.

Talent Screening

One of the tasks undertaken by project personnel was the development of a screening instrument in two versions, one for parents and another for teachers. Since there were no prior preschool programs for the gifted/talented handicapped, no such instruments existed. Moreover, a review of the literature revealed no instruments for screening nonhandicapped preschool gifted children.

The Teacher and Parent Checklists currently used, the result of several revisions, took shape initially through a search of the literature for lists of characteristics distinguishing older children in the six talent areas and through the input of teachers who had experience working with young gifted/talented children and professionals and students with expertise in one of the talent areas. Teachers rate the children in the six areas and their subcategories.

The reliability and validity of the checklists have been established. Cut-off scores for each area identify approximately 9.2 percent of the children as potentially or functionally talented. Parents tend to rate their children higher than do teachers; consequently, the number of eligible children exceeds 10 percent and may run as high as 15 percent. Since the make-up of classes varies considerably, making it difficult to determine precisely which children should receive RAPYHT programming, we have felt it more humane to err on the side of inclusion than to risk overlooking potentially gifted/talented children. The approach is positive, and the programming in areas of strength can only be beneficial, even though in the end some children turn out not to be gifted or talented.

We are often asked, "How long do you program before you determine whether the child is gifted?" It is difficult to answer this question precisely; however, when children are periodically reviewed by an interdisciplinary team and information is shared, a concensus does emerge.

The checklist for creative talent, for example (see Fig. 1), illustrates the specific observations by which teachers determine whether a child exhibits a preponderance of the characteristics associated with potential or functional giftedness or talent. Such observations are far more pertinent than merely asking a teacher to nominate children who seem talented or gifted.

Talent Identification

To determine whether a child is eligible for RAPYHT programming, a multidisciplinary team reviews the results of the Talent Checklists, observations of children using the RAPYHT list of common characteristics as criteria and results of standardized tests. In a class of 10 to 15 mildly or moderately handicapped children, one or two children may be identified as potentially gifted/talented.

In-Depth Assessment

To assist teachers in carefully examining abilities within given talent areas, RAPYHT developed an instrument called TAPP (Talent Assessment for Program Planning). TAPP is designed to assess a child's level of functioning in components of a talent area, provide information for program planning and implementation and evaluate a child's progress. In the art assessment portion of the instrument, for instance, the talent area is divided into four skills: visual sensitivity, technical skill, aesthetic expression and appreciation, and originality. A teacher is thus able to weigh strengths or weaknesses *within* a given talent area.

The teacher uses TAPP to assess a child's talent as delineated at the interdisciplinary staffing, where specific goals are generated for the child. Through the ongoing assessment process, the teacher can match a child's stage of talent development with programming. This enables the teacher to develop objectives and activities to achieve the goals set for the child. To facilitate this match, activities that link assessment to programming have been developed. In art, for instance, the following activities are suggested to enhance a child's aesthetic expression and appreciation: talking about paintings and colors and how different colors make him or her feel; making abstract pictures through blob painting; and using colored chalk or dry tempera paint expressively.

Talent Programming

As indicated, programming based on assessment in a talent area is the heart of the program. There is little value in identifying the gifted/talented handicapped child unless the child is provided with an appropriate curriculum. The teacher has a TEP (Talent Education Plan) for each handicapped child identified as gifted/talented and, to assist in implementing, draws upon the *Talent Activities Manual*. Each activity or lesson plan specifies objectives, materials, procedures, an activity and suggested follow-up activities, and the lessons can be adapted to meet a child's individual needs. In addition, the Nurturing Talent guides give the teacher suggestions for enhancing a child's skill or knowledge in each talent area.

The RAPYHT model can be incorporated into programs espousing a variety of approaches. In its first years RAPYHT was used in an informal classroom following the orientation of the British Infant School and in a teacher-directed classroom using an instructional model derived from Guilford's Structure of the Intellect.[5]

Family Involvement

An educational program for young children must involve the family. In RAPYHT parents are involved in the identification and special programming for their child from the very beginning. Parents need to understand what gifted/talented children are like and especially how to foster the development of their own. Many of the alternatives found useful in working with parents of young handicapped children are equally useful in working with parents of young gifted/talented children.[6]

Evaluation

Although we are interested in assessing parental needs, helping parents set goals for themselves and determining their satisfaction, the heart of the evaluation effort is the child's progress. The evaluation concentrates on how well the child achieves the following goals: increased ability to engage in divergent thinking; refined basic skills within the talent area; broadened or extended interest within the talent area; increased willingness to persist at a task; and a positive self-concept.

Short- and Long-Term Effects

To determine the short-term effects of RAPYHT programming, pre- and post-data on self-concept, motivation, creativity and talent functioning were gathered at three replication sites across the county.[7] The results indicated that the program had

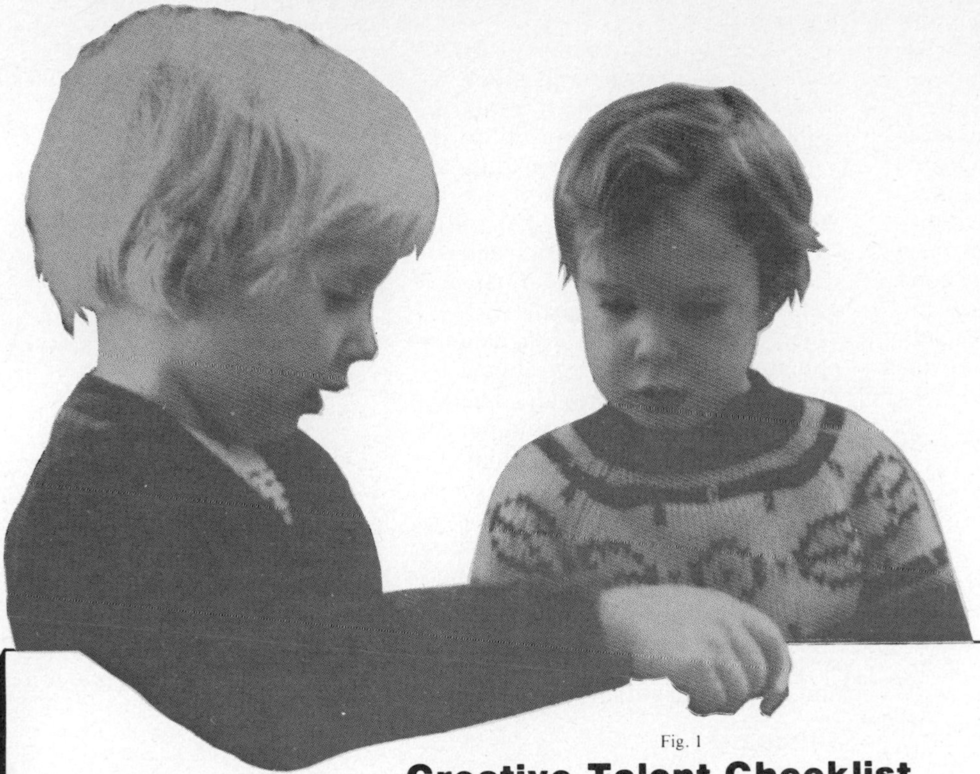

Fig. 1

Creative Talent Checklist

1. Strongly disagree
2. Disagree
3. Neutral
4. Agree
5. Strongly agree

Teacher _____

School _____

City, State _____

Date _____

Children's Names

1. Is very curious, often examining things closely or asking many questions.

2. Has a good sense of humor and sees humor in situations that may not appear funny to others.

3. Is often busily involved in work of great interest to him/her.

4. Likes to make and is interested in a lot of different things.

5. Often does things in his/her own way, is independent or non-conforming.

6. Is highly imaginative in art work, play, use of materials or ideas.

7. Often has many ideas for a given situation.

8. Is able to approach a problem or use materials in more than one way (flexibility).

9. Often has original ideas or makes original products; often has unusual, "way-out," or unique responses.

10. Elaborates in great detail in art work, play, or conversation.

Creative Talent
TOTALS

significant impact on all four areas. A follow-up study of elementary school children who were formerly enrolled in RAPYHT at the University of Illinois revealed that they were performing at or above the level of their non-handicapped classmates in such areas as listening, self-assurance, memory, counting, independence, attention span and self-concept.[8] The study concluded that RAPYHT does indeed have a lasting effect on children identified and served at the preschool level.

The Replication Process

At the University of Illinois, a skeletal central staff—a part-time director, a full-time assistant director/coordinator and a part-time evaluator—oversees the replication process. The key persons in this process are specialists who live in the areas of the replication sites. The specialists, typically former students at the University of Illinois, are trained in implementing the model and are supplied with training materials. They make 12 to 14 visits to the sites over a 9-month period, conducting training workshops, conferring with personnel, visiting the classrooms and demonstrating techniques for the teacher. Training is based on a needs assessment, and progress toward replication is jointly assessed by site personnel and replication specialists. Personnel from the sites, as well as others considering replication, are welcome to visit the demonstration program at the university.

In order to ensure a high probability of successful replication, several criteria have been established to assist in selecting sites. There must be a high-quality early childhood program for mildly to moderately handicapped children in place, and there must be evidence of financial resources to continue the program. We ask that sites designate one staff member to coordinate the efforts and to provide time for personnel to receive training. In addition, sites must be willing to demonstrate the program to visitors and to continue the program after training is discontinued.

The model can be implemented at a nominal cost—simply the costs of assessment instruments and curriculum guides.

Summary

Perhaps the greatest impact of the RAPYHT program is the change it brings about in the way that parents and teachers view young mildly and moderately handicapped children. Instead of being preoccupied with the handicapping condition, the program stresses the importance of observing a child's strengths, nourishing them and, at the same time, helping the child overcome or compensate for the handicap. Short- and long-term data on children's progress in school reinforce our belief that early identification and programming do make a difference.

[1]Further information on the replication sites—located in California, Colorado, Connecticut, Florida, Illinois, Iowa, Louisiana, Michigan, Minnesota, Missouri, New Hampshire, New Jersey, New York, Pennsylvania, Utah, West Virginia, Wisconsin and Wyoming—may be obtained from the RAPYHT Project, University of Illinois, Colonel Wolfe School, 403 E. Healey, Champaign, Ill. 61820.

[2]M. B. Karnes, "Identifying and Programming for Young Gifted/Talented Handicapped Children," in A. Fink (Ed.), *International Perspectives on Future Special Education* (CEC World Congress, Stirling, Scotland), Reston, Va., Council for Exceptional Children, 1977.

[3]C. J. Maker, *Providing Programs for the Gifted Handicapped*, Reston, Va., Council for Exceptional Children, 1977.

[4]These and other RAPYHT program materials discussed in the article are published by the Institute for Child Behavior and Development, University of Illinois, Urbana.

[5]J. Guilford, *The Nature of Human Intelligence*, New York, McGraw-Hill, 1967. For a comparison of these approaches, see M. B. Karnes and J. D. Bertschi, "Identifying and Educating Gifted/Talented Non-Handicapped and Handicapped Preschoolers," *Teaching Exceptional Children*, Summer 1978.

[6]M. B. Karnes and R. R. Zehrbach, "Flexibility in Getting Parents Involved in the School," *Teaching Exceptional Children*, Fall 1972.

[7]M. B. Karnes, A. M. Shwedel and G. F. Lewis, "Short-Term Effects of Early Programming for the Young Gifted Handicapped Child," *Exceptional Children*, Oct. 1983.

[8]M. B. Karnes, A. M. Shwedel and G. F. Lewis, "Long-Term Effects of Early Childhood Programming for the Gifted/Talented Handicapped," *Journal for the Education of the Gifted*, Vol. 6, No. 4, 1983.

A 'Social' Social Studies Model for Gifted Students

Diane E. Willard

Diane E. Willard *teaches elementary gifted students in the public schools of Quincy, Massachusetts and is presently involved in curriculum development.*

"The only freedom that is of enduring importance is freedom of intelligence . . . freedom of observation and of judgment exercised in behalf of purposes that are intrinsically worthwhile."

John Dewey

■ Men have questioned the nature, purposes, and forms of freedom since at least the fifth century B.C. when Plato and the Sophists debated in the forum of ancient Athens. In contemporary America, democratic living in the public school classroom can serve as the superstructure for building social studies programs to develop the thinking and problem-solving abilities of academically talented students.

Quincy, Massachusetts, birthplace of the second and sixth presidents of the United States, and the critical professional "home" of progressivist Francis W. Parker, has explored alternative options in democratic education for gifted students for over a quarter of a century. The fifth grade offering is a one-day-a-week pull-out program open to all qualified students throughout the city. John Dewey's philosophy of experience provides the theoretical and practical core of curriculum organization and instructional design in the Quincy program, as the following social studies model indicates.

The model described is a full-year course of study for the 65 students who participate in the enrichment program one day per week. The study of economics and urbanization comprises the first 3 months of the school year; the study of culture, social organization, and adaptation comprises the next 4 months; and the completion of community service projects occurs during the final 3 months of the academic year.

Developing the social studies model involved a number of variables, including children's interests and significant community events, as well as a conceptually oriented curriculum model developed by the professional staff of the Quincy Public Schools which included the comprehensive concepts of economics, urbanization, social organization, culture, and adaptation. Working from these reference points, the teacher introduced the study by directing students' attention to the meaning of *social*. Investigation of this question led students and teacher to set up learning centers and contracts which included problems, questions, activity cards, and resources. Problem-solving led students to explore the issues at hand through literary interpretation, creative writing, philosophical analysis stimulated by computer designs, and individual research projects.

DEWEY AND SOCIAL PROCESS

"Social," for John Dewey, meant "shared activity" (Dewey, 1916). For him, "shared activity is the greatest of human goods" (Dewey, 1925). Applied to education, this umbrella term includes at least the concepts of experience, communication, and reflective thinking; these, in turn, become the center of democratic life—in and out of school. Young children experience life, and learn from it and through it, by actively participating in forming goals and solving problems that they perceive as "real"—problems that demand the need to know. Forming goals and solving real problems require potential problem-solvers to share ideas, collect data, form hypotheses, try out possible solutions, verify results, and restructure goals in the light of consequences obtained (Dewey, 1933). Freedom to think, through reflective inquiry, is a social process leading to growth through experience.

Dr. Joseph S. Renzulli's *Enrichment Triad Model* (Renzulli, 1977) is today at the forefront of model programs for the gifted emerging from Dewey's philosophy of shared activity. The social studies model which follows is an example of the application of Renzulli's Triad in a class of elementary-level gifted students. Type I exploratory activities, Type II specific skills activities, and Type III problem-solving activities form the core of the social studies program.

DEVELOPING A "SOCIAL" SOCIAL STUDIES MODEL

One morning, following a heated discussion of the pros and cons of Proposition 2 1/2, a tax-cutting measure approved by the Massachusetts electorate in November, 1980, I asked my fifth graders this question: "What is 'social' about social studies and how does our discussion of Prop. 2 1/2 apply here?"

A brainstorming session about the meaning of "social," followed by a foray into various dictionary and thesaurus explanations, led to question-writing regarding the nature of "social" and its applicability to Proposition 2 1/2. Students next made a "web," or relationship diagram, of topics related to the question. Included here were the themes of economics, the development of cities, uses of tax money, reasons for different kinds of societies, and ways in which people can help other people.

Economics and Urbanization

Students decided that the first task was to clarify the problem and break it down into manageable components. Accordingly, they prepared a list of types of resources, materials, and agencies that might be of assistance. After a preliminary investigation, students tentatively decided that "social" had to do with people and the way they live, and that, with regard to Proposition 2 1/2, the social issue at hand was an economic one. They further subdivided the topic into five major areas: supply and demand; goods and services; production and consumption; inflation and recession; and primary and secondary resources.

Next, students decided to form problem-solving groups on the basis of interest, with each group initially posing a series of questions to be explored. An economics interest center was set up in the classroom which included questions, brainstorms, print and audiovisual resources, new questions, tentative answers, types of ongoing activities, and "new leads." Student activities developed at three levels of investigation:

- general exploration of major ideas (e.g., inflation, production, goods and services);

- specific exploration of economic issues in Quincy (e.g., unemployment, layoffs, five-year projections); and

- indepth probing into social issues underlying the economic malaise (e.g., waste of primary resources as a fundamental problem of production, education as an economic resource).

In searching for solutions to their problems, students developed original games in economics, took part in a simulation called *Merchant* (1974), which explored the rise of small-town businesses competing in the free market, and interviewed the mayor of Quincy, a banker, and a tax accountant.

Investigation of waste of primary resources led to a study of urbanization, the problems of cities, and the nature of physical/social adaptation. During the final week of the study of economics and socialization, students visited field sites in Quincy and Boston where they examined, firsthand, the rise of industrialization in an urban area, its economic impact, and the continued development of technology in a postindustrial society.

At the conclusion of this study, students were alive with ideas about the meaning of "social" and its relationship not only to Proposition 2 1/2 but also to the broader field of economics. Among their conclu-

Students explore cultural implications of the ''Manysquare'' computer design.

Students exchange ideas about the meaning of *social.*

sions was that ''social'' is a huge idea that includes many interrelated aspects of community life—a conclusion that set the stage for the next investigation.

Social Organization: The Nature of Culture

Having examined some of the economic effects of waste of primary resources, these academically talented fifth-graders began to question differences in occupations and lifestyles around the globe. The new problem emerged into a study of human adaptation; the key concept was unity and diversity: how are people the same and how are they unique? In addition to brainstorming characteristics of culture and webbing issues related to each characteristic, small groups began to investigate specific culture-related questions,

including reasons why man is able to build a progressive, sequential cultural chain. Individual students investigated the development of specific characteristics (e.g., family life, government) in societies of their choosing.

Not only did this study lead to extensions in philosophy, literature, history, and sociology, but it also provided students with a genuine need to learn formal research skills: notetaking, outlining, using primary as well as secondary resources, interviewing, and report-writing that contained a synthesis of ideas and original conclusions. Students prepared individual research studies and a group slide presentation entitled ''Culture Is. . . .'' They examined folk literature with its universal themes and unique settings and characterizations and created their own contemporary folk tales. They then organized and presented their findings in a program for parents.

At the conclusion of their study of cultural adaptation, students began to synthesize their knowledge of the process of socialization. The vehicle for synthesis emerged out of a design created on a computer screen! "Manysquare" was a multicolored polygon made up of a union of squares of many sizes and colors. In breaking down the components of "Manysquare" into line segments, angles, and points, students discovered the Gestalt conclusion that "the whole is greater than the sum of all its parts." Transferring this notion to the nature and characteristics of culture, they interpreted that culture—like "Manysquare"—is a whole greater than the sum of its parts: each cultural group is unique in its specific mode of environmental adaptation, but all groups share common characteristics which unite them in a global community that evolves from the interaction of physical, psychological, and social factors. Students discovered that "social" involves many kinds of shared activity.

People Helping People:
Community Service Projects

Having shared many kinds of activities in their studies of economics, urbanization, and social organization, and having transformed the classroom into a community of shared ideas, interests, and resources, the fifth graders next decided that they must look for ways to be of service to people within the community in which they lived.

One student had seen a television news story highlighting the American Humane Society's pet therapy program. Couldn't the class conduct a similar program at a Quincy nursing home? Another group wanted to conduct weekly story hours for primary grade students in the school, while a third group chose to make math, reading, and spelling games for children who were sheltered at a local center for battered women and children. A fourth group decided to prepare "readable" science booklets for second graders in another school.

In completing their service projects, the children soon discovered the requirements of careful planning, organization, and, in some cases, research. They also discovered that successful completion of the projects demanded careful attention to detail, delegation of responsibility according to strengths and interests of group members, and group cooperation. Not only did this program build a variety of leadership skills, but it also provided a catalyst for developing a sense of commitment to the needs of others, as well as insight into the special gifts that all people have to share within the human community.

EVALUATION

This model social studies program for academically talented fifth graders proved to be highly successful in building the students' concept of "social" as an active, ongoing process that is an integral part of life, both in and out of school. Children experienced classroom life as the core of shared activity, out of which a continuous progression of social studies concepts and programs emanated. In addition, growing out of a genuine need to find out, students extended their skills in problem-solving and in critical and creative reasoning. They expanded their research skills and their leadership skills. Through their individual and collective efforts, these academically talented fifth graders shared an experience in democratic living—an experience in "freedom of intelligence . . . exercised in behalf of purposes that are intrinsically worthwhile" (Dewey, 1938).

REFERENCES

Dewey, J. (1916). *Democracy and education.* New York: Macmillan Company.

Dewey, J. (1925). *Experience and nature.* LaSalle IL: Open Court Publishing Company.

Dewey, J. (1933). *How we think.* Lexington MA: D. C. Heath.

Dewey, J. (1938). *Experience and education.* New York: Macmillan Company.

Merchant, a simulation game. Lakeside CA: Interact Co., 1974.

Renzulli, J. S. (1977). *The Enrichment Triad Model: A guide for developing defensible programs for the gifted and talented.* Mansfield Center CT: Creative Learning Press, 1977.

Will the Gifted Child Movement be Alive and Well in 1990?

Joseph S. Renzulli

Joseph S. Renzulli, Bureau of Educational Research.

The beginning of a new decade, like graduation ceremonies, elections, and other "passages," is a time when we are likely to reflect upon some of the collective wisdom of the past. At these times, we attempt to chart new courses that will guide us through the uncertainties that are the only universal characteristic of the future. The decade beginning now is an especially important time for such reflection because we are in the midst of enjoying the strongest amount of acceptance and public support that has ever been accorded to the gifted child movement in America. The question that is continually being raised, however, is whether the movement will grow and prosper, or whether it will once again fade into obscurity as has happened so many times in the past. The answer to this question is obviously very complex, and yet at the same time it seems that the entire future of the field revolves around one "big" issue and its related creative challenges for program development. Oversimplifications of important issues are always dangerous; but perhaps by bringing the larger issue into focus around a single problem the thoughts presented here will help to establish a common target towards which many people can take aim in the decade ahead.

What is this big and important issue? Simply stated, the field of education for the gifted and talented must develop as strong and as defensible a rationale for the practices it advocates as has been developed for those things that it is against. Perhaps an analogy will help to clarify both the issue and the reason for its importance.

During the 1930's and 1940's the Progressive Education Association was the biggest and strongest educational force in the United States. Today it is virtually unknown. Why did this pioneering attempt to reform American education, this revolution in educational thought inspired by John Dewey, fade into oblivion? Most historians attribute the demise to the fact that the progressives knew more about what they were against than what they stood for. Like educators of the gifted, this innovative group was against the content-centered, memory-oriented curriculum. They were against schools that were more subject-centered than child-centered, schools that were lock-step in even the smallest detail, and a curriculum that was based on a philosophy of functionalism rather than humanism. To be certain, many of the ideas of the progressives were integrated into the mainstream of American education, but the movement bogged down and lost its punch as a major reformation because it failed to follow through on its criticisms with a solid and positive course of action. A similar analogy could also be presented using the open education movement of the 1960's.

Let us now turn our attention to the present day gifted child movement. First, most educators of the gifted would agree on the types of educational practices we are against. Second, many of the things we stand for (e.g., more emphasis on cognitive and affective process development) have been integrated, or at least accepted, by persons in general education. Finally, in spite of several years of increased activity within the field, very little attention has been given to the development of systems, theories, or models that can be used as defensible rationales for the day-to-day activities that we advocate for gifted youngsters.[1]

At this point I feel certain that the practical-minded reader is ready to give up on this article! Why, he or she might ask, is the writer making a pitch for more of "that theory stuff" when what I need are some Monday-morning activities to use with my gifted students? The answer to this question is a difficult one, and having been a teacher of the gifted, I can readily identify with the urgency of learning (usually quickly) how to "do something" to keep a dozen or so active minds busy for two and one-half hours. But therein lies the dilemma. Suppose that I were to complete this article by carefully describing four or five of my favorite no-fail activities for gifted youngsters. This approach would certainly have popular appeal, but I fear that it would also be a disservice to the reader unless it was accompanied by a defensible rationale for why such activities are being recommended for gifted youngsters. Unless the teacher of the gifted or program director can stand before the board of education or curriculum council and answer what I have described elsewhere as "those haunting questions" (Renzulli, 1977), we may be in danger of winning the battle but losing the war. The most frequently raised haunting question is familiar to almost all people working in this field: "Isn't what you are doing for the gifted good for all youngsters?" If we deal only with Monday-morning realities and do not give equal attention to the development of systems, theories, and models, we may never be able to answer this question in a defensible manner.

Let us examine one example of how the development of systems and theories can help us to win the war. Another haunting question that both critics and people within the field are beginning to raise relates to evaluation. How, they ask, do we know that our programs are having any payoff or that one approach to gifted education has certain advantages over another? The sad but true fact is that we can't really develop respectable evaluation designs when our programs are little more than patchwork collections of random practices and activities. Researchers and evaluators can only obtain effective results (and hopefully gain maximum support for programs) when they are testing a model or a comprehensive and integrated approach to programming. Then the program director can stand before the board of education and say, "Our program is based on (this or that) model, and within this framework, our evaluation data reveals (thus and so)."

Before going on to some specific needs related to the development of rationale, there are two final concerns about the general issue that should be mentioned. First, I am not advocating esoteric systems, theories, or models. Any theory that is not rich in examples and suggestions for practical application is as valueless to an applied science or field of study as are specific activities without an accompanying rationale. I believe that "practical theory" is the best of both worlds, because the two approaches (theory and practice) working together side-by-side can provide actual learning activities that will help to validate the theories and models, and provide a framework within which numerous creative people can contribute practical applications of a given theory or model.

Second, if the field is to advance, we need competitive and even conflicting theories so that we may test one against the other in a never-ending search for better ways of serving gifted and talented youth. There is an old saying in science about the accepted theories of today being tomorrow's outmoded ideas. Just as Einstein's work largely disproved many of Newton's "laws" of physics, so also must we challenge conventional wisdom and existing ways of doing things. This challenging attitude is exactly what we advocate for gifted youth. Perhaps the time is long overdue for us to begin practicing what we preach. In order for our field to advance we need to create systems, theories, and models that will serve as the vehicle for a great in-house dialogue directed toward providing a true meaning for our most frequently used (and abused) concept; "qualitative differentiation."

Four Related Issues

Following is a discussion of four areas in which there is a need for the development of more defensible systems, theories, and models. The four issues that follow are particularly interesting because of past or present efforts and

because they may stimulate a little of the controversy that is needed in our field.

The Identification of
the Gifted and "Gifted Hypocrisy"

Although most people will not admit it, up to this point in our history we have continued to view giftedness as an absolute concept — something that exists in and by itself, without relation to anything else. For this reason, most of our identification efforts are directed toward uncovering the magic piece of evidence that will tell us if a child is "really gifted." The absolute conception causes us to act as if giftedness is something that "you have" or "you don't have," and consequently, we still think in terms of a child being "in" or "not in" a program. Any mistakes in the selection (or rejection) process, according to the absolutist, are attributed to deficiencies in identification instruments rather than to giftedness being a relative or situational concept.

Although there is a great deal of platform rhetoric about multiple talents and multiple criteria for identification, the sad fact remains that most students participating in special programs are preselected for time periods of at least one year, and in most cases the major criterion for selection is a predetermined cut-off score of 125 or 130 on an intelligence test.[2] One need only survey the identification procedures for a cross section of special programs or review several states' guidelines to affirm the continued reliance upon high test scores.

Our reliance upon intelligence test scores has resulted in pupil selection on an all-or-nothing basis. Students are either "in" or "out" of a program for an entire year and seldom are nonselected students given an opportunity for special services even when very valid indications of superior potential arise. This approach is roughly analogous to selecting students on the basis of hair or eye color because it assumes that giftedness is some sort of absolute and predetermined condition rather than a set of behaviors that emerge when certain traits interact with one another in relation to a particular topic, area of interest, or specific talent.

A large amount of accumulated research (Renzulli, 1978) clearly indicates that the type of gifted behavior displayed by creative and productive persons is always the result of interaction among three clusters of traits; above average ability, task commitment, and creativity. Outstanding accomplishments occur when these interacting traits are brought to bear on one or a combination of specific performance areas (i.e., the numerous ways and means through which human beings express themselves in real life situations). Research and plain old common sense tell us that gifted behavior is both topical and temporal in nature. That is, such behavior emerges in relation to a sincere area of interest and it operates at maximum efficiency during given periods of time. It is at such times as this — when a strong interest emerges and the child is unquestionably eager to put forth maximum creative effort — that supplementary services and resources should be made available to the child. It goes without saying that an important part of overall programming is the encouragement (indeed, the creation) of task commitment and creativity. But if we restrict our efforts for such encouragement to students who have been preselected (on the basis of test scores) for a special program, we may fail to "turn on" the child who has the greatest potential for benefiting from interest development and creativity producing activities.[3] Gifted behavior emerges as a result of certain youngsters (generally of above average ability) taking advantage of opportunities that are made available to them. We can serve gifted students more effectively if we (1) expand the number and variety of opportunities, (2) make the opportunities available to more students, (3) do not require every child to follow through on every activity, and (4) provide supplementary services at the time and in the areas where a child shows the eagerness to follow through. In other words, our identification procedures should place as much emphasis on the ways in which children interact with experiences (i.e., action or performance information) as they do on the ways in which children respond to structured questions or ratings (i.e., status or psychometric information).

Before discussing the characteristics of a more relative concept of giftedness and our need to think in terms of "gifted behavior" rather than "being gifted," consider one other reason why giftedness has traditionally been viewed as an absolute concept. There are in fact certain abilities that are more pervasive and enduring than others and it is precisely these abilities that have resulted in our rather narrow conception of giftedness. Essentially, these abilities include being a good test-taker and/or lesson-learner in a traditional learning situation. In most cases, good test-takers are also good lesson-learners, although there are many examples of youngsters who "go to school well" but who do not "show up" well on intelligence, aptitude, or achievement tests. There are also many cases of youngsters who score well on tests but who, for one reason or another, do not achieve well in traditional learning situations. Let us assume for a moment that being a good test-taker or lesson-learner is a certain type of "giftedness." These types of giftedness should obviously be respected and provided for to whatever extent possible in the school program. In fact, it is these types of giftedness that are most easily provided for through modifications and adaptations in the regular curriculum. Any child (regardless of test scores) who can cover regular curriculum material in a more compact and streamlined fashion should be given the opportunity to do so provided, of course, that it does not present the child with undue stress or emotional problems. If there is one important area in which regular classroom teachers might be legally actionable for negligence, it is in their lack of providing youngsters with appropriate modifications in the coverage of regular curricular materials.

If we consider test-taking and lesson-learning ability as certain types of giftedness, there are at least three important considerations that must be kept in mind. First, being a good test-taker or lesson-learner does not necessarily guarantee that a child will display gifted behavior in the creative and productive sense of that term. Creative and productive endeavors are the result of combining particular abilities in certain areas (including but not restricted to general intelligence) with task commitment and creativity. A second consideration is that one need not necessarily be a good test-taker or lesson-learner in order to display creative and productive behavior which emanates from high levels of task commitment and creativity. Our limited conception of giftedness, however, has often precluded entrance into special programs or supplementary services to good test-taking and lesson-learning ability and therefore highly creative youngsters or youngsters who have displayed unusual amounts of motivation to pursue topics or talent areas have been systematically excluded from special programs.

Our third consideration is simply that no one is "born with" task commitment or creativity. Rather, these are clusters of abilities that we should seek to develop in all students. Obviously, good test-takers and lesson-learners have high potential for benefiting from experiences designed to develop creativity and task commitment, but once again, these abilities are no guarantee of success nor should they preclude youngsters who do not have the test-taking and lesson-learning abilities. In a certain sense, activities that are conscientiously and systematically designed to develop task commitment and creativity could be viewed as the situations or occasions whereby we can spot examples of gifted behavior. In other words, performance in these situations should become part of our identification procedure, and the entire identification process should be built around a "revolving door" concept that allows children to flow into and out of the special program as the need arises.

The main difference between this approach and the traditional method of having the same students in the program for the entire year is that there is a specific *raison d'etre* for a child (or small group of children working on a common problem) to be in the program for a given period of time. The period of time may be a few weeks or several months, the major determining factor being the amount of time necessary for completing the project or solving a particular problem. In a certain sense, this approach means that a child "earns the right" to obtain special services by showing some or all of the "necessary ingredients" of giftedness (that is, above-average ability, task commitment, and creativity). The concept of "earning the right" to obtain special services will obviously be a controversial one, but this approach will certainly help to overcome some of the very valid criticism that has recently been expressed by parents about the identification process (see especially Weiler, 1978). This approach also helps to insure continuous involvement on the part of the regular classroom teacher. In the traditional approach (in which the child is preselected and placed in the program for an entire year), the regular and special programs frequently operate as two separate entities and it is not uncommon for the regular classroom teacher "to forget" about advanced expressions of ability once children have been placed in the gifted program. The revolving-door approach, on the other hand, requires the regular classroom teacher to be constantly on the look-out for signs of interest, creativity, task commitment, and advanced expressions of ability. In addition to becoming a more sensitive "talent spotter," the regular classroom teacher can become more involved by providing certain types of enrichment experiences that will become useful as the situations or occasions for spotting children who should be "fed into" the resource room. The resource room becomes a place where extensions of the regular curriculum and more advanced levels of involvement can occur.

This approach can also help to overcome one of the main deficiencies of special programs that are organized around the resource room or itinerant teacher model. Most resource room teachers are not resources — they are teachers in the traditional sense of the term. In far too many instances when I have visited resource rooms, the teacher is teaching predetermined, prescribed lessons to the entire group. The content of the lessons may be different from the content of the regular curriculum, and the atmosphere may be a little more relaxed, but otherwise, the learning or instructional model is exactly the same as the type of teaching that goes on in any good classroom. If resource teachers want to become real resources to gifted and talented children, then they must drastically reduce the amount of time that they spend instructing students and "teaching lessons." A real resource person serves an individual student (or small group of students working on a common project) in much the same way that a graduate advisor serves a doctoral student working on a research project. The teacher helps the student to focus or frame the area of interest into a researchable problem; suggests where the student can find appropriate methodologies for pursuing the problem like a professional inquirer; helps the youngster to obtain appropriate resources (persons, equipment, reference materials, financial support); provides critical feedback, editorial assistance, encouragement, and a shoulder to cry on; and helps the child find appropriate outlets and audiences for his or her creative work.

But how, you may ask, can the revolving-door approach help to accomplish these types of behaviors on the part of resource room teachers? The answer to this question lies in the greater emphasis that this approach places on the individual child, the child's particular area of interest, and his or her commitment to work on a certain problem. In other words, the *raison d'etre* that caused us to send children to the resource room becomes the basis for the supplementary services that are provided when they are working under the direction of the resource teacher. The revolving-door approach, in a certain sense, "forces" the resource teacher to deal with the individual child and the specific reason that the child was sent to the resource room.

This approach also will help us in matters of accountability and program evaluation. If we know the specific reason why a given child was sent to the resource room, and if we have some documentation about the specific services that were provided, then we can review the youngster's work and make determinations about growth in relation to the objectives set forth for the individual student.

By way of summary, the revolving-door approach can help to overcome many of the problems and criticisms that have been associated with programs for the gifted and talented. This is especially true for relatively affluent school districts where large numbers of parents feel that their children are gifted. This approach allows us to serve more students, to avoid the IQ cut-off score game, to place the rationale for advanced level services on characteristics that are unequivocally supported by the research literature, and to shift the emphasis of special programs from lesson-oriented, whole group activities to the development of individual strengths and interests.

Curriculum Hocus-Pocus

A second area in which we need to examine the rationale underlying special programs is concerned with the so-called "process models" that form the most sacred part of the litany in the area of education for the gifted and talented. Bloom's *Taxonomy of Educational Objectives* (Bloom, et al., 1956) and Guilford's *Structure-of-the-Intellect* (Guilford, 1967) model are almost universally offered as the rationale for special programs. If we examine these models carefully, however, two almost obvious conclusions emerge. First, the models point out mental processes that should be developed in all children. Indeed, when Bloom referred to his taxonomy as a classification of "higher mental processes," he was merely calling attention to the distinction between these processes (which are common to all humans) and the lower processes of sensation and perception (which humans share with other members of the animal family). One of the reasons we cannot defend programs for the gifted by simply saying that focus should be placed on the upper end of Bloom's continuum (analysis, synthesis, and evaluation) is that the taxonomy is a hierarchical structure — one cannot engage in advanced levels of analysis or creativity unless one has dealt with advanced levels of knowledge and comprehension (the two lowest levels in the taxonomy). Contrary to what the prophets of process would have us believe, knowledge is important, and for the person who is going to make a significant breakthrough in his or her field, knowledge of methodology (Bloom's level 1.20) is perhaps the most important skill that one can possess. Failure to understand this hierarchical arrangement has undoubtedly resulted in gifted education's over-reliance on the cute games and situational-specific training activities that purport to develop creativity and other thinking skills. Suffice it to say that there is a vast difference between the types of mental growth that result from a thirty-minute exercise in creative ways to paste macaroni on oatmeal boxes and the kind of disciplined inquiry and task commitment that sparked the work of Marie Curie, Rudyard Kipling, Martin Luther King, or anyone else that history has recognized as a truly gifted person. Our major theory development need in this regard is to learn how situational training activities can be used as stepping stones to more advanced kinds of inquiry rather than as ends in and of themselves.

A second conclusion that becomes apparent if we carefully examine the process models is the large amount of rigidity that such models place on learning activities. In their seemingly noble goal of focusing on particular processes (rather than content), such activities tend to fractionate learning into the highly structured kinds of experiences that we criticized in the content-centered curriculum. So now, rather than filling kids' heads with isolated facts and figures, we are filling each "cell" of the Guilford model with isolated processes according to a structured and predetermined lesson plan. Reliance upon the process models has undoubtedly resulted from a popular but completely unsupported belief that the gifted person is "process oriented." The reality, however, is that authors, inventors, designers, and anyone else engaged in the creative aspects of art or science attack a problem because they are attempting to produce a new and imaginative product. In the act of writing the story or designing the new piece of machinery certain processes undoubtedly are used and further developed. But gifted persons are highly product oriented—processes are the paths rather than the goals of their creative efforts. Unless we view process activities in this manner, there is a danger of trying to ram them down students' throats in much the same way that we force-fed youngsters with facts and figures.

My concern about a preoccupation with process models started to emerge a few years ago when I worked on a curriculum development project (for the gifted) that involved several scholars from the academic disciplines. When we tried to "sell" these scholars on the Taxonomy and the Structure-of-the-Intellect models they flatly stated these approaches where a kind of phony educationese or "curriculum hocus-pocus." They accepted the processes as psychological phenomena and even agreed that certain kinds of elementary training activities could be built around the models. But when it came to our target population—gifted persons—they said that these models simply were not reflections of the ways in which first-hand inquirers pursued knowledge in their respective fields. If we are to overcome our naiveté in this regard, perhaps the starting point should be a careful study of the ways in which creative people attack real problems within the various fields of knowledge.

Some additional curriculum hocus-pocus has also resulted from the almost obsessive concern that many educators of the gifted have had for speed and efficiency in learning. Although we do know that brighter students can cover curricular material faster and more precisely than those of lesser ability, our knowledge about the contri-

butions of other important factors such as task commitment, individual interests, and learning styles is far less sophisticated. Our lack of understanding about these factors has frequently resulted in quantitative rather than qualitative approaches to educating the gifted. In other words, we have simply dealt with the gifted by speeding up the traditional approach to learning.

Let us briefly analyze a typical learning situation. Almost all traditional learning experiences are characterized by the step-by-step pursuit of curricular material that is planned and administered by the teacher. Students engage in predetermined exercises with generally prescribed procedures for problem solving and generally agreed upon standards of acceptability for success. Thus, the curriculum from the early grades through most college-level courses consists of one long progression of exercises after another, and the student is cast mainly in the role of a "doer of exercises." Are we really doing anything that is qualitatively different when we merely accelerate students or the rate at which we expose them to a never-ending diet of prescribed exercises? Simply removing youngsters from one exercise-learning situation and placing them in another similar situation (albeit at a more advanced level) does not change the role of the learner. Unless appropriate modifications are made in the ways in which advanced material is taught, I fail to see how an accelerated learning experience differs qualitatively from the regular curriculum. Providing highly able youngsters with opportunities to learn at advanced rates of speed is certainly an important objective of special education for the gifted, but what is equally certain is that the great accomplishments of mankind have always resulted when bold and adventuresome persons have dared to go beyond predetermined and step-by-step progressions through traditional material. The "stuff" out of which greatness is made can only result from experiences in real discovery, inquiry, and creativity rather than presented exercises in these important processes. It is for this reason that I am somewhat skeptical when people tell me they are "writing curriculum" for the gifted, even if the curricular material is in a nontraditional area or related to an esoteric topic or process. If the epistemology of the learning experience remains the same (i.e., the role of the learner and the ways in which he or she pursues knowledge), then I believe that writing curriculum for the gifted is yet another example of self-deluding hocus pocus. "Writing curriculum" implies more prescribed and presented exercises rather than starting with the child and his or her interests, and then providing the conditions, resources, and guidance that will result in first-hand investigative activity and real creativity. We will only make a breakthrough in our quest for qualitative differentiation when we learn how to "de-exercise" at least a portion of the school experience for gifted and talented youth.

The Teacher of the Gifted and American Pie
One of the more fortunate developments in the last few years has been a greater emphasis on identifying those

characteristics and behaviors that help to define the so-called "teacher of the gifted." There are at least two groups of persons to whom we refer in discussing the "teacher of the gifted." The first group is obviously specialists — those individuals who have, by job designation, been assigned to work with gifted students at particular times and under particular circumstances.

The second group consists of regular classroom teachers when they are dealing with a child in whom we are trying to promote gifted behavior. It is sad but true that in the foreseeable future most gifted youngsters will spend most of their time in regular classrooms, and in the majority of school districts, they may not have access to any supplementary services or specialists in gifted education. It is in these situations that we must attempt to provide at least some of the services as those proposed in special or "pull-out" programs. There is no magic in being a specialist who is assigned to work with gifted children. Certain of the teaching behaviors employed by such specialists can also be used very effectively by regular classroom teachers, provided of course such teachers learn the competencies and have the time and resources to bring them to bear within their classrooms.

Let us now turn our attention to the question of what some of the special competencies of teachers of the gifted and talented are. On several occasions I have asked people in the field to list the most important characteristics of teachers of the gifted. The resultant lists can best be described as pure "American Pie"!

That is, such lists always contain very general and highly idealistic truisms with which very few people would disagree. Items that always show up high on such listings are: flexible, democratic, considerate of individual differences, open-minded, has a sense of humor, sensitive to the affective needs of students, varies the learning environment, etc.[4] (Just for the fun of it — if you were asked to list the characteristics of teachers of the gifted, would not the above items appear relatively high on your list?)

This is not to suggest that these traits are not characteristics of teachers of the gifted. Let us assume, however, that you are the parent of a so-called average (or even below average) child. Does this mean that your child's teacher can be inflexible? undemocratic? inconsiderate of individual differences? closed-minded? lacking in a sense of humor? insensitive to affective needs? does not vary the learning environment? etc.? I would hesitate to tell the board of education in my home town that these are the kinds of things we seek in teachers of the gifted but not in other members of our teaching faculty.

An even bigger problem with the "American Pie" lists is that the items are too general or highly inferential to be of any practical value so far as teacher training is concerned. The "American Pie" list is really a list of personality variables, perhaps far less subject to modification (through teacher training) than specific teaching behaviors which relate more directly to the instructional process. We should, quite obviously, attempt to select teachers on the

bases of these characteristics and to do whatever training we can to promote them further. But once again, we should select and train all teachers with these characteristics in mind.

If we are ever going to make progress in defining the characteristics of the teacher of the gifted, I think it is important for us to get serious about specific teaching behaviors that promote specific kinds of learning and especially creative/productive behavior. To be certain, we can train all (or almost all) teachers to be more flexible, to ask higher level questions, and to teach lessons that promote creativity and affective development. At the same time, however, there are certain teaching behaviors that should be brought to bear upon youngsters who have transcended the role of merely being lesson-learners (at whatever advanced levels they are learning lessons), and it is these behaviors that are most crucial in helping youngsters develop their true creative and productive abilities.

Evaluation and the Absurdity of the Hard Data Mystique

A final area in which we need to give more attention to the development of a defensible rationale is program evaluation. Because of the relatively unique objectives of programs for the gifted and talented (Renzulli, 1975), the traditional models, instruments, and procedures that have been used to evaluate programs in other areas of education are largely inappropriate for evaluating programs that serve gifted and talented youth. In recent years there has been a great deal of concern about the specification of objectives in terms of observable and measurable student behaviors. Many evaluators have looked upon the "behavioral objectives models" as a panacea for conducting evaluation studies. The nature of gifted programs, however, and their concern for developing more complex behaviors and more comprehensive types of creative products may make this model too cumbersome to be practically applied to programs for the gifted and talented.

The rigid behavioral objectives model is mainly inappropriate for programs that serve gifted youngsters because it forces us to focus primarily upon those behaviors that are most easily measured, but also the most trivial. Such a situation may well result in the tail wagging the dog — that is, our programs may tend to focus on lower level (basic skill) objectives because of the neatness and precision with which they can be measured. Michael Scriven, the single-most influential person writing on educational evaluation today, has pointed out that "putting pressures on [a person] to formulate his goals, to keep to them, and to express them in testable terms may enormously alter his product in ways that are certainly not always desirable" (Scriven, 1967, p. 55). Other writers (Stake, 1973, pp. 196-199) have pointed out that the errors of testing increase markedly when we move from highly specific areas of performance to items which tend to measure more complex processes and youngsters' attempts to strive toward more unreached human potential.

Although the testing industry has provided us with a vast array of instruments for measuring the mastery of basic skills and general achievement, there has thus far been an absence of technology when it comes to evaluating the more complex types of learning and the creative accomplishments that oftentimes characterize programs for the gifted and talented. The constant call for "hard data" has undoubtedly been the reason for limited technology and the development of alternative evaluation models that can better serve the types of programs advocated by persons in this field. On the one hand, persons are [in effect] saying, "Go forth educators of the gifted and develop in this special population of students the upper levels of their most creative and productive behavior!" At the same time, however, the persons who offer us this creative challenge frequently also request that we show the results of our efforts in terms of some nice, neat scores on a standardized test. Unfortunately, the complexity of our objectives and the neatness and precision of the evaluation data requested do not go together. Tests simply do not exist to tell us the amount of growth that takes place when a youngster's work is instrumental in changing a state law, stopping the construction of an environmentally unsafe interstate highway, producing an award-winning film, publishing a special-topic newspaper, or bringing about the erection of a monument at a place with important historical significance. These types of creative products are the right and proper types of data upon which our evaluations should focus. They may not be as precise and objective as scores on a standardized test; however, if we are to make any important breakthroughs in evaluation, the products of children must be viewed as data. Our evaluations of such data may be more imprecise than test-score data; however, it is far better to have imprecise information about the right type of objective than precise information about the wrong objective.

What is most surprising about the hard data mystique is that very few persons calling for such objective data would question the more comprehensive types of objectives that we advocate for gifted youngsters. Using these objectives as our starting point, the first and biggest job in evaluation is to convince persons receiving evaluation reports (state departments of education, boards of education) that our special efforts require — indeed, demand — new evaluation models.

Although I can only speculate about some of the major characteristics of such models, one certainty is that we must develop better means for assessing the quality of all types of students' products. Such assessment will require that we seek the advice of specialists within particular fields (architects, furniture designers, choreographers, etc.). Through their knowledge, appreciation, special insights, and "connoisseurship" we may be able to learn about benchmarks of quality that will assist us in program evaluation.

Footnotes

1. Six notable exceptions to the lack of theory and system development can be found in the work of Ward (1961), Stanley (1974), Feldhusen & Kolloff (1978), Treffinger (1975), Renzulli (1977), and Renzulli and Smith (1979).
2. Indeed, the well-known Pegnato and Birch study (1965) validated multiple criteria approaches to identification by comparing the alternative approaches with individual IQ test scores. In other words, a child was judged to be "really gifted" only if he or she met this ultimate criterion on a single measure. This being the case, one wonders why we should bother with alternative criteria and merely use individual IQ scores! Alternatives to the type of research design used by Pegnato and Birch can be found in Renzulli and Smith (1977) and Jenkins (1979).
3. Space does not permit a detailed discussion of how interest and creativity development activities are related to developing gifted behavior. The reader is referred to sections on Type I and Type II Enrichment in Renzulli, J. S., *The Enrichment Triad Model: A Guide for Developing Defensible Programs for the Gifted and Talented.* Mansfield Center, CT: Creative Learning Press, 1977.
4. Some of these lists of characteristics have been used for research studies and can be found in the literature. See for example, *Instructor*, May, 1977, p. 20.

References

Bloom, B. S. (Ed.). *Taxonomy of educational objectives, handbook I: The cognitive domain.* New York: David McKay Co., 1956.

Do you have to be gifted to teach the gifted? *Instructor*, 1977, May, 20.

Feldhusen, J. F., & Kolloff, M. B. A three-stage model for gifted education. *G/C/T*, 1978, 4, 3-5; 53-57.

Guilford, J. P. *The nature of human intelligence.* New York: McGraw-Hill, 1967.

Jenkins, R. C. W. The identification of gifted and talented students through peer nomination (Doctoral dissertation, University of Connecticut, 1978). *Dissertation Abstracts International*, 1979, 40. (University Microfilms No. 7914161, 167-A)

Pegnato, C. W., & Birch, J. W. Locating gifted children in junior high schools: Comparison of methods. In W. B. Barbe & J. S. Renzulli (Eds.), *Psychology and education of the gifted: Selected readings.* New York: Irvington Press, 1975.

Renzulli, J. S. *A guidebook for evaluating programs for the gifted and talented.* Ventura, CA: Ventura County Superintendent of Schools, 1975.

Renzulli, J. S. *The enrichment triad model: A guide for developing defensible programs for the gifted and talented.* Mansfield Center, CT: Creative Learning Press, 1977.

Renzulli, J. S. What makes giftedness: Reexamining a definition. *Phi Delta Kappan*, 1978, 60, 180-184.

Renzulli, J. S., & Smith, L. H. Two approaches to identification of gifted students. *Exceptional Children*, 1977, 44, 512-518.

Renzulli, J. S., & Smith, L. H. *A guidebook for developing individualized educational programs (IEP) for the gifted and talented.* Mansfield Center, CT: Creative Learning Press, 1979.

Scrivan, M. *Perspectives on curriculum evaluation.* AERA monograph series on curriculum evaluation, No. 1. Chicago: Rand McNally, 1967.

Stake, R. E. Measuring what learners learn. In E. R. House (Ed.), *School evaluation: The politics and process.* Berkeley, CA: McCutchan, 1973.

Stanley, J. C., Keating, D. P., & Fox, L. H. (Eds.). *Mathematical talent: Discovery, description, and development.* Baltimore: Johns Hopkins University Press, 1974.

Treffinger, D. J. Teaching for self-directed learning: A priority for the gifted and talented. *Gifted Child Quarterly*, 1975, 19, 46-59.

Ward, V. S. *Educating the gifted: An axiomatic approach.* Columbus, OH: Charles E. Merrill, Inc., 1965.

Weiler, D. The alpha children: California's brave new world for the gifted. *Phi Delta Kappan*, 1978, 60, 185-187.

Index

Credits/ Acknowledgments

Cover design by Charles Vitelli

1. Mainstreaming
Facing overview—UNITED NATIONS/photo by S. Dimartini. 17-19—*Teaching Exceptional Children,* Winter 1985.
2. Attitude Change Strategies
Facing overview—UNITED NATIONS/photo by S. Dimartini. 33-35—*Teaching Exceptional Children,* Winter 1984.
3. Teaching the Visually Impaired Child
Facing overview—UNITED NATIONS/photo by S. Dimartini.
4. Teaching the Hearing Impaired Child
Facing overview—UN photo by L. Solmssen. 89—*Music Educators Journal,* April 1978.
5. Teaching the Physically Impaired Child
Facing overview—UN photo. 115—*Teaching Exceptional Children,* Winter 1983.

6. Teaching the Mentally Retarded
Facing overview—UN photo by L. Solmssen. 137-138—*Teaching Exceptional Children,* February 1982.
7. Teaching the Learning Disabled Child
Facing overview—UNITED NATIONS/photo by Marta Pinter.
8. Teaching the Emotionally Disturbed
Facing overview—WHO photo by K. Kalisher. 196-198—*Teaching Exceptional Children,* Spring 1985.
9. Teaching the Gifted and Talented Child
Facing overview—EPA Documerica. 222-224—Photographs are provided courtesy of The Chicago Public Schools Gifted Program. 229—*Children Today,* September-October 1984. 233—*Teaching Exceptional Children,* Fall 1984.

ANNUAL EDITIONS:
EDUCATING EXCEPTIONAL CHILDREN, Third Edition

Article Rating Form

We Want Your Advice

Here is an opportunity for you to have direct input into the next revision of this volume. We would like you to rate each of the 46 articles listed below, using the following scale:

1. **Excellent: should definitely be retained**
2. **Above average: should probably be retained**
3. **Below average: should probably be deleted**
4. **Poor: should definitely be deleted**

Your ratings will play a vital part in the next revision. So please mail this prepaid form to us just as soon as you complete it.
Thanks for your help!

Annual Editions revisions depend on two major opinion sources: one is our Advisory Board, listed in the front of this volume, which works with us in scanning the thousands of articles published in the public press each year; the other is you—the person actually using the book. Please help us and the users of the next edition by completing the prepaid article rating form on this page and returning it to us. Thank you.

Rating	Article	Rating	Article
	1. Executive Summary—Sixth Annual Report to Congress on the Implementation of Public Law 94-142: The Education for All Handicapped Children Act		23. Children on Medication: A Guide for Teachers
	2. The 1984 Annual Report to Congress: Are We Better Off?		24. Comprehensive Microcomputer Applications for Severely Physically Handicapped Children
	3. Where Is Special Education for Students with High Prevalence Handicaps Going?		25. Learning About Disabilities
	4. Staff Development: A Key Ingredient of Effective Mainstreaming		26. Is There a Child with Epilepsy in the Classroom?
	5. Don't Stare—I'll Tell You Later		27. What Is Mental Retardation?
	6. Changing Attitudes		28. The Child with Down's Syndrome
	7. Providing Opportunities for Interaction Between Severely Handicapped and Nonhandicapped Students		29. Learning Through Outdoor Adventure Education
	8. Toward More Success in Mainstreaming: A Peer Teacher Approach to Physical Education		30. Changes in Mild Mental Retardation: Population, Programs, and Perspectives
	9. Integrating Disabled Children		31. An Analysis of EMR Children's Worries About Mainstreaming
	10. The Parent Connection: Enhancing the Affective Component of Parent Conferences		32. Speaking for Themselves: A Bibliography of Writings by Mentally Handicapped Individuals
	11. It's My IEP: Involving Students in the Planning Process		33. Recognizing Special Talents in Learning Disabled Students
	12. Books About Children with Special Needs: An Annotated Bibliography		34. Teaching Learning Disabled Children to Help Themselves
	13. Mainstreaming Children with Visual Impairments		35. How Do We Help the Learning Disabled?
	14. Some Thoughts on the Education of Blind Children		36. Mainstreaming: How Teachers Can Make It Work
	15. Teaching Partially Sighted Children		37. The Psychology of Mainstreaming Socio-emotionally Disturbed Children
	16. Technology and the Handicapped		38. Skill-Streaming: Teaching Social Skills to Children with Behavioral Disorders
	17. The Visually Handicapped Child		39. Educator Perceptions of Behavior Problems of Mainstreamed Students
	18. Poor Learning Ability . . . or Poor Hearing?		40. Reducing Stress of Students in Conflict
	19. The Hearing Mechanism		41. Child Abuse and Neglect
	20. Notetaking: A Necessary Support Service for Hearing-Impaired Students		42. Our Most Neglected Natural Resource
	21. There's A Deaf Child in My Class		43. The Teacher as Counselor for the Gifted
	22. Integrating the Physically Handicapped Child		44. Special Children . . . Special Gifts
			45. A "Social" Social Studies Model for Gifted Students
			46. Will the Gifted Child Movement Be Alive and Well in 1990?

(cont. on next page)

ABOUT YOU

Name _____ Date _____

Are you a teacher? ☐ Or student? ☐

Your School Name _____

Department _____

Address _____

City _____ State _____ Zip _____

School Telephone # _____

YOUR COMMENTS ARE IMPORTANT TO US!

Please fill in the following information:

For which course did you use this book? _____

Did you use a text with this Annual Edition? ☐ yes ☐ no

The title of the text: _____

What are your general reactions to the Annual Editions concept?

Have you read any particular articles recently that you think should be included in the next edition?

Are there any articles you feel should be replaced in the next edition? Why?

Are there other areas that you feel would utilize an Annual Edition?

May we contact you for editorial input?

May we quote you from above?

EDUCATING EXCEPTIONAL CHILDREN, **Third Edition**

BUSINESS REPLY MAIL		
First Class	Permit No. 84	Guilford, CT

No Postage
Necessary
if Mailed
in the
United States

Postage will be paid by addressee

The Dushkin Publishing Group, Inc.
Sluice Dock
Guilford, Connecticut 06437